A theory
of history

Also by Agnes Heller

Renaissance Man

A theory
of history

Agnes Heller

Routledge & Kegan Paul
London, Boston and Henley

First published in 1982
by Routledge & Kegan Paul Ltd
39 Store Street,
London WC1E 7DD,
9 Park Street,
Boston, Mass. 02108, USA and
Broadway House,
Newtown Road,
Henley-on-Thames,
Oxon RG9 1EN

Set in Plantin by
Saildean Ltd, Surrey
and printed in Great Britain by
St Edmundsbury Press, Suffolk

Library of Congress Cataloging in Publication Data

Heller, Agnes.
A theory of history.
1. Historiography.   2. History-Philosophy.
I. Title.
D13. H4145 1982   907'.2   81-12173

ISBN 0-7100-9010-2   AACR2

Contents

Preface

In this book I wanted to avoid references and quotations to the extent that it was possible. Historiographical works and works from the field of the philosophy of history which are regarded as *classic* belong to the subject matter of this study; accordingly, I made adequate references to them. However, where both authors and works were generally known, I omitted quotations except for some very short and representative ones. I am fully aware of the fact that the notion 'classic' is very vague and that it partially depends on the author's position as to which works are considered members of this cluster. There can be some reasonable disagreement about my treating Weber, Durkheim, Croce, and Lukács as 'classics' in the field, while omitting others. On the other hand, I have mainly referred only to authors from whom I have borrowed certain theoretical proposals and solutions, and also occasionally to some whose concise and ingenious formulations I considered to be illuminating in a particular aspect.

The problems I have dealt with here are basic issues of our times, and they have been addressed by many distinguished scholars of our century. Even so, I felt it inappropriate to bring into the discussion the recapitulation of the proposed solutions only in order to show that I do not share them. But I am indebted to all of these people because they have put their fingers on the very issues and induced me to think them over in my own way. If I am now going to list their names with gratitude, this is not an empty act of courtesy, but the expression of my obligation to the scientific community of yesterday and today. Irrespective of whether or not I have quoted their works and names, I am especially indebted to: Adorno, Aron, Apel, Becher (L. C.), Berlin, Blake (C), Bloch (E.), Bloch (M.), Gallie (W. B.), Gellner (E.), Beard (C. A.), Danto, Gurwitch, Gadamer, Gardiner, Goldmann (L.), Habermas, Hempel, Kuhn, Luhmann, Meyerhoff (H.), Murray, Meinecke,

Foucault, Lovejoy (A. O.), Nagel (E.), Marquard (O.), Mandelbaum (M.), Mesarovic, Lévi-Strauss, Pestel, Service, Schulin, Spuhler, Troeltsch, Sauvy, Schmidt (A.), Toynbee, Sorokin, Russell, Walsh (W. H.), Wittgenstein, Whitehead, Popper, Scriven (M.), Pirenne (H.), White (M.), Leach, Sahlins, Polanyi (K.).

One author and one book stand out with their considerable impact on this undertaking: Collingwood and his work, *The Idea of History*. Before I read this book there was chaos in my thoughts regarding my subject matter: having finished it, I knew perfectly well what I was going to argue for. My deepest gratitude is due to this unjustly neglected author. This book is dedicated to his memory.

Here I wish to express my gratitude to Ferenc Fehér for his conscientious criticism and good advice which enabled me to correct the manuscript, to elucidate certain dark spots, and make some arguments more convincing.

I wish to thank Freya Headlam and Brett Lockwood for the stylistic revision of the text. They have spent a great amount of time and energy with their work on the manuscript. Finally, I thank my colleagues of the administrative staff of the Department of Sociology, La Trobe University, for having typewritten the manuscript.

Agnes Heller

Part I

Historicity

Chapter One

The stages of historical consciousness

1 Consciousness of unreflected generality: the myth.
2 Consciousness of generality reflected in particularity: consciousness of history as prehistory.
3 Consciousness of unreflected universality: the universal myth.
4 Consciousness of particularity reflected in generality; consciousness of history proper.
5 Consciousness of reflected universality: world-historical consciousness.
6 Consciousness of reflected generality – as a *task* (of overcoming the discomposed historical consciousness): planetarian responsibility.

From unreflected generality to reflected generality

Once upon a time there was a man. There he was *once upon a time*. He *was* since he is no more. He *was*, so he *is* because we know that 'once upon a time there was a man', and he *will be* as long as someone is going to tell his story. It is a human being who was there 'once upon a time', and only human beings can tell his story because only human beings know about 'once upon a time'. 'Once upon a time' is the time of human beings. It is human time.

A man was 'there' once upon a time. He was *there*, and not here. But he *is here* and will remain here as long as someone tells his story here. It is a man who 'was there'. Only human beings can locate him 'there' since only human beings know about 'here' and 'there'. 'Here' and 'there' is the space of human beings. It is human space.

Historicity is not just something which happened to us. It is not a propensity we 'slip into' as into a garment. We are historicity; we are time and space. The two Kantian 'forms of perception' are nothing

3

but the consciousness of our Being. The consciousness of our Being is our Being. The Kantian categories *a priori* – of quantity, quality, relation and modality – are secondary from an ontological aspect. They are not the consciousness of our Being but the expressions of the conscious reflection *on* our Being. Human beings can conceive of time and space without quantity, quality, relation and modality (as the 'tohu bohu', the void, the universal vacuum), but they cannot conceive of categories outside time and space. Even absurdity is temporal and spatial because we are time and space.

'Every human being is mortal'. The animal perishes, but it is not mortal. Only those are mortal who are *aware* that they will perish. *Only human beings are mortal.* Since we are time this is why we have not *been* and we shall not *be*. Since we are space, our not-Being means not being *here*. When we shall not be, we shall not be here but *there*: in the air, in the wind, in the fire, in Hades, in Heaven, in Hell, or in Nothingness. But even Nothingness is space, just as never is time. We are mortal but we are not dead. We cannot conceive of our 'being dead' for we are time and space.

That we have not been and we shall not be, that we have not been here and we shall not be here, *means* that when we had not been, *others* were, and when we shall not be, others will be; that when we shall not be 'here', others will be 'here'. It is imaginable that we were not and were not here in the times of Caesar and Napoleon, but it is unimaginable that we were not and were not here when *no one was*. It is imaginable that we shall not be and we shall not be here when others shall be, but it is unimaginable that we shall not be when *no one shall be*. 'Not-Being here' is only meaningful if others are here. Being nowhere is only meaningful if there is a 'somewhere', not-Being, if there is a Being. 'Once upon a time there was a man' *means* that there is someone who tells his story and there will be someone who will tell it. Historicity of *one man* entails the *historicity of humankind*. The plural is *prior* to the singular: *I am if we are, and I am not if we are not.* The primary question of historicity is the question of Gauguin: 'Where have we come from, what are we, where are we going?'

From the moment of mortality, from the moment of time and space, we have always raised that same question and therein expressed the historicity of humankind to which the historicity of our Being (of the Being of each individual) has been and always is related. The question never changes but the answers do. The answer to the question, 'Where have we come from, who are we, where are we going?', will be called '*historical consciousness*', and the answers to it, different in substance and structure, will be *the stages of historical consciousness,*

(a) First stage: unreflected generality: the genesis

In the beginning there was the beginning.

The sentence 'in the beginning there was...' does not mean that *there* is no more, not even that it cannot be anymore, only that *so* it was at the beginning.

The threshold of humanity is crossed at the moment when regulation by norms had been substituted for regulations by instincts. Only those beings can be called human whose actions and forms of behaviour develop through systems and institutions of conduct which exist externally to the given member of the species in the moment of his or her birth. At the beginning we are born into a clan, a tribe. Even though there is no social institution without change, alterations can be slow and minute, and therefore imperceptible. The norms and rules of social coexistence are constant and repetitive, not only within the lifespan of one single person, but for all generations which can 'meet' each other. The existing order is the order of existence, and it cannot be otherwise. But this order calls for justification, and normally it is legitimated by its *genesis*. And, for mankind, the most ancient form of legitimation via genesis is that accomplished by *myth*. To be more precise, it is the primary function of myth to legitimate genesis.

According to Lévi-Strauss all true myths perform a basic task: they account for the contradictions and tensions within the framework of the world of customs by explaining them in a repetitive way. Systems of values are never free of contradictions and inconsistencies. If they were, one would assume that a tiny group of people has developed norms of its own without any contact with various other groups – a genetically absurd assumption because the combination of genetic pools is the precondition of human survival. Such contact between different human groups brings about the combination, the synthesis of various systems of conduct. No process of homogenization is able to smooth out divergences completely, particularly with respect to sexual prescriptions. These latent contradictions have to be justified and are in fact legitimized via the myth of their genesis. Of course, we do not know, and can never know, whether all human groups have developed the myth of the genesis 'in the beginning'. The sentence 'in the beginning there was the beginning' does not refer to actual phylogenesis: it is rather a theoretical construction: the consciousness of beginning *is called* (defined as) beginning.

It is on the level of *unreflected generality* that historical consciousness expresses itself in the myth of the genesis. *Generality* means that the genesis of the system of values, habits, and institutions of the group in question encompasses in its projects the genesis of the world, the universe as such. Why and how a particular system of conduct came about and why it *should* have come about exactly as it did involves the answer to the question of why and how existence as such came about and came about exactly as it did. The end result of existence is *this* existence; 'once upon a time' is *'here and now'*. 'Unreflected' means that 'man' is identical with the clan or tribe of the myth. Our species has been very reluctant to strip this 'primitiveness' during thousands of years of high civilization. For the Hellenes, every 'barbarian' was born to be slave. Several languages have only one word for 'man' and 'human being', and the civilized Caucasian traveller often referred to the Aborigines of many lands as 'monkeys'.

The notion of the 'elected people' is only a more refined version of the primordial identification of 'man' and 'member of my tribe'. The myth of the Old Testament legitimized the Jewish people as the 'chosen' one in contrast to all other human groups, who became second-rate products of the Creation.

On the level of unreflected generality, *time is infinite in retrospect*. Infinitude is drawn here as an *image*: it is *not* conceptualized. The historical consciousness expressed in these myths concludes in the *present*. Future, past, and present are not distinguished. (Future-directed myths are already beyond the stage of unreflected generality.) Likewise, the image of space is not distinguished from the image of time. The present is not only 'now', it is also 'here': the 'here' of a clan or tribe.

But already the first answer to the question of historicity contains either in a latent or an explicit way all principles and modes of self-understanding which later on characterize *all stages* of historical consciousness *but one*.

The answer to the question 'where have we come from?' contains a causal explanation in a latent way. The stories of origin are also stories about the 'why'. At the same time 'there' and 'now' is the end result in which the 'origin' concludes. In all myths there is a hidden teleology. Although myths do not apply notions of 'laws' and 'regularities', *analogy* is one of their outstanding features, and assumes a valuable explanatory role in them. The analogical repetition of actions and events (we repeat the past and make it present) is the embryonic form of the notion of 'regularity'.

The motive of *'lesson'* is omnipresent in myths. Since genesis legitimizes the existing order as the order of existence, myth tells us what we ought to do and what we have to avoid, what we should fear and what we can hope. The transgressions committed by mythological figures are *warnings* for the believers. The interplay of fate and human activity gains momentum. It is fate that prevails, but a fate that can be influenced by human practices: it can be induced to show mercy. The practices (healing, human sacrifices, initiation rites, etc.) are prescribed and strictly regulated, but they can be performed both on behalf of the individual and the community.

The myth of genesis is also *the image of the world order*. It not only explains our being, it also arranges our experiences. These patterns are rational in so far as they ensure the smooth process of reproduction for the individual and the collectivity. One understands the world and acts in terms of this framework. *Understanding* and *action* are potentially divided.

Myth is storytelling. The explanation of our Being and the legitimation of our world and systems of conduct is *interesting*. The stories about the genesis are *representative* stories, and their attraction is not lost by repetition. But it is reasonable to suppose that even 'at the beginning' there were other stories beside the myths. Lucky hunting, fights, or deliverance could have equally been recounted. Were these stories incorporated in the myth or related to it, they would not embody any particular new tendency. But if not so incorporated, they would have needed a specific momentum. The stories of the myth are expressions of a collective consciousness. They cannot be deliberately 'corrected', though they cannot be falsified either. However, 'everyday stories' can always be corrected, even refuted. If someone narrated the story of a lucky hunting, the other could remark: 'it did not happen this way but that way', or, 'not only this happened but also this'. We may assume that *verification* and *falsification* first appeared *outside* historical consciousness.

(b)   Second stage: the consciousness of generality reflected in particularity. The consciousness of history

Kronos devoured his own children. As Hegel remarked, *time as history* (that is to say, politics, state, civilization) *has been born* with Zeus.. Above all, the consciousness of history is the consciousness of *change*. Not only 'once upon a time' is confronted with 'now' and 'here', but also yesterday and the day before yesterday are confronted with today. Rulers succeed each other, though these rulers are not all alike. There are the powerful and the weak, victorious and vanquished, 'better' and 'worse'. A ruler of today can be greater than another of yesterday or vice versa. No longer are all institutions legitimized by the genesis. Some were installed by particular rulers in a particular time and these rulers themselves then become the protagonists of certain myths: these are the myths of history.

The deeds of great rulers, heroes, bygone times, have to be put on record, rendered immortal. Future generations have to know about them. Of course, future means the future of the same body politic. But since 'ups' and 'downs' within the continuity are surmised, oral transmission cannot be trusted. As it never fades, *writing* has to bear witness to the immortal deeds. 'Putting on record' is not yet historiography as it is not yet *interpretative* (see Collingwood), but it *is* with writing that the consciousness of history emerges.

Being means from this moment on not only 'Being-in-time' but also 'Being-in-a-particular-time'. Every human being is mortal; so is every body politic. Naturally, *not our* body politic: its constancy and continuity is posited in advance (our descendants are the addressees of the hieroglyphs). But the body politic of 'others' most certainly is. *Our* pharaohs, *our* monarchs have wiped out *others*. These others existed, but they exist no more.

In Heidegger's view, the Persians were the first to develop a consciousness of history; the Jews and Greeks only followed suit. The Persians, Heidegger then argues, comprise the first historical nation. Though the consciousness of history emerged with writing, it was really the Jews and the Greeks (probably under Persian influence) who expressed it explicitly and on a higher level. For them, this consciousness implied more than the mere consciousness of change and of the mortality of the body politic of *others*. They reflected *on their own* body politic (their state) as on the upshot of human decision. Men (citizens) created the state, and have defended it, though they could have created it in a different way, and defended it in a different way. So it is that the image of the *alternative* appears. This image could only break through completely with the Greeks since the political historiography of the Old Testament, in the last instance, combines human decision and divine providence.

Should the state be, as it appears, the upshot of human decisions, then its survival or ruin is equally dependent on human decisions. The image of a possible collapse or destruction of one's own body politic has emerged simultaneously with the idea of alternatives. Be it expressed in philosophical considerations or in prophecies, the threat invites contemplation and action: we have to find out what to do in order that our state will survive and flourish.

On the level of unreflected historicity, human beings must comply with the prescriptions of traditional habits. The 'content', that is to say, the interpretation of good and evil, of correct and incorrect, is fixed: as modes of conduct are legitimized by myth, no room exists for personal interpretation. Basically 'that which we ought to do' is traditionally fixed even on the first level of the development of historical consciousness (for instance, Amenhotep's reforms could not break through), even though the personal initiative is already present as far as the 'how' of the action, and mostly of political action, was concerned. But it happens only on the second level of this stage of historical consciousness (most explicitly with the Greeks) that both that which we ought to do and the way in which we ought to do it become a matter of consideration. Although consensus regarding the basic values is preserved, their *interpretation* is more and more individualized. From this time onwards, individuals could declare: 'not that is good, but this is good; not that is just, but this is just; not that is true, but this is true.' Moreover, should I say 'not that is good, but this is good', I am obliged to *argue* on behalf of my interpretation, to justify it, verify it. This is exactly what philosophy does, what rhetoric does, what Thucydides' protagonists did.

In this stage of historical consciousness generality is reflected in particularity. The supreme good is the good of state (of my state, my people), whilst the good and the happiness of men (of individuals) derives from it. But, within limits, individuals are free to define what the good of the state is, how this goodness can be procured; how it may ensure the goodness and happiness of the citizens, and what has to be done in order to maintain it. Both verification and justification of the interpretation of good, just and true aim at the persuasion of the actors. The individual assumes that if he could persuade others to accept his interpretation, the state would be rescued from the ill fate it is doomed to, or else the best of states could be realized. Thus the consciousness of change entails the intention of change (of perfecting or restoring). Is change good at all? Do we have to choose dynamism or stagnation? Which kind of change is good and which is bad in relation to ensuring the being and well-being of the state? These are the questions raised. (The sons of Israel pondered in a similar fashion on whether or not to elect a king as other peoples did.)

Consciousness of history thus implies a new form of rationality. Whereas in the state of unreflected generality rational action meant guarding and observing the homogenous norms of conduct, the reproduction of society being in this way ensured, reflective consciousness queries these very systems of conduct. The norms of rational argumentation develop and the correct and incorrect *forms* of argumentation are distinguished. According to Aristotle's *Rhetoric*, the convincing argument is logical, demonstrative, and aims at the good. It distinguishes between essence and appearance, between true knowledge and opinion. Yet where there is rational argumentation, there is its abuse as well. Rational argument and demagogy are twin brothers; they can only emerge together. Reflected generality entails both possibilities. If a new norm of rationality is established, the possibility of its violation is equally established.

In the state of unreflected generality the existential question of historicity ('where have we come from, what are we, where are we going?') is raised and answered by one single objectivation: the myth. But in the second stage of historical consciousness, the objectivations which raise and answer this very question are already differentiated. Even the Bible contains myth, historiography, poetry, penal code, and rhetoric in the same breath, though due to all of them being subjected to religion, philosophy is pre-empted. The clear-cut distinction between the various objectivations of historicity is the merit of the Greek culture. Even though myth does not disappear, but in fact remains preponderant in popular belief, it can be more or less individually interpreted. Myth is no longer the immobile and closed system of a collective world-view, but rather a medium through which changing, particularized and individualized world-views can be expressed and formulated. It also becomes a medium for art and philosophy, and not an obligatory medium, but one open to choice. Not all tragedies used myth as their medium (for example, *The Persians*), even less have comedy or poetry. Side by side with the sculptures of gods stand the sculptures of athletes. Plato made use of the medium of myth, Aristotle did not. The explanation of genesis is shared between myth and philosophy. 'At the beginning' there was the water, the *apeiron*, the four elements, the fire, the reason, the numbers, the matter, and the form. The secular explanations of genesis are individual and competitive. Argumentation, justification and verification are also increasingly applied to the understanding of genesis. But if genesis is made a philosophical subject matter, the explanation does not lead any more *directly* towards the legitimation of one group of people or one state. *Apeiron* does not legitimize the systems of conduct in Miletus. The hidden or explicit goal of genesis could not be Miletus, Athens, or Syracuse, for history had been thought of as the result of human deliberations and actions. The *particular genesis* thus becomes disconnected from *general genesis*, and the former is made subject matter by *historiography*. So it is that *true knowledge* of history (history as episteme) was born. Jews and Greeks are no longer mere chroniclers of the great deeds and victories of monarchs. They tell stories about peoples and citizens. But neither are they merely storytelling: both the interpretation of motives and the explanations of events gain momentum. Since history is not a myth, its being a 'true story' requires verification with facts. Events have to be described as they really happened. The facts are, as a rule, testimonies of eye-witnesses (such as with Herodotus) or testimonies consensually accepted within a given culture. Historical *space*, in comparison to the image of space on the level of unreflected generality, *widens*. All peoples have to be understood (their motives interpreted, their fate explained) who had once been or who are now, our friends or foes. Roman historiography subsequently embraced the whole of the then known civilized world. Yet because generality is always reflected in particularity, the *time* of historiography is limited by the lifetime of the city, the people to whom the historian belongs. For Collingwood, '*ab urbe condita*' is the most distant horizon at this stage.

The existential question of historicity is answered by historiography mainly through the question: 'where have we come from?' The two questions: 'where have we come from, and what are we?' with emphasis on the second, is the issue raised and answered most powerfully by *tragedy*. This is why, after comparing historiography to tragedy, Aristotle decides in favour of the latter. Tragedy not only expresses our 'Being-in-a-particular-age' but it also expresses the challenge of the age to Being. The challenge is answered by the whole personality of the actors, their reflections, passions, their virtues and transgressions. Similar representations in the Bible are the stories of

Judith, Esther, Job, and several tragic episodes in the Book of Kings. Granted this, the consciousness of history in tragedy does not always express the final reconciliation of age and Being. In Euripides' tragedies fear becomes all-embracing and the reconciliation is only formal. The end of history casts its dark shadow on the fate of the actors. We are the women of Troy. Perhaps we do not head in any direction. If we go nowhere, there is nothing left. To be in a particular age means to be in a people, in a state, in the age of *this* people and *this* state. If Being and age cannot be reconciled, they perish together. The last part of the existential question of historicity can be answered in only two ways: in terms of reconciliation, or in the *negative*. In answer to 'Where are we going?', there is either the perennial present, or nowhere.

Ancient philosophy provides an answer to the question of 'who are we?' Contrary to tragedy, in philosophy, Being challenges the age, virtuous man society. In tragedy, the situation is concrete; in philosophy it is abstract. Since in philosophy the virtuous man is the challenging party, the question 'where are we going?' can be answered in a positive sense; from the standpoint of the individual; from that of individual Being. The realization of the idea of humanity is the incipient goal of all Being, or at least it *should be*. The nihil of historicity is death, but as long as there is life there is no death. Epicurus rightly said that there is no necessity to live in necessity. In brief, the notion of *personal freedom* becomes increasingly disconnected from the Being-in-a-particular-age. The outcome of ancient philosophy makes it clear that it was *generality* that had been reflected in particularity. Particularity ('my city', 'my people') lost ground and the conscious Being (man as free person) finally challenged the age absolutely: *he abstracted from his Being-in-a-particular-age.*

But generality never ceased to be reflected in particularity. This is why the question of 'where are we going?' could be answered in a darkening age from the viewpoint of Being. This Being could never construct an age adequate to his virtues and his freedom, not even in his imagination. Being could abstract from its own Being-in-a-particular-age, but there were only two courses open through which it could be aware of this age: either as perennial Being or the coming collapse of the world: the end of history.

(c)   Third stage: the consciousness of unreflected universality

Whereas in the previous stage of historical consciousness the collapse of a particular world meant the collapse of the world as such, with this collapse becoming subject matter only in the form of the limit of human possibilities, the universal myth owes its conception to the collapse itself. The destruction of Judea gave birth to Christianity; the destruction of Rome marked the latter's final triumph. Particularities had been relativized and generality could be reflected in them no longer. The 'King of the Jews' became the redeemer of *humankind*.

When generality is unreflected, the question of what man really is cannot be raised, for the answer to this question is fixed in the myth: we are (our tribe, our group) *homo sapiens*. When generality is reflected in particularity, this question can be, and indeed is, raised. Inquiry into human nature, motivation, essence, substance, is launched, although from the perspective of the particular body politic in which generality is reflected. Once again, universal myth is unreflected. We cannot raise questions as to what we really are (and where we really come from and where we really are going) because the myth offers the complete answer and this answer cannot be challenged. Human nature is *created* according to the intention of the Creator. This Creator is *universality per se*. Generality (human essence, humankind) is dependent on universality and contingent on the same. Heavenly and earthly kingdoms are divided. The consciousness of unreflected universality excludes particularity. No matter which people you belong to, your salvation hinges solely on your relation to universality. Even pagans are potential Christians – one only has to convert them to the greater glory of God to make possible the salvation of their immortal soul. Heroes and heroines of Christian legends are unlike the heroes and heroines of ancient myths in that they do not conquer countries, but souls. And even if they did so conquer, they won souls thereby. The hermit withdraws to the seclusion of the desert in order to find salvation for *his own soul*. Penitence for sin is not required (as with Oedipus) in order to save a community; the atonement of the person is a goal in itself and does not serve as a means for something else. The *person*, even if only in respect of his sin and salvation, is destined to be involved with his own end whilst being directly related to the universality embodied in the church.

Consequently, every person's personal salvation is the 'royal road' to universality. The redemption of humankind is nothing but the *aggregate* of everyone's personal salvation. Humankind is intrinsic in each human being, and the person observing God's commandments realizes the possibilities of humankind. (Christian) man is equal in so far as every man has equal access to universality and every man is equally free not to realize this possibility. Sartre evidently had this in mind when (in his play *Bariola*) he declared, in the voice of his protagonist, that freedom was born with the teaching of Christ.

The consciousness of universal myth is the unreflected consciousness of *historical totality*. It offers a homogeneous and final answer to the existential question of historicity ('where have we come from, what are we, where are we going?'). The history of human beings (humankind) is arranged from the *beginning to the end* (creation-fall-redemption-Last Judgment), and is divided into two stages (one before, one after the redemption). The first stage is prehistory, the second is past, present, and future. Future is not only part of, but is also the *purpose* of history; it is its *accomplishment* and its *end*. It is no longer an uncertainty, the threat of collapse that may be avoided, but the certainty, the unavoidable outcome. But the person embodies history *as a whole*. He lives after the redemption, and so the end (the Last Judgment) can bear the meaning of promise and fulfilment for him. The fulfilment of times is the fulfilment of historicity. But Man is born with the original sin as well (with the sin that precedes redemption), and so the same end can bear the meaning of threat and final damnation for him. In this case too, fulfilment of times is fulfilment of historicity. Being-in-time is here identical with Being-in-all-times.

The consciousness of unreflected universality is the consciousness of ideality (in the sense that this consciousness does not take recourse to the empirical). This is its distinctive feature as compared to both the consciousness of unreflected generality and the consciousness of generality reflected in particularity. In the former, the contradictions within the norms of conduct had been summarized and legitimized by the myth, but there was no contradiction between particularity and generality since consciousness expressed them as identities. In the latter, the conflict between particularity and generality is depicted in art and conceptualized in philosophy. Generality is nothing but the utmost possibility of particularity, its Ought as juxtaposed to its Is. Common to both stages is that consciousness refers to *reality*, though the consciousness of universal myth derives from the interrelation of the notions of God – humankind. 'Humankind' is not a real entity as Athens, Jerusalem, or Rome had been – humankind resides in the personal soul. 'Real' societies (as opposed to the *spiritual* community of Christendom) in the period of the late Roman Empire or in the Middle Ages were not less particular than their predecessors. Their particularity was embodied in their customs, traditions, estates, political institutions and was expressed by the consciousness of these particularities. They even transmitted the myths of the beginning via their practices and superstitions. But these particular types of (real) consciousness *cannot* formulate themselves *historically*, but only through the medium of universal myth. In cases of serious conflict, the church either assimilates these particularistic types of consciousness into the universal myth with a great amount of elasticity, or it accuses them of heresy and annihilates them. There is only one form of objectivation which is capable of harmoniously expressing the ideality of universal myth and the reality of particularistic life: this is art. (Not only in stories such as those about Roland or Cid but also in lyric poetry and painting). Redemption of humankind cannot be painted, only the Saviour can; nor can the salvation of our soul be painted, only the human being's suffering and struggling.

For as much as consciousness here originates from 'ideality', it transforms real time and real space into ideal time and ideal space. Medieval chronicles are nothing but the repetition of the consciousness of history on its first level. If they entail explanations at all, these are pseudo-explanations. The reference to the ideal time and the ideal place by a simple (and final) gesture suffices; it speaks for itself. Being-in-a-particular-age is *conditional* as compared to our Being-for-eternity. The particularistic entities (political bodies, peoples, states) have no *real future* in real time and real space. Future is the future of the person (the representative of humankind) – and so it is the future of ideality.

In this way, universal myth answers the question as to what man is, what humankind is, what history as a whole is about, and it encompasses the past, the present, and the future. The person is the addressee of universal myth, but the same person is not allowed to reflect upon the myth; the myth demands *belief*. But belief does not completely exclude the interpretation of the myth. The more the person becomes aware of the *problems* of real time and space, the more he offers a new interpretation about universal time and space as 'idealities'. The triad of Joachim of Fiore – the epoch of the Father is that of obedience, the epoch of the Son is that of love, and the future epoch of the Holy Spirit is that of freedom – imagines future as the realm of freedom, Heaven on Earth. This is philosophy of History *in statu nascendi*. As the consciousness of generality reflected in particularity, in its final formulation (stoicism and epicureanism), pointed already towards the consciousness of particularity reflected in generality, so pointed the consciousness of unreflected universality in its final formulation towards the consciousness of reflected universality.

(d)   Fourth stage: the consciousness of generality reflected in particularity

Within this stage one has to again distinguish two levels. The first is the consciousness of a *new beginning in history*, the second the consciousness of generality reflected in particularity proper. But generality is reflected upon already on the first level. 'Human being' is no longer identical with the citizens of a particular state or with the bearers of one specific culture. Human being *means every* human being, *human nature as such*. This is why the following question can be raised: which societies and which kinds of state or systems of belief are adequate to human nature, and, of these, which are *more* and which are *less* adequate to it. Past is being slowly transformed from *prehistory* – from a construct of artistic fantasy, from myth – into *history*. Sartre remarked that we are able to *choose* our history, but this has not always been true. It is a historical consciousness that transcends the prehistory of our institutions which enables us to choose our history. Consciousness *about* history differs from consciousness *of* history in that the former allows for a choice of our past. The consciousness of a new beginning of history has chosen the city-states of ancient times for its own past, regardless of whether the choice fell on Rome, Athens, or Jerusalem. All that happened in *those* times and cities became our prehistory to a *greater extent* than what happened in centuries preceding ours. All that happened *there* was of greater importance for us than what happened *here*. Present is reborn from times bygone. Times bygone become the source of knowledge, and, at the same time, paragons. The spontaneous identification of times bygone and the present (for example, in medieval Italian city-states) is queried and is replaced by *analogy*. Vasari was well aware of the fact that the art inspired by Greek sculpture is not identical to original Greek scupture, just as Machiavelli knew well that Florence was *not* a mere continuation of Rome, and as Grotius had no doubts that the Netherlands were *un*like Jerusalem.

As far as the choice of history is concerned, there is more continuity than discontinuity between the two levels of the consciousness of generality reflected in particularity. The consciousness *about* history does not really change, only the scope of our-chosen-history widens. Consciousness about history implies the comparison of various periods and societies. It also implies keeping distances clear: if I choose times bygone, I choose a history which exists no longer; which has terminated (this is why it is times bygone). That which has already been terminated can only be understood viewed from its *end*. This vision of the end of a particular culture, of its collapse, becomes the vision of the past. It is for this reason that it can be relativized: the end of *one* world is no longer identical with the end of the world. Once upon a time there was a people, there was a state, but they exist no longer; they existed in their space and time but not in ours. However, it is we who understand them, who revitalize them, who restore them to the present. Past cultures do not exist in that they have disappeared,˙ but they exist still in that we are able to imagine and re-imagine them; to reflect on them. They live in us, with us.

If cultures, states and peoples can be understood when viewed from their respective ends; if, also, they can be compared when so viewed, then 'history' assumed *plurality* as *histories*. Consciousness about history was to begin with consciousness about histories. The comparison of different histories involves statements about *regularities*. In this conception, every civilization (history) covers the same stages of development: ascent, flourishing, and decline. Civilizations resemble organisms. They have their childhood, adolescence, and manhood, and finally they all die. This metaphor, having already emerged sporadically in ancient periods, now becomes dominating. But now the questions regarding the common and the particular causes of these sequences are raised and answered differently. Further, present civilization too is put under scrutiny when surveyed from the same patterns. Where do we stand now? Are we at the stage of childhood, adolescence, manhood or senility? Shall we repeat this sequence in the same way or not? Even Hume believed that England had already passed the peak of her civilization.

The *real time* of historical consciousness widens continuously. Vico, at his time, had already turned back to *archaic* Greece, the Jesuits and Voltaire discovered that China had an even more ancient history. This widening of real time finally leads to the attempt at *unifying* all histories in question. Civilizations are, it is now assumed, interconnected in some way or another. Regularities are not only inherent in each civilization, but the consecution of civilizations shows an equal regularity. The spirit of the Vicoean *corsi e ricorsi* accounts precisely for this regularity. The end result is the notion of 'world history' as

coined by Voltaire. The *ideal time* of history disappears simultaneously from historical consciousness and survives only as a private faith.
History is no longer the history of redemption. The future inherent
in universal myth, the vision of a rupture, of a collapse of the present world, as the promise to the good and the warning for the evil,
loses all its relevance. Even if historical consciousness has to come
to terms (consistent with the circular regularity) with the decline of
a present culture, the birth of a new culture in a future is simultaneously projected with it. But the future is increasingly grasped
in terms of realizing the models of rationality. The image of *universal genesis* is equally buried. The world has no longer 'originated'
from a common substance: water, *apeiron*, forms, etc.; it has not been
created either.

The great metaphysical systems are static and timeless. One single
substance *exists*, infinite substances exist, things exist (from 'past'
infinities to 'future' infinities). The Almighty is a watchmaker who
winds up the world-clock. The universe is being ushered out of
history. The 'disenchantment of the world' begins its tortuous
journey. Consciousness about history promotes the distinction
between *cultural* product on the one hand, and *'natural'* product on
the other; between *our lives and our life-conditions*. The laws of the
universe are static; the laws of culture (of histories) are changing.
Time is culture: *we are time*. The history of the ancient can be
exemplary, but not their metaphysics. In regard to the latter there is
no new beginning, for the beginning is absolute. Only the evidence of
human reason or human senses can be the fountainhead of knowledge.
But consciousness mirrors particularity in *generality: human nature* is
the focal point of world construction. It is (a kind of) 'nature' and it is
'human'. Since it is nature, the temporal has to be reintegrated with
the eternal (human being into nature). As far as it is nature, human
being is 'eternal'. But human nature is *human*, temporal, dynamic,
changing, as well. In order to resolve the contradiction, qualities had
to be attributed to human nature which, even though being eternal,
could account for change, dynamics, and history. These propensities
are freedom and reason: Human beings are born free and they are
endowed with *reason*. Man is free, and therefore can change himself
and his world. He is endowed with reason, and therefore can produce
and increase his knowledge, and can create a *rational society* by
applying this knowledge. There was no consensus about the *motivational* system of human nature. The controversial matter was whether
our basic passions were evil or good. But it became consensually

accepted by the consciousness of generality reflected in particularity that human nature is basically characterized by freedom and reason.

In the consciousness of particularity reflected in generality, man's essence was his being a citizen, and the question of 'what are we?' was answered by ethics. In the fourth stage of the development of historical consciousness, freedom was no longer identified with political or ethical freedom. Even evil could be considered a creative force in human history (egotism, vanity, crime). But a society will finally have to be established in which personal and social freedom can be reconciled. The model of social contract can easily (and rightly) be declared a naive abstraction; nevertheless, it is a wise construction. It suggests that human nature is both the source and the limit of our possibilities and that we have to make the best of it. Particularity was reflected in generality in all self-expressions of the fourth stage of historical consciousness. The new European culture was identified with the dawn of rational humankind, bourgeois civil society with rational society, bourgeois and citizen with freedom and reason, thus with human nature.

It has been mentioned that real time progressively widens and ideal time disappears. Real space widens as well, and, in fact, in a double sense; as the space of history and as the space of the universe. Contrary to ideal time, ideal space had been preserved, even though transformed into the infinite eternity of metaphysical systems. Ideal space only disappears simultaneously with the resurrection of ideal time (with Kant's 'Copernican turn'). Geographical space and the space of history become distinct. The first encompasses the whole globe, the second the territories of 'high cultures'. Travellers gave accounts of the life of peoples in remote and hitherto unknown places of our earth. They were considered peoples 'outside' histories, but became more and more the objects of curiosity. Their incorporation into a common history (of humankind) already points towards the consciousness of reflected universality.

At the stage of the consciousness of unreflected universality the objectivations were hierarchically organised; the all-embracing objectivation was religion. At the fourth stage they became symmetrical and developed independently and simultaneously. In their entirety they expressed the consciousness of generality reflected in particularity. Historiographies chose their own past, reflecting the generality in particularities, and answering the question: 'Where have we come from?' this way. The new natural sciences start to treat our world as an object, and this is legitimate because the subject (history) is disconnected from nature and human reason is *authorized* to reveal the secrets of our space. Philosophy queries human possibilities anew (now as possibilities of 'human nature'), and offers answers to the question: 'what are we?' Art does this also. But the fact that generality is reflected in particularity is even clearer in art than in philosophy. The world of art is not simply a 'situation', a challenge to which individuals react in a good or evil, an extreme or less extreme way; here they react always passionately. The situations themselves become heterogeneous. Social life is far from being identical to the political sphere: society and state are divided, and private life as such becomes the topic of art. Generality is constituted through particularity and not vice versa. History can be identified with historicity. The individual creates fate and thereby his or her own fate. The protagonist of the novel is not 'ready made' at the beginning of the work: he or she makes himself or herself. To apply Lukács's term, the individual becomes problematic in that he or she *solves problems* of the environment, of his or her own character, and this is seen from Robinson to Tom Jones. All new topics involve discoveries of new problems, and art becomes sensitive to exploring new topics; everything that is 'humane' can become its subject matter. But the themes are always taken from the *present*. History and myth are only mediums through which to grasp the present. Art travels in the depths of the present. Its adventures are means through which we can come to grips with 'what we are'. Its past is the past of the present and its future is the future of the present. The questions: 'where have we come from' and 'where are we going?' are of no use for art. The particularities of the present offer all the opportunities necessary to explore the potentialities of human nature.

(e) Fifth stage: the consciousness of world-history or the consciousness of reflected universality

Theater mundi is already set in the period between the siege of the Bastille and Waterloo. Junius Brutus made his appearance on the stage of Rome: Danton coined his final catchwords whilst already in front of the limelights of world history, and being fully aware of his presence on the stage of *theater mundi*. Goethe's dictum truly expresses the feelings and ideas elicited by this experience. 'It is appropriate to these times to measure our small private affairs on the immense scale of world-history'.* There are no longer histories in the plural, there is only 'History' (with a capital H), universal history, world history. World-historical consciousness *relativizes* our culture in so far as it reflects upon the *historicity* of the present, but it also makes it *absolute* in so far as it reflects on itself as the *only true self-consciousness of historicity*.

World-historical consciousness becomes again the consciousness of universality. All human histories are unified under a universalistic concept which contains past, present, and future. The future is no longer the future of one or the other culture but the future of humankind. It is not thought of as the perennial presence of the existing order either. It is that which is *different*: the world of salvation, the world of doomsday or of the eternal process of perfection. In all of this there is the recurring image of redemption, but it is not in the form of a homogenous belief. The consciousness of universality is now *pluralistic*. It can cherish the messianic idea of the unification of individual and species, or make a cast for the 'invisible hand' of economic relations, or for reason, for industry, for legal institutions as the repositories of future perfection. The despairing cry that no redemption exists because evil is ineradicable from our nature is also one of the several expressions of the new consciousness of universality. World-historical consciousness constitutes the world just as much from the viewpoint of its final issue as did Christianity. The final issue may be the end of history or of prehistory or the endlessness of eternal perfection – in all cases present is relativized *because* it is illuminated by the beam of light of the future.

However, the new consciousness of universality is reflected. As it is pluralistic, the variations on the same theme have to argue with each other *rationally*. They must defend and verify their own *images of future* against the images of others. Future is of no aid in this since it is future that has to be verified. The time of universal history is *ideal time*, but *real time*, that of the present, is an inexhaustible source of argumentation. Because present proves future, present has to be known, described, reflected on. Just as the analysis of civil society (bürgerliche Gesellschaft) *proves* the self-development of world-spirit, so the critique of capitalism *proves* the relevance of the society of associated producers, the critique of mass-culture the Superman, and the critique of society the superiority of community. This is why

---

* Quoted in F. Meinecke, *Die Entstehung des Historismus*, Verlag von R. Oldenburg, München/Berlin, 1936, vol. II, p. 518.

the consciousness of reflected universality embraces *Kulturkritik* on the one hand, and *social science* on the other. World-historical consciousness is *secular*. It is neither religion nor myth: it is primarily philosophy of history. It dwells not only in the 'recesses of history', in the studies of philosophers, but also on the streets and battlefields. Political revolutions are fought with this consciousness: 'le jour de gloire est arrivé'.

The universal myth had no collective point of reference. It addressed the person. There was no particular 'here and now' in it; all moments 'here and now' between salvation and the Last Judgment were alike. The way to repentance had always remained open. Reflected universality has reference to *representative* subjects: the collective subjects or the 'great man'. 'Here and now' gains emphasis: dozens of Waterloos were not enough to shake this belief. 'Here and now' of the barricades and battlefields is reverberated by philosophy of history and vice versa.

Thus the emphasis on *real time* (within the framework of ideal time) stands out both in the theory and practice of world-historical consciousness. The past (that-which-is-not-yet-present) is construed as 'different' in comparison to our times. The habits and values of the past are subsequently devalorized. The present has to be grasped *scientifically*; so has the past. The only valid knowledge is scientific knowledge, and *values* become the *objects* of research, not its *limits*. The idea that reason has to establish an *ethical* (or moral) state or society in the future (an idea still decisive in Kant, who stood on the borderline between two historical epochs) is ever more relegated to the background. The 'dialectic' of virtue (*'Tugend'*) and 'world-process' (*Weltlauf*), the primacy of the religious attitude as against the moral one, the emphasis on 'beyond good and evil' or on 'value-free science', all of these express basically the same concern. The universality of 'ideal time' and the methodology of real time are akin. Of course, private life can be directed by traditional systems of conduct as before, and even ancient types of moral philosophies (such as stoicism and epicureanism) may further organize the various ways of life without becoming theoretical components of a universalistic reflection.

The question of what man is becomes subordinated to other questions. The consciousness of reflected universality understands our existence in terms of its varying social setting. What history is, what civilization is, has to be answered. Man *became* what he is in history, in civilization. Motivation, good or evil, is explained by history. Evil is due to the repression of human passions. Should a civilization come about which would allow for the free manifestation of all our passions, we would be good and happy, so Fourier and Kropotkin argue. Our passions (instincts) demolish the framework of human coexistence, and so civilization has to control them, Freud argues. Darwin's work had been exploited for quite different kinds of argumentation: struggle for life or the co-operation of the species justify two contradictory theoretical proposals. In all these and similar theories the genesis of present man is the genesis of historical man, of civilized man. The universalization of man is the universalization of history (or civilization).

In this way man becomes the subject *of* history, but not the *person*. The person becomes subject *to* history. Man is universal, but not the person. The person is identified with the universal called 'the man' only if he or she becomes the subject of history or *resigns* history completely. The person is either seen as contingent or as the *man of genius* or as the *man of resignation* (from history). This 'contingent person' pursues his or her goals, does his or her duty as a means for 'higher' aims (of the world-spirit, of historical laws, of unconscious structures). It is through him or her that History, the uncionscious, the 'laws' realize themselves. The protagonists of nineteenth-century novels are mostly contingent persons. They are defeated by superior powers, and even their happiness is not their own deed, but befalls to them by the grace of the 'cunning of reason'. The genius, the great conductor of history, is not subject to rules, but is their arbitrary creator. Men of genius in politics, in art, or in abstract ideas are worshipped. Human sacrifice is welcome on their altars; contingent persons are so much raw material for them. Heine's grenadiers express this life-feeling in all its grandiose inhumanity:

> Was schert mich Weib, was schert mich Kind,
> Ich trage weit besseres Verlangen!
> Lass sie betteln gehen, wenn sie hungrig sind
> Mein Kaiser, mein Kaiser gefangen!*

The resignation (from history) means at the first stage the solidarity of small communities or the choice of personal relations or the withdrawal into the symbolic (though not always into the symbolic)

---

*What matters child, what matters wife?
There is a loftier pulse in my veins;
If they hunger, let them go begging through life –
My emperor, my emperor's in chains!
(Heinrich Heine, *The Two Grenadiers*, translated by Aaron Kramer.)

frugality of the *chambres de mansard*. At the second stage it is equivalent to the authenticity of Being-towards-Death. Finally, one way or the other, universal Man (man of history) becomes Superman, in the present or in the constructed future, whilst the person remains creature (created by history as 'nature').

While the person becomes created nature (creature), nature equally becomes created. It will be demystified, dehumanized, de-anthromorphic, de-anthropologized. The Creator of ancient times finds shelter and abode in our innermost soul. History creates nature to the extent that it changes nature (both theoretically and pragmatically). Knowledge is power: the universal man possesses power, but not the person.

World-historical consciousness progressively universalizes the *taste* and makes it thereby the subject matter of the judgment of taste. The works of art are scrutinized in their capacity of being embedded in time. Art is conceived of as *historical* product. The choice of a particular historical past determines the choice of a particular genre of art, style, creative vision of the world. It expresses a preference of a way of life. Every way of life and the genres, works of art, etc. adequate to it can be gradually appreciated: the art of knighthood (Hurd), that of the peasantry (the cult of folk song, folk tale, folk art), the pre-Raphaelite painting, the Orphic mystery, African sculpture, Chinese painting, Egyptian architecture, and the like. The emphasis on the *new* and the choice of an *ancient* artistic form are interconnected. The various preferences are shifted at an ever-increasing speed and they are increasingly individualized as well.

The consciousness of reflected universality envisages particularity as the bearer of universality. Just as the person had to become the universal person (the man of genius) in order to be worshipped, integrations have to embody the goal and message of universality in order to be justified. Particular nations, peoples, and classes were supposed to embody universality *per se*. The culture or the 'spirit' of certain peoples became the repository of human culture; nations were acclaimed as 'world-historical nations' and classes as 'world-historical classes'. The message of the former stage of development of historical consciousness, according to which *every* human being is born free and is equally endowed with reason, is now dismissed with contempt as historical and naive. Generality (man as humankind) will no longer be reflected upon *directly*, only indirectly. It does not exist, it can only come about, if at all, via universality realized through the deeds of world-historical particularities.

But the stage of the consciousness of reflected universality is not homogeneous; perhaps even less so than the former stage of consciousness. More precisely, it never becomes all-embracing since the consciousness of particularity reflected in generality does not fade away. It remains prominent in the struggles *for political democracy*. Every movement (from working-class organizations to feminism) which aims at the realization of political democracy insists on the presupposition that every human being is born free and endowed with reason; this is why everyone should be entitled to participate in political decision-making. In the sole traditional democracy of this period (in the United States) the consciousness of reflected universality did not even emerge. It became dominant in the semi-feudal German states (and later in the unified Germany), and in Bonapartist and post-Bonapartist France. But those who struggle for political democracy turn away from the consciousness of reflected universality even in these states. This explains Sorel's hatred against those French socialists and democrats who were active in the struggle against the trial of Dreyfus: he opposed to them the idea of universality in the secularized but unreflected form of a new myth. Nietzsche's hatred against the narrow-minded 'grocers' of his time was the manifestation of the same hostility against the consciousness of generality from the perspective of an unreflected universal and secular myth of different provenance.

Although the consciousness of particularity reflected in generality has not faded away, its formulation has undergone basic changes. In the previous epoch man was identified with the bourgeois; now human being becomes identified with the worker and the woman as well. It is easy to reflect generality in particularity since the real human being usually has his or her identity as bourgeois, worker, woman, and the like. Identification becomes difficult or even impossible only for those who have lost their particular identity, and amongst these are the *intellectuals*, increasingly disconnected from their original background of class and estate affiliation. Intellectuals do not belong to classes and they do not constitute a class of their own. They are constituted *qua* intellectuals through their knowledge, through the task they perform in the division of labour: the task of creating *meaningful world-views* in an ever more *pragmatic* age. In a world where knowledge has become general, where it can be used by anybody, and is therefore used indiscriminately, the job of producing knowledge creates social identity, but not *class identity*. This is why intellectuals become the bearers of the consciousness of universality. Universal knowledge is impotent without identity. This is why intellectuals impute universality to various identities. The intellectual *identifies* himself or herself with an existing integration (class or nation) constituted through this identification as a 'world-historical' nation, people, or class. The intellectuals' other option is to turn their backs to history and particular societies (as unworthy of universality) and to mystify themselves and their being as the ontological absolute, as the identity in negativity. Intellectuals are 'problematic individuals' *par excellence*, and as such they become the scourge of God.

Both types of consciousness have their own truths. The version of the consciousness of particularity reflected in generality creates some progress; the consciousness of reflected universality judges it as petty, irrelevant, banausic as measured with the absolute standards of universalistic ideas. The consciousness of reflected universality is a problematic one because its will is *the will to the absolute*, but it is precisely for that reason that *it can perform its mission as the 'scourge of God'*. Even the fairly sceptical Weber formulated it this way: 'Certainly all historical experience confirms the truth that man would never have attained the possible unless time and again he had reached out for the impossible.'*

Faust is the problematic individual. Because he cannot face old age or death, and he cannot accept limited knowledge, he appears as such from the first scene of the play. He wants to know everything and live every experience. His existence is nothing but the will to the absolute. It is here that, as against practical reason, there is founded the primacy of theoretical reason combined with the totality of life-experience. The world-historical excursion is led by Mephistopheles. Nevertheless, at the end of this world-drama the problematic individual finds his way back to the consciousness of reflected generality:

> Yes - this I hold to with devout insistence,
> Wisdom's last verdict goes to say:
> He only earns both freedom and existence
> Who must reconquer them each day.
> And so, ringed all about by perils, here
> Youth, manhood, age will spend their strenuous year.

---

* M. Weber, *Politics as a Vocation*, in H. H. Gerth and C. W. Mills (eds), *From Max Weber: Essays in Sociology*, Oxford University Press, New York, p. 128.

Such teeming would I see upon this land,
On acres free among free people stand.*

'Freedom' does not stand here for the self-realization of the
world-spirit or for absolute redemption. 'Earthly paradise' is nothing
else but our earth, where freedom and life have to be conquered daily,
where honest work has to cope with dangers, where life becomes
completed in its finitude. Goethe, as well as Kant, stood between two
epochs.

But very soon the problematic individual becomes the protagonist
in art, and not only as the 'contingent person' of the novel. The artist
himself is increasingly problematic, and so is poetry at its best (Byron,
Shelley, Baudelaire, Verlaine, Rimbaud). Reflected universality in its
purest culture can be detected in Wagner's musical dramas. In Ibsen,
the only non-problematic individual is a woman. Owing to the
problematic individual being forever present in the world-vision of
intellectuals, it can only have one fulfilment: the creation of a work of
universal validity. There is fulfilment for the problematic artist, but
not for the problematic person created by the artist. All Peer Gynts
(be they called Rastignac or Rubempré or Madame Bovary) end up in
the melting-spoon of the Great Button-Founder. If creation itself
becomes problematic for the artist, his or her creature undergoes a
transmutation from the problematic to the inauthentic individual: it
becomes a 'man without qualities'.

Dostoevsky, as Lukács suggested in his *The Theory of the Novel*,
already belongs to a new epoch. The consciousness of reflected
universality is unmasked again as a devilish principle. But the
individual bearer of this consciousness is no longer gigantic, no longer
the man of genius who seeks the impossible. He is identified as the
creature, as the contingent individual, as inauthenticity incarnate. The
counterpoint to inauthenticity is goodness, though goodness is
impotent. But although impotent, it is also exemplary and imperative.
Categorical imperative remains alive even in the chaotic soul of
inauthentic man. Faust could not face death; the Superman already
enjoins us to subdue fear. But Dostoevsky knew that Life-to-Death is
the *inauthentic* Being. The fear of death does not have to be subdued:
the fear of moral transgression has to be regained. He belongs indeed
to a new epoch, but will this new epoch come?

---

* J. W. von Goethe, *Faust*, trans. Walter Arndt, New York, 1976, Part II, Act
V, lines 11573–11580.

**(f)   Sixth stage: the confusion of historical consciousness.
The consciousness of reflected generality as a task**

The confusion of historical consciousness as a general phenomenon
has been generated by the First World War and intensified in the
traumatic experiences of the Second World War, the Holocaust,
Hiroshima, and the Gulag. These events have shaken the belief-
system characteristic of the consciousness of reflected universality as a
whole. The world-historical consciousness and its theoretical absolu-
tism has been made into a theoretical problem prior to the traumatic
experience of our century (for example, in Weber), but both the
general confusion of consciousness and the attempts to overcome it
have been brought about by these experiences. The 'positive'
philosophies of history based on science or a new mythology proved
to be destructive in practice, at least so it seemed. Powers which
understood themselves as the repositories of the world-historical class
or the world-historical nation populated the old Europe with
concentration camps. The new gods turned out to be bloodthirsty
idols. Philosophies of history were brought to trial for having
allegedly been responsible for everything that happened. Nietzsche on
the one hand, and Hegel and Marx on the other, were accused of being
instigators or at least accomplices of mass murders. Yet these
ideological trials were equally the offspring of philosophies of history.
The attorney-general was the intellectual who accused the theories of
fellow-intellectuals of being the main causes or instigators of the
cataclysms. The intellectuals supposedly 'betrayed' history with their
false promises. Had they constructed the future in a different way, the
cataclysms would not have occurred. Had human mind been rational
or dialectical (instead of being irrationalist and metaphysical), had it
opted for an open society, history would have taken a different course.
Morality, having already been once relegated to the background by
world-historical consciousness, remains in the background. *False* or
incorrect knowledge is blamed, and not the shortcoming in moral
values and norms. The notion of 'objective responsibility' (so in vogue
in philosophies of history) will be emphasized here, as against moral
(subjective) responsibility. The agio of values decreases rather than
increases.

All consistent philosophies of history collapsed simultaneously, and
contrasting one with the other would not (and did not) provide us
with any remedy. After Hitler and Stalin, can we say with Ranke that

all historical periods are *equally* immediate to God? Can we speak about organic development – or development at all – if the relapse into barbarism and despotism is no longer an abstract alternative but a fact of the time that we have to face? Can we emphatically state again that 'the time is ripe', that a future paradise is within our reach, when all of 'here and now' proved to be false promises? Can we subscribe even to the theory of eternal repetition when the threat of nuclear catastrophe, the end of all repetitions, the unimaginable, has to be imagined? Can we turn our back to history and cultivate our authenticity if history totalizes us; if it does not allow us to escape? Can we prophesy the doomsday, the end of our civilization, if it is no longer a prophecy but a sober forecast? The confusion of historical consciousness expresses the feeling that history is a sort of computerized mastermind about to make its last play on the chessboard, with historical consciousness standing one move from checkmate. Even the belief in our modern god of instrumental rationality becomes shaky. Natural sciences, once the rationalist enemies of oppressive, this-worldly powers, have gradually become tools of those same powers. The technology of modern warfare is the product of natural science; the gas chambers and crematoriums of Auschwitz are inventions of the scientific mind. Equally, the two hundred thousand dead from the nuclear explosion in Hiroshima and Nagasaki are the victims of the 'progress' of natural science. There are no longer closed doors and closed souls: bugging devices record our most intimate encounters, lie-detectors break through the inhibitions of the Freudian 'censor'. We have become gods in the blasphemous sense that the trumpets of last judgment and the paraphernalia necessary to bring about doomsday are in our hands; we can set them in motion at a moment's notice. In all of this, when did we take the wrong course? Perhaps with Galileo? The indictment against natural sciences as such is an expression of the confusion of consciousness to a no lesser extent than the indictment against the consciousness of reflected universality. Philosophy of history has not been overcome here either. The problem of moral values and norms is hardly raised. Again, Mind, and not Man, is made responsible.

But how about the consciousness of generality reflected in particularity? How about radical anthropology with its unassailable belief that man is born free and is endowed with reason? How about the emancipatory consciousness which has not waned in the nineteenth century, and which penetrated certain philosophies of history as well? After the Second World War, political democracy won the day, at least in Western Europe. Its rules have been introduced and have kept functioning more or less as quasi-nature. But the institutions and organizations which have introduced these rules and kept them functioning do not induce us to reflect upon generality. There is no party and no union which would make us raise the question of what man really is. Pragmatic politics is in no need of any radical-positive anthropology. Weber's prediction has come true: rationalization impedes rationality, and there are only institutionalized answers to human suffering. The feeling of threat is externalized. The irregular answer of individuals is denounced as 'irrational'. Health and longevity became the new myths of a world devoid of the meaning and sense of life. Guilt became illness and we pay the psychoanalyst to cure us. The slogan that nothing is worth dying for has its obverse: that nothing is worth living for. Life is worshipped as the perseverance of a carefully balanced metabolism.

Philosophies of history in the age of the confusion of historical consciousness worked out three alternative theoretical proposals. All of them express the situation described above and all of them contribute to it. They can be labelled as 'Research Institute Facticity', 'Grand Hotel Abyss', and 'Mental Asylum of the Radicalization of Evil'.

'Research Institute Facticity', basically, stands with the consciousness of pragmatic particularity. It neither turns values into its subject matter nor relegates them to the realm of contingent subjectivity (decisionism). It does not reflect on generality, and it refuses radical anthropology. As a rule, it has no anthropology at all. It identifies freedom either with the acceptance of existing institutions as a mere ideology of *adjustment* or with the elimination of their occasional dysfunctions. Rationalization becomes an article of faith and rationality becomes mere problem-solving. The riddle of genesis is not rendered into the theme of research, the dream of the future is marginalized. Nothing is left but the present and the future of the present, painted in rosy colours. The optimism of the *Kitsch* and of science fiction is substituted for the much despised prophecy. Faust is transformed into Sherlock Holmes.

Neo-positivism inherited the worship of science. But in the period of the consciousness of reflected universality science has not yet become problematic: the true knowledge of science was not grasped in terms of instrumental rationality. Science suspended values in order to pursue 'true facts', but the scientists related their truth back to their values. What was scientifically true was not necessarily good for them and they were very much aware of this: tension was implicit in their endeavours. This tension is now gone, and has been replaced by the self-complacency of the engineers of life.

If neo-positivism identified with the pragmatic consciousness of particularity, the philosophy of history of 'Grand Hotel Abyss' expresses the opposite extremity: pragmatic consciousness with all its life-preserving activities is reflected by it as the mere object of contempt. The view from 'Grand Hotel Abyss' is cast on a *totality* – on a *negative* totality. The present once again becomes, as earlier in Fichte's time, a theme as the age of radical sinfulness (*vollendete Sündhaftigkeit*), but this time without redemption. History has missed the bus. Earlier, perhaps, there was a 'here and now', but it is gone and will return no more. The consciousness of the individual is completely fetishized – there are no individuals any more. Human beings have become one-dimensional: completely malleable, completely manipulable. We are nothing and shall be nothing but dust and ashes. Our sensual abilities are dried out, and we became incapable of authentic experience and incompetent in immediacy. The vision is catastrophic to the extent that it becomes questionable whether it is catastrophic at all. If we are nothing and shall equally be nothing, it is questionable whether there is much to regret about it. If nothing really can be done, it is open to debate whether the best option might not be to sit back in our armchairs enjoying the frightful vision, or to write essays about doomsday. Last Judgment without the hope of grace relieves us of moral commitments. The landscape of a total catastrophe is an irretrievable aesthetic vision: it pleases or displeases without interest. It is legitimate to raise the question whether this vision of the world with its contemptuous treatment of all particularities is not suspiciously akin to the everyday attitude of the 'man in the street' who enjoys TV dramas about space wars and the destruction of our earth while peacefully consuming his dinner.

Well then, does not *this* Faust resemble Mephistopheles? Indeed he does, though he is not identical to him. Contrary to the unhappy consciousness of ancient times, the unhappy consciousness of reflected universality does believe that it is a necessity to live in necessity, but it echoes the self-expression of its predecessors that it is misery to do so. This is why it is open to all kinds of anthropological radicalism, despite its totally negative conception of the world and its aesthetical attitude. Even the slightest and most modest movement with some degree of anthropological radicalism is interpreted by it as a *sign*, as an angelic salutation, as the annunciation of hope that perhaps it is still not necessary to live in necessity. The transfiguration of this Mephistopheles into Faust can happen any minute. The unhappy consciousness of reflected universality is *ambiguity*.

The third philosophy of history in the age of the confusion of historical consciousness is 'Mental Hospital', 'the radicalization of Evil'. If violence and force transformed us into their objects, we have to practise violence in order to find our personality. If society marginalizes us, we have to cultivate marginality. If our ego is crushed, we have to confine ourselves to the egocentric daydreams of addictions. If instrumental rationality turns out to be irrational, we have to resign every form of rationality and plunge into the abyss of private myths, religions, cults, mystical contemplations. If we are deemed 'sick', we have to declare sickness, psychosis, madness to be real revolution. The radical deed is a healing rite, the redemption of others is a mere means of the restoration of our mental health: with the aid of terrorism we can cure our headaches, with the drug we can get over our sexual disturbances. It is legitimate to ask whether this vision of the world is not suspiciously similar to the despised consciousness of adjustment and conformism? Is the contrast of health to sickness not central to both? Does not this Faust resemble Raskolnikov, who killed in order to liberate himself from the feeling of guilt? Moreover, does he not also resemble Kafka's hero who, for having been treated as a worm, has indeed become a worm?

Where have we come from?

The discovery of planet, our earthly space, has been accomplished. We keep discovering our earthly time, the past. Within the last two hundred years our earthly history has expanded by about 7000 years. The prehistory of *homo sapiens* has been traced back five million years. We have learned to read the messages of the remote past, and not only the Romanic cathedral, but also the faded cave drawings, the stone axe and the skeletons of vanished human species bear witness to this past. The 'world-history' of the consciousness of reflected universality, once the yardstick of our particularistic acts, became itself but a moment of world-history. In comparison with the Paleolithic period, even the Neolithic revolution belongs already to our present. Nature, once the precondition and the source of history, becomes better understood as its limit. Ecological balance is no longer a fact to be studied but a problem to be solved. Listen to De Vore:

> It is still an open question whether man will be able to survive the exceedingly complex and unstable ecological conditions he has

created for himself. If he fails in his task, interplanetary archeo-
logists of the future will classify our planet as one in which *a very
long and stable* period of small-scale hunting and gathering was
followed by an apparently *instantaneous* affluorescence of technology and society leading *rapidly* to extinction. 'Stratigraphically',
the origin of agriculture and thermonuclear destruction will appear
as essentially simultaneous. On the other hand, if we succeed in
establishing a sane and workable world-order, the *long evolution* of
man as hunter in the past and the (hopefully) *much longer* era of
technical civilisation in the future will bracket an incredibly *brief
transitional phase of human history* - a phase which included the
rise of agriculture, animal domestication, tribes, states, cities,
empires, nations and the industrial revolution.*

Philosophy of history has thus been reintegrated into philosophy of
nature. Ecological consciousness, involving the notion of our natural
limits and the idea of our being 'contaminated' because of our
transgressions against nature, is the consciousness of the restricted and
fragile existence of our civilization. In this light, the distinctly
subsequent ages are perceived as coeval.

Not only because we strike ever deeper into the well of the past do
we have the consciousness of being coeval with periods long gone.
The present population of our globe is equal in number to the sum
total of its inhabitants throughout all human histories. And, more
importantly, humankind as an idea has become a fact. What happened
in El Alamein or Pekin became vital in London; what happens in
Washington is crucial for Papua-New Guinea. Our present history is
in fact world history.

This planet is our home. It will either be a home for everyone, or
for no one.

The confusion of historical consciousness is not absolute. A new
consciousness, the consciousness of *reflected generality*, is about to be
born. Our being here and now is no longer identified with humankind;
humankind is understood as *everyone's* 'here and now'. In one version
of this reflected generality, every civilization has been built of the
same units. Even though the mosaic is always different, we are
all - and always have been - essentially the same. The human universal is language, and no language is superior or inferior to the others:
all fulfil their functions adequately. The theoretical triumphal march

* Richard B. Lee and Irvin De Vore (eds), *Man The Hunter*, Aldine,
Chicago, 1976, p. 3.

of language and speech already expresses the birth of the consciousness of reflected generality.

Humankind exists in fact but does so only 'in itself', for its existence comes about through the interest conflicts of particularistic nations, states, powers, classes. It is still *abstract*. Modern art, the first objectivation to adequately express the consciousness of reflected generality in its pure form, is therefore also abstract. The creator, the artist (the particular personality), directly reflects generality (humankind). But people confined to particular integrations do not recognize themselves in this art: they cannot, since humankind exists only 'in itself' and not 'for itself'. The commitment as (in Apel's terms) a planetarian responsibility, is missing.

For the first time in history human beings have to take a planetarian responsibility. But planetarian responsibility in itself is not yet planetarian commitment: it can evoke and reinforce the feeling of impotence, the confusion of consciousness, unhappy consciousness.

Theory and practice (ideas and needs) have to meet halfway in order for the consciousness of reflected generality *not* to become just another expression of the confusion of historical consciousness.

There are movements committed to a radical anthropology, but the world cannot be redeemed from one day to the other; in fact, it cannot be redeemed at all. Is it possible to combine anthropological radicalism with socio-political realism?

Planetarian responsibility as commitment is *ethics*. Are we still able to differentiate between good and evil? Are we ready to work out the ethics of a planetarian responsibility together? Can we give a positive answer to Dostoevsky's question? Have we got sufficient resources to achieve a world in which good is no longer impotent? The temptation for good is enormous, Brecht rightly remarked.

Both the consciousness of particularity reflected in generality and the consciousness of generality reflected in particularity have been morally founded. The latter stressed that the good citizen must be virtuous; the former, that we need institutions within the confines of which even a 'race of devils' (Kant) would behave in an ethically acceptable way. Can the primacy of practical reason become constitutive in society, indispensable for society, and indeed, for *all societies* sharing our planet with us? The consciousness of reflected generality is obliged to answer exactly this question.

And it does answer the question.

Human beings are born free and they are endowed with reason. Hence they must *become* what they *are*: free and rational beings. The theory as the adequate expression of the consciousness of reflected generality offers theories for both radical anthropology and socio-political realism.

It is pointless, or rather misleading, to declare in the habitual manner of philosophies of history that 'the time has come', that 'the time is ripe'. The simile suggests an *organic* process which provides *but one* (irretrievable) instance in which we can act in a fertile way. But in history responsibility (the moment of 'fertile action') is ever-present. We always can and we always should live up to it, but we are not compelled by any kind of necessity to do so.

The awareness of the task stemming from the consciousness of reflected generality is again and again countered by the awareness of the incommensurability of this same task. Widening the present into the absolute presence of all humankind now shrinks the persons present into powerless nonentities, and not only the persons, but also the movements, institutions, communities of particular provenance. The necessity inherent in the consciousness of reflected universality was dynamic: it marched forward and backward. The necessity inherent in the consciousness of reflected generality is static: it weighs heavily on the shoulders of those acting and suffering. Even if we reflect on it, we can hardly bear it. It is only the weight of responsibility that can tip the scale.

Castoriadis recounted the story of his Greek peasant great-grandfather who planted oil trees for his grandchildren in the certain knowledge that the grandchildren would enjoy their yield. This was no self-denial on his part, but pleasure: he watched the trees growing. Planetarian responsibility resembles planting oil-trees, even if those who do the planting cannot know for sure whether there will be anyone to enjoy the yield; we can only hope that there will be. There is no self-denial in this gesture either; in fact there is pleasure, since planting *these particular* trees means putting aside necessity. Man is born free and endowed with reason: it is in this way that he or she shows it.

Once upon a time there was a woman. The good fairy granted her three wishes. Her first wish was banal, her second wish was motivated by anger and was irrational, and so she could not help revoking in the third wish the second one. In the main, irrational wishes may be revoked. But those who have learned from the wise allegory of human history, will try to wish rationally, in order that the result need not be revoked.

Chapter Two

Present, past and future

(a) The present, past and future of historicity

The various forms of present of historicity can be circumscribed by
the following terms: 'just now', 'now', and 'being now'. The first term
is related to the past and the future in their ordinary sense; the second
to 'times bygone' and 'times to come'; the third to the beginning and
the end.*

'Just now' denotes action.   Any life-experience (felt, dreamt,
uttered in a proposition) containing 'just now' is tantamount to the
commitment that I am in fact performing the action 'just now'.
Life-experiences containing 'just now' are usually (with the exception
of borderline cases such as dreaming) 'many-jointed': they signify
more than one action of a 'just now' character, some of them *en route*
towards the past, others *en route* towards the future. (This is largely
promoted by the criterion that the duration of 'just now' can be one
minute or a few hours but not a considerably longer time.) The
following descriptions will elucidate this constellation. I am sitting on
the train and I am thinking of you: here both actions are of a 'just
now' character. I am sitting on the train but I am no longer thinking
of you. A certain action can irrevocably become past within the 'just
now' duration of another action. *Every* action of 'just now' character
will become past: they must pass. From the viewpoint of every
'just-now' action the next action of 'just now' character *is future*.
Every 'just now' action has a future. This is the *rhythm* of our
historicity.

---

* Every reader of Heidegger will realize that when using categories like 'just
now' I draw on (even if not directly use) this writer. This also explains the
lingual difficulties of rendering these categories in English.

The future and the past related to 'just now' is time passing ('backwards' or 'forwards'), not life changing (as in the case of now). I pass from one action to the other and nothing changes. More correctly, if something does change, this change is not caused by my passing from one action to the other. The life-rhythm is the rhythm of *repetition*. This is why the past and future related to it are only *relative*: I am going to school; I did so yesterday, and I shall do so tomorrow. The past related to 'just now' is therefore not time bygone. Similarly, the future related to 'just now' is therefore not 'time to come'.

The present as 'just now' is the ontogenetically primary present. The newborn is crying, sucking, sleeping; he or she has a life-rhythm. However, not having had times bygone, he or she has not got a 'now'.

'Now' is a frontier, a line of demarcation between that which has already happened and that which has not yet happened; between the object of recollection and the object as purpose; between that which is known and that which is unknown. Now is not an object of recollection, nor is it a purpose of action. At the same time, I recollect times bygone just as I set goals departing from my presently given now. I pass to somewhere from that which exists just now, but I transcend what is now.

Within given limits, 'now' is always transcended. I transform my present into my past, into times past, into the object of recollection. I always transform my future into my present (in that I 'design', as it were, 'a' future for myself in the present, on the ground of the present). I transform my present into the future (the obverse side of the above procedure) via decisions, plans and projects and I transform my past into my present through the will to bring it back into my memory. I equally transform my past into my future in that I build my experiences into the process of deliberation and decision about my future, and I transform my future into my past in that – in so far as becoming present – my decisions regarding future already lie in the past. But there are limits to this transcendence. We cannot recollect what is to come, and no purposive action can be directed towards times bygone. Yet it is the very expression of our historicity that we cannot be content with these limitations: we want to know our future and we want to change our past.

The restlessness of our historicity is self-contradictory. If we knew our future we would not have a future, and if we could change our past we would not have a past (it would not be *our* past any longer). We would only have our now, but as now is the only line of demarcation between that which is bygone and that which is 'to come', we would not even have a 'now'. But the statement that we cannot know our future and cannot change our past has only relative validity. Every recollection of what is bygone is an interpretation: we reconstruct our past. What we reconstruct, how we reconstruct it, what kind of sense we attribute to the reconstructed, all this changes with our experiences, with our interest, with the measure of our sincerity and insincerity. In brief, we change our past via selective interpretation.

This is exactly the procedure of psychoanalysis, in that this reconstruction leads us to work out a new 'bygone' (*contradictio in adjecto* as it may be) by transforming the supposedly unconscious experiences into conscious remembrance. Even those having never heard of psychoanalysis at all, or who do not accept consciously its theoretical framework, reconstruct their past again and again in many different ways in order to connect organically the present with the past. We may well have as many personal 'prehistories', as many periods bygone, as 'now'. On the other hand, knowledge of what is 'to come' is not completely excluded either. Although we cannot know our fate, we can know *ourselves* well enough to *exclude* at least certain possibilities from the potential events of the years to come, and the older we grow, the more possibilities we exclude. In a traditional society in which the patterns of behaviour and curriculum are fairly repetitive, we can hardly change our past, but we can almost exactly know our future. In an open and dynamic society we can repeatedly change our past, but if our self-knowledge is not good enough we may hardly know our future at all. Consequently, 'now' is secondary to 'just now' not only ontogenetically, but also philogenetically. Once we can imagine a small clan with very rigid life patterns, we can then imagine a social life without 'now' and with only two types of present: 'just now' and 'being now'.

'Being now' comes about by inserting 'now' into the context of 'Being', by inserting it into the sequence between the beginning and the end – the sequence of childhood, youth, adulthood, old age. Our present is always our 'being now'. 'Being now' defines us, encloses us in a circle of limited possibilities. The extension of life-expectations has only modified the yardstick of identification but we are identified by 'being now' to a no lesser extent than we had been before. Neither the past nor the future of 'being now' can be changed, and both are known.

We are always, in every minute, 'just now' and 'being now'; equally, we are 'just now' in every 'being now'. We are always enclosed in the time and space between the beginning and the end, between the past and the future. But just as the newborn has no 'now' because he or she has nothing bygone, there is a time for everyone when there is no longer anything 'to come'. The man saying 'I am dying' is in the present of 'just now' and 'being now', but is no longer in the present of 'now'.

The result of distinguishing that which is bygone and that which is 'to come' from beginning and end is called *personality*. If what is bygone is 'mine', if the years 'to come' are 'mine', in other words if I transcend my present, then I am a personality. If I reinterpret my past and reconstruct its organic unity with my 'now', if I build my future on the foundation of this 'now', I am a personality. Goethe formulated this in the following way: 'Volk und Knecht and Überwinder, Sie gestehn, zu jeder Zeit:/Höchstes Glück der Erdenkinder/Sei nur die Persönlichkeit./Jedes Leben sei zu führen/Wenn man sich nicht selbst vermisst;/Alles könne man verlieren, Wenn man bliebe, was man ist.'*

The identification of what is bygone and what is 'to come' with the past and the present of 'just now' is the alienation of personality, and so is the identification of what is bygone and what is 'to come' with the beginning and the end. The authentic personality is characterized by the primacy of 'now' as against 'just now' and 'being now'. The authentic personality subjects his or her 'just now' and 'being now' to 'now'. He or she interprets beginning as a possibility and abstracts from the end, because there is nothing bygone in the former and nothing to come in the latter. 'As long as we live, there is no death', Epicurus remarked: the wise man thinks about life, not death, so Spinoza opined. In an authentic life 'just now' is but a moment of 'now'. What is bygone and what is 'to come' makes sense of the past and of the future of 'just now'. The domination of 'just now' over 'now' makes human beings one-dimensional. The domination of 'being now' over 'now' makes them inauthentic.

---

* Goethe, *Poetische Werke*, vol. 3, *West-östlicher Divan*, Berlin 1965, p. 95. English translation: The slave, the lord of victories,/The crowd, whene'er you ask, confess/In sense of personal being lies/A child of earth's chief happiness./There is not a life we need refuse. If our true self we do not miss, There is not a thing one may not lose/If one remains the man he is.' Johann Wolfgang von Goethe, *West-Eastern Divan*, trans. Edward Dowden, London and Toronto, 1914. Terminologically, the chief problem with the translation is, of course, that Goethe's main point: *Persönlichkeit* (which is called in my text personality) is rendered by the vague words 'personal being'.

Once upon a time there was a man. He was there when we were not there. Yet we shall not *be* when others tell of *our* story taking place 'once upon a time'. Our beginning and our end, as well as our times bygone and our times to come, our past and our present, relate to *others*. Our past is the future of others and our present is the past of others. We are the others. Historicity is history.

We are born humans and this is why we are mortal. Socrates is mortal because every man is mortal. Being born human and being born mortal *means* carrying in us millions of years. We carry them with our genetic code. We appropriate these millions of years via socialization, and first of all via the mastery of the system of objectivations 'in-itself', of language, customs, rules regulating the use of objects. Content and scope of the system of objectivations is also historical: it changes. Through its mastery, we learn a particular past, *one* history. But as there is no human life without the mastery of the system of objectivation in-itself, when learning to master this system we appropriate human history as such, and thereby our own humaneness. All our actions are oriented towards the future, but this future is not identical with our future or the times 'to come': it transcends them. We mediate our socially inherited language, customs, use of objects to the forthcoming generations, whose times 'to come' and whose end is the absolute future as compared to ours. When planting a tree, we plant it for this absolute future.

Every 'just now', every 'being now' and every 'now' refers equally, even if not in the same way, to the past and the future of *others*. Writing a letter (just now) presupposes the institution of correspondence (others wrote letters before and others will write letters later). I am upholding the institution (just now) and in doing so I am mediating between past and future human beings who did and will do the same. The simple observance of a custom is a *latent generalization*. The deliberate infringement of a custom is not 'just now' but 'now'. It points towards a possible *future* generalization in an implicit or explicit manner. Here the past carries a *negative* meaning: what is infringed has to exist. My 'now' is not only mine; I introduce it into the future, which may recognize my 'times to come' as its own past. My 'being now' presupposes others' 'not-being now'. I can be old because others are young. I can only die because others before me were born and have died.

We are products of one society, but we are at the same time not products of one society. We do reproduce one society, but we do not only reproduce one society. Historicity is historical, and in reproducing society we affirm our historicity as history. But this society which we live, struggle, create, think, suffer and enjoy, is merely one moment of eternity. This is our world. There was a man once upon a time because we made him our contemporary. In the future, 'there will be a world'. In uttering this sentence, we make it *our* world. Our faith belongs to our world to no lesser an extent than our remembrance does.

(b) Historical present, past and future

Every 'just now', 'now', and 'being now' is 'being-together', *Togetherness*. We are together with those living since we too are living, since we act and think for them and against them. We are together with the dead in so far as we tell their stories, and we are together with those not-yet-born in so far as they live in us as a promise or as faith. Togetherness is contemporaneity. The Incas and the Englishmen of 1312 AD lived 'simultaneously' but they were not contemporaries. They were not even aware of each other. They did not share a Togetherness. A Togetherness is constituted by those living – living for and against each other. Its confines are flexible. Various generations live together, some who in fact share a Togetherness with some others, but who will not share a Togetherness with yet others with whom their former 'consorts' would. One can share a Togetherness to a larger or smaller extent. But despite the flexibility of the confines of Togetherness, everyone knows what all this is about. We are being together with those with whom we *can* be acquainted even if we are not in fact acquainted with them; together with those whom we *can* help even if we do not in fact help them; together with those whom we *can* confront in various conflicts even if we do not, in fact, confront them.

Togetherness has no past and no future: it is the *absolute (present) now*. Those who are together now were not together in the past, and they will not be together in the future. The past is the Togetherness of *others*, as is the future.

Historical present is *not* an absolute present, but a *structure*: more precisely, it is a *cultural structure*.

There is no cultural structure without a *consciousness* of itself. Togetherness is always conscious. We cannot even imagine a human society without the consciousness of Togetherness. However, consciousness about a cultural structure presupposes the contrast of *old* to *new*. Abraham begot Isaac and Isaac begot Jacob. But Abraham is not Jacob's 'historical past'. The *covenant* with God, the culture, the institution which came about through Abraham, the new as against the old and alien customs of idolatry – all this is Jacob's *historical present*. The historical present is identical with the *new*: new social structures, cultural structures, structures of beliefs. All historical presents are *discontinuities*. Whereas Togetherness is contemporaneity without a past (it only has origins), historical present is discontinuity which contains *its own continuity*. Historical present has its *own past* (the past of present) and its *own future* (the future of present) which are related to continuity within discontinuity. Abraham's covenant with God was *present* for Jacob (as compared with the epoch before the covenant); it was also *the past of the present*. The past of present is *yesterday*, the future of present is *tomorrow*. Both can be distant in time. What makes them yesterday and tomorrow is the fact that they 'occur' within the framework of a structure which is constituted, understood, and reflected upon as an identity.

To reiterate: historical present is a cultural structure, but its own past and its own future are not structures; they cannot be, since historical present (as against historical past) is conceived of as discontinuity. The past of present and the future of present are *events*; they are usually, but not always, actions. For instance, 'King X died' or 'The storm destroyed the enemy's ships' are not actions, but events. However, historical present is not an action or an event.

I have described historical present as the new as against the old culture structure. But the construction of historical present varies at different stages of historical consciousness. At the state of the consciousness of generality reflected in particularity the notion of *genesis* was already related not only to the old (to the past), but also to the *emergence* of the present (the given cultural structure). Similarly, the future was not only envisaged as the future of present, but also as the *decay* and possible disappearance of the historical present (and all historical presents). Thus the notion of 'emergence' mediates between the historical past and the past of present, whereas the notion of 'decay' mediates between the future of present and historical future (the future of a past present). The confines of discontinuity are destabilized without ceasing to exist: discontinuity not only has its own continuity, but becomes more and more entrenched in the continuity of human history. It is this tendency that later dominates the consciousness of reflected universality.

The reconstruction of historical present now also undergoes several changes (in light of the experiences of Togetherness). On the one hand, the historical present is absolutized; on the other, it is relativized. It is absolutized in that structure (the historical present) is being abstracted from the 'flow' of continuity of the past and the future, and equally from its *own continuity* (from the past of present and the future of present). It is relativized in that the historical present is accepted neither as the quasi-natural framework of our lives nor as the bearer of a new historical present (in the future). The relativity of past historical presents is also reflected upon. In the case of conflict or co-operation between two cultural structures, these structures no doubt share the same historical present, but they do not share it simultaneously. The European conquerors belonged to the historical present of American Indians only to the extent that they destroyed their cultural structures – their present – completely. The world-market and the World Wars represented a common 'historical present' for the inhabitants of our earth, even though the latter live in different historical presents, though their past presents were completely different. These acts of absolutization and relativization may eventually, though not necessarily, lead to a total cultural relativism. In addition, the tendency described above is complemented by another one. Because it became clear that 'historical present' is a construction, one can equally abstract from the structure. It is only a matter of one's position on what is deemed as 'belonging' to our present. Everyday institutions disintegrate and new ones emerge. Every event is a real change: there is nothing but change. How far was Theseus' ship really the ship of Theseus? 'Flow' is the only reality and 'durée' is *inside*, not 'outside'. Togetherness is substituted for historical present. But if there is no historical present, there is no historical past or future either, only the void of 'Time'. It is this void, Time, that was, is, and will be the iron cage for historicity.

When I now undertake the task of an analytical distinction within the notion of 'historical present', it will not be performed for the purpose of a mental exercise. In attributing various nuances to the same general concept, I will try to reconstruct this category from the viewpoint of Togetherness.

In fact, I distinguish between *present history*, *historical present proper*, and *present age*. This also involves the distinction between past history, historical past and past-present age; future history, historical future and future-present age. For the sake of clarity it is best to start with the past.

Past history encompasses all events and happenings (or the absence of such happenings) whose consequences are no longer alternative in character, as well as events which do not threaten us or fill us with hopes. Here, the events *and* their results are outside the scope of our action: we have neither pragmatic nor practical relation to them. Our relation to past history is explanatory.

As has been argued, *historical past* is the 'old'; in other words, it is a socio-cultural structure that we have already transcended. 'Historical past' is not characterized by the absence of practical-pragmatic relations, but by non-identity. We are outside of it.

The past-present age is the historical past *understood* by the present (or eventually, past history understood by the present). The past-present age is an age whose symbols and values have become *meaningful* for us. It can threaten us or fill us with hopes, even if it is beyond our power to alter it. It is identity, even if at the same time non-identity.

Present history encompasses all events and happenings whose consequences are alternative in character, and also events which can threaten us or fill us with hope; events to which we can relate both practically and pragmatically. Historical present is the cultural structure that we are 'inside'. The present-present age is the sum total of meaningful objectivations, systems of belief, and values which are essential to our way of life; which direct and 'steer' our attitudes to our world. It stands to reason that these three types of 'present' are by no means isomorphic, in space, or in time. We can have a pragmatic or a practical relation to events which occur outside our socio-cultural structure; for example, to the life of peoples who share the same globe with us but who live in a different 'historical present', say, in a tribal society. In this case, the present history is common, the historical present is different. On the other hand, works of art or of philosophy from the historical past and past history may belong to our present-present age, as may religions emerging in a different 'historical present', and yet, belong to our present to a no lesser extent than the events within and outside our cultural structure. There are events which occurred within our socio-cultural structure (within the past of our present) to the results of which we no longer have pragmatic and practical relations; and again, events within the framework of an 'old' socio-cultural structure (the historical past) the results of which may trigger off practical and pragmatic interest (for instance, centralization in France). Abolished institutions do not belong any longer to our historical present, but they may belong to our present history (if our actions are aimed at reintroducing them) and they can equally belong to our present-present age. Historical future, or, in other words, the image of a new socio-cultural structure that would make ours old, does not by definition belong to our historical present. But it can belong to our present history if our actions are so aimed. It may also belong to the present-present age as a meaningful image, a value, or an idea.

If we regard our present only as the 'historical present' then we abstract from the present history (the constant flow of events) and from the present-present age (from the meaning we attached to objectivations) and, in doing this, we abstract the historical present from *Togetherness*. However, structures only exist as structures for Togetherness (for the living subjects of contemporaneity). On the other hand, should we identify the present with present historical age, the upshot will only be isolated actions of (individual or collective) subjects and the relations between them will be 'before', 'after', and 'simultaneity'. Thus history becomes an uninterrupted chain of events without a world; without the institutions and forms of conduct that any Togetherness needs to appropriate. Whereas the identification of the present with present history means abstracting the 'flow' from the structure, its identification with the present-present age means abstracting the 'eternal' (the world of meaning) from the structure.

'Eternalization' (creating meaning and attributing it to objectivations) takes place within historical present, even if it is not historical present that is being eternalized. In the latter case we 'eternalize' something *against* the historical present, and this also presupposes historical present.

Indeed, we live in three presents (and distinguish between three pasts and three futures). This does not mean that all humans *equally* live in all three presents, but that we all more or less *live in all three*. Equally we can (and do) reconstruct the past from the viewpoint of all three presents. This is how we construct the future.

It was the Enlightenment's standard charge against religion that it poisons the human mind. In the twentieth century it is history that should be charged with the same crime. Generations have been infected in their school years by the subject called history. School texts and all sorts of books about history did their utmost to legitimize irrational actions, hatred, revenge, violence, force, and the feeling of superiority, in their relations with the 'past'. Hero-worship, the glorification of mass-murders, and the vilification of the ever-given out-group have been the common course taken by various ideologies of history. In such an atmosphere the question inevitably arises: how could the reconstruction of the past (the present and the future) be achieved through rational communication? It was one of Max Weber's greatest achievements to pinpoint this problem and suggest a de-ideologized understanding of histories. In this he referred to social science and its norm. Now we should go even further and seek a solution for everyday historical consciousness as well.

The norm of a de-ideologized historical consciousness (a norm which cannot be completely observed, only approximated) is the injunction to construct our pasts as *past-present ages* and our future as *future-present ages* from the viewpoint of *Togetherness* conceived of as *absolute present*.

To start with the latter, what does it mean to reflect upon our Togetherness as on our absolute present?

Firstly, it means to assume that neither the past nor the future justify *anything*. The fact that a particular social stratum enjoyed privileges in the past will not serve to justify its privileges in the present; the fact that a piece of land belonged to a country in the past will not justify the claim that it should belong to that country in the present; the fact that a certain people violated our rights in the past does not justify our violation of their rights in the present. No image of future abundance justifies present starvation; no image of future freedom justifies present oppression; no fear of future justifies Machiavellian politics here and now; no uncertainty about the future justifies indifference today.

All our present actions, goals, endeavours, and attitudes can only be justified by rational arguments. And, for a rational argument, the past can only play the part of a *lesson*, and the future, the part of a *regulative idea*.

Furthermore, to reflect on our Togetherness as on the absolute present involves the awareness that we are responsible for those living now, for the present (and the future of the present). We have no responsibility whatsoever for the past. We can only be responsible for the future if and in that we are responsible for the present.

As well as this, we have to accept our Togetherness, our contemporaneity, as our own. To contrast the greatness of the past to the pettiness of the present or the (projected) purity of the future to the sinfulness of the present is at best sterile. It usually leads to theories of catastrophe, which themselves may well contribute to catastrophes. To understand our present as the 'highlight' or 'peak' of history is equally sterile, and might lead to indifference towards the wounds, the sufferings of our present, and so, again, to catastrophes. To reflect upon our Togetherness as to our absolute present means the assumption that our world is neither better nor worse than any other worlds have been. We have to accept this present, but without reconciliation. This is the world we are destined to live in: we have to make sense of it.

Our Togetherness is our contemporaneity. Contemporaneity is always simultaneity, but simultaneity, as we already know, is not always contemporaneity. 'Planetarian responsibility' presupposes that simultaneity is understood and lived as contemporaneity. 'Planetarian responsibility' is a meaning, a value attributed to simultaneity by the consciousness of reflected generality. It is equivalent to the present as present-present age. The latter is dependent on the historical present, but is far from being identical to it. We can reproduce ourselves socially, and we can work and act without failure in our historical present, and do all this without achieving the enormous consciousness of planetarian responsibility. But if we reproduce historical past, either from the perspective of mere historical present, or from present history, we would reconstruct past histories and historical pasts, not past-present ages. 'Planetarian responsibility' commits us to the reconstruction of the past as past-present ages. We may call this reconstruction 'radical hermeneutics', though this is a somewhat sophisticated category for such a simple procedure.

'Radical hermeneutics' means a generalizable approach to histories on the level of everyday consciousness. It is 'not yet' scientific, even though it provides the point of departure for historiography. Hermeneutics has a dialogical relation to the past. Radical hermeneutics is also dialogical: it mediates the consciousness of planetarian responsibility towards the past. It approaches the past not only in order to find out the meaning, the sense, the value of former historical actions, objectivations, and agents, but also in order to disclose what is *in common* between them and us. We communicate with past beings as with *equally* human beings. In approaching each past history we communicate with humankind. Thus each historical period will be equally close to humankind which does not mean that each of them is equally *valuable* for us. Lukács once described art as the organ of memory and the self-consciousness of humankind. Art enables us to incorporate all past-present ages into our present-present age, either with cognitive love or with cognitive resentment, but without authorising the use of them to justify the present. By the same token, the understanding of all histories *sub specie* their common humanity implies their *alienation* as past histories or historical pasts.

This simple procedure prevents us from approaching histories with the biases and prejudices of our historical present. Our cognitive love or hatred will not be elicited by this historical present but by present-present age; in other words, by the values and meanings pertaining to planetarian responsibility. It needs to be repeated that these values and meanings are also the 'products' of historical present (and of the past of present) but they can, of course, relate critically to the historical present (and the past of present). It is for this reason that I have described this approach to histories as *radical* hermeneutics.

Should our Togetherness be reflected upon as the absolute present, and should we relate to the past as to past-present ages (from the viewpoint of our present-present age), we see future as a *future-present age*. For this reason, future-present age becomes an image – a Utopia – to which meaning (values of the consciousness of planetarian responsibility) has been attributed. The ethic of responsibility (for the future) cannot simply rest, as Weber assumed, on calculations about the predictable consequence of actions, because even the best calculation can (and normally does) fail, and since responsibility is planetarian, it is not concerned about the victory of one or the other particular integration or particular goal but about the future-present age that it has a dialogical relationship with. If we think in terms of common humanity, we have to make our image of humanity (our meaning attributed to it, our values inherent in it) common. The image of a future-present age can be upheld as long as it is wide-spread and shared by the present-present age. This is why, as Apel put it, the consciousness of planetarian responsibility has to be dialogical in the present. Those taking planetarian responsibility on their shoulders will not precipitate 'the future'. They are not going to will that which cannot be willed – that the future should be 'here and now'. Infants excitedly ask every morning whether today is already tomorrow, and they cannot be placated without the answer that today *is* today and tomorrow will be the next day. Then they ask the same question again the next morning. Likewise, we may say that it is only infantile humankind which despairs over the fact that we are destined to die without seeing the future. We are indeed enclosed in our Togetherness. The future is never today. If we share the planetarian responsibility we project a future-present age that we can love. We also commit ourselves to live, act and think in such a way that a lovable future-present age should be able to understand us with cognitive love.

According to Russell, it is *logically* not impossible that the world was created five minutes ago. But Danto rightly countered this with the submission that be it logically not impossible, it is still unthinkable. All the same, it is thinkable (and had in fact been thought several times) that the world will soon perish, cease to exist (even within that five minutes). The past of 'being now' is the beginning, the future of 'being now' is the end. Togetherness has no past and no future of its own (it is the absolute present). But the continuous chain of Togetherness that 'we were begotten by X-Y who were begotten by X'-Y',' etc. and the equally continuous (anticipated and so imaginary) chain of Togetherness that 'we shall beget $a - b$ who on their part will beget $a' - b''$, are conceived of together with the image of 'beginning' or 'end' as well. But the images of the beginning and the end differ both ontogenetically and philogenetically, though not in the same way.

The analysis of the stages of historical consciousness started with the notion of genesis. In emphasizing that in the *beginning* there was the genesis, I *defined* beginning via the consciousness of the beginning. All instances of Togetherness understood themselves as 'outcomes' of a beginning. From this perspective it is irrelevant whether humans believe in creation, transfiguration, or the 'evolutionary' origin of our species. All agree that there was a time when there were no humans, and another time henceforth from which they existed. We are forever aware that there was a beginning of the 'chain', but the 'when' is uncertain, and for some of us it is inconsequential. The world was created in six days – but when? For us, the knowledge about 'when' became highly important even though it is of necessity uncertain. Contrary to the 'beginning' of humankind (or of the group which is identified with it), the beginning of 'being now' is known and it is certain. Everyone knows that he and she was born, and everyone knows when, at least approximately. It is unthinkable that all men were created five minutes ago.

'The 'beginning' of 'being now' is therefore taken for granted, but not its *end*. We know that we are going to die, but we want to – and often do – think in terms of our eternity. The projected image of our (future) eternal life presupposes the image of the eternal life of others (at least of certain others). Yet because we have to cope with the threat of our own future non-existence, we are able to imagine humankind's future non-existence as well. It is paradoxical but nevertheless true that the idea of the *end* of the world (within five minutes) can only appear within the framework of eschatology: we can only accept its possibility as real if we believe in eternal life. No *secular* idea of 'Doomsday in five minutes' can be formed since *it would destroy the present*. The agony of 'being now' does not destroy the present. The *last* wish of those dying is addressed to a Togetherness *in vivo*. It is a wish that, by its very nature, can only be granted in the future (of others). Togetherness is the absolute present, but the absolute present is the absolute continuity. It contains future in its present. Whitehead rightly remarked: 'Cut away the future and the present collapses, emptied of its proper content.'* Every action is goal-oriented. The goal is that which is not yet achieved; it is the future, and without future there is no present. If we project any future for ourselves, we must at the very least picture it at a distance tantamount to that between us and our everyday goals.

The end of 'being now' is just as certain as its beginning. The end of all cases of togetherness is just as certain as their beginning. There is no reasonable action directed at preventing the end of 'being now', but there is reasonable action to prevent the termination of the unbroken continuity of the chain of Togetherness. That finally even this end cannot be prevented is of no concern to our Togetherness; billions of years are just as unthinkable as the end of the world in five minutes time. We cannot act either for or against the unthinkable.

Once upon a time there was a man. He was and he is, for we tell his story. He had been because we are. Once upon a time there will be a man since we plant oil trees for him and we wish that he should enjoy their yield. We know that our life is a limited enterprise. So is the life of humankind. Both extend from the beginning to the end. But at least the end of the life of humankind – its terminal date – is unfixed.

---

* Quoted in A. C. Danto, *Analytical Philosophy of History*, Cambridge University Press, 1965, p. 152.

Chapter Three

Everyday historical consciousness as the foundation of historiography and the philosophy of history

Historical consciousness is the consciousness of historicity: it is all-embracing. At all its stages historical consciousness manifests itself in every cultural objectivation created and absorbed by Togetherness. History as the object of interest is but one manifestation of historical consciousness from amongst many. However, a theory of history has to restrict itself to the analysis of such objectivations that have history as their specific subject matter. It has to examine how (past and present) histories understood themselves in their capacity as histories, how the various stages of historical consciousness have been reflected upon by the understanding of history. Owing to this, a theory of history cannot come to grips directly with historical consciousness, but only with its reflections: it has to reflect on reflections. Should it set the task of analysing historical consciousness before itself, it would be no longer a theory of history, but a theory of culture. Historiography ('writing history' in the broader sense of the word) and the philosophy of history are the objectivations proper which aim at the understanding of history. They reflect upon history; the subject matter of their inquiry is history *sensu stricto*. This is why a theory of history has to deal with them, and not only with the purpose of giving an account of the theoretical procedures, the modes of verification and falsification, the inherent ends of historiography, and the philosophy of history. The theory of history has to understand the roots of various historiographies and philosophies of history as inseparable from the various stages of historical consciousness that they actually express. It has to fathom their function in the life-world of historical periods, their being related to these periods. This is why their structure and the specificity of their message ought to be grasped simultaneously.

'Just now', 'now', 'being now' and Togetherness are the various presents of historicity. The presents of 'just now' and 'being now' (with their corresponding pasts – 'past' related to 'just now', 'beginning' related to 'being now') do not yet elicit the need for historiography and the philosophy of history. The need for understanding history and the inquiry elicited by this need pertain to the 'now' and Togetherness of historicity, which in part mean the *awareness* of (personal and social) *alternatives* and of the *responsibility* that persons and social groups have to take in their decisions and actions.

Togetherness as shared responsibility presupposes the possibility of *interpreting* values in harmony with the exigencies of the historical present.

Thus 'now' and Togetherness – as shared responsibility – are indeed cradles of the need for historiography, philosophy, and speculative religion. (Weber termed them 'intellectualized' religions.) The need for a philosophy of history as related to the future-oriented Togetherness is unique.

Even though 'just now' and 'being now' do not in themselves embrace the need for historiography and the philosophy of history, they do reinforce and amplify these needs, should they be triggered by 'now' and Togetherness. But the function of 'now' and Togetherness alters – in the main ontogenetically, but philogenetically as well – with the various ways in which they are constituted.

For the time being we must, at least relatively, *abstract* from the variety of relations between historical consciousness and the objectivations which elaborate history as their subject matter. I am going to discuss 'life-world' in a manner whereby only vague distinctions will be made between its general features and the particular features peculiar to our historical present.

(a)   Storytelling*

Once upon a time there was a man; we tell his story. Once upon a time there was a king, and he had three sons; we tell their miraculous stories. Once upon a time there was a hunter. He shot the game, brought it home, cooked it, ate it – we tell his banal stories. 'During the time I was a prisoner of war, the following thing happened to

---

* Since I analyse here 'storytelling' in everyday life, the meaning of the word cannot be completely identical with its categorical use as applied to historiography (social science).

me...': we tell our own miraculous stories. 'I wanted to buy a frock last week but...': we tell our own banal stories. The past, the remote and recent past, the past of others and of ourselves, is above all a tale, a story. History is a story ('*Geschichte ist Geschichte*').

The hunter shot the game, thus we know of his rifle. He cooked the game, thus we know that he could kindle fire. The king's sons met the wolf, the dragon, the fairy, the princess. In the POW camp our fathers met other prisoners of war, met warders and guards (good and evil ones); they coped with the punishment, with hunger, with frost. In order to buy a frock, I went to the shop; I drove my car, I parked, and was then served (in a good or bad way). A story means 'being-in-the-world'. *It is an organized unit of information* about a world in which the event took place. It informs us in a coherent way about what happened, how it happened and why it happened. If the account is not coherent, it is not yet a story: it cannot be *repeated* (or it is not worth being repeated). A real story involves *repetition. Originally it is repetition.*

'Tell it again!', implores the child, and we tell the same tale for the hundredth time, bored by the repetition. We believe ourselves to be *different* from the child, forgetting that we have told *our* stories about our POW camp and about our misfortunes in shopping a hundred times *without* being bored by the repetition. Moreover, we feel an almost irresistable urge to tell these stories again. Everyone repeats and induces others to repeat stories relevant to their lives, no matter whether they happened with 'others' or with us.

The older a child gets, the less hĕ or she wants to hear exactly the same stories: the child becomes selective. So do we. There are stories that we only tell for a few days or weeks after they happen and we forget them very soon. Then again, there are stories which we like to recount again and again all our life. Sometimes we are bored by a story unknown to us; other times we will listen to the same story many times with complete attention. The wish of frequent repetitions, the imploring sentence 'tell it again!', indicates that the story is *important* for us. It distinguishes the important from the less important and the unimportant. But what is important?

That which is 'important' has a bearing on 'now' and on Togetherness. If the storyteller or the listener is involved in the questions of 'what exists, why it exists, how it exists', and if the story offers a coherent report about times bygone and/or the past-present ages, then the subject turns to the past, departing from the participant's 'now' and Togetherness, and reveals an important message to him or her. We get bored by the repetition of Little Red Riding Hood not because we are acquainted with it, but because it is irrelevant for our present 'now' and Togetherness. It is, to be sure, most relevant for the child's 'now' and Togetherness, otherwise the child would not insist on its being repeated. Should the story become relevant once again for our 'now' (for example, if we become involved in the times of our childhood for analytical or other reasons), we recall and retell it, at least for ourselves. That which is *only* related to 'just now' is, by definition, the *unimportant*. People who primarily draw their stories from the past of their 'just now' are usually terrible bores. It can be assumed of them that they have not got any 'now' (times bygone and times to come); in other words, that they have no personality.

A story can be more or less important depending on our personal relationship to the storyteller. The same story (or a similar one) can be more important if told by a representative 'other' than if it is recounted by a non-representative one. The 'other' can be representative in two respects: either in regard to our *now*, or in regard to our Togetherness. First, if we identify ourselves with someone (for instance, we love him or her), then whatever happens to this Other is of the greatest importance to us. Second, stories about certain famous personalities of the age we live in, about political events, about catastrophes, are important without any kind of involvement with the personality of the speaker. In the first case we are dealing with 'now', and in the second case with Togetherness, and they become paramount in our involvement.

If we repeat the same story to our children with any variation, we are normally caught redhanded. 'Why have you left out this or that?' children ask with suspicion or irritation. They often retort to our paraphrasing the story with 'It did not happen this way but that way.' Should we tell our story (stories) to a psychoanalyst, the analyst might voice the same objection: yesterday you told the story differently; please, repeat it again. In fact, an important and complex story cannot be told often, not even twice, wholly unchanged. It is difficult to memorize a meaningful poem without changing one single word when repeating it, and it is important to understand that this has little to do with our memory. With certain things, perfect reproduction is easy. Once we have memorized it, we repeat the Lord's Prayer according to the ritualized text without fail. The sum total of the phone numbers and addresses we repeat correctly contain more bits of information than the stories we 'vary'. But the more important – the more *meaningful* – the story is, the more it involves our 'now' and our Togetherness, the more selectively we retell it. Selection means omission, change, addition. If a 'fixed text' is repeated (the most extreme case being a poem), the possibilities of variation are very limited. If we tell our own stories, the scope for change is much wider. Selective repetitiveness is often unconscious, though it can be conscious too.

Storytelling presupposes *listeners*. The most extreme case is if we are the listeners of our own stories. It is the listener(s) who will decide on the *authenticity* of a repeated story. If a text is recited, authenticity can be very easily decided by comparing the recited with the 'original' text. But which variation should be accepted as the 'authentic' version if there is no text to refer to? In the objection of the child when confronted with a new version of the story and in the remark of the psychoanalyst the *aim* of the child and of the psychoanalyst is not identical. The child wants to hear the story in exactly the same way he or she heard it the day before; the psychoanalyst has greater interest in the *variations* – he has the story repeated in order to find out what really happened (or perhaps, which story makes more sense to him and the patient). For the analyst, the *last* and final version is the authentic one. To sum up: the listener accepts either the *first* or the *last* version of the story as the *authentic* one. The authenticity of the first one, if we accept it, is *absolute*, but the authenticity of the last one is only relative: there can always be new repetitions as long as the storyteller lives.

But not only the same person can tell the same story in different versions; different persons may recount the story in various versions as well. And which variation is accepted by the listener as the authentic one in this case? Definitely not the last version. Should the last be accepted at all, this is not because of its being the last. It is either the first storyteller's story (the primal source) or the version related to *the most representative personality* which is regarded as authentic. The more significant the personality of the storyteller, the greater the extent to which he or she induces us to believe that the story happened exactly in the way recounted.

The problem of authenticity is distinct from the problems of objectivity and true knowledge. We do not judge jokes by applying the criteria of true and false, objectivity and bias, but it is appropriate to say that they have more or less authentic versions. Moreover, authenticity and truth may collide. Should we be informed that a story did not really happen in the way it has first been told to us, we often stubbornly resist this information because we cannot 'unbind the spell' of the 'original'. We may consider the first as more beautiful, more convincing, more evocative, than the 'true' one. Why else would we reread the stories of ancient historians when we know that things did not happen in the way they described them?

All this does not purport that authenticity has absolutely nothing to do with objectivity and truth. Should the personal biases (interest, hatred) of the storyteller be too explicit, we do not normally regard the story as an authentic one. Also, a conspicuous lack of objectivity evokes suspicion of inauthenticity. Whether the report in question was true or false becomes a matter of authenticity only if we are theoretically or practically involved in the consequences of the story, in other words, only if we listen to the story *in order* to find out the truth about somebody or something we want to act for or against. But in desiring special involvement, we are interested in events which might have happened within the given framework, and should the storyteller paint us a lively picture then we accept the story as an authentic one, even if we are aware that not everything happened 'exactly' that way.

We listen for a while, and then we interrupt the storyteller impatiently: 'Do not go on about it, come to the point.' The 'point' is the essential as against the inessential, the substantial as against the immaterial, the relevant as against the irrelevant. 'Come to the point!' means 'Speak about the essential, the substantial, the relevant!' Every story has its 'real object'. If someone tells us the story of his marriage, and starts with describing at length the vicissitudes of his life in his parents' house we may interrupt him with 'come to the point!' He may react by cutting the long introduction short but he might also say, 'Wait a minute, all this is very much part of the story.' If the relevance of the recounted events does not become evident later, we shall stick to our judgment that the story was loaded with superfluous details.

Every story is recounted from the perspective of its *ending*; a narrative is a story only if the narrator is *aware* of its ending. It often happens that the listener, too, is acquainted with the ending. But even if the listener is not, he or she has to assume that the storyteller is. Whether we are curious (because we are not acquainted with the end) or whether we are not curious (because we are so acquainted), the *tension* of listening to a story is due to the expectation that the story itself proceeds towards an 'end'. If our expectation is betrayed (if the story has no end or the ending is not a proper one), then we are disappointed. 'And what happened afterwards?' we would ask. If the answer is 'I do not know', or 'there is no afterwards', we experience a deep dissatisfaction. The ending of a story is ceremonial, often ritual, like the end of a sermon. The 'amen' of a story is 'the end'. Even a personal story has to be concluded ceremonially: 'And this was the end of our friendship', 'This was the end of our vicissitudes.' A story *becomes past* by being narrated from its ending, and the end is *absolute*, but also *relative*. It is relative because the narrator speaks in the present: we listen to the narrative in the present, we cry and laugh in the present. We relive the times bygone in the present, making them our present.

It is the story that guides us to reliving and understanding *what* happened, *how* it happened and *why* it happened. Merely narrating 'what happened' can only be called a story if all possible addressees of the narrative are aware of how and why it happened. Stories narrated from the perspective of 'just now' are usually of this type. Customary action (I got up yesterday, I went shopping, and the like) do not call for explanation. But the description of 'how it happened' may occur already at this stage. There are people with the talent of narrating even the most banal events in a colourful and funny way. It is important to note also that there is no narrative whatsoever without *selection*. The instances of 'just now' of yesterday are practically infinite in number, so I cannot recount them all. But if the narrative's point of reference is 'just now', then the selection will normally be a schematic procedure: we simply enumerate the instances of 'just now' that we share with everyone else (in a similar social situation). It can also happen from the perspective of 'now' (for instance, in a *curriculum vitae*) that one restricts oneself to the retelling of the instances of 'what happened', thereby abstracting 'how it happened' and 'why it happened', but this will not make up a story. The selection will be schematic in this case as well, in so far as one only enumerates the items which are relevant to 'whom it may concern'. But if we make a genuine attempt at this process then it is never easy to omit the 'how' and the 'why': these are marks of our personality.

Contrary to a merely functional description of times bygone, real stories about them are always *evocative* in character. Expressing the personality as a whole, they affect other personalities as wholes as well. They simultaneously elicit feelings, reflections, and occasionally decision. They create their own situations, for they transform a person or an agglomerate of people into an *audience*. The audience listens to the story, the storyteller tells it. And the roles become interchangeable. The listener can start to tell a story, and in return the storyteller becomes a listener. Nor does the listener only listen: he or she interrupts the speaker, raises questions, asks for further explanation or elaboration, and sometimes causes the storyteller to remember something that would otherwise have been neglected. The listener becomes a *participant*, with his or her personality being 'built into' the story of the other. If someone listens to the same story several times, complete identification with the subject of the story may take place, and it might happen that one will later tell the same story as if it had happened with him or her. This is not dishonesty, but the outcome of a continuous interplay between narrator and listener; an interplay evidenced by the very process of identification.

We are historians. We all are.

There are stories about history. They were born together with the consciousness of history like the story of the wolf and the lamb, of the puffed-up frog, of the raven and the fox. But there is even a story about storytelling, that of the cricket and the ant. This tale is not only unjust, it is outrightly stupid, since each and every ant cherishes a cricket in its internal self. We want to hear the tune, the song, the tale; we want to chant, to sing, to tell our stories. We need to tell the stories of our contemporaries and the stories of those who lived 'once upon a time' and who will not die as long as we recall and narrate their mournful or happy fate, their stories.

(b)   Objectivity, true and false; the facts

The discrimination between authentic and inauthentic stories is evaluative. Evaluation does not always involve passing value-judgements. Inauthentic stories often simply stir uneasiness in us, and emotionally we reject them without further ado. Should the storyteller greatly lack objectivity, this would contribute to a latent feeling of inauthenticity. The opposite of objectivity is, though, not subjectivity, but particularistic attitude. If the listener is able to share the narrator's passion and commitment, or at least accepts them as justified and well-founded, then this passion may be very apparent without endangering authenticity. The story elicits the feeling of inauthenticity only if the passion or commitment seems to be unfounded (for instance, if there is apparent contradiction between the passion and the 'facts' of the narration). An intention that the listener should believe everything about the teller – that all this has happened to him, that he is always right and others wrong, that he is kindly and others mean, unjust or base – will induce an inclination in the listener to disbelieve, to refuse the authenticity of the account on the grounds of the insincerity, vanity, or bitterness of the storyteller, who is obviously full of rancour. As a result, the listener will spontaneously reconstruct the story in a different way. (Even objective stories can elicit the feeling of inauthenticity if they strike us as 'particularistic'. Innocent victims of conspiracies, if they are realistic enough, know this perfectly well and are prepared to tell their stories only to those they have known for a long time and who have a prior confidence in the authenticity of their personality.) Thus objectivity does not exclude subjectivity (for instance, subjective commitment) but it does exclude particularistic motivations like rancour, envy, jealousy, vanity and rigid prejudices. If the listener assumes that the reconstruction of the 'how' and the 'why' of a story is motivated by one or another of these feelings or character traits, he or she will judge the story (and perhaps the storyteller) as inauthentic because of the lack (or perceived lack) of objectivity.

The problem of objectivity is raised not only in narratives, but also in *every* reconstruction of past events. If two children have a fight, the parents on both sides are inclined to say that it was 'the other kid' who started it. They make up their mind *before* testing the facts, in keeping with their particularistic interests. In such cases we assume that the parties involved are not 'objective' and we summon impartial (disinterested) witnesses in order to decide the matter (if we wish to have a decision at all). But the 'non-objective' statement is not necessarily an 'untrue' one. For instance, in this example, if one of the children deliberately started the fight, the statement of one of the parents has to be true. Yet if it is unclear as to who started it, we may even conclude that both interpretations are true or that both are false, or that there is some truth in both, even though both are non-objective (motivated by bias, decided before testing the facts, etc.). In this and similar everyday cases, objectivity has a very simple meaning: it is the readiness, as far as is possible, to test the facts before judgment, and to abstract from our vested interests and particularistic motivations in the interpretation of these facts. We may accept a statement as authentic if it evokes the impression of objectivity, and a witness as authentic if his or her attitude to the events in question is mainly critical, logical, and if he or she *prima facie* has a greater likelihood of an objective judgment transcending all vested interests.

Not only the narrative and the reconstruction of a single past event raise the question of objectivity; so does the *judgment of character, of institutions, of activities*. If the object of judgment is a person, if this judgment is related to a person or persons, then objectivity belongs to the family of 'justice'. If, for instance, the reconstruction of the children's fight just mentioned (the question of 'who started the fight') does not affect the children in any respect (they are neither scolded nor punished), the objectivity of reconstruction does not belong to the family of 'justice'. However, if one child started the fight, and is scolded or punished, the objectivity of reconstruction already belongs to the family of 'justice' because it entails the *judgment of persons*. On the other hand, if X refers to Y as a 'mean person' and we consider the judgment to be non-objective, we may remark, 'you are unjust'. But if X states that progressive taxation is a harmful institution, we may answer: 'You are not objective – you defend this position as you are on a high salary and have a vested interest', and we may even add that the statement is false (in that we argue on behalf of the *rationality* of progressive taxation), but even so, we definitely cannot say 'you are unjust'. Our preference for objective judgments is like our preference for objective stories. Not knowing personally the persons or institutions disapproved of by the narrator, not having had personal experiences with them, we are far more inclined to accept the disapproval at its face value if the narrator does not relate his or her *own* vicissitudes but discusses the distress of *others*, even if such vicissitudes as are known to us would provide sufficient evidence of the objectivity of this negative judgment. Partial and biased people are perfectly aware of this tendency, and try to disguise their biased judgment by referring to injustices allegedly committed to others. They *rationalize* their judgments. Both the non-objective 'average man' and the non-objective historian rationalize their biased judgments, giving them the appearance of objectivity.

I have already hinted at the possible divergence of 'objectivity' and true knowledge in stories and in everyday statements, in testimonies and judgments. Now this brief reference needs elaboration.

A story is called 'true' if it is not fiction. The child asks 'Tell me, dad, is this story true?' and wants to find out whether the events narrated happened indeed 'in life' or have only been invented by father in order to entertain them. 'Don't be afraid, this is only a tale.' We soothe our children. 'Dragons and witches do not exist, things like that do not happen "in life", in reality.' The *function* of a 'real story' and a fictitious one is different, even if the purpose of the storytelling is often identical (to entertain).

We do not expect *the same* thrill from a real story that we do from a fictitious one: it can be rough, unpolished, badly composed, but it usually has an irresistible attraction simply by the virtue of its being

'real', 'true'. We cannot read a short story without being bored or
disappointed if its only merit is that of being a 'story', but if we *know*
that it indeed happened, that it is 'true' in this sense, we give it our
utmost concentration from the beginning to the end. Is this so because
we recognize ourselves in a 'real story' rather than in a fiction? I do
not think so. Normally, we are more likely to recognize ourselves in a
fiction. But 'reality' has a value of its own: it is the *primary* object of
our *curiosity*. A fiction is *interesting* for us. Curiosity is *aroused* by the
writer, but he *makes* us curious only if the novel is a good one. But
curiosity for reality, for 'true stories', need not be aroused: it is
primordial. We cannot resist the temptation to watch the activity of
completely *unknown* people (through an illuminated window, in a
cafe, in an assembly). In coming upon a street accident we make
enquiries about what happened, we listen into conversations: we are
born eavesdroppers and *voyeurs*. We love and practise gossiping. Our
curiosity is therefore primarily related to reality (reality value – the
status or quality of being real), so we are curious about history as well.
If we read a novel about real historical personalities with excitement
and later are informed that the story was partially fictitious, we feel
some disappointment, even if the novel was interesting. We are
curious about the real actions of real historical personalities; about
their real life, real calamities, even their loves and hatreds, and, of
course, their real 'end'. The *true* story is the *real* story.

The 'true story' can be *checked*, the fiction cannot. A real story can
be falsified, and we may later realize, on the basis of comparing the
story to 'reality', that its *essential facts* were not the case. By essential,
we generally mean 'the gist of the matter', the events which comprise
the 'point' (*Die Sache selbst*). If our father describes his safari
adventures in Africa and we later discover that he has never been
there, the 'thing itself' is falsified and we no longer accept the story as
'true'. But should a reliable witness inform us that our father shot
tigers, not lions, and he did it in February, not in April, this has no
bearing on the gist of the matter, and the original story is only
confirmed as a 'true' (since 'real') one.

Falsifying the 'real' character (the reality value) of a story does not
necessarily lead to its general devaluation. If it satisfies the criteria of
good fiction it will survive as a fictitious story; this is expressed in the
well-known Italian proverb, *si non è vero, è ben trovato*. But if it fails
to meet these criteria it simply becomes *false* and loses its relevance
as an object of curiosity. Furthermore, the critical distinction between fiction and a 'true', a 'real' story, presupposes the ability

to discriminate, which develops in childhood very slowly. Children integrate fantasy and reality; they live in a world characterized by both, and they often feel offended, and justly so, if adults contemptuously dismiss their 'real stories' as mere lies. Also, we act in vain if we tell them that witches do not exist: they won't believe it. There are certain people who never acquire this discriminative ability. They become either swindlers or writers.

We do not always want to check whether a story that we listened to was 'true', 'real', or not. But there are typical circumstances in which the *will to checking* is preponderant. In everyday life, this will is not motivated by theoretical interest or consideration. (The theoretically motivated checking of 'reality content' of life stories is related to sciences like psychology or sociology.) We go 'after things' if we are *practically* motivated; in other words, if we are practically involved with the narrator or the characters of his or her story. Practical motivation can be practical proper (ethical) or pragmatic. We check the stories if they have a bearing on our behaviour (actions, decisions, feelings, attitudes, deliberations).

In the case of a statement of fact (a statement concerning 'what happened') about everyday life, one is not usually theoretically motivated either. Let us return to the simple example of the fighting children. The fact to be decided here is 'who started the fight'? In our example, the parents were biased and each accused the *other* parent's child with starting it. They had a pragmatic interest in *not* checking 'reality'. In this and similar cases, *practical* motivations (for example, to do justice) make it important that we *check* the 'reality content' of the statements. The court procedure is the formalization and rationalization of this everyday interest in 'reality content'. Like the court procedure, we, in everyday life, take into consideration the testimonies of eye-witnesses (preferably disinterested ones), and if we can, we check the statement by producing evidence (for or against it). If X states that he never vilified Y, we may produce a letter by X full of slander about Y, and so on.

But 'that which happened' (the fact) can hardly be discerned from 'why' and 'how' it happened even in the simplest case. To separate 'what' from 'how' and 'why' is already an abstraction. It is a pragmatic abstraction (performed in order to obtain the 'pure' facts) and it is a relevant abstraction for a point of departure. When we find out who started the fighting, we usually proceed thus with our questioning: 'Is it true that X started the fight because he had constantly been humiliated by Y?' In this and similar questions we already interpret

facts and evaluate them. 'Starting the fight' as a fact appears in a
different light depending upon whether it was a matter of aggression
or a requital for some previous humiliation. But the eye-witnesses
(even the most impartial ones) who were of great help as long as we
simply wanted to find out 'who started the fight', are no longer reliable
when it comes to 'why' and 'how'. Even if they can give a testimony
about *post hoc* (and even this is very rarely the case), they cannot give
any testimony about *propter hoc*. The answer to 'why' is always
interpretation, which can be replaced by at least some other (equally
relevant) interpretations.

Attributing motivations to the actors of a story can make the
interpretation plausible. *Plausibility* is the verisimilitude of everyday
life, thinking, and judgment. We normally accept *the most plausible*
interpretation. The interpretation of any event is most plausible if it
provides an explanation of the event by creating a connection between
the characters and the situations of all persons involved in the event,
and does so in a coherent way. The most plausible interpretation
becomes a *theory*: it implies that we interpret all particular facts of the
event (and all particular motivations attributed to its actors) within the
framework of a theory; that we transform the interpreted facts (and
the imputed motivations) into the facts of our theory. In addition, it
stands to reason that the more complicated an event is, the greater is
the number of theories which can explain it in this manner. With
complexity there come several 'most plausible' interpretations. Should
something like this happen in science or philosophy, we may (and
often do) suppose that *more than one* theory can be true; that, for
example, two theories can be *equally true*. This is not the case in
everyday life. Even if we subscribe to one of several 'most plausible'
interpretations, we accept only this one as 'the true' and reject the
others as 'erroneous', 'false' ones. We select either according to our
consciously chosen values or our particularistic motivation, our vested
interests. If we select from equally 'most plausible' interpretations we
are *never objective*. This lack of objectivity blocks the quest for true
interpretation only if we stick to our theory despite the circumstance
that new facts have been discovered and interpreted which can no
longer be coherently explained by the previously chosen theory.

It has been assumed that our interest in mere statements of fact in
everyday life is pragmatically and practically, but not theoretically,
motivated. The more interpreted and evaluated the facts are, the more
we intend to understand the obvious 'what' together with the related
and more subtle 'how' and 'why'; the stronger becomes our theoretical

involvement *within* the given practical and pragmatic ramifications. Almost always when we must cope with something 'unusual', something 'out of order' (at least from the viewpoint of our lives), we start to make the event a theoretical subject matter almost feverishly. If a child catches cold (an event only *slightly* out of order), the parents immediately construct theories – both of a causal and a predictive nature – about the virus. The temptation for speculation is irresistible, and this is not only confined to events which concern us directly. Why our boss has chosen an elderly personal secretary, why our team has lost the final match, why and how our neighbours have adopted a child – events of this nature provide inexhaustible raw material for speculation. We are not only born historians, but we are born theorists as well.

(c) Making sense of something

We are born into the 'historical present'. 'Historical present' has been defined as the 'stock' within the 'flow', as structure. We start our lives with the appropriation of this structure through the appropriation of some *segments* of the structure. As individuals we never appropriate our total historical present, but we cannot rationally reject or suspend it either (as we are within the structure). Our experiences, items of information, actions, interpretations, are guided and shaped primarily by historical present. By placing, conceptualizing, expressing them, we *make sense* of them. If we fail to insert certain phenomena or experiences into the explanatory framework of our historical present, they seem to be 'senseless' or even 'inexplicable'. If 'senseless' and 'inexplicable' experiences are not by and large residual, but become overwhelming, the personality creates for himself or herself a 'secondary' order: the order of delusions, the order of madness.

In a homogeneous and static world humans usually accept the ready-made reality without further ado. 'Making sense' is a mere subsumption. The more heterogeneous and dynamic a world-order is, the more that mere subsumption and 'making sense' are ever less identical, although even then we cannot 'make sense' of experiences, actions, phenomena without some kind of subsumption. (Even in the present subsumption is an overwhelming fact). The differentiation between the present as historical present and as present-present age (elaborated in the previous chapter) is itself an historical product. Only if the procedure of 'making sense' of something can (at least partially) be disconnected from the procedure of mere subsumption; only if we are able to query certain segments of our 'present age'; only if we can criticize them, reject them, and denounce them as 'senseless' from the standpoint of objectivations, values of past-present ages and the ideal of an imagined future – only then can we reasonably distinguish between 'historical present' and 'present-present age'. It has to be added that subsumption too has become a far more comprehensive category nowadays than it was in homogeneous societies.

Making sense of something means to insert phenomena, experience, and the like into our world; it means to transform the unknown into the known, the inexplicable into the explicable, *and* to reinforce or alter the world by meaningful actions of various provenance. Whether the transformation from unknown into known is prior to meaningful actions, or vice versa, is something that cannot be decided in general terms. Moreover, making sense does not inevitably require both components. If we learn the *name* of something, for example, 'oak tree', we place this oak tree in our universe even without any meaningful action taken for or against it, and it is a meaningful act indeed to turn on the light, even if we cannot insert 'electricity' as such into our known universe.

Every story (excepting the restricted stories of 'just now') 'make sense' of our world. It is obvious that all theories and interpretations do this. They use certain procedures of 'making sense' that are applied on various levels by everyone in everyday life.

I have already hinted at the elementary forms of 'making sense of something': it is the procedure of *giving name* to something. The 'name' has a spell, the magic of knowledge. We can make sense of something by *giving name* because we thereby subsume the unknown under a well-known category. 'What is this?' the child asks, and we ask the same question again and again. The doctor makes his diagnosis: 'This is small-pox.' By combining the symptoms, he recognizes the syndrome, and the unknown illness becomes *known*. One can also make sense of the *inexplicable* by giving it a name: we call it a *miracle*, and insert it thereby into our universe.

We can make sense of something by *analogy*. We say: 'X is like Y' or 'X resembles Y' and, given that Y is known, we have inserted X via analogy into our universe.

We can make sense of something by *causality*. We ask: 'I do not understand why you neglect your work. Has something happened? Are you ill?' Generally, we do not desist until we get an answer to our question, for the simple reason that, unless we know its cause, we cannot make sense of a behaviour. In this and similar cases, 'cause' is not a clear-cut scientific concept. It can practically be anything (a motivation, a previous event, a state of mind, a state of organism) the knowledge of which enables us to understand the behaviour in question. The principle of making sense through causality is the principle of *sufficient ground*. Both motivation and *causa efficiens* can equally serve as 'sufficient ground'. It depends on the phenomenon (event, behaviour, and the like) that we want to make sense of. Likewise, it depends on our interest in the phenomenon, and which kind and how many items of information are needed, in order to make the phenomenon 'known' through the 'sufficient ground'.

We can make sense of something by all categories of *modality*.

We often say: 'It happened by chance'. The components of something 'happening by chance' can be expressed as *two* opposites: the result of a *voluntary* (intentional) action, and *fate* (destiny). The statement that 'we did not meet by chance' can express two distinct meanings depending on the situation and the context in which we utter it. The first meaning is equivalent to this: at least one of us *intended* meeting the other. The second amounts to this: our meeting each other has been predestined, was inevitable (it 'has been written in the stars'); wittingly or unwittingly, we had to meet. If we describe events as contingent, we make sense of them in so far as we *deny* their being either intended or inevitable. But if we term an event 'contingent', we have not yet said anything of its *importance*. Sometimes, despite its being contingent, we intend to reveal its 'sufficient ground'. One may die in a car crash (which was neither intended, nor, obviously, predestined) and its cause still has to be traced (for instance, the steering-wheel of the car broke).

If we make sense of something, we in fact distinguish 'essential' from 'inessential'. Here, 'essential' means 'important' or 'real', and so, 'inessential' may mean either 'unimportant' or 'apparent'. Every event or action of grave or far-reaching consequences is regarded as essential (important). If we say that X went berserk because of the avarice of his brother, we impute importance to the brother's avarice from the aspect of X's whole fate (it was essential). But if we warn someone not to be deluded by X's complaisance, as X is not what he seems to be, then we do not distinguish between 'important' and 'unimportant', but between 'appearance' and 'reality' (the 'essence' of character).

We can make sense of something through the categories of

'possibility' and 'probability' (impossibility and improbability) irrespective of whether the event happened in the past or is going to
happen in the future. But when applying these categories to past
events, we *mean* things that are completely different from the
application of the same notions of the future. If applied to the past,
possibility and probability have an affinity with 'true', whereas
impossibility and improbability have an affinity with 'false' (the lie). If
someone tells us that X has killed his wife and we react with the
exclamation 'Impossible!', the meaning of the exclamation is that 'this
cannot be true'. I mentioned 'affinity' and *not* 'identity' with regard to
the categories of 'true' and 'false', and it stands to reason why. Should
we *know* that X has not killed his wife, we would not answer with the
exclamation 'Impossible!'; we would simply remark that the statement
was not true. Similarly, if we react to an account of a past event with
the statement that 'yes, it is possible', or 'yes, it is very probable' (that
this and this was the case), we do not confirm the 'truth' of the
account; we simply mean that 'it is imaginable that this and this was
true' or that 'this might have been the case'. If applied to the *future*,
possibility and probability have an affinity with 'realization'. If I say
to someone that he has undertaken an impossible task, I mean by this
that going by my experiences, he will not be able to succeed in it.
Something is probable if 'it is very likely to happen'. Again, I mention
affinity, not identity. If I have undertaken a task, and all conditions of
its realization are met (or so I think), I shall not apply the categories
of possibility and probability.

I can make sense of single events and modes of behaviour by the
application of *'general sketches'*. General sketches usually combine
subsumption, analogy, and causation. They can be applied both to the
past and the future, and this, in terms of the tense in which they are
employed, is why they annul the distinction of the categories of
modality. Formally, a general sketch is a statement about facts, but it
always entails hidden valuation. This is why all general sketches can
become imperatives. Last but not least, we assume that they are true
statements and we employ them on the basis of this assumption. Only
their application can be interpreted, not the general sketches themselves.

Proverbs are typical general sketches; for instance, 'Who sows the
wind, reaps the whirlwind'. We can 'make sense' of various different
events by the application of the proverb ('X harassed his neighbours
until he was ostracized by them', and the like). We subsume the event,
but this subsumption is in itself an analogy. The event will become

analogous with all other events and patterns of behaviour which can be subsumed under the *same* general sketch. The implicitly *causal* character of the proverb is self-evident. The proverb 'Who sows the wind, reaps the whirlwind' means that *if* someone sows the wind, *then* he or she will reap the whirlwind. It also means that *everyone* who sows the wind will *always* reap the whirlwind. In this context, causality is turned into *necessity*. Causal nexus does not only mean that if someone 'reaps the whirlwind' then we can make sense of this event by discerning the *causa efficiens* of the event in the prior event that someone 'has sown wind'. It also suggests that if X has sown wind, he will *inevitably* reap the whirlwind. And, if it is true that whoever sows wind will inevitably reap the whirlwind, then it is also a certainty that if I sow wind *now*, I shall inevitably reap the whirlwind in the future. The outcome of 'sowing wind' is not only possible or probable, it is absolutely sure, since it is a necessity. Furthermore, this statement of fact ('who sows the wind, reaps the whirlwind') is at the same time a value-judgment. It can easily become an imperative: that you should not sow the wind!

General sketches are general in that they refer to '*everyone*' and '*any time*'. At the same time, they are *not* open to falsification. Even if it happens a hundred times that someone 'sows the wind' and does *not* 'reap the whirlwind', the proverb will still be considered *true* thereafter, and will be employed as a true statement of fact.

General sketches mediate traditional experiences in a concise form. Proverbs are only the classic examples of this genre. Mothers who tell their children that 'anyone' who drinks cold water when overheated will get a sore throat, also employ a general sketch. So did Aristotle in stating that *all* extreme democracies lead to tyranny. All facets of the proverb 'who sows the wind, reaps the whirlwind' can be found in both the previous statements, which are of very different character.

'Making sense' is not only the fitting of events and forms of behaviour into one's universe. The transformation of the unknown into the known automatically increases self-knowledge. But one acts for and against the surrounding world as well. A person must dovetail action with personal knowledge and vice versa; interactions with the knowledge of others and about others, and vice versa. By the various – but in the main interconnected – procedures of 'making sense', *one makes sense of one's own life*.

In a homogeneous and static world-order the *specific* question of making sense of life is not yet raised. The person applies himself or herself to his or her historical present and adjusts thereby to his or her

Togetherness. The sense of life is *given* and no specific effort or intention is needed for making sense of one's *own* life. But if the forms of life are open to interpretation and the mere subsumption may be replaced by critical (and individual) choice, the problem of 'making sense of my life' is already raised, but without being problematical, or only occasionally so; for example, in times of social crises and catastrophes. For the individual of ancient times, the problem of 'making sense of my life' was basically a moral issue. Humans had 'been given' a task or they had chosen one. But whether the task was given or chosen, the individual was neither too 'little' nor too 'great' for it: he or she knew of the obligation to accomplish it and of the need to be virtuous in order to do so. The individual knew that by observing the norms 'during his whole lifetime' (Aristotle), his life would be meaningful; that life became void of sense after severe moral transgression, just as Judas lost the sense of his life in betraying the Master. Life was also regarded as senseless if there has remained no task to accomplish. But as *norms* pertained to every task, the empty life and the immoral life were identical notions. If fate was hard, the individual could only blame himself. Moral transgression, *hubris*, sinning against the Almighty, failing to rectify the fathers' sins – in short, vice – was the only explanation. If there was no vice to be blamed, fate could not harm one's 'sense of life'.

'The time is out of joint; O cursed spite – That ever I was born to set it right'. Hamlet's words are giving voice to the life-experience of modern individuality. Man's life is no longer written in the stars. Being the creator of his own destiny and of the destiny of his world, he can take fate into his own hands, or so Machiavelli argued, giving voice to the life-experience of modern individuality. The modern individual makes sense of life with categories other than those of his ancient predecessors.

One of the modern individual's basic experiences is the discrepancy between the personality and the task. 'I am destined for great deeds but must cope with subaltern and banal tasks', means 'I cannot make sense of my life.' 'I have missed the great possibility of my life' equally means 'I cannot make sense of my life.' To find the adequate task to recognize it, to create it, to make use even of misfortunes in order to grow, to develop, to constantly progress; this is precisely the meaning of 'making sense of modern individual's life'. Virtue is not a main concern. The desire is to make sense of life through freedom.

Freedom is merit. Merit is attributed to anything as long as it increases freedom; as such, it accrues not only to the morally commendable act. Even bonds linking people together can be construed as a limit of freedom, and individual development towards freedom must be unlimited. But this process *is* inevitably terminated: it is limited by 'the end'. Thus the end is also relativized. The task becomes adequate to the person if it makes the person immortal, and so the task itself has to be immortal. Death is no longer 'natural', since its mere existence ridicules 'Captain Forward' (as Feuerbach put it). But if we ask the moment to linger, we will lose the sense of our lives. Tomorrow makes sense of today and yesterday; times to come make sense of 'now' and of times bygone. A strong grasp of the present enables its transformation into the future. Every soldier carries the marshal's baton of the future, and should he miss the appropriate moment, should he fail to recognize his proper task and fate, he will never marshal life itself; he will not make sense of his life. But if a man becomes indeed the field-marshal of life, if he succeeds in transforming life into fate, if he increases his freedom day by day, making good use even of *bad* luck, if *his destiny becomes his merit* (whatever this merit may be), then, reflecting on times bygone, he will both feel and know that everything that happened to him happened *of necessity*, and did so because everything contributed to the final goal – to the totalization of his own future. Everyone who has failed to make sense of life usually asks the empty question 'where have I missed the mark?' and thus ruminates, 'Had I decided otherwise at this or that juncture, my life would be meaningful now', or 'Had certain people behaved or acted otherwise, my life would make sense now.' Conversely, success in making sense of life prompts the thought that 'Everything that happened to me, happened well as it did. Had it happened otherwise, it would have been disastrous. But it could not happen otherwise – under the given circumstances I was the author of my own life; I was a free author of fate.'

We are philosophers of history, we *all* are. We are philosophers of history whenever we do not blame failures on bad luck, but on our decisions of yesteryear, on our worldly institutions, or on the conscious (or unconscious) motivations of others. We are philosophers of history whenever we succeed in harmonizing our Being and our Togetherness and whenever we understand our times bygone as links in the chain of necessity, as constitutive of our self-created destiny. The statement that 'everything should have happened otherwise', or that 'I am sure in the victory of my ideals' are statements of the philosophy of history.

We are, then, born historians, born theorists, born philosophers of history. This is why historiography, theory, the philosophy of history exist: they express, formulate and satisfy our needs. If we blame these objectivations for their blunders and shortcomings, the blame reverts to us. Be their consequences good or bad, blissful or disastrous – we bear the responsibility – we *all* bear it.

Part II

Historiography as
episthémé

Chapter Four

Introductory remarks

The title of this part describes historiography as *episthémé*: as true knowledge. The choice fell on the Greek word in order to emphasize that the *norm* of historiography has always been true knowledge, although the *criteria* of 'true knowledge' have changed in the sciences in general, and no less in the historical sciences. In the framework of this book I am not going to offer any theory about 'true knowledge', not even as far as *our* historical understanding is concerned. I have to add that in my view different objectivations and different spheres of life make use of different criteria of true knowledge, although all of them are of a normative nature. I discussed the problem of true and false as categories of value-orientation in my book *Towards a Marxist Theory of Values*: the problem of true knowledge in everyday life in my *Everyday Life* and the notion of truth in philosophy, in *Radical Philosophy*. However, none of these works analysed the problem of the criteria of true knowledge in the modern sciences. But here I will restrict myself to historiography, since in a series of works elaborating my theory of anthropology, to which this volume is the third contribution,* I also plan to write a book on the theory of true knowledge.

My conception of true knowledge in historiography is a combination of three elements. As far as 'applied theory' is concerned, in the main I have accepted Popper's theoretical proposal, with certain modifications which will become obvious to the reader. These modifications stem from the dependence of the 'applied theory' on the 'higher theory' that I argue for, and to an equal degree on the emphasis on the values which co-constitute the 'applied theory'. As

---

* *On Instincts* and *A Theory of Feelings*, Assen, Netherlands, Van Gorcum, 1979 are the first two.

regards the 'higher theory,' the second element of the combination, Kuhn's theory of true knowledge becomes decisive. Although it is well-known that the theories of Popper and Kuhn are controversial, they can be, and indeed are, homogenized when applied on *different levels* and dovetailed in their transformation through my *theory of values*. The latter, my own theory of values, is the third element of the combination. It goes without saying that all the responsibilities for the theoretical proposal are mine.

The Children of Captain Grant*

On 26 July 1864, a new ship, the *Duncan*, was crossing the Northern Canal. One of the sailors caught sight of a fish which seemed to be *unusual* in those waters. It turned out to be a shark. The ship's passengers decided to catch it, for such an endeavour might be *useful* and at the same time exciting. While the crew was throwing the carcase back into the sea, one of them observed that there was an *unusual object* in its gut. One sailor suggested that it might be a piece of rock, another an undigested cannonball (an uninteresting finding), but a third identified it as an old bottle. 'Get it out carefully', the owner of the ship commanded, 'for *often valuable documents are contained* in bottles found in the sea.' The thing became an *object of curiosity*. The ship's passengers started to act as *investigators*. First of all, they identified the *make of the bottle*, and found out that it came from *far away*. Then they opened it. There were indeed *papers* in the bottle, and they were called *documents* by the discoverers on the assumption that they bore a message from somewhere, from someone (or some-'ones'). There were *three* documents in the bottle, written in three different languages, but water and time had blotted out the writing; there remained only a few words or fragments of words in all three of them.

The first paper looked like this:

62	Bri	gow	
sink			stra
aland			
skopp	Gr		
	that monit		of long
and			ssistance

---

* A novel by Jules Verne.

The message *did not make sense*. After having deciphered the other two fragments of text (written in German and French) the investigators combined them in order to get some clues. They succeeded in obtaining the following message: a ship called *Britannia*, which had embarked on 7 June 1862, in Glasgow, had sunk somewhere. It was the captain and the sailors who had thrown the bottle into the sea at latitude 37° 11′ South, seeking help. Everything else, and most importantly the longitude, was unknown. By using another document (the *Mercantile and Shipping Gazette*) they found out that the captain's name was Grant.

The passengers of the *Duncan* did not stop here, but went further. They thought that the gaps of the message could easily be filled and proceeded to complete the words and sentences. In so doing they came to the conclusion that the *Britannia* sank near the coast of Patagonia and that the captain and two sailors were captured by Indians. Apparently everything *was fitting together*, the message seemed to have been read correctly.

They placed an advertisement in *The Times* stating that information regarding the fate of Captain Grant was available from them. As far as they were concerned, the story of the *Britannia* had ended.

However, the *search for the story* did not end at that stage. Captain Grant had left children who were *personally* interested in the fate of their father. They persuaded the owners of the *Duncan* to launch an *expedition* in order to find Captain Grant. In this act, curiosity was combined with *involvement*. En route they discovered a passenger, who was unknown to everyone, named Jacques Paganel. He had studied geography in the solitude of his chamber for twenty years, and joined the expedition in order to *test* his knowledge.

Off they went to Patagonia where they *did not find* Captain Grant. They realized that what they thought to be a *fact* was but the *interpretation* of the message in terms of the 'Patagonia-theory'. They re-read the documents again and again until they came to the conclusion that the theory was false. Captain Grant had to be in Australia. By elaborating the new theory, *everything seemed to be fitting together again*. The message appeared, once again, to have been understood. So off they went to Australia, but they did not find Captain Grant there either. By *chance* (glancing at a New Zealand newspaper) Paganel came to the opinion that the 'Australia-theory' was false too: Captain Grant had to be in New Zealand. He read the documents in the light of this theory and *everything seemed to be fitting together again.* The expedition went off to New Zealand – but they did not find Captain Grant there either.

Of course, all novels of adventure have to have a happy ending. The passengers of the *Duncan* did eventually find Captain Grant. They found him by chance, at a place that no one had thought of. The captain explained the document to them. *Everything was fitting together again.* Everyone came to know how the story actually happened.

The story of Captain Grant's children describes everything historiography and the philosophy of history is about, though with one difference: if we travel in time and not in space, we can never find Captain Grant *alive*. No one *can tell us* what really happened and how. There is no happy ending, because there is no ending at all, as long as the *Duncan* (the symbol of the present) embarks towards the ocean of the past.

Chapter Five

Past, present and future in historiography

Historiography was conceived of as *episthémé*, that is *true knowledge*, by Herodotus, in contrast with mere *opinion (doxa)*. In a similar (even if not identical) way, philosophers of several epochs contrasted true knowledge, represented by philosophy, with the *doxa* of everyday thinking.

In the first part of this book I tried to define historical consciousness (the consciousness of historicity) in general, hence I could not differentiate everyday knowledge and understanding from the two types of true knowledge and understanding. The distinction was at that stage irrelevant from our viewpoint. In order to go further, one has to be aware of problems not yet raised because of the synthetic nature of the discussion. A more analytical methodology is required.

While speaking of the roots that both historiography and the philosophy of history have in everyday thinking, I argued for the theoretical proposal that not only is the need for historiography and philosophy deeply embedded in everyday consciousness, but that their basic determinants are as well. By this I did not mean to identify the structure and function of everyday understanding with those of historiography and philosophy, nor did I intend to disregard the differences in the *content of knowledge* in regard to the various levels of objectivation. In spite of the distinction between true and untrue, objective and biased (as far as the intention is concerned), in spite of spontaneous theorizing, everyday knowledge does not transcend the level of understanding called 'opinion' in ancient times, due to the direct - unreflected - identity of theory and practice in which practice may be pragmatic or practical proper.* As far as the content of

---

* The distinction between pragmatic and practical interest respectively activity was made clear by J. Habermas. I apply the two concepts in the same way that he does. If historiography is used as a means for the successful

knowledge is concerned, the difference between the two levels is even more obvious. Everyday knowledge is never coherent and it mostly encompasses the conclusions of the objectivations of *episthémé* without their argumentation, by selecting fragments fitted to practical and pragmatic use. However, in spite of the partial character of reception, it is to be assumed that everyday historical consciousness is -the basis of both historiography and philosophy (of history). More precisely, the problems formulated on the level of *episthémé are* the problems of everyday life and consciousness. We may describe them as the forms of 'imputed consciousness' in Goldmann's sense of the word: they make the implicit explicit, the vague clear, the covert overt, the incoherent coherent. There is no cause-effect relationship between the consciousness of historicity and its two forms of *episthémé*; the latter belong to the former as its extreme expressions. Yet the forms of *episthémé* may influence everyday consciousness in a very special way, and in modern times they do this in an ever-increasing manner: they offer a *language* absorbed quickly by everyday self-understanding. People who have never read Condorcet or Hegel or Marx or Nietzsche or Ranke or Toynbee or Block *speak* their language. Even most scholarly historical writings can be 'spoken' by the mediation of belletristic literature and the mass media.

Historiography is *episthémé* by contrast with everyday knowledge because it does not aim at any pragmatic or (immediate) practical application. If one wants to know the truth about a fight in the eighteenth century, one does not do it in order to punish or reproach the responsible party as in the case of the children's quarrel described in the preceding chapter. Neither does one do it in order to entertain. Moreover, for the *norm* of historiography, the pragmatic application of knowledge is excluded on principle. The justification by history of a present action belongs to history as ideology, not to history as *episthémé*. This does not mean that historians have never done this, only that according to the norms of historiography they should not have done it. The *mediated* (i.e. never direct) *practical* intent does not contradict, however, the norms of historiography. History proper has served for a long period as a 'lesson' for the present. Hence it is not

realization of any concrete social goals or for the rationalization of any actions taken, then its use is a pragmatic one. If it is used to 'enlighten' the actors of the present, to make them learn from history and change or reinforce their attitudes and behavioural patterns through insight and rational deliberation, then its use is a practical one.

simply its orientation towards truth and objectivity that characterizes historiography as 'true knowledge', but also its norm which detaches truth and objectivity from pragmatic action and behaviour, and from direct practical use.

Historiography is and always has been *critical*. It does not take opinions of witnesses at their face value, but selects from them in order to distinguish the authentic from the inauthentic. Of course, this can also be done on the level of mere 'opinion'. The norms of historiography hold that there must be a *general principle* of selection. Everyday procedures of selection cannot serve as general principles in historiography. (We cannot ask a witness from the past to look deeply into our eyes in order to find out whether or not he lied.) Different historians of different times have opted for different general principles of selection, but all genuine historians have had to find and apply them in a coherent way.

Historiography always deals with the *past*. This statement seems to be a commonplace but it is not. Croce and Collingwood, for instance, challenged it in stating that historiography always deals with the present. Their arguments have to be taken seriously, and so my statement above has to be *proved*.

Plainly, the problem is not whether the *subject matter* of historiography is the past or the present, but whether this subject matter serves only as a *medium* in order to deal with the problems of the present. For example, in *Julius Caesar*, Shakespeare dealt in fact with his own present, and not with the past, although the subject matter of the tragedy was taken from the past. Can historiography be understood in this manner or not: that is the question?

As far as the subject matter is concerned, historiography always excludes the *past of our present* and only deals with *historical past*. During the Second World War no one could write a *history book* on a battle that happened yesterday. All stories of the past of present are *reports* of a kind (in oral or in written form). Historiography chooses subject matters which can be reconstructed and understood from the standpoint of a (relative) *end*. For instance, in the case of Captain Grant's children, the ship *Britannia* had already experienced her fate when the search for survivors started.

Nevertheless, what belongs to the past of present and what belongs to the historical past is determined by historical consciousness itself, that is to say by the consciousness of a present age of which historiography is only one expression. Hence, by the statement that the subject matter of historiography is the past, the other is implied as well: that it is not historiography alone which decides on the simple question of *what past is.*

This is not only relevant as far as the distinction between the past of the present and the historical past is concerned. Historical consciousness has to reflect upon itself as the 'new' against the 'old' in order to construct a historical past at all. Moreover, the past – that is to say, the subject matter of historiography – is an expression of a collective consciousness from different aspects. These aspects are the following: where does the past begin, does the present have *only one* past or many, and if the latter is true, *how many,* etc.? In the case of Captain Grant's children, the past 'started' with the *Britannia's* putting to sea at Glasgow; everything which had happened prior to this was outside the interest of the passengers of the *Duncan.*

In this way the subject matter of historiography is constituted by the present. But even so, what is constituted by the present is something which is no longer present but belongs to the past. The question is whether it *really* belongs.

The past has to be contained *in the present* in the form of messages and signs. What is not *here* and *now,* cannot be deciphered at all. Without traces (documents, things), there is no past. The ship *Britannia* (and whatever had happened in relation to it) existed only from the moment when the message was received by the *Duncan* (the present age).

The message has to be here and now but this is not sufficient: it has to be understood as a message. First of all, it has to be *identified* as such. The bottle was already on the *Duncan* but as long as it was identified as a piece of rock or a cannonball, it was no message, not even a trace of a message. It became a trace (of a message) when it was identified as a bottle.

Further, in order to recognize a trace of a message as such, one has mentally to connect the trace with the possibility of a message. The possibility (or probability) of this connection is again contained in the present. The bottle (the trace of the message) was already identified when one of the sailors remarked that the fish swallowed the wine together with the bottle – in other words, when he identified the trace without relating it to any kind of message. But when the owner of the ship made the comment that 'often there are valuable documents in bottles found in the sea', the trace was connected with the notion of a message, and it was connected in a *generalized* statement. The trace may be a message, because *traces like this often are* messages. The preceding statement presupposed the following elements: (a) there is knowledge in the *present* regarding the possible interconnection of a concrete trace with a message, (b) the message is conceived of as a *document*, again in the present, and (c) *value* is attached to the documents (to some of them at least) in the present.

Thus the trace has to be in the present. The trace is only contained in the present if it is identified by the present as such. The trace is the trace of a message only if the notion of a message is related to it by the present. The message is received as a *significant* one only when it is understood as a document by the present. In order to become significant, value has to be attached to certain documents by the present. The trace is in the present and it is only the present that constitutes the trace.

The attitude of the passengers of the *Duncan* to the bottle (as a trace with a possible message) was *curiosity*. We usually want to know what is 'inside something'. If the story of the sailor, by which the fish swallowed the wine together with the bottle, had been accepted, no one would have wanted to know what was inside the bottle, because everyone would have *known* that it was wine. The motivation of curiosity (a general human motivation) was aroused by the knowledge about the possibility of a message. Thus curiosity as such does not account for curiosity-for-something, in this case: curiosity-for-the-content-of-the-bottle. We do not open the bottles of the past just because we are curious. We are curious, yes, but this curiosity is prompted by our reckoning with the possibility of finding *valuable documents* in them, documents-for-the-present, valuable ones for the present.

By connecting the notion of a message with the trace and being motivated by the curiosity-for-the-message, human beings are in the state of *readiness-for-the-message*. The readiness-for-the-message can be prior to the trace. There are epochs (such as ours) in which the ship *Duncan* undertakes the cruise in order to find the bottle which might contain the messages we are looking for.

The readiness-for-the-message is mostly a readiness to receive concrete types of messages. For another crew with different intentions, even a cannonball in the gut of the fish could be relevant as a trace of a message (though this was not the case with the *Duncan*).

Readiness for a particular message is the general characteristic of historical consciousness. The first step that historiography as true knowledge undertakes is deciphering the message from the trace or looking for traces in order to obtain messages to be read. Such a procedure has to be *methodical* and *critical*. The owner of the ship

Duncan commanded that the bottle should be opened cautiously (because often there are valuable documents in bottles like this). A message is a message only when it can be *read*. Even if we connect the notion of a message with the trace, even if there is a 'readiness-for-the-message', if nothing can be read (understood), we are confronted with a trace but not with a message. In the case of Captain Grant's children, had the water totally blotted out the words, the papers would have never become messages, only traces of unknown people and unknown events which would never have become known unless a new bottle with a readable message about the same people and the same events had been found by another crew.

By deciphering the four papers together, the historians of the ship of the present named *Duncan* read the message. To read the message means to obtain a certain amount of *information*. To read a historical message means to obtain a certain amount of information about *what happened in the past*.

Up to this point, I have always referred to the present. The trace is a trace contained in the present, the readiness-for-the-message is again in the present, the message is read in the present. What must also be understood is that the message itself reveals the past. While reading the message one deciphers the past. Historiography is involved in reading messages about the past; its readiness-for-the-message is methodical and its reading of messages critical. Hence the conclusion that the subject matter of historiography is the past (the historical past).

The historians of the ship of the present named *Duncan* deciphered not just any random information but *new data*. No one knew about the fate of the *Britannia* before they read the message. Naturally, the new item of information was related to the old. In this case, everyone knew that the *Britannia* had put to sea at Glasgow. Historiography reads messages of the past while relating new items of information to old ones.

'Reading a message about the past' is not a single act but a process involving different and heterogeneous procedures. The 'historians' of the *Duncan*, first of all, agreed on the items of information which could be taken as given. It could be taken for granted (it was *sure*) that a ship called *Britannia*, which put to sea on 7 June 1862, at Glasgow, sank somewhere, and also that the captain and two sailors threw the bottle into the sea at latitude 37° 11' South, and that they were seeking help. This information was regarded as *historical fact*. The second step was to 'fill the gaps' in the message. This 'filling the gaps' led them to the acceptance of the 'Patagonia-theory'. It served to explain events in the past. They explained the past for the present (for themselves) and thereby expressed the readiness-for-the-message from the standpoint of the present (historical consciousness). They wanted to find out what in fact happened and how it happened in the past – nothing else. True knowledge about the past was desired.

We know from the story that the Patagonia–theory had to be replaced by another one, the second theory again by another, and so on. But all these theories lived up to the criteria of scientificity, constitutive of the endeavour to obtain true knowledge about the past.

The 'historians' of the *Duncan* deciphered the message without being motivated by any pragmatic or practical interest. Also, their procedure was methodical and critical. Their interest was at the same time invested in the knowledge of something which happened in the past. They wanted to know the truth about this past.

To go a step further, the *future* did *not* play any part at all in their theoretical interest. They never thought that the fate of Captain Grant might play any role in *their* future – in *their* personal future and that of the ship of the present named *Duncan*. But it did.

Herein lies the paradox of historiography. It wants to find out the truth about the past from the standpoint of the present. It does not deal with the future at all, not even with the future in the present. Even so, it influences the future (mediated by the future in the present) contrary to its own intentions. If this influence is intended, historiography is not historiography proper. It is either not true knowledge at all (it is ideology) or it is a different kind of true knowledge: philosophy of history. If, however, historiography does *not* lead to the unintended effect, it is again not historiography proper but historical philology. Genuine historiography is not constructed from the standpoint of the future (future in the present) and though it deals with the past, it has to have a *feedback* to the present and so it has to influence the future in the present. It is precisely reception that mediates historiography to the pragmatic or the practical intentions of the actors.

It has already been mentioned that these two types of mediation are not of equal value. If historiography is mediated in the direction of pragmatic goals, it is absorbed as ideology. If it is mediated in the direction of practical goals, historiography proper comes about.

When the 'historians' of the *Duncan* deciphered the message, they put an advertisement in the newspaper. They suggested that anyone who wanted to know anything (get any sort of information) about the fate of the *Britannia,* could get it. The advertisement offered knowledge; information about the present. This information *met* a practical interest, the need and personal involvement of Captain Grant's children. They had a *purpose* (to find their father) which was internalized as an *obligation* by the ship of the present named *Duncan.* The future of the *Duncan* did change, although this was not intended by its 'historians'. The change resulted from the feedback of knowledge to the practical interest.

Captain Grant *existed* from the moment the message was read. He existed in the *minds* of the actors of the present (the passengers of the *Duncan*). Moreover, he started to *act,* to *participate* in the present since his whereabouts was a practical concern of his children. He also participated in changing the future of the present (the *Duncan*). This was the real resurrection of the past called *Britannia,* a miracle that happens every day in and through historiography.

The historical past is *not what is forgotten, but what can be recalled.* In this sense past is indeed exclusively contained in the present. But only what is forgotten can be recalled. Historians are the psychoanalysts of the human species in that they transform what is forgotten into what is recalled. If we do want to remember, they enable (and instigate) us to remember. They can only enable us to remember because something had been forgotten. In this sense, the past is not what is actually remembered, but what *can be* recalled. Thus *our* historical past is what can be recalled. *The* past of humankind is everything that can be recalled in the subsequent present ages of the future up until the final days of the limited enterprise, humankind, is subject to recollection. Heidegger put it in this way: 'The past does not primarily exist in what is recalled but in what is forgotten.... Only because the past has this forgotten existence, can it be preserved and recalled at all.'*

According to a memorable simile of Dilthey, history is the autobiography of peoples and humankind. In the way we re-write our life-story again and again, humankind re-writes its life-story anew as well. Although the simile is apposite in one way, it does not distinguish between historiography and the philosophy of history. Both participate in re-writing the autobiography of peoples and humankind, but from different aspects, with different intentions and following the different rules of their respective objectivations.

---

* Quoted in H. G. Gadamer, *Kleinere Schriften,* vol. I, Tübingen, Mohr, 1976, p. 160.

In order to make this difference clear from the viewpoint of the past, present and future, let us turn back for the last time to the history of Captain Grant's children.

Up until now, one of the protagonists of the novel and his actions have been left out of the discussion: this personality is Jacques Paganel.

Jacques Paganel was not on the ship when the trace of the message was found. He did not participate in the methodical and critical work of the travellers on the *Duncan*. He did not relate the notion of a message to the trace. The message was first read *without* him. The consensus regarding certain statements (facts) was achieved before he made his first appearance. He joined the *Duncan* (uninvited) at the moment when the ship embarked on its trip towards the future. His goal was threefold. First, he wanted to test his ideas in reality; second, he had decided to communicate with foreign peoples and that is why he learned their language (it should be noted that he learned Portuguese *instead* of Spanish and was embarrassed that no one could understand him); third, he wanted to rescue Captain Grant.

The subsequent reinterpretations of the text were accomplished by Jacques Paganel. The first interpretation (undertaken without him) was motivated, as noted earlier, by readiness-for-the-message; by a desire to find out what in fact happened in the past. The second and third interpretations, undertaken by Jacques Paganel, were motivated, however, by the *goal* and *obligation* to do something in the future, to *change* the course of the *Duncan* in order to find Captain Grant. The knowledge of the past was no more a goal in itself; it became a means for practical purposes; the theory served as a regulative practical idea for action. Jacques Paganel did not offer any new *information*, any new facts; what he did was to arrange the facts according to a theory-for-action. He *did not deal with the past*, he dealt with the present-for-the-future, although the *subject matter* of his interest encompassed the past as well; his concern was the past, and thus the present and the future of the *Britannia and its crew became* interconnected with the present and the future of the ship *Duncan*. This way of theorizing is *philosophy of history*.

Historiography can be called *episthémé* and contrasted with mere opinion only if it disconnects knowledge about the past from all kind of pragmatic and immediate practical goals. Philosophy of history disconnects knowledge from pragmatism as well, but it *relates it to practice*. As philosophy in general, it wants to find out what is true *and* good. Hence what is true is at the same time Good – it should lead our behaviour and actions; what is untrue is at the same time Evil: it cannot or should not lead our behaviour and actions. In the philosophy of history the past is always the past-in-the-present. It is interconnected with the 'good'; it is a reconstruction of the past in order to reconstruct the unity of true and good in the present and for the future. The philosophy of history *speaks* about the past, but it does not communicate anything about it; it tells us something about the present, with the intention to influence it, to maintain or to change it. Yet this does not mean that philosophy of history offers us true knowledge to a lesser degree than historiography. Jacques Paganel succeeded in reconstructing the message as skilfully as did the 'historians' of the *Duncan*. Although he took the facts as given and did not consider reconstruction as a goal in itself, although he did not offer any kind of new information, he transformed all the facts into those of two subsequent theories, homogeneously and without logical contradictions.

At any rate, Captain Grant was not found by either following the predictions of the 'historians' or those of the 'philosopher of history'. But several things happened: new knowledge (information about the past) was offered to a historical consciousness ready to receive it, and the fate of the *Duncan* changed indeed.

The autobiography of peoples and humankind is written both by historiography and philosophy of history. The first makes us recall something which had been forgotten, the second changes our lives or at least our attitude to our lives by re-arranging everything which had been recalled. The first never intends to change our lives; the second never intends to make us recall what has been forgotten. Both what has to be recalled and the way recollection can be related to our lives are expressions of the historical consciousness of the present. The subject matter of historiography is the past and it deals with the past no less, motivated by the readiness-for-the-message. The subject matter of philosophy of history is the past, the present and the future-in-the-present but it deals with the present from the viewpoint of the future.

It became a commonplace that the relation of the present to the past is but a form of *communication*. But if the above distinction between historiography and the philosophy of history holds true, the only medium with which we are able to communicate with the past on the level of true knowledge is historiography. If one speaks of the past without telling anything about it, telling something new only about the present (and the future-in-the-present), one does not communicate with the past, but with the present. Actually, philosophy of history *queries* the past, but it raises only those questions to which the answers are already known by the interrogator. Consequently, the questions are pseudo-questions as far as the past is concerned, they are real questions only in regard to the present. As a result, the past as such does not provide any new information for the philosophy of history, it speaks the tongue of the present. On the other hand, historiography does communicate with the past. When it queries the past, it does not know the answers to its questions in advance. To be more correct, it has a preliminary notion about the character of the possible answers (otherwise it would not raise precisely those questions which it does) but the actual answer granted by the past cannot be predetermined. It might even happen that historiography gets an answer it never thought of, or that it gets no answer at all. At the same time, historiography has to 'induce the past to ask *its* questions' as well. This is a norm of historiography which can never be completely fulfilled but the fulfilment of which has to be always intended. It cannot be fulfilled because the resurrection of the dead is accomplished by those living in the present and the past can only speak with the tongue of the present. But speaking with the tongue of the present and spelling out the message of the present (which is the assignment of the philosophy of history) differ considerably from each other. Historiography is a kind of psychodrama, where the interrogator is compelled to take the position of those whom he wants to understand. The historian has to take the position of past present ages, of people acting in past institutions, without assuming that he/she knows anything better than they did. Communication can be real only if there are at least two interlocutors, if they differ from each other, if they can ask different questions and answer them in different ways, if the result of the communication differs from its starting point, if we come to know something more after the communication than we knew before, or if we come to know at least something different.

Chapter Six

Values in historiography

In the preceding chapter two statements were made without making the reader aware of the antinomy hidden in them. Both statements attempted to grasp the *episthémé-character* of historiography. The first statement reads as follows: historiography is always an expression of historical consciousness, it is one form of its imputed consciousness. The second statement reads as follows: historiography has to disconnect knowledge about the past from pragmatism and direct practical involvement in the present and for the future.

This antinomy is *not* the antinomy of historicity in general, it appears at a concrete stage of historical consciousness. As long as reason's ability to grasp the essence of the world was taken for granted, no self-reflection was needed and antinomies did not emerge. Antinomic thinking emerged with Kant through the consciousness of reflected universality. Hegel solved the antinomy by the assumption that human understanding develops historically and that all epochs have their own truths. Still, due to the progressive self-development of the world-spirit, the *last* truth, that of totality, is, at the same time, the genuine one, the synthesis of every particular truth expressed necessarily in the course of history. Philosophy can take this stand, because it deals with the present, but historiography cannot. Historiography has to take the antinomies of reason seriously because it is not allowed to identify the subject of the present with the subject-object of the past. The controversy between Ranke and Hegel was the controversy between the theory of historiography and the philosophy of history.

When Herodotus defined historiography as 'true knowledge', the concept of 'true knowledge' was not self-reflective and therefore not antinomic. Storytelling was related to *consensual values* and the self-understanding of the city-state. These values could be interpreted in different ways, but their validity was beyond doubt. Being critical and methodical did not imply a critical stance on values, it meant solely the elimination of hearsay-evidence. No matter whether this consensus in regard of values is called *sensus communis* or *conscience collective* or *Vorurteil*, the only thing that matters is that it was taken as given. The limits and scope of this readiness-for-the-message were set by this *sensus communis*. The consciousness of history was a consciousness of *pre*history because the readiness-for-the-message was identical with the readiness for the message of the prehistory of a city-state. Even when changes in mores were reflected upon, consensus about the exclusivity of basic values was taken for granted (as in Roman historiography). Consensus regarding basic values had to become problematic in order for the historian to get interested in a prehistory different from his own.

According to the consensus regarding the basic values, and thus the readiness-for-the-message as the readiness for the message of prehistory, a disconnection from immediate practical interest was not only not required, it was impossible. The history of past events and personalities could only serve as a *moral lesson* for the events and persons of the present, because history exemplified the same mores recognized as valid in the present. The 'alien ones' (barbarians, pagans) were either the 'repugnant ones' or – in times in which the valid moral norms were infringed by the bearers of the same norms – they were the examples of the realization of the very norms neglected by their representatives proper. The disconnection of true knowledge from pragmatic interest could not serve as a rule in historiography either, because pragmatic and practical action was not yet differentiated in the socio-political sphere. If there is consensus regarding values, then the goal rationality of human actions is always subordinated to their value-rationality, though, of course, not factually, but according to the norm – to the world-view of the age. Hence the distinction of pragmatic and practical interest cannot be conceived of as a *problem*, but is seen as an anomaly, irrespective of how frequently it occurs. The imputed consciousness of historicity has to express direct practical interests and cannot take into consideration the discrepancy of practical and pragmatic intentions. It is interesting that the first thinker who differentiated theoretically between practical and pragmatic interest (Machiavelli) failed to apply his distinction to historiography (*The Prince*, on the one hand, *Discourses* and *The History of Florence*, on the other).

And so the norm of historiography as true knowledge, according to which it ought to disconnect the reconstruction of the past from any kind of pragmatic and direct practical intention in the present is also a product of history. In the wake of the emergence of civil society based on contract and as a result of the loosening of communal ties, the firm *sensus communis* regarding the pattern and hierarchy of values started to disintegrate. The universalization and *abstraction* of some (few) values on the one hand, the *particularization* of the concrete *sensus communis* on the other, and the emergence of different, often contradictory mores in the same society at the same time led to the dislocation of individuals in their value-orientation. Hence pragmatism and practical intention (success and good) were disconnected and 'good' itself became plural (different supreme goods). All these gave rise to a pluralism of world-views. Awareness of the tendency described above led to the imperative both to *ensure* the universal validity of our morality by – seemingly – making it void of every material content, and to ensure the scientificity of our knowledge by censuring world-views as the sources of insoluble logical contradictions on the one hand and to universalize one particular world-view (and ethics), on the other.

To cut a long story short, the dissolution of the *sensus communis* and the pluralization of the world-views (due to the emergence of civil society) transformed the readiness-for-the-message in different although interconnected ways. First of all, the readiness increasingly became a readiness for different kind of *pasts*. Second, different world-views became interested in different *types* of message (wars, communal institutions, law, forms of states, heroes, everyday life, etc.). Third, 'diving' into the past started. The well-known characteristic of historiography – making us recall what has been forgotten – was due to this interest; traces for the messages were sought for. However, historical consciousness, which triggered off historiography's 'dive' into and reconstruction of many histories in line with many world-views, was the soil of the imperative to abstract from the *same* world-views in order to become 'scientific'. This is why historiography has to be disconnected from direct practice and pragmatic interest.

It can be seen that it is not too difficult to resolve the antinomy of historiography *theoretically*. The thesis that historiography is the imputed consciousness of our historicity and the accompanying thesis that its true knowledge should be disconnected from direct practical interest and the pragmatic one, *are not two separate theses*, but only one, because the imperative of disconnection is the expression of our historical consciousness no less than the insight that this very disconnection cannot be accomplished. Although the tension between 'Ought' and 'Is' is inherent in the categories themselves, which is why "Ought" is always counterfactual, it would be a misconception to state that everything that ought to be done cannot be done. In fact, we usually suppose just the contrary; that what ought to be done, can be done. In case of modern historiography, however, Ought is counterfactual in a reflected way: we know that Ought cannot be realized and we still demand that it should be. Thus the theoretical resolution of the antimony of historiography does not lead us one step further in the practical solution of this antinomy. Both the postulate of scientificity (this ought to be done) and the self-reflections of our historicity (this cannot be done) express our historical consciousness.

Before proceeding with the discussion, I want to summarize briefly three typical theoretical proposals formulated as intended solutions of the aforementioned antinomy. In awareness of all their individual subdivisions, I will emphasise only the *directions* of the theories concerned, without making an attempt at a thorough criticism of their particular way of argumentation.

(a) The disconnection of historiography from pragmatic and practical interest can be accomplished if one avoids all kinds of evaluation. Hence no categories with inherent value content should be applied in historiography. Historiography is able to grasp what the case really was only if it has no overt or covert idea about how it ought to have been, since all yardsticks are rooted in present-day practical interest (what and how something ought to be *here and now*).

(b) Historical material cannot be organized in a meaningful way without the application of a set of values; even periodization would be impossible in this case. However, being 'in history' ourselves, our set of values cannot carry out the task. Past periods have to be understood via their values and not ours - if we apply ours to them, we cannot help but violate truth and the norm of scientificity. There is only one system of values whose application enables us to organize historical material, to make sense out of it without violating the norm of scientific truth, and this is a value system which is *outside* history, which is *not* historical, but eternal. As Rickert put it: the 'value formula' (*'Wertformel'*) itself should be 'ahistoric'.

(c) Even the attempt to rid our reconstructions of history of our values, world-views, prejudices is in vain. What we cannot do, we should not try to do. We have to become conscious that there is no material available for leading principles except that of the historical present (Dewey). In another formulation: we have to be aware of the circumstance that historiography always deals with the present (Croce). As a third formulation has it, in our society there are different patterns of values embedded in different (often controversial) world-views related to different classes. To take the standpoint of one class means to reconstruct history from the standpoint of one world-view and one pattern of values inherent in it. We ought to take the stand of that class or social stratum which by virtue of its social position has the greatest (or absolute) access to truth and scientificity.

Let us consider all three proposals.

It is obvious at first sight that irrespective of the solutions offered there is an explicit *evaluation* in all three theoretical proposals: they do not merely describe what historiography *does*, but formulate what *it ought to do* in order to become something (really scientific, meaningful, able to perform its *task*). All three imperatives (for that is what they are) formulate in one respect exactly the *same* postulate: that what is formulated by historiography has to be *true* (true knowledge). It is the interpretation of the concept of true knowledge that makes the difference.

At the present stage of analysis, it is sufficient to point out some basic weaknesses of each theoretical proposal outlined above. The question partly concerns whether their requirements can be met, but is primarily directed to whether they should be accepted as norms.

(a) It has often been argued that evaluation cannot be circumvented. The attempt to strip our concepts of any value content and to apply only so-called 'exact' ones to historiography is in itself an expression of *our* historical consciousness. The type of interpretation of the notion of 'truth' which is inherent in it is no less imbued with a world-view than any other one. This world-view is in time and space and has no better claim to eternal validity than world-views of another kind. Even if we accepted that the adherents of this approach recognize only one value, that of scientific truth, their claim of being value-free could not be accepted. But this is not the case. The fact that the norm of scientific knowledge is based on a particular interpretation of the notion of 'true knowledge' implies that the concept of 'true knowledge' itself is evaluated by the world-view in which it is embedded, and that the evaluation (interpretation) of 'true knowledge' is transcendent to the value of true knowledge. Moreover, the differentiation of 'evaluative' and 'exact' (scientific) concepts is no less an expression of this world-view-being-in-time. The distinction itself evaluates. Also, whether a social concept can be applied as a non-evaluative one has no other criterion but the world-view itself whose concept it becomes. So, for instance, 'progress' is, for Pareto, an evaluative concept, but 'elite' is a scientific and non-evaluative one, although it is not difficult to imagine another world-view wherein 'elite' has a value connotation. (The same can be said of notions like 'technology', 'prognosis', 'monarchy', 'party', 'charismatic legitimation', and the like.) There is nothing *in* the concepts themselves which would make them void of evaluation. Consequently, to accept a notion as non-evaluative and to refuse another as 'evaluative' makes sense only within the framework of one world-view among many others, all of which express the historical consciousness of our times. The suggestion that the interpretation of the notion of 'true knowledge' is embedded in different world-views challenges the theoretical proposal that the choice of values is an 'irrational' act beyond the possibility of explanation. Undoubtedly, the choice of value, and even that of a world-view, cannot be accounted for as far as the choices of single individuals are concerned. The lack of explanatory evidence is, however, in itself nothing but the expression of our historicity, that of the disappearance of the *sensus communis*, that of the confrontation of dislocated individuals with controversial and particularistic value-systems. Thus the lack of explanatory evidence in regard to the value-choice of individuals can be explained. Yet world-views are not private affairs, and the choice of values (world-views) occurs only inside the framework of historical consciousness. As such, this choice is more limited than it seems to be.

All the same, if one accepts, as I have, the norm that historiography has to divorce the quest for true knowledge of the past from any kind of pragmatic and direct practical interest, one is, by the same token, not entitled to reject the *norm* of positivism as nonsensical, even if the objection can be raised that this norm can never be *observed* in positivist approaches. Positivism cannot avoid the direct intention of pragmatism and practice (not even the former) for the simple reason that it takes the standpoint of one *particular* world-view and at the same time that of one *particular* evaluation, that is, one imputed form of our historical consciousness while contrasting it, as the only legitimate access to scientificity and truth, with all others, and refusing at the same time to argue rationally for the values concerned. Thus positivist theories contradict the very norm that they themselves formulated.

If positivist theory is applied to historiography, the avoidance of evaluation usually involves the avoidance of theoretical hypotheses as well. Disconnection from direct practice leads to disconnection from practice altogether in such a way that theory cannot be related back to practice at all. At the same time, positivist historiography is not disconnected from pragmatism; the quest for true knowledge becomes a mere means for the justification of the profession, of its allegedly exclusive scientificity. Without denying certain scholarly merits of this school, one is entitled to describe it as a cul-de-sac of human enterprise called historiography. What cannot be related back to practice is dull and what serves the goal of self-justification is functionally ideological, no less ideological than the works of the type of historiography which aims at the justification of particular existing socio-historical goals.

(b)   The proposition that historical material cannot be organized in a meaningful way without the application of a set of values has been formulated again and again in the foregoing analysis. Once we accepted that historiography deals with the past and not with the present and the future, we have to agree (up to a certain point) with the imperative of the second typical theoretical proposal for the solution of the antinomy of historiography too: with the postulate that past historical periods have to be understood according to *their* own values and not according to ours. None the less, the above mentioned two assertions only *formulate* the antinomy without resolving it, for the applied set of values and the set of values to be understood are not identical with one another. In order to resolve this contradiction as well, the theory turns, as has been mentioned, to supra-historical, *general-universal* values which can be used to evaluate all historical times, all historical value-systems, the ancient ones as well as our own.

Turning to supra-historical values is in itself no novelty; all variations of natural law theory did basically the same thing. What is new is the *reflected* rejection of identification of supra-historical values with the valid values of *our* historical consciousness, or at least with the valid values of one world-view imputed to this historical consciousness. In this respect it does not matter whether the theorist in question wants to elaborate a set of material values of this propensity or only invents a universal 'formula' *(Formel)* of supra-historical evaluation.

One cannot deny that certain values *become* universalized historically and that certain values became abstracted from their original concrete content and preserve their binding character throughout various histories. But the quest for universal values *outside* and above history is doomed to failure, unless one turns to God as the only possible fountain-head and guarantor of these values. But even in this case, the God of modern theories is individually constituted and the values guaranteed by him are those which have to be conceived of as universal ones from the standpoint of modernity and especially from that of the author. The approach itself is therefore an expression of *our* historical consciousness to a degree no less than the approach of positivism. As we have seen, differentiation between universally valid values and *our* valid ones is rooted in our historicity which we cannot 'strip'. More precisely, by constructing a set of universal values or a universal 'formula' of evaluation, we cannot help but universalize the values of the time we live in, together with our readiness to acknowledge the universality of certain values retrospectively. Hence the second attempt to resolve the antinomy of historicity is caught by the same trap as positivism. While being aware of the problem that evaluation cannot be circumvented, the theories in question opt for the circumvention of the historicity of evaluation, the impossibility of which has been correctly recognized by positivism. Again the aforementioned theorists are tied up with one world-view among many, whereas they raise the claim to timeless universality.

Although the historicity of evaluation cannot be circumvented, the postulate of the second theoretical approach should not be considered as completely irrelevant. If all past present ages have to be understood via their own sets of values and the respective world-views in the framework of which they occurred, then our time, our set of values and their respective world-views should not be exempted from this procedure either. The more that universal values organize the material of the past *and* the present, the more we might be able to put an end to the uncritical application of our set of values embedded in our particularistic world-views to the understanding of bygone times. Although the universalization of our values in our times cannot be accomplished entirely either, it can serve as a regulative idea for historiography. As I am going to argue, this is a reasonable postulate and free from the fallacy involved in the construction of supra-historical values. Several theories of Kantian provenance suffer not from the malaise of postulating something which is counterfactual (this being the status of *all* postulates), but - like positivism, although in a different way - from the ambiguity of postulating something which contradicts our historicity.

(c) The different types of the third theoretical approach for resolving the antinomy of historiography emphasize our historicity, the infixation of our values and world-views in historical consciousness.

Furthermore, even the formulation of an imperative to transcend our historical consciousness is understood by the adherents of these theories as misconceived. Different values are the values of different world-views which on their part express different practical and pragmatic goals for action and behaviour. The attempt to look for any universal values *outside* concrete world-views, constructed for practical and pragmatic action is, according to them, in itself an expression of false consciousness, hence an illusion.

Consequently, in this conception historiography (just as social science in general) should *not* be disconnected from direct practice and pragmatism. It has to clarify our goals in the present or has to serve as a means for our goals or has to initiate communication between two particularistic world-views without any claim to universality.

Needless to say, this approach, too, is an expression of our historical consciousness. Yet in this case – and contrary to those analysed before – there is no contradiction between the assumption that the theory expresses our historicity and the very conception of the theory, because the theory understands itself as the reflection of historicity. The self-contradiction of the theory reveals itself on another level, namely in the explanation of the concept of 'true knowledge'.

If knowledge is nothing but the expression of a definite world-view of a given historical time, and cannot and should not be divorced from direct practice and pragmatism (always particularistic in nature), how can we become able to differentiate between 'true' and 'untrue' knowledge? True-untrue, Good-Evil, successful-unsuccessful, useful-harmful are value-orientative categories of different provenance and the lack of their distinction pre-empts the solution of the problem of 'what is true' *independently* of successful, useful or correct actions taken on the grounds of the knowledge. Different actions can be furthered by different understandings of society and history. What is useful or proves to be successful for one group can be harmful for another. Moreover, what is useful or proves to be successful in one situation can be harmful in another. If historians of French-German relations reconstruct this history so that the Germans were always right, their historiography may be very useful for Germans in a war against France, but definitely not for the French, and vice versa. If the pragmatic use of historiographical theory had anything to do with the truth of the theory, every particular interest-group would have its own truth and this would mean the renunciation of truth altogether.

In the abovementioned case the theory *intends* its direct practical and pragmatic use by a particularistic interest-group, (it is formulated in order to promote French or German interests in the war). To draw the conclusion that if the Germans win the war, then the historiography which promoted the success is *true*, and vice versa, is no less nonsensical than the statement that both theories are true, because both promote action in the war. Rather, it can be suggested that both theories are false precisely because they intend direct practical and pragmatic use, independently of the fact that they did promote actions and contribute to their success.

One could argue against these considerations that the example picked at random is an extreme one. Alas, if one takes a look at school textbooks of history written in our century, one will immediately realize that this is rather the rule than the exception. One could object to it, however, from two different standpoints. First, one could state, that even if pragmatic and direct practical use is *not* intended by the historian, his or her theory can be used practically and pragmatically. This is in fact the case. But if the intention of the theorist is not aimed at direct practice and pragmatism, but something else, this something else can only be *true knowledge* itself, and the theory can then be measured only with its own yardstick, that is, with the yardstick of true knowledge disconnected from direct practice and pragmatism. Second, one could argue that at any rate, the *direct* intention of practical and pragmatic use is a pretence, because all such use of theories is in fact *mediated* by reception. All theorists intend the reception of their theories, otherwise they would not proffer them. In addition, they always have in mind an addressee to whom they speak. Again, this is a fair argument. All historians unquestionably intend the reception of their theories, and mostly not only by a scientific community, but by the broader public as well. Disconnection from pragmatic and direct practical use means only one thing: they offer not a pleasant, flattering, exciting knowledge to the public, but a *true* one: they want the true knowledge to be received *because* it is true. Whether or not the reception is co-constitutive in the truth of a knowledge is another question. One has to assume that the constitutive character of reception in the truth of a theory can be accepted only in a *negative formulation*: if a social theory (in this case a historiographical theory) is not *received at all by any addressee*, it cannot be true knowledge. If we accept the thesis that historiography as true knowledge is one of the forms of the imputed consciousness of our historicity, we should also accept the conclusion that if no single world-view of our historical consciousness recognizes itself in the theory offered, it cannot be true, because it cannot be the imputed consciousness of historicity. This statement, though, does not imply any positive formulation of the same interconnection, namely the identification of the truth of a knowledge with the width and depth of its reception. The wide and deep reception of a certain kind of reconstruction of history might be due to the *particularistic character of its values* applied in the organization of the material. The assumption that we can apply only our values to the reconstruction of history does not mean that we should apply the most particularistic values, even if the width of reception depended on it. If we accept reception as one of the criteria of truth in historiography, we are exposed to the danger of giving preference to particularistic values as against universal (or at least, more universal) values. The objection could again be made: who (what) decides on the universality of the values, if not reception? But, what kind of reception? Reception for what purpose? Whose reception? Historiography is the imputed consciousness of historicity. Still, imputed consciousness aims at attaining and expressing the *maximum*, not the minimum, consciousness of an era.

There have been various attempts to resolve this contradiction of the criterion of reception and the claim to the universality of values, at least in some particular formulations of the theory discussed. The most sophisticated among them is, in my judgment, Marx's theoretical approach as reformulated by Lukács. As is well known, this theory reaffirms our historicity and regards consciousness as historical: as we *are* historicity, true knowledge cannot be but the imputed consciousness of our historicity. At the same time, it argues that our era is a particular one: it is the final, the last period of the historical past, called 'prehistory of humankind'. It is this period that gave birth to a particular class (the proletariat) which has the mission of transcending *this* history. The being of this class is *inside history*; its goal and task is, however, *outside* this history (it is in so-called *real* history). In view of this the standpoint of the proletariat enables us to resolve the antinomy of historiography (and the social sciences in general) because it is the expression of our historical consciousness through the act of reflecting on the being of the class. It is at the same time the expression of humankind, universality *per se*, through the act of reflecting on the mission of the class transcendent to our history. Subsequently, the imputed values of a particularistic class are also the universal ones: the historical material can be organized by them without running the risk of relativism. Since the practice of the proletariat concludes in terminating prehistory (to which the past belongs) and is universalistic *per se*, knowledge can only be true if it is related to the practice of this class and at the same time disconnected from the practice and pragmatism of all other social classes.

In what follows I wish to disregard the socio-political fact of whether the proletariat has lived up to these promises, and instead to criticize the aforementioned solution solely from a theoretical aspect. To conceive of the present as the last period of a past called 'history' is, again, an expression of our historical consciousness. When enumerating different pragmatist, hermeneutical and historicist theoretical proposals I came to the conclusion that they reflected on their historicity without contradiction and that the unresolved contradiction was translocated into the notion of truth. The claim of the Marxian-Lukácsian theory is to resolve this contradiction as well, at least up to a certain point, by answering the question raised above, that of whose reception, whose practice, can be regarded as co-constitutive in the truth of a knowledge, and reaffirms the claim that true knowledge can only be achieved if universal values are applied. Thus this theory is able to differentiate between true and untrue, the more or less true reconstructions of history and society. The price paid for this solution is, however, that the contradiction is translated back into the same problem with which all types of positivism and all theories of Kantian provenance are confronted, although in a different way. If one expression of historical consciousness explains its time as 'the last', it construes the 'future in the present' as if it *were* the future and starts to speak of *its* own present in the *past tense*. A period can be the last only from the standpoint of *another* present period and not from the view of a future era *in* the same present. As such, the understanding of a present era as being the last (in one or the other respect) is false consciousness.

The intended correction of the Marxian-Lukácsian theory by Mannheim was less consistent and no less contradictory. In fact, his statement that in the present era it is the intellectuals who have access to scientific truth can be accepted as correct, but it brings us not one step closer to the solution of the antinomy of historiography (and the social sciences in general). Nowadays it is intellectuals who have access to truth, but it is equally intellectuals who have access to untruth as well, for in the division of labour the creation and mediation of meaningful world-views has become their task. More correctly, intellectuals are the products of specialization in a modern, pragmatically oriented society in which the creation of meaningful world-views became allocated according to professions. Hence *all* world-views are created by intellectuals, all reconstructions of history and society are their accomplishment. Meaningful world-views can either be directly related to pragmatism and practice or divorced from them. Their respective sets of values can be more or less particularistic, more or less reflected. They can be purely ideological, they can be also scientific. Hence it is completely erroneous to ascribe universality *per se* to the values of intellectuals.

Granted this, if Mannheim's descriptive statement was transformed into an imperative, the postulate would run as follows: everyone who creates meaningful world-views, *should do* so by applying *universal values*. Intellectuals today are specialists in creating meaningful world-views, thus intellectuals should apply universal values in their theories. This is certainly a reasonable and valid postulate. Should the application of universal values belong to our being intellectuals, the postulate would be meaningless. It only makes sense because this is not the case.

The historian is an intellectual; so is the philosopher of history. All those who write this kind of book are intellectuals and almost all those who read them are intellectuals as well. They exist in time; they express our historical consciousness but they have to overcome this limitation, although they cannot overcome it. To make the best of our historical consciousness, we should obey the imperative and thereby transform our limitations into our possibilities, which we have to exhaust. The task is given and the basic question of how we can live up to it is not raised by one or another particular theory alone but by all of them that are ready to observe the norm. It is in this spirit that I am going to make my proposal.

The problem will be discussed in three steps. First, I am going to broaden my argument against positivism by showing to what extent all our categories are value-laden. Second, I shall plead for the universalization of our values to the upper limit of our historical consciousness. In the third step I shall raise the problem of communication with the past, concentrating the analysis around the basic issue of whether we are able to pass relevant moral judgments about actions which have taken place in the past.

As has already been mentioned, all traces of the past can be viewed as possible messages if the readiness-for-the-message, the curiosity-for-something, is present in historical consciousness. The simple proposition that knowledge is valuable contains two evaluations: an open and a hidden one. The open one is formulated in the predicate, the hidden one in the subject of the sentence. 'Knowledge' means understanding, explanation, information considered as 'good', no less than 'beauty' or 'justice' are considered as 'good'. The notion itself is evaluative. We can know only if we can *not* know. This hidden evaluation contained in the concept of 'knowledge' does not contradict the open one ('it is valuable') of *our times*. This has not always been the case. In different preceding ages there have always been things a mortal *should not know*. Knowledge of certain things was considered to be demonic, devilish, a form of moral transgression. 'Demonic' and 'devilish' things are repulsive but at the same time attractive. This contradiction can be explained by another one between two evaluations: knowledge itself is a value in spite of the negative evaluation of this or that kind of (forbidden) knowledge. The myth of the apple of knowledge expresses the contradiction in question very clearly. The disappearance of this contradiction from *our* historical consciousness makes us forgetful of the evaluative character of the notion itself and induces us to think that it is only the predicate of the sentence that 'knowledge is valuable' that attaches values to knowledge.

The readiness-for-the-message-of-the-past becomes, as far as *knowledge* is concerned, less and less selective in *our* history: everything that happened can be worth knowing. To put it in a better way, selection is personal and determined by the world-view of historians. Several competing world-views select in various ways, they do not observe any taboos in common. No one tells the historian; 'We do not want to know this or that, it is dangerous, it is sacreligious to know it. Let us forget it.' Curiosity no longer has inhibitions. It turned into curiosity for *everything*. The statement that 'knowledge is valuable' is a value judgment which simply formulates the fact that curiosity has become universalized and that selection (from the standpoint of knowledge) has disappeared.

The uninhibited quest for knowledge (about the past) is a value taken as granted, as 'natural', or at least as adequate to human *rationality*. The growth of knowledge is understood as infinite *per se* and this infinitude is evaluated as adequate to rationality. Inhibition is obviously value-rational and that is why the lack of this inhibition (and the positive evaluation of knowledge *per se*) may lead to the illusion that we are free of all kind of evaluations or that value-rationality is (and has to be) replaced by a different kind of rationality. If, however, inhibitions are value-rational, the negation of inhibition is not less value-rational: the liberation of inhibitions involves value-rationality too.

The value of knowledge *per se* is a product of the disappearance of the *sensus communis* (of *conscience collective*). We do not know whether a new *sensus communis* could or would again narrow down the field of knowledge to be attained or whether it would and could make questionable its infinitude anew. It is not too difficult to imagine a new *conscience collective* narrowing the readiness-for-the-message even as far as historiography is concerned. Living in my time and space, I could hardly accept this limitation which does not mean that such a limitation cannot arise. Thus I would argue on behalf of the uninhibited readiness-for-the-message-of-the-past on the ground of value-rationality, and would do so because in my world-view the maxim that I am human and nothing human is alien to me is a maxim having special significance.

It has been repeatedly noted that the disappearance of *sensus communis* opened the way for different particularistic world-views; controversial and often contradictory ones. Historians cannot step outside these world-views because 'stepping outside' all world-views contradicts the function of the objectivation in question. The more someone rejects the guidance of a world-view, the more one's work ceases to be a work of historiography and becomes mere philology. Without the perspective of a world-view, the feedback of the work of historiography to practice is impossible, and knowledge can only serve as raw-material for historians proper, who absorb them in keeping with their world-views.

Although, as mentioned, knowledge of the past became indiscriminative on the level of *society as a whole*, it also became more discriminative than it had ever been in any particular work of historiography. All the historians of ancient Greece and Rome and of the Christian ages selected the messages but the basis and the norm of selection was generally shared. Selection was determined by the *sensus communis* and not by the historians themselves. In our age, however, there are numerous kinds of entirely different selections. It is the number of dominant world-views that accounts for the number of different types of selection. But even one world-view which is shared by a group of people can be interpreted in different ways by them, and this accounts for individual selections.

This particularistic type of selection is co-constitutive in *all phases* of reconstruction of the past.

The readiness for all kind of messages, the value attached to every kind of knowledge about the past, is an expression of our historical consciousness. Here, though, the norm is observed indirectly, namely in the readiness for *exclusive* messages and the hierarchism of different kind of knowledges. Every historian is ready to read certain messages and refuse to read others. Every historian *assesses* the messages by labelling them as 'important', 'unimportant', 'decisive', 'indecisive', 'primary', 'secondary'. Even a decision regarding the *authenticity* of historical sources is – inside a given framework – dependent on the world-view of the historian. What is 'primary' or 'decisive' for one world-view can be 'indecisive' or 'secondary' for the other – indeed, it may not even merit a mention. If one takes a very well-known and simple document of the past, the tapestry of Bayeux, for example, it becomes obvious that the erotic-pornographic scenes scattered all over the third section of the work and sewn with a remarkable gusto might be read as 'important' and 'decisive' messages only within the framework of certain world-views and can easily be left unmentioned by others. Selection is evaluative even in the seemingly most value-free domain of investigation. But if we envisage the sum total of the works of historiography, we are made aware of the fact that in them everything is considered worth knowing.

All world-views have an anthropological stance, in other words, an image of man. The question raised by all of them is: What is man like? If the historian asserts: 'I describe human beings such as they are and not as they ought to be', he/she expresses a value-judgment, that they are *not* as they ought to be. Historical explanation and understanding undoubtedly presuppose the evaluative reconstruction of human nature or at least one type of human behaviour. This is obvious in all cases when historians *order motivations* (rational or nonrational ones) to the historical actor (actors) in question. If they do not do this, but instead explain actions as determined by the self-development of structures of institutions or by extra-historical powers (God, epidemics, population density), they evaluate human nature no less, although in an indirect way (as inactive, malleable, as being a mere object of or overpowered by destiny, as creature-like, and so on).

It is a commonplace that the subject matter chosen by a particular historian is within the sphere of (subject to the judgment of) his or her system of values. The evaluation takes place from the standpoint of the present but it can be twofold: it might be related to something which is important *in* the present, or something which is important *for* the present, as determined by the set of values of the historian. The former induces the historian to choose a problem or story resembling those of the present; the latter induces him/her to choose a problem or story which can be contrasted with the present.

(As a typical example, let me mention that in Marxist historiography the two main poles of interest are the times of revolutionary explosions, heydays of class struggles, peaks of technical revolutions, *and* the so-called 'primitive', 'communistic' societies, examples of communal ownerships, of participation, harmony, etc.). Both that which is decisive *in* and *for* the present depends on answering the question of the present: what ought to be done, what ought to be changed, what ought to be conserved, what ought to be rejected, and in all of this, *how* to go about it. The historian may have the conviction that the present ought to be rejected (evaluation of the present as an irrevocable decline), or that something ought to be done but only if a special condition is met (a new leader, or hero is born, etc.). If the change or conservation of the present is understood as a possible outcome of political actions, the historian will reconstruct his epoch as political history. If it is primarily understood as a possible outcome of a particular economic behaviour, the historian will see his past epoch in terms of economic history. If it is understood as a cultural achievement (of an elite or a collective), the historian will reconstruct his chosen epoch in terms of a cultural ethos and change of cultural patterns. If it is understood as the outcome of the struggle of certain unconscious psychic forces, the historian will reconstruct the subject as a story of repressed instincts in the process of socialization. Hence everything is open to knowledge and everyone reconstructs history differently from a different value-system and world-view.

But the question becomes obvious: Why should history deal with the past at all? Why should the reconstruction of the past be disconnected from direct practice and pragmatism? If every historian deals with the present, if they do not disconnect historiography from direct practice and pragmatism, we would get out something about the past anyhow while reading all the works together. The antinomy of historiography seems to be but an expression of a false expectation; it seems as if the problem itself should not have been raised.

Both possible objections are relevant, but from different aspects. Of course, there is nothing wrong with historians' reconstructing history in various ways according to different world-views and different value-systems. Yet it is not true that if we put together differing reconstructions all dealing with the present, we might then acquire knowledge about the past. But the acquisition of knowledge about the past is the need of our historical consciousness and that is why the question of the scientificity of our knowledge about the past has to be raised. The problem lies not with the *different* possible reconstructions of the past but with the question of how these different solutions can claim scientificity without abandoning evaluation which cannot be accomplished.

Undoubtedly, the scientific character of a historiographical work does not reside exclusively in the values applied in and by it; there are other additional conditions to be met in order to fulfil that requirement. In the subsequent chapters they will be discussed in detail. Since the proper method of evaluation is the first, even if not the sufficient, condition of the scientific reconstruction of the past, the analysis has to start at this point.

The triple dilemma of historiography can be then reformulated as follows. As the imputed consciousness of our historicity, historiography attributes value to knowledge *per se* and so the sum total of the historiographical works encompasses all possible knowledge about the past without discrimination. However, each particular historiographical work distinguishes between relevant and irrelevant and important and unimportant knowledge in *every aspect* departing from *particular* world-views and their respective sets of values. And all this happens (this is the third element) despite the norm that, according to the imputed consciousness of our historicity, historiography has to disconnect knowledge about the past from pragmatism and direct practical involvement in the present and for the future, in order to become true knowledge.

Even if this series of contradictions cannot be resolved, rules for its resolution can be observed. It is the values themselves which define within what framework this norm can be observed. If a method of checking the values applied in historiography could be suggested (from the standpoint of observing the aforementioned 'rules'), one would get an answer to the main question about the precondition of scientific true knowledge in historiography.

Values applied in historiography can be:
(a)   conscious or unconscious;
(b)   non-discriminative or discriminative;
(c)   reflected or unreflected;
(d)   false or true.

The norm of rendering our values conscious was clearly formulated by Max Weber. The unconscious application of values makes it impossible to reflect on the values employed and the question of non-discriminative or true evaluation cannot even be raised. Unconscious values are always of particularistic provenance and they go into the theory with the false consciousness of nonevaluation, the result being that one particularistic reconstruction of the past is unquestionably regarded as the only possible true knowledge. The solution of historical problems is taken for granted without even an attempt to disconnect the knowledge gained thereby from direct practice and pragmatism. The assumption that the question of conscious evaluation has been circumvented if the method of inquiry follows patterns borrowed from some of the procedures of the natural sciences is mistaken. If evaluation is not methodical, methodical inquiry itself cannot decide on the truth or falsity of a theory.

The discriminative or non-discriminative application of values is a far more intricate issue with manifold implications. Generally speaking, the use of a certain value is always discriminative, if it is related exclusively to the *we-consciousness*. If an historian attributes the highest value to the concept of 'nation', he/she must not apply this value solely to his/her own nation but to virtually all. The historian should not censure the nationalism of other nations while admiring his or her own. If the historian chooses 'culture' as the supreme evaluative concept, this value must not be exclusively related to the historian's own culture but to virtually all cultures. The discriminative application of values has a non-conscious aspect as well. Values themselves may be rendered conscious, but their identification with the we-consciousness may remain unconscious.

To be sure, historiography can operate with evaluative concepts related to *specific goods* in various ways. For example, in the realm of culture an historian can opt for 'Western culture' or for 'tribal culture' or for 'technical culture' or for 'emotional culture'. Or in the realm of 'power' the historian can opt for one type of power against other types, or can evaluate the use of power as positive when exercised by certain actors in one situation and as negative when exercised by others in other situations. Even so, should the values be specified according to particular goods, the specified values *should not be the highest ones*. If they are used as the highest values (no matter whether consciously or unconsciously) the evaluation will be discriminative and therefore ideological. But if the specified evaluations can be subordinated to higher values without contradiction, and if these higher values are themselves not discriminative in nature, the specified evaluation of particular goods will not become discriminative either. To give some idea of what I am talking about: if the specified evaluation of a particular culture can be subordinated to values such as 'equal access to the products of culture' or 'pluralism of cultural objectivations' or 'social cohesion of culture', values which are applied in a non-discriminative way because they serve as evaluative yardsticks for *all cultures* equally, irrespective of whether they are 'ours' or not; and, further, if the subordination does not imply any kind of contradiction, then the specified evaluations cannot be considered to be discriminative ones either. One might object that the usual procedure is just the opposite: first we have our specified values and then we look for non-discriminative – higher – ones in order to justify the application of the former, according to practical interests. This may well be true, but it does not contradict the assumption that in following the norm of the application of non-discriminative values we are in fact already disconnecting historical evaluations at least from pragmatic interest, and partly from direct practical interest as well, because we are committed to apply the highest (non-discriminative) values in *all cases*, in other words, not only in the cases in which our direct practical interest is vested.

This second method of avoiding evaluative discriminations already involves reflection.

Values are applied in an unreflected manner:

(a) if the values themselves are not reflected upon;
(b) if the concrete evaluations are not reflected upon.

The first stage of reflection can be grasped and explained in unsophisticated terms because the obligation to reflect upon the values in historiography is a simple one, even though it is difficult to live up to in practice. Reflection on the values itself consists of two elements. It involves reflection on the inherited values of various traditions (traditions of everyday life and traditions of historiography, the theory of history, the philosophy of history) and reflection on the theoretical framework, the categorical system of the re-inherited traditions which are the crystallizations of preceding evaluations absorbed.

The first element is divided, again, into several, although interconnected, parts.

We are educated in keeping with a definite pattern of values in everyday life and in a particular milieu (culture, social class) reproduced by it. In everyday life the proof of the relevance of values is always pragmatic and practical; in the process of learning them we become able to find our way correctly. The evaluation acquired fulfils its proper task if it enables us to move in our milieu with ease or at least to avoid catastrophes. In all kind of theoretical attitudes to which historiography obviously belongs, the umbilical cord of personal survival and evaluation has to be cut. The theorist who follows and applies value simply in order to be successful in everyday life excludes himself from the ideal community of scientists, irrespective of whether he really intends to be successful or not. Thus the first norm of reflection on values requires us to disclose whether the values we apply fulfil the requirement of personal disinterest. The self-surrender proposed by Peirce is the first step in reflection on values.

The evaluative concepts and behavioural patterns internalized from early childhood are manifestations of one specific form of life, in itself an outcome of specific traditions and of the social division of labour. Human beings start to view the world through the spectacles of ready-made evaluations. Although our world offers heterogeneous spectacles of this kind, with the consequence that the possibility of comparison, selection and choice is open to everyone, the first and most intensive learning process has an impact on the mind which is hard to alter. This is so not only because we mediate values with our gestures, language and customary attitudes too, but because their evaluative character can remain hidden in the quasi-natural character of these life manifestations. Thus the second rule of reflection on values requires the denaturalization of the evaluative patterns and concepts inherited by tradition and their transformation into the expressions of one particular, even though incoherent, world-view. This does not necessarily mean that the process of reflection has to conclude in the rejection of our quasi-natural evaluative patterns but rather that it must, of necessity, lead to rendering them conscious, thereby making them open to acceptance or rejection.

Anyone who lives in a world of social division of labour, in a society of subordination and hierarchy, has to be aware of the affinity of all social theories and their respective sets of values to various and often conflicting social projects and expectations. The conflicting projects and expectations have, on their part, an affinity to different social classes, strata, groups, to the interests or needs of one or several of them. This awareness implies the third negative norm of reflection on values which prescribes that we should not naively generalize a set of values interconnected with particularistic needs and interests. The same norm has to be extended to the comprehension of the traditions of historiography and the philosophy of history, since it has to be assumed that their set of values express an affinity to particular world-views, projects, and particular needs and interests as well.

Reflection on the values of inherited scientific enterprises involves an inquiry quite different from the procedure of self-reflection. Self-reflection ought to be accomplished before theorizing; reflection on the values of inherited objectivations can only be reconstructive. In order for a true reconstruction to come about, it is far from sufficient to merely trace back the affinity of the theory in question to particular projects or to needs of particular social forms. The inquiry has to be extended to include a reinvestigation of the categorical framework of this same tradition. Evaluation being intrinsic in them, categorical systems cannot be applied uncritically in the cases in which our evaluative system differs from that of the inherited corpus of knowledge. No historiographical work of any consequence can be written if the re-evaluation of the applied categories is not undertaken. If one accepts and applies, e.g. the distinction between party and faction, caste and class, first and second serfdom, one must be aware of the value connotation inherent in them, and if one's own set of values differs from those of the authors who have made these distinctions, one either has to drop the distinctions completely or has to re-evaluate and to re-define them in order to fit them into the new world-view without generating inner contradictions.

Here we have already arrived at the second problem of reflection on values described above as the reflection on the *application* of values in the theory. The imperative for the application of values reads as follows: in historiographical works all *concrete evaluations have to be reflected on*. This is a form of self-reflection again, but is a *second* step within the process which cannot be accomplished *before* proceeding to write the work, but only while working on it, and often only *after* having written it, as one element of revision.

The conscious, non-discriminative and reflected system of values has to be applied in a historiographical work in a conclusive and coherent way, without contradictions. But no historian, however hard he/she might try, can successfully observe this norm in isolation. The work has to be opened (either during the process of writing or in the completed form) for discussion, and not only for a theoretical discussion in a narrower sense of the word, but for a value discussion as well. It is difficult to distinguish between theoretical and value discussion in practice, although only if the theoretical discussion is a discussion about theory and if it surpasses the level of verification and falsification of (interpreted) facts. Nevertheless, such a distinction has to be made, for reasons of principle.

The values of a historiographical work can be criticized in a legitimate way as non-reflected, and hence wrong, if one of the following is proved:

(a)   that although the same highest values (value ideas) are applied in it, they are applied in *different* interpretations;

(b)   that there is a contradiction or discrepancy between the professed values and the applied ones (or some of the applied ones);

(c)   that non-discriminative values are applied in a discriminative way;

(d)   that the categorical system applied by the writer implies evaluations which do not conform to the writer's professed system of values;

(e)   that the writer has made his/her evaluation consistent only by ignoring the consideration of certain facts without arguing for their being ignored within his/her theoretical framework;

(f)   that the writer has made his/her evaluation consistent only by referring to facts not accepted as such by the consensus of the scientific community without offering a new interpretation of the message in question according to the principle of sufficient cause;

(g)   that the writer has carried out specific evaluations without relating them to higher values without contradictions;

(h)   that the set of values embedded in the categorical system reveals internal contradictions in the application.

If any one of these items is proven, the historian is obliged to right the wrong by making the evaluative framework consistent or by arguing for either ignoring certain facts or introducing new ones. If the historian fails to do this (it does not matter whether this is 'will not or cannot'), his/her set of values can justly be rejected as *wrong*. In this way the norm of reflection on values entails a readiness to *eliminate all contradictions of the application of values* and, if this turns out to be impossible, to *reconsider the system of values* itself and replace it with another one. Of course, this kind of readiness involves the separation from pragmatic and direct practical interest. Whenever the historian wants only to prove the validity of his/her values through the historical material, he/she will not be ready at all to open the work for any kind of criticism as far as the contradictory application of the values is concerned, because the readiness to do so might endanger the pragmatic or directly practical goals inherent in the set of values. The readiness for value discussion appears as part of practical interest too, but in an indirect way. It is not that the existing and accepted practice has to be legitimated by history, but that a relevant (true) understanding of the historical past (or one period of the past) must be seen as a condition of the *right* practical feedback.

To sum up the norms of evaluation: values have to be conscious. They have to be non-discriminative, that is, general. They have to be reflected on from different angles, such as:

(a)   personal disinterestedness;

(b)   the suspension of their quasi-natural character;

(c)   awareness of the affinity of values (and world-views) to the interests or needs of specific social groups;

(d)   reconsideration of the value content of inherited categories and categorical distinctions applied;

(e)   commitment to value discussion in which the system of values can be proved to be consistent or contradictory in its application, and thus right or wrong.

All these are only *preconditions* of the enterprise, which I promised to analyse here. Although certain aspects of the separation of knowledge about the past from pragmatic and direct practical interest have been formulated as imperatives, one aforementioned imperative made it reasonable to assume that this preparation is only an illusion; the imperative which prescribed the consciousness about the affinity of theory with the interests or needs of one particular group and project. What is the significance of rendering this relation conscious if the affinity of values to any kind of particular interest makes the assumption reasonable by itself, that knowledge about the past can never be divorced from direct practice and pragmatism? If the system of values (and world-views) always has an affinity with a particular kind of interest, commitment to value discussion cannot lead to a real disconnection from pragmatism and direct practice but only to their suspension.

Only when the connection with pragmatism and direct practice is suspended can it be proved whether the values are right or wrong. If all values are checked methodically and are proved to be right, a historiographical theory can be regarded as true knowledge if all the other conditions of true knowledge are met. Hence the suspension of direct practical and pragmatic interest in theorizing on history can be regarded as a *sufficient* criterion for the possibility of true knowledge. Nevertheless, the norm of permanent separation from direct practice and pragmatism should guide historians because this is the only way that suspension can be achieved. Observing this norm implies a resolution on the part of historians to look for the true values.

For these reasons, the application of right values involves the acceptance of the norm of true values.

But which values can be called 'true'?

Every practice is related to the interests and needs of a particular group and its particular projects. Hence if values could be constructed from the standpoint of the practice of humankind and if historiography can be led by those values alone, it would be disconnected from any kind of particularistic practice and pragmatism and its feedback to universal practice would become possible. We have seen that – being historicity ourselves – we cannot construct any value-systems *outside* history. Can we then construct them *inside* history, or at least work out the norm of such a construction?

There are various value-systems, various world-views on the ground of which various pasts can be reconstructed. It has been mentioned that in principle there is nothing wrong with this. Should all historians suspend practical and pragmatic interests while aiming for feedback to the universal practice of humankind, all specific reconstructions of history would have to be considered as equally true (providing, of course, that all other criteria of true knowledge were met). This could only be achieved if all value-systems were related to the *same universal value* without contradiction.

In my book on philosophy I have worked out a theoretical proposal for the solution of the problem, which I will here summarize briefly.

There is one empirically universal value in our historical consciousness – it is the *value-idea of freedom*. The value-idea of freedom is an empirically universal one since it is shared by everyone, and no one can choose its *opposite* (unfreedom) as a value or regulative idea. Thus the value of freedom has universal validity, which, of course, does not mean that it is not infringed. If true values are universal ones and as such are related to human practice *per se*, the criterion of the truth of a value can only be its consistency with the value-idea of freedom. If a value can be related to the value-idea of freedom without any contradiction, it has to be accepted as true. Naturally, the value-idea itself is always *interpreted* in different ways. The realization of freedom interpreted in one way may contradict the realization of freedom interpreted in another way. If the realization of different interpretations of freedom exclude each other, the interpretations cannot be universal ones, and equally cannot be the values of universal human practice. Consequently, if a value can be related to the value-idea of freedom without contradiction, it is not necessarily a true value. It is only a true value if its realization can be thought of together with the realization of all other values related to the same value-idea of freedom, and this occurring without contradiction. If we want to universalize our evaluations, we should apply in our theories only values which can be related without contradiction to the value-idea of freedom, and which can be realized (observed as norms) without excluding the realization of all other values (their being observed as norms) related in a contradiction-free manner to the value-idea of freedom.

Living in a world of subordination and hierarchy, in a world of conflicting interests and world-views, *we do not apply* true values. The only thing we can do is to accept the idea of true values as a regulative one. This means checking our values continuously, using them in a conscious, non-discriminative and reflective way and suspending direct practice and pragmatism in our research while approaching (more or less) universality inside our history; a history that we cannot transcend. The norm of true value is the highest norm of true knowledge, even though it is not the only one.

If we formulate things in this way, the perspective of our historical consciousness cannot be transcended, the knot can never be undone. But to fathom the maximum possibilities of our historical conscious-ness may be the utmost we are able to achieve. To live up to the imperative formulated above *means* precisely to fathom the maxi-mum possibilities of our historical consciousness. It opens the way for a pluralism of perspectives and world-views liberated from the burden of particularistic biases, in other words, from the use of the past as a means for the justification of particularistic goals. It opens up the way for rational communication with each past from the standpoint of an ideally existing humankind. All histories are human histories and thus they may be regarded as equally close – not to God, but to humankind. If we put it this way, the knot can be undone.

It is exactly here that the last problem has to be realized: how can all histories possibly be regarded as equally close to humankind, if true values are the ones which can be related to the value-idea of freedom without contradiction? If this value-idea is taken as the highest value, then human histories cannot be grasped as all equally close to humankind. The status of freedom has greatly varied in different societies: a great amount and variety of liberties has been present in some, and much less in others. However, to communicate with each history from the standpoint of an ideally existing humankind, and to evaluate as equal everything that is human, are two different questions. The first goal can and should be achieved; the second cannot and should not. We cannot and should not avoid being partial.

Without a certain kind of partiality the past would not interest us at all, and while burying this interest we could not help but bury historiography as well. Readiness-for-the-past is motivated by the partiality of historical consciousness. Partiality for freedom is, however, partiality for humankind, partiality for universality. It is the ultimate readiness-for-the-past, for the resurrection of the dead called historiography.

Chapter Seven

Moral judgments in historiography

The double task of historiography has been analysed from different aspects. To sum this up again: on the one hand, past-present ages have to be understood in terms of their own systems of values embedded in institutions and in the consciousness of actors socialized by these institutions; on the other, we have to communicate with the actors of all past-present ages on equal terms, as human beings with human beings. There is a particular aspect of this double task left unexamined up until now: the problem of *moral judgment*. The question I am going to explore in the following discussion is that of the possibility or impossibility, the desirability or undesirability, of passing moral judgments on actors or actions of the past. It has to be mentioned at the beginning that not all works of historiography are confronted with this problem to the same extent.

I am going to discuss this issue from four different angles:
(a)   morality as the subject matter of historiography;
(b)   moral decisions as explanatory principles in the reconstruction of a past-present age;
(c)   the possibility or desirability of judging the actors of past-present ages in moral terms;
(d)   the question as to whether moral judgment is co-constitutive in the reconstruction of a past period and whether it *should* be co-constitutive.

If we internalize the abovementioned second task of historiography, in other words, if we are ready to communicate with all human beings who lived before us on equal terms – as human beings (should do) with human beings – we cannot answer the question of the desirability of moral judgment without formulating *our expectations*. That is, we have to ask ourselves whether we wish to be judged morally by the historians of the future, and whether we *expect* them to so judge us (the actors of our present). Both questions have to be dealt with briefly.

Anyone who undertakes to write historiography in line with the most elementary norms of this venture, such as personal disinterested-ness (the non-discriminative application of values and reflection upon the values), is aware of the responsibility. Responsibility in itself is a moral commitment; and in this case it is a double commitment. It is responsibility for true knowledge, and responsibility for the possible reception of the same knowledge, thus for its 'reinvestment' into practice. Anyone who is committed does not regard themselves as merely imprinted upon by circumstances and genetic codes, but as a (relatively) free actor. Even if the author conceptualizes society in deterministic terms, the same terms cannot be applied to his/her own activity. The historian is ready to accept moral judgment in the present and that is why he/she has to accept the moral judgment of an ideally existing future historian as well. Yet if a historian who is observing the norms of historiography professes consistency, he/she has to impute the *same* relative freedom, commitment and responsibi-lity to all contemporaries and so judge *them* in moral terms, accepting thereby the moral judgments of all virtual future historians too. The historian must assume that actors of past-present ages would raise exactly the same claim, were they alive. As a result, while communi-cating with them on equal terms, the historian is obliged to judge them morally also. Barraclough formulated this problem in the simplest terms: it would be infamous if we refrained from judging Hitler morally; as a consequence, we should judge Nero morally too. The formulation is simple, and perhaps that is why it is not generalizable, though it is apposite. In passing moral judgments we usually take into consideration two aspects: the motivation of the action and its social-personal consequences. Whether a particular human action was motivated by goodwill or not cannot be known; it can only be assumed, and the probability of a correct assumption increases with the knowledge of the person in question, and with the knowledge of his subsequent actions in similar and different situa-tions. The socio-historical consequences of the deeds of one single actor are at the same time usually not decisive: whether good or bad, the devastating balance-sheet of an epoch can seldom be ascribed to individuals alone. The case studies of Hitler, Stalin, Pol Pot or Idi Amin are beyond doubt the simplest ones. The horrifying conse-quences of their actions are not only enormous but they can also be totally ascribed to them for the very reason that their death or removal was in itself sufficient to put an end to mass murder and other criminal activities. The same holds true of historical monsters as well. Although they are unfortunately not infrequent, they are not normal historical phenomena either. In the case of historical monsters it is convenient to attribute certain typical motivations to them such as thirst for power or sadism, but as far as moral judgment is concerned motivation does not really matter: the misery they caused, the outrages they provoked would outweigh even the best motivations. If we then exclude historical monsters, the question is not only whether we are *entitled* to pass moral judgments but whether we are *able* to do it, whether we can avoid arbitrary judgments as far as average historical actors are concerned.

Let us now return to the four problems posited above.

(a) It is obvious that mores (in other words, the norms and patterns of approved - or disapproved - behaviour) are part of the subject matter of historiography. As Apel puts it, 'The data of the humanities have themselves the attribute of following rules subjectively'.* It is only 'following technical rules' which does not have anything to do with mores, but mores *can* be related to technical rules as well. Following social rules, though, is *equivalent* to observing mores. Whenever historiography reconstructs different rules, and also their interconnections and structures, it reconstructs mores no less when it tells the story of a war or a reform than when it deals with historical personalities such as Alkibiades or Richelieu. Mores as the natural subject matter of historiography do not, however, necessarily involve morality, that is to say, the personal relation to mores, in the subject matter of historiography. There are *no* works of historiography which *do* not deal with mores, but there *are* works of historiography which *do not* deal with moralities (e.g. the comparative reconstruction of the English and French system of serfdom in the twelfth century). Morality can become the subject matter of historiography in *any case* where the historian reconstructs a particular historical *event* as the outcome, the consequence of human will, individual or collective. An event is one event because it is *not repetitive*, hence the actions resulting from these events are not repetitive either. Wars have taken place in all times, and particular social structures usually involve particular types of wars, but the Peloponnesian War happened only once, the three Punic Wars were

---

* K. O. Apel, *Transformation der Philosophie*, vol. II, Frankfurt, Suhrkamp, 1973, p. 385.

different in character, and so were the two World Wars. Assuming that human decisions played at least some part in these events (in launching the war, in fighting, etc.), and that their effect cannot be reduced to nil (or if so it has to be argued for), the different kinds of personal (individual or collective) *motivations* may be taken into consideration and the outcome of the event can eventually be grasped as the outcome of these motivations, as the consequence of various human wills. And again, morality can become the subject matter of historiography if not only the rules (and their structures) are reconstructed, but if it is the historian's intention to find out to what extent these rules were observed, by how many people, and with what kind of intensity. If there is a discrepancy between the system of rules and the way people observe them, one is again confronted with cases which cannot be explained only by mores unless the historian can prove that the lack of observance of certain rules was only the expression of the emergence of new ones, that new mores were in gestation. If this cannot be proved, the historian has to take human (individual and collective) motivations and their possible conse- quences into account. For example, whether or not the dissolution of mores can really be deemed to have been a decisive factor in the fall of the Roman empire, it still became a matter of consensus in historiography that traditional rules were massively infringed in the last centuries of Roman history, and this is a statement about morality.

(b) There were times in which morality has been the main explanatory principle of historiography. Wars have been lost due to cowardice, vanity and greed, won due to heroism, self-sacrifice, asceticism and devotion for the cause. If a people of high moral standards was vanquished, the fateful turn was only partially ex- plained by the numerical or technical superiority of the enemy: it was mainly attributed to the ruthlessness and dark intrigues of the adversary or by treason. Present-day historiography has a different attitude, although the man in the street has not lost the inclination to explain historical events in terms of morality.

The statement that morality had to lose its explanatory value because morality itself has to be explained by other factors, is not as obvious as it seems to be. At any rate, whether the explanatory principles of historiography have to be the same in all concrete cases, is a debatable matter too. Why historians should renounce explana- tion by morality (that is, in all possible cases) is a problem which cannot be settled by a condescending professional smile, especially as even the historian must accept the authenticity of plays and fictions in which the motivations of the historical actors (individual or collective) are always depicted as central in the turn of historical events.

The inevitable conclusion is that morality cannot have explanatory value in any historical reconstruction, not because it may not serve as sufficient grounds, but because it is *beyond our reach*. The motivations of historical actors can only be assumed, never known, we cannot even pretend to know them. Imputing motivations is the prerogative of fiction, at least today, for the simple reason that mere assumption (a point of departure for fiction) is not open to falsification. In ancient times, though, when historiography was not disconnected from direct practice and pragmatism (and there was no postulate that it should be), the imputation based on the *sensus communis* of a community was a *collective* one. It then fulfilled the function of sufficient explanation which it can no longer fulfil for us.

(c) How are we able to pass moral judgments on historical actors if we can only impute motivations to them without knowing them? The question itself already implies a negative answer. Yet we are obliged to do so because we want future historians to pass moral judgments on the actors of our times as well. In order to meet this expectation, we can only judge the moral content and not the motivation of actions; in Kantian formulation, *legality and not morality*. This is an incomplete moral judgment, but it is a moral judgment because it goes beyond the reconstruction of mores and raises the question of personal responsibility.

Moral judgment concerning 'legality' involves a comparison between a real and an imaginary action regarding what an actor has done and what he ought to have done in a given situation. If he did what he ought to have done (if there was the identity of a real and an imaginary action), moral judgment involves approval; if he did what he should not have done, the moral judgment involves disapproval, and this is so according to the difference or contradiction of the real and imaginary action.

The procedure seems to be a simple one but it is not. Historiography reconstructs the deeds of an actor (or actors). But how is historiography able to tell us anything about an action which never occurred?

But the action referred to is not the only one which historiography often has to consider. One may also ask whether historical actors could have acted in a different way from the way that they in fact did act; in other words, one may compare a real action with another (not less possible) one. Of course, one cannot write 'alternative' history, and the question of what the world would look like if something had happened differently from the way it did happen belongs to the realm of fantasy, not to that of true knowledge. Even so, the assumption that nothing could happen otherwise than it really did again has nothing to do with true knowledge: it is a belief in predestination or some other kind of finalism. Accordingly, historiography cannot avoid taking imaginary actions into account as well, irrespective of the theoretical consideration whether or not an alternative action might have altered anything at all in the long run. Historiography which fails to operate with imaginary actions (in the above sense of moral expectations) would also fail to adopt the standpoint of 'togetherness' of past-present ages, and of those having suffered in them because a certain decision was taken which should not have been taken or which could have been avoided.

For our purposes, let us now leave out of consideration the imaginary action of the second type ('what could have been done') and stick to the problem or moral judgment only with regard to another imaginary action ('what should have been done'). The assumption that whatever should have been done also could have been done is far from being excluded. Historiography may try to combine these two questions, even in being aware of the fact that the second one does not entail any moral judgment.

The imaginary action can be defined as a deed which would meet the moral expectations of the 'togetherness' of a past-present age: the actor should have acted in harmony with these moral expectations, but he did not (because of motivations unknown or assumed), and that is why the actor's real action should be criticized. This is a simple case. The historian adopts completely the standpoint of the 'togetherness' of a past-present age and passes moral judgment according to the mores of that age.

However, this is only possible when the action in question took place in a historical period with a homogeneous system of values. If the historian tells the story of an action which happened *after* the dissolution of a homogeneous value-system, he is confronted with different (often contradictory) expectations. If he/she is ready to pass moral judgments on historical actors *and*, again, is prepared to assume completely the standpoint of the past-present age in question, he/she has to identify with *one* type of expectation and ignore the others, or even disapprove of them. In this case, however, the historian only *pretends* to assume totally the stance of the evaluative systems of past-present ages because his/her *choice* itself – the identification with one or other expectation is not rooted in the bygone times upon which the judgment is passed, but is rooted in the present from the standpoint of which the judgment is actually being passed, in the historian's own system of values, in his/her own personal world-view. A seemingly relevant solution could be to limit the scope of imaginary actions to the ones which met the expectations of the social group, class, or integration to which the historical actor belonged. Yet this approach presupposes that the actor had no opportunity whatsoever to act in keeping with different expectations, and this, again, cannot be reasonably assumed. We would not like it either if the historians of future-present ages acquitted a war criminal of our times on the consideration that obedience was a virtue recognized by his social milieu.

The situation of the historian who chooses to pass moral judgments on actors of the past is awkward. Whether the historian is involved in epochs of homogeneous or heterogeneous value-systems, he/she cannot live up to the task in an unambiguous way in either case.

In the first case our judgment cannot be unambiguous if the infringed ethical rule itself contradicts our present moral convictions and habits. For example, it would be ahistorical to judge morally the actors who killed an adulteress as long as this act conformed to the then contemporary mores when reconstructing a historical period in which adultery was punished by death. Nonetheless, if we are confronted with actors who refused to observe this norm, who did not kill a person caught at adultery and who, as a result, had to face the disapproval of their community, we are reluctant to adopt the position of the mores and echo such disapproval. We may even be inclined to do the opposite. We cannot help being ahistorical; we cannot manage to abstract ourselves entirely from *our* morality.

In the second case the moral judgment cannot be unambiguous either. If the historian adopts the position of a particular social integration, class or stratum and identifies with its expectations (motivated by his/her choice in the present), the *mores* of the particular integration will serve as the solid ground of judgment. Anyone who acts according to them will be lauded; anyone who acts against them criticized. However, in all cases in which an actor of another social integration has to be judged, a completely heterogeneous yardstick will be applied. If the actor of another social integration acted in keeping with the historian's and not the actor's mores, the mores will have to be disapproved of. The disapproval of mores is, though, not only ahistorical by definition, but also self-contradictory from the standpoint of the above demonstrated methodology which claimed to judge correctly the actors of a period according to their own value-systems. In a paradoxical way, in order not to apply a double standard (as far as moral judgment is concerned), the application of totally different (contradictory) yardsticks is essential.

I started my analysis with the assumption that I wanted the future historian to judge the actors of our times morally and that is why we too are obliged to judge past historical actors morally. Being fully conscious of the fact that moral judgment cannot be but fragmented, I left the individual motivation of an action out of consideration and restricted myself to the moral judgment of the action itself. It has also been asserted that virtual and real actions can be compared – thus we are able, in principle, to compare an action committed with an action which should have been committed. However, at the end we were left with empty hands. The problematic of passing moral judgments over the actors of the past lies not in the impossibility of comparing real and imaginary (expected) actions, but in the ambiguity inherent in grasping the imaginary action itself. In trying to find out what should have been done, we either relapse into a total relativism (in spite of the protest of our moral feeling) and so fail to accomplish the task we expect future historians to do, or else our methodology is confused and self-contradictory, the approach unclear; an unreflected mixture of past and present evaluations.

One has to conclude that except for historical monsters, and at least according to our historical consciousness and its limits and theoretical norms, we are unable to pass moral judgments over actors of the past consistently and methodically. All the same, it would be desirable if we could do so, for we cannot set down norms for future historians we are not ready to follow ourselves. This conclusion is not only unsatisfactory, it is alarming.

(d) Histories are *criminal cases*, and so is ours. All histories are stories of murder, looting, plundering, violence, oppression, exploitation, stories of suffering. They are very particular kinds of criminal cases. In them, it happens very rarely that *the* murder can be pointed out: still, it happens even more rarely (practically never) that someone can be pointed out who bears no responsibility at all for what happened. The myth of Jesus Christ is *not* history and that is why it is exemplary. Only someone who took all the sins and sufferings of humankind upon himself has the right to judge the living and the dead. No one else has.

Moralizing historiography is wrong. Not wrong in general, but wrong for us who in modernity inevitably see history as a chain of criminal cases. We withhold moral judgment (except when it comes to historical murderers who can be pointed out) not because it is 'more objective' and 'more scientific' to do so, but because it is *more moral as well*: judgment is not ours. No living human being can take upon himself the suffering of humankind.

But how can we refuse to moralize historiography and plead for the withholding of moral judgments in history if we still expect future historians to pass moral judgment on the actors of our times?

If the refusal to moralize historiography meant of necessity the neutrality of the historian towards the message read and interpreted, it would be wrong historiography no less. But only passing moral judgments in exceptional cases, and being completely neutral are far from identical attitudes. Even if the criminals cannot be pointed out, one can always know who *suffered the most*. The gesture of Raskolnikov is the gesture of historiography: it has to bow before the suffering of humankind. The partiality for those who suffered the most is not moralizing. Those who suffered the most cannot be regarded as the morally better ones; they usually are not. They cannot claim moral approval but they can claim *empathy*. And they ought to get this empathy from historiography proper.

Cannot the task we expect future historians to fulfil be translated into this language too? Would our need be satisfied if future historians bowed to our sufferings and to those of our contemporaries? Obviously it would and, in my opinion, no more should be expected, simply because there is nothing 'more' that *could* be expected. If both victors and victims are beneath the earth, no punishment can be meted out, nor any award granted them. But justice can be done in retrospect.

Collingwood compared historiography to the detective novel. Poirot reconstructs the crime and no moral judgment plays any part in the reconstruction itself, though when the case is solved, he pronounces his judgment: 'I do not approve of murder.' But the comparison is not wholly apposite. We are entitled to say: 'I do not approve of murder, I do not approve of looting, exploitation, plundering, oppression', and we perhaps even *should* say this. Yet all histories are stories of murder, looting, plundering, oppression and exploitation, and the statement 'I do not approve of history' would rather fit Molière's pen. Yet even though not wholly apposite, the comparison still makes some sense. Not everyone was a murderer, not all historical actors looted and plundered, and not all did it to the same extent and in the same way. If a concrete historical drama can be reconstructed as the story of particular historical actors, whose participation in and responsibility for a concrete action and its consequences can be established, in this case (and only in this case) moral judgment is not misplaced. I use the notion of 'drama' deliberately. If a historiographical work accomplishes this task, it is *literature*. The difference between historiography as scientific knowledge and historiography as literature (or literature written about history) is not that between the 'real' and the 'fictitious'. Historiographical literature can often stand the most critical test as far as the 'reality' of its story is concerned. The fundamental difference is the fact that in historiographical literature action is completely ascribed to actors, to their will, motivation and personal character traits, whereas in historiography proper this is not the case. The fact that motivations can only be assumed and not claimed to be known does not hinder historiographical literature in its quest for motivation for the very reason that 'true' and 'good' might be grasped together. The unity of true and good must be achieved in this case not only in the reconstruction of the deeds of prominent actors of the past. It might even go so far as to impute concrete motivations and actions to people whose actual deeds are not recorded in the chronicles of history. This is fiction, but at the same time it is something else, because all the actions are really the actions of actors who once existed and all these actors had indeed a story of their own: anyone who suffered did so individually, and anyone who killed, committed the act individually as well. The separation of true knowledge from direct practice is *not* the norm of historiographical literature. While the resurrection of the dead is accomplished by historiography in general, historiographical literature does something else too: it transforms the dead into our contemporaries with whom we can communicate on equal terms (as human beings with human beings) on the basis of *our* morality. Historiographical literature judges the actions and the actors morally by inviting the reader to judge, by guiding the reader in a way that he/she *should* share the judgment of the writer.

It would be futile to raise the question of superiority. Historiography proper and historiographical literature accomplish different tasks, although the interconnected endeavours of instigating communication with the protagonists of the past on equal terms and the reconstruction of the mores of the past are pursued by both of them. Priority lies, as far as reconstruction is concerned, with the former; as far as communication is concerned, with the latter. They cannot replace each other.

In spite of these differences, there is no Chinese wall between historiography proper and historiographical literature such as there is between historiographical literature and the philosophy of history. This is not only because historiography is storytelling while the philosophy of history is not, but because historiography proper and historiographical literature are complementary genres whereas the philosophy of history and historiographical literature are opposing ones. Owing to this, memoirs of the witnesses of great historical events always lie between historiography proper and historiographical literature. Their writers usually impute motivations to their protagonists, they do not refrain from moral judgments, they address an audience simultaneously contemporary to the storyteller and to the events described, they preach sound and honest behaviour and wish the addressee to learn lessons and to draw the proper consequences. There is no basic difference between Thucydides and Xenophon on the one hand, and De Gaulle's or Churchill's reports on the history of the Second World War on the other.

Consequently, if the past of the present is reconstructed, moral judgment cannot and should not be avoided for the simple reason that reward and punishment, praise or censure are related to the living, and so are not misplaced. The wounds are not yet healed and the consequences have to be faced here and now. Communication and the reconstruction of mores cannot be two separate matters: they constitute the same issue. The more deeply we ponder on the past, which is no longer the past of present, the more that task becomes divided between historiography which primarily reconstructs the mores of the past, and historiographical literature which enables us to communicate with the dead as with our contemporaries. In the first case moral judgment has to be withheld, in the second it has to be passed. And both have to be done.

Chapter Eight

The concrete norms of historiographical research

The concept of objectivity has been interpreted in different ways in the literature. There have been theorists who have even challenged the value of objectivity in social sciences. For this reason, in what follows I have to deal with three problems. I have to clarify my understanding of objectivity, I have to answer the question of whether objectivity should be regarded as an absolute norm in historiography, and I have to consider whether the norm, if accepted, could be observed at all, and if so, to what extent.

In the first part of the book a distinction was made between the notion of objectivity and that of true knowledge in everyday thinking and practice. This distinction was clarified in a general discussion about the roots of historiography and philosophy of history in everyday life. The problem was exemplified by a quarrel between two children. The spontaneous reaction of the parents (i.e. blaming the other parents' child for starting the quarrel) was denounced as a *non-objective attitude*, although one of the statements had to be true for the simple reason that the quarrel had to be started by one or the other child. Thus a non-objective statement can be true and untrue. But regardless of this obvious fact, objectivity gets credit in everyday life, it is even distinguished by the rules of civility. We are expected at least to affect objectivity in the meaning of the word above.

Following this path, the differentiation between objectivity and true knowledge seems to be at hand. One has to have in mind at the same time that even though the procedures of the social sciences are deeply rooted in everyday life, they do not yet follow everyday patterns. The distinction of *'episthémè'* and *'doxa'* should continuously be borne in mind. Taking into consideration the self-imposed limits of the present enterprise, I cannot explore all the manifold implications of this basic distinction. Objectivity and true knowledge will be examined here only from the standpoint of historiography.

Objectivity can be defined in terms of the subject-object relationship. In historiography, the subject is the historian as the repository of the historical consciousness of his times. The object is a past-present age; in other words, a past historical consciousness, and in this sense, the object is a subject. A headstrong subject indeed, which does not yield easily to our superimpositions. The more we are involved in it, the deeper we dive in order to grasp it, the more it superimposes *its own* values and ways of understanding upon us – but being headstrong ourselves, we do not want to yield either. The resurrected dead wish to turn us into their own contemporaries just as much as we wish to turn them into ours. And all this is more than a figure of speech: it actually happens in this way. It happens not only with the historian but with the enthusiastic reader of historiography as well. What, then, is objectivity so far? It cannot mean forcing the subjects of past-present ages into silence in order to manipulate them and use them for our purposes – this is exactly why historiography has to be divorced from all kind of pragmatism. It cannot mean forcing ourselves into silence either. It is *we* who read the messages, who ask and answer the questions, who cannot organize the historical material without being led by *our* values. Our readiness-for-the-message is in itself the expression of *our* historical consciousness. So, as far as the subject-object relation is concerned, objectivity can only mean the proper balance of the two superimpositions. By organizing the historical material with non-discriminative and reflected values, and by understanding past-present ages according to their own mores, and thus communicating with their actors as human beings with human beings, we *are* objective. In terms of this first approach, objectivity in historiography is the Aristotelian 'medium' between two extremes: between mere ideology and mere philology.

This notion of objectivity as the proper balance of two superimpositions is a conclusion drawn from different premises. One of them is the application of non-discriminative and reflected values. However, this premise is far from being an obvious point of departure. Let me refer back to the analysis of the antinomy of historical consciousness, where non-discriminative and reflected values were described as the 'right' ones by virtue of generalization. We may imagine a proper balance of superimpositions even though particularistic values were applied, for even here the historian can grant the 'freedom to speak' to certain actors of past-present ages. But only some of them are granted this right, and that is why objectivity is curtailed. In applying discriminative values, we do not allow *our* contemporaries to speak and, as a result, we discriminate in regard to the actors of past-present ages as well. While granting some of them the 'freedom of speech', we exclude certain others from the discussion: we only have ears for what we want to hear. As a result, past-present ages cannot express *their* historical consciousness and evaluations in a proper manner. Communication becomes distorted because the requirement of proper balance is only seemingly met.

Thus the norm of objectivity in historiography implies the application of non-discriminative and reflected values; in other words, the application of 'right' values. It implies, by the same token, the suspension of personal interest and bias, the elimination of all contradictions in the application of our set of values and the obligation to make conscious the affinity of our values to the needs and interests of particular human groups. Without this temporary self-surrender, the minimum requirement to make our values non-discriminative and reflected, the norm of objectivity in terms of a proper balance between our historical consciousness and that of the past-present ages we intend to understand, cannot be observed.

It has often been emphasized that objectivity must raise the claim of impartiality. When suggesting the application of right values in order to achieve the proper balance between our historical consciousness and that of past-present ages, I did not question the validity of this claim. On the other hand, when discussing the problem of moral judgment in historiography, the conclusion has been drawn that impartiality is not allowed and it has been suggested that partiality for those who suffered the most must be a norm in historiography. It would seem that I have manoeuvred myself into a contradiction.

Well, can not one argue that impartiality and partiality do not exclude each other; after all, one can be partial *and* impartial about the same matter, though from different aspects? This is the case in everyday life as well. In the example of the children's quarrel, impartiality means the readiness to find out who, in fact, started the quarrel, irrespective of our personal attachments. Naturally, it would be totally nonsensical to ask for the suspension of the *attachment* itself as well. The attachment to one person or the other should not impede justice, but justice does not involve impartiality as far as attachment is concerned. The same holds true in historiography. No historian can be expected to exercise impartiality in his or her attachment. The preference for one culture above others, caring more for the fate of

one social class than for that of others, loving one nation more than
the others – these things cannot be eliminated. One can only pretend
that they are. Self-surrender does not mean the suspension of
empathy, it simply means that no empathy, no concern, no attachment
should become co-constitutive in the reconstruction of a historical
case. While not suspending attachment (partiality) in general, we have
to suspend it as a motivation for explanation (impartiality).

The norm of objectivity is finally challenged by the argument that
the observance of this very role does not bring us closer to the real
aim, namely, the achievement of *true* knowledge. It has even been
argued that – since there is a contradiction between objectivity and
true knowledge – the former impedes the latter.

Those who plead for the neutrality of the norm of objectivity could
refer to the case of the children's quarrel. It is obvious that if two
children fight, one of them must have started it. If both parents insist
that the other's child did it, one must be telling the truth without
being objective at all. And this biased interpretation of events is not an
isolated case, it is an *attitude* taken in numerous subsequent cases. It is
reasonable to assume even in everyday life that biased attitudes
generally lead to untrue statements, at least more often than unbiased
ones. In historiography *all cases* (all interpreted facts) are interconnected within the framework of a theory. *The general attitude has a
priority*, unlike the prevailing situation in everyday life. If theory is
based on bias, access to true knowledge is no longer possible.
Objectivity is far from being neutral in the question of truth. The lack
of objectivity excludes even the possibility of true reconstruction of
histories.

The argument that objectivity impedes a true account of history is
based on two different considerations. The first is due to the unclear
use of the concepts I have already dealt with, to the lack of distinction
between partiality of judgment and partiality of attachment. 'Objectivity' is thus contrasted with 'subjectivity'. Subjectivity is, however,
partiality in attachment, and it does not involve partiality in judgment
and explanation. The statement that the greater the subjectivity then
the greater the objectivity holds true only if the subjectivity means
attachment. The second argument against objectivity refers to the
plurality of explanations. All historical events can be explained in
various ways and these explanations may contradict each other. This
contradiction cannot be accounted for except by subjectivity as the
motivation for explanation. To anticipate the results of a subsequent
analysis: it is beyond doubt, that there can be different interpretations

of the same historical events. This does not mean that *all* different
interpretations of the same events are true or *equally true*. In order to
give an interpretation (one among many) which may be regarded as
true, subjectivity should not serve as motivation for explanation.

In view of this, the norm of objectivity (the application of
non-discriminative and reflected values in order to work out the
proper balance between our historical consciousness and that of
past-present ages) involves both partiality and impartiality. Values
themselves have to be proved right in discussion, and from then on
they become binding. Both our attachment and our self-distancing
from that same attachment as motivation to explanation can be
achieved if our historical reconstructions are related to the above
values without contradiction. Thus there is no objectivity without
value-guidance. Those who believe that values prevent us from being
objective are like the birds in Kant's metaphor who believed that it
would be much easier to fly in a vacuum.

Walsh made a reasonable distinction between personal bias and group
prejudice on one hand, and conflicting theories of historical interpretations on the other. Different non-discriminative and reflected values
imply different theories of historical interpretation. All these theories
have to be considered as objective ones, they all *can* be true.

Objectivity is the precondition of true knowledge in historiography,
but not its sufficient condition.

For Ranke, historiography should disclose and describe 'how
something really happened'. It cannot be true knowledge unless it
lives up to this task.

Ever since Ranke's provocative formulation, the matter has been
repeatedly brought into question. Present-day discussions equally
reconsider his controversial dictum. Diverging standpoints are extreme. Certain theorists reject Ranke's norm on the ground that it
cannot (and, accordingly, should not) be observed; others accept it,
but not as a norm, counterfactual by definition, but as a methodological principle.

Going by the first argument (here, of course, I describe only general
trends, not one particular theoretical proposal), historiography deals
with the present and so cannot reconstruct how something really
happened in the past. The application of values makes our historical
reconstruction meaningful – but precisely because we apply our
values, no true statements about past events can be formulated. A true
statement is one which everyone accepts, or should accept. The

presenting of a history that cannot meet with general consensus involves by definition the giving up of the claim to a 'true' reconstruction of the past. (Or, in another version: a statement is true when tested in action; what cannot be tested in action cannot be proved either true or false.) It is not only impossible to describe 'how something really happened', it is a nonsensical norm as well. It is exactly the merit and not the shortcoming of historiography that it is unable to observe this norm. As Dewey put it: historical sentences are not true or false, but better or worse.

But to state that we cannot formulate true statements about history is in itself a statement about history. If some one asserts that true statements are impossible in regard to history, his statement cannot be true either. But leaving aside this well-known logical counter-argument and trying to grasp the substantial message of the theory, one has to confront two elements embedded in it. Both have already been discussed. It has been argued for sufficiently that historiography deals really with the past and not with the present; therefore, there is no reason for further analysis of this matter. The thesis that value-guidance does not hinder, but rather promotes true knowledge in historiography has equally been argued for. Yet this latter argument was left incomplete because it only dealt with the precondition of true knowledge, with objectivity, and it left out of consideration just that question of what 'true knowledge' really means, whether it means to live up to the norm formulated by Ranke or something different. So further discussion seems to be necessary.

The second extremity in the present-day debate is supported by theorists who accept the proposition that historiography deals with the past but who refuse the relevance of value-guidance. Ranke's norm is taken by them as an instruction to formulate one single verifiable statement regarding all historical issues and this excludes the plurality of true understanding. For example, Hempel suggests that one method of the natural sciences should be accepted. One must construct general laws and deduce statements about concrete historical events from them. Following this pattern, we obtain true statements from the historical material presumably in the same way as the natural sciences do.

The full answer to this theoretical proposal will be elaborated later in this book. For the time being, it will suffice to point out its major fallacy. The elimination of values from the study of history and the treatment of history as if it were nature transform the subject-object of the investigation into a mere object. In this case, the past cannot speak at all; it becomes merely the raw-material for the consciousness of the present. The application of 'general laws' to historical material is an invention of the present, and by pursuing this method, it superimposes itself on the past. Consequently, the proper balance required by the norm of objectivity thus cannot be achieved, not even seriously aimed at. Now, if objectivity is the precondition of true knowledge, then, following this pattern, no true knowledge can be achieved. Moreover, with the elimination of evaluation, the theory in question pretends to be outside history and becomes unable to reflect upon its own historicity. As a result, the procedure is based on false consciousness.

If historiography really dealt with the present and could not offer any true statements regarding historical past, it would be a bad argument to characterize its statements about the past as 'arbitrary', because they should be seen as disguised statements about the present. Conversely, if historiography deals with the past, and does not offer true statements about it, one is entitled to assert that its statement are arbitrary. Arbitrary statements are incompatible with *episthémé*. Thus everyone who accepts the premise that historiography deals with the past (even though from the standpoint of the present), must also accept the conclusion that it ought to reconstruct events in the way 'they really happened'. But this conclusion does not mean any. concession to, or confirmation of, Hempel's arguments.

The crux of the matter seems to be tied up with how Ranke's norm is understood. What does it mean to grasp 'how something really happened' - this is the question to be raised.

The statement that one can never know or disclose how an event really happened would only make sense if contrasted with statements regarding 'how something really happens'. Unless this distinction is clearly made, we would be obliged to take the standpoint either that all statements concerning 'how' in society can be *neither* true *nor* false, or that all statements concerning 'how' - in the present as well as in the past - can be *either* true *or* false.

There is one fundamental difference between statements regarding how something happened and those regarding how something happens. The first grasps events of a past historical consciousness from the standpoint of the present one while in the latter case both cognizant and cognized are the expressions of the same historical consciousness. This difference has been previously dealt with and a particular interpretation of objectivity was established as its outcome. This is why the abovementioned divergence can be dismissed for the time being. The problem to be solved is related to the possibility or impossibility of offering two equally true reports on something which happens.

Wittgenstein gave a very profound account of one particular happening: 'jemanden zum Tee erwarten' – waiting to have tea with someone. Waiting to have tea with someone is a symbol that stands for various occurrences and actions. These occurrences and actions differ from each other, but if I wait to have tea with someone they all become part of the symbol. Even though 'waiting to have tea with someone' is a very simple event, if someone intends to give a true account of 'how it actually happens', many different true accounts of this simple event can be given, because of the multifariousness and divergence of actions and occurrences related to this symbol. If someone gives the account in the following ways: when waiting to have a particular person for tea, I put on the kettle and slice the cake, or: I tidy up and dress myself properly, then both statements are true. If someone gave the following account: while waiting on a particular person for tea, I dig a hole and take out my gun from the drawer, it becomes immediately obvious that the 'how' contained in the account refers to a different symbol and not to 'waiting to have tea with someone', and as a report of the latter event it should be considered as untrue. If the person in question argued in a court procedure that by digging a hole and taking out a revolver from the drawer he/she was merely waiting to have tea with someone, he/she would be properly rebuffed on the grounds that such activities do not belong to the occurrences and actions comprised in 'waiting to have tea with someone', and so the account must be untrue.

Reports on what actually happens are usually far more complicated than Wittgenstein's example. 'Giving a party' is a symbol of definite and well-circumscribable occurrences and actions. Nevertheless, there can be heated discussions during the party, love affairs may begin, strangers can make friends, and everyone can give an equally true account of the party according to what was the most important occurrence for him or her. Not only will the ones who started their love affairs not give account of the arguments and vice versa but even the most uncommitted observers would give selective accounts of either one or the other occurrence by emphasizing the most interesting or notable scenes. If someone in the future was to say that 'that was the party at which the discussion on statistics started' or that 'that was the party at which X and Y met', both statements should be regarded as true, and, accordingly, both subjects could describe how it actually happened in an equally true way.

During the discussion of the roots of historiography in everyday life and thinking it has been observed how difficult it is to describe *what* actually happened without giving an account of *how* it actually happened. If it comes to the 'how' of an event, an additional problem arises which we have not yet faced. It is often very important to abstract the 'what' from the 'how', although the difference itself is fluid and this is why the distinction, in the majority of cases, can only be done with a definite purpose in mind. 'There are bruises on the body of the child' is a 'what-fact'. 'He was beaten up by his parents' can be a statement about a 'what-fact' and a 'how-fact', depending on the purpose of questioning. In the latter aspect, the statement can have various different meanings; 'he was tortured', etc., and what the statement really means as a statement of 'how-facts' depends to a large extent on the interpretation. I would argue that all 'how-facts' regarding social issues can be replaced by *evaluative sentences* in a functionally equivalent way; more correctly that all 'how-sentences' bear a hidden evaluation (or various kinds of hidden evaluation). This evaluation can be generally accepted by the prevailing social rules or accepted by a particular group or embedded in a personal selection of the one who gives account of something. The less consensual the rules are, the more individual (personal) the selection becomes. The *mental reconstruction of 'how it happens' is part and parcel of 'what happens'*. In a period of fragile and multifarious social rules, the reconstruction of 'how it happens' depends increasingly on the viewpoint of the individual.

To sum up, the answer to the question: 'how does it happen?' contains the following elements even in everyday life: selection from the happenings and occurrences related to a symbol, selection from the parallel and subsequent occurrences and happenings related to different symbols according to evaluation, emotion, interest. It is an evaluative statement or series of statements with a hidden evaluation – the evaluation may be collective and/or individual; the mental procedure becomes part and parcel of the object itself. However, it follows from the preceding analysis that a report on 'how something actually happens' always involves a report on 'how something actually happened'. Even the symbol 'waiting to have someone for tea' implies that it always happens in the same way. As far as a report on a particular event is concerned (to wait for X for tea at Y time), the present and the past of present cannot be distinguished at all. In the moment one describes what actually happens, it already *has* happened.

The same problem has to be faced if we turn to socio-historical events of our present (or past of present). We may replace 'waiting someone for tea' by 'general election', which is equally a symbol of related actions and occurrences. But, if we speak of a particular general election which had a bearing on the future (or might have had a bearing on it) from different aspects, the everyday example of a particular 'party' might be more apposite. As a model case, we can take the general election in Great Britain of 1935 and Winston Churchill's account of it, first, in the present tense in 1935, second, in past tense in 1948. In 1935, on having been re-elected, he said: 'I take it from your vote... that you desire me to exercise my independent judgment as a Member of Parliament.'* The fact of being re-elected (the 'what') was interpreted by Churchill (the protagonist and the historian of the account in the one person) as approval of a particular kind of politics, a very unorthodox one in the given case. The 'how' was grasped together with the 'why' and this is why the event made any sense at all: it made sense exclusively through and by the interpretation. Yet, the present tense referred already to a past action (past of present), to the ballot of the previous day. In analysing the same event retrospectively (as the past of present), Churchill remarked: 'The result of the general election was a triumph for Mr. Baldwin.... All who had opposed him... were stultified by this renewed vote of confidence.... Thus an administration more disastrous than any in our history saw all its errors and shortcomings acclaimed by the nation.'* It is superfluous to replace Churchill's statements by evaluative and functionally equivalent ones – they are sufficiently evaluative and explicitly so. But we could replace this interpretation by different or even contradictory ones which would give equally true accounts of the same election.

The inevitable conclusion is that the more complicated the events we are faced with (and socio-historical events are always complicated), the less we are able to reach consensus regarding 'how something actually happens and happened'. But if there is no unanimous statement about how something happens now, it is more than doubtful that it is worth even trying to offer statements about past events as the only possible true account of how something actually happened. Different histories are different past-present ages. How something

---

* W. S. Churchill, *The Gathering Storm*, Bantam, London, 1977, p. 161.
** Ibid., pp. 161-2.

actually happened can only be known from the accounts of those who lived in these ages. There is and was no 'how' independent of its evaluative reconstruction. By pretending that there can be but one single true account of how something actually happened, we not only superimpose our will on the subjects of past-present ages and thereby violate the norm of objectivity, but we also manoeuvre ourselves into an epistemological deadlock, accepting a statement as true *which cannot be true* because the *case never existed*, since it is obvious that nothing happened in history in this or that way *outside* the consciousness of the actors involved. Thus any claim that something is the single true account of how an event actually happened is a *false* one. The hypothesis that objectivity as the proper balance between the past and the present consciousness is a precondition for true statements about history is thereby reaffirmed.

If there are different true accounts of how something happens now, there should be different true accounts of how something happened in the past as well. Every statement regarding the 'how-fact' is either evaluative or can be replaced by an evaluative one. If we are ready to describe how something actually happened, we have to evaluate. We also have to be aware that there is not just one true description of how something actually happened, but many.

But two basic problems, those raised at the beginning of this discussion, remain still unresolved. First, if the answers to the questions: 'how does it happen?' or 'how did it happen?' can only be given *in the plural*, is there any yardstick left for differentiating between true and untrue statements? Can or should Ranke's norm be observed at all?

Those who pronounce statements on happenings – on how an event actually happened – are *witnesses*. Historiography has to rely almost exclusively on the statements of witnesses. In everyday life a witness can be proved unreliable by personal experience (it is *we* who witness his or her unreliability); in regard to the socio-historical events of the present this holds true as well, even though in a lesser degree. Nevertheless, if we are confronted by the past, the unreliability of one witness is confirmed or contested only by another witness, and so forth. Marx's suggestion that we should not judge people by what they believe they do but rather by what they actually do is highly problematic in historiography because what certain people 'actually did' is only contained and communicated by the testimonies of other witnesses equally expressing 'beliefs'. We can only have access to testimony.

In so far as historians reaffirm the norm of objectivity and recognize thereby the actors of past-present ages as equally human beings, they apply the *same criteria* to the witnesses as to their own approach. In other words, they will check the reliability of different witnesses on the grounds of the objectivity of their testimony. To test witnesses by the objectivity of their testimony already suggests the observance of Ranke's norm: to describe events in a way they actually happened. How something actually happened can be approached at the first instance through the accounts of objective witnesses.

There are various procedures to test the reliability of witnesses. For example, M. Bloch holds that if two witnesses give completely identical accounts of an historical event or if their accounts are diametrically opposed, they are, in both cases, unreliable. One has to test, first of all, whether the witness could have had access to the confidential intelligence he gave his testimony about. Personal biases and group prejudice have to be taken into consideration as well, in order to find out in what respects the witness may be trustworthy, in what respects not. At the end of these procedures, certain witnesses have to be selected as reliable, and these are mostly the people who tell the same story differently but not in a totally contradictory way. The difference should and can be accounted for by the characteristics of all statements about how something actually happened (discussed above). Once more, the selection of witnesses in keeping with the norm of objectivity leads back to the assumption that there is no single true description of the 'how' of an event.

To test the witnesses' objectivity is a task all historians have to fulfil. Their chosen theory will depend on which one they confide in most from among many trustworthy ones. All theories have to be built around the testimonies of trustworthy witnesses, but the theorist chooses from among them not according to their objectivity (since there are several objective witnesses), but according to their own *attachments*. The so-called principle of confidence is not based on a 'fingertip-feeling', but on a bet. Historians bet on one particular objective witness to whom they are attached.

To this point there has not seemed to be a fundamental difference between a true statement regarding the present (and the past of present) and a true statement regarding the past. The same difficulties have to be faced and they can be resolved in a similar way. Nevertheless, if one suggests that it is not impossible to make true statements regarding the past, one has to be aware of the special kind of obstacle that must be removed as far as possible, in order to make true statements regarding the past, obstacles which never arise (or at least not in the same form) when making a true statement regarding the present or the past of present. While pondering on the past and testing its testimonies, we have to understand, first of all, the content of the testimonies concerned. One has to understand the symbolism of a past-present age and assume that a sentence may then have had an entirely different connotation to what it has here and now. A certain amount of preconception (and knowledge) about the symbolism of an age is the precondition of the proper reading of a testimony of that age. Even so, here one cannot completely escape a vicious circle. If one has a preconception (and all historians do) then the testimonies read will be subject to this preconception, otherwise, they could not be read at all. Then, however, the preconception leads the historian in his reading and becomes co-constitutive in the testimony itself. Moreover, Bradley's statement that no historical testimony can establish the reality of facts that have no analogy in our present experience is entirely correct. We may assume that there are testimonies whose proper reading is beyond our reach. In such a case we are unable to prove the reliability of the witness in question and cannot be objective either, because we either ought to superimpose our historical consciousness on the past-present age under scrutiny or give up the undertaking itself. Thus we have to restate the interconnection of objectivity and true knowledge again, even though from a negative aspect: if we cannot be objective, we cannot make true statements regarding the past. It has to be emphasized, though (and this is the new problem one is confronted with), that the obstacles in the way of the proper balance between our historical consciousness and the past ones may not necessarily reside in our attitude, but in the character of historical testimonies as well.

In view of the foregoing, we may conclude that Ranke's norm can be neither superseded nor circumvented. Once we accept the norm of objectivity, we have to apply the same norm to our own witnesses. Hence we are obliged to reconstruct historical events in order to find out how they really happened. We ought to make true statements regarding the past. Historiography fails to become true knowledge (*episthémé*) without doing everything within its reach to live up to this norm. True knowledge in historiography is the observance of this norm.

I stated earlier that the choice among equally trustworthy witnesses is made according to the attachment, or, to put it better, according to the affinity of attachment of the witness and of the historian. Thus the particular set of values of the historian proves to be decisive in the choice. It is known that different sets of values are related to different world-views. The statement that the selection from among several trustworthy witnesses is guided by a particular set of values is identical with the other; that it is led by the world-view of the historian. The set of values, hence the world-views, accomplish even more: they 'interrogate' the witnesses. If this interrogation goes as far as imputing the answer to the witnesses the historian cares to hear, the objectivity of the procedure is violated and the result falls short of true knowledge. But if the historian allows the witnesses to speak and to give their own testimony, as it were, then good questions do not impede true knowledge. Good questions are asked by good world-views, that is to say, by ones which express our historical consciousness in a radical and coherent way. It was even an understatement to say that good questions do not impede true knowledge: true knowledge can only be attained if good questions are asked.

As long as the discussion about true knowledge was centred around the problem of reliability of witnesses, how it can be tested, which testimony should be accepted, and the like, the analysis was mainly concerned with historical *facts*. Not wholly, of course, for socially relevant facts are always interpreted ones, and the interpretation itself is mostly guided by a theory. Like all sciences, historiography has to transform facts into the facts of a theory, the testimonies of different reliable witnesses have to be linked together in order to explain each other and to serve as points of reference, basic sentences,* evidence to which the theorists can have recourse. Theorists do not have to connect all the facts, but are free to select only those which are relevant from the standpoint of the particular theory under the proviso that the testimony accepted as reliable by the scientific community must not be neglected by the theorist even if it contradicts one of his or her statements. 'Must not be neglected' means in the given case that the theorist is obliged to argue rationally on behalf of the omission. The facts are properly interconnected:

(a)   if they have an explanatory character;
(b)   if the theorist refers to all of them;
(c)   if the explanation and understanding of the chosen subject matter becomes a coherent one;
(d)   if the evaluations are not contradictory.

---

* Of course, the observation is not carried out by the theorists, but by reliable witnesses.

These well-known considerations have only been repeated in order to widen the framework of the initial problem. Ranke's norm, according to which we ought to describe an event in the way it really happened, may be challenged if we have in mind that historiography is always theory (as we shall see later, even in a double sense: it applies one theory and implies various theories). In the discussion of everyday knowledge and thinking it has already been argued that the 'how' cannot be grasped without the 'why'. Even if it is a reliable witness who provides an answer to the 'why', this answer is embedded in his world-view, historical consciousness, and possible theory, and the historian who explains structures or events or both in terms of his own theory, cannot usually accept the explanations of times bygone. For example, Aristotle was a highly reliable witness, but no historian is obliged to accept his explanation of emergence of Athenian democracy as due to homosexuality. All theories are the works of fantasy. They bridge gaps – and sometimes quite wide ones – with the aid of imagination while enlightening us, and they make us understand and experience the intellectual enjoyment we are in need of, the so-called 'Aha-experience' rooted in *our* historical consciousness.

We may again refer back to the story of Captain Grant's children. The message has been read three times: in terms of the Patagonia theory, the Australia theory and the New Zealand theory. In all three reconstructions of the text, everything was fitting together perfectly. Captain Grant was, in fact, not in Patagonia or in Australia or in New Zealand. There was a fourth way of reading the message, but it had not been read this way at all. And this happened in a case in which only one single testimony was read. Actual historical reconstructions are far more complicated; theories implied in them far more sophisticated. Should we conclude, then, that Ranke's norm cannot become a valid and guiding idea and that we will never know how something really happened?

The question raised here has to be divided into two separate ones.

When summing up the discussion on true statements about historical events, I came to the conclusion that historiography fails to be true knowledge unless everything within its power is done to live up to Ranke's norm. The criterion of *how* this can be done was clear: one has to apply the norm of objectivity to the witnesses. Going by this criterion, a *consensus* among historians can be achieved, at least a temporary one. There are always dubious cases and testimonies can always be re-assessed from the aspect of reliability, but there is always a body of knowledge in historiography which is cumulative and which consists of basic statements accepted by everyone. Observing Ranke's norm may not always produce true knowledge, but it mostly does. Even if the reconstruction of 'how it happened' may slightly differ there are several relatively consensual interpretations, the so-called 'raw material' for various theories. To refer back again to the story of Captain Grant's children: all the passengers of the *Duncan* agreed that the *Britannia* had put to sea at Glasgow, had sunk somewhere, and that the captain and two sailors had escaped and were looking for help. This knowledge was consensual and was never challenged in the subsequent theoretical reconstructions. And at the end of the novel it was verified by Captain Grant himself that everything which happened, happened exactly that way.

It is clear that Ranke's norm cannot be observed in the same way in theories. It is obvious that only objective testimonies can become the facts of a theory, but this is no additional criterion, only the reaffirmation of the old one. Still, I did mention that *good* world-views can ask *good* questions of the witnesses and I described a good world-view as one which expresses our historical consciousness in a radical and coherent way. All world-views go into historiography as theories. All theories have to meet the four requirements enumerated above (points a-b-c-d). I wish to make the following theoretical proposal: all theories which fulfil the four requirements must be regarded as true, but not all theories are true to the same extent. The 'better' a world-view is (in terms of asking 'better' questions), the truer the theory becomes.

First, we need to have in mind the meaning of Ranke's norm as regards theories. All theories are expressions of *our* historical consciousness, the utmost embodiments of *our* values. Every theory is a commitment. Anyone who organizes facts in a theoretical framework commits himself or herself to one interpretation of how something really happened. The norm functions as a *regulative idea* in its theoretical and practical use. It regulates theorizing in so far as it leads us to meet the four requirements of a coherent theory, and it regulates our practice as well because the theoretical use of the regulative idea is not only the precondition of successful problem-solving, but also an *obligation*, a postulate. As long as we commit ourselves to one interpretation of 'how something really happened', we wish everyone else to live up to the same commitment. A regulative idea, however, is always and by definition counterfactual. Ranke's norm is valid if everyone accepts it as a norm. Its validity has nothing to do with the question of whether in fact we reconstruct how an event really happened. But we must follow the norm.

As already noted, all theories which meet the four requirements while interconnecting the testimonies of objective witnesses, are considered as true. If different theories offer different explanations of the same historical events *on the same level* and all of them meet the requirements of a true theory, they have to be considered as *equally true*. In this case, different theorists commit themselves to various interpretations and they equally follow the regulative idea of historiography. To return once again to the case of Captain Grant's children: had the Patagonia, the Australia and the New Zealand theories been offered at the same time, all of them should have been considered as true. The theories were falsified subsequently by experiments (they did not find the captain in any of the three countries), a procedure very unlikely to be applied in historiography proper, even if not completely excluded (to mention just one example, archeological investigations). Usually the statement of witnesses is all we have got, hence various interpretations like the Patagonia, or the Australia, or the New Zealand theories have to be accepted as equally true ones.

In all of this, the restriction that theories are equally true only if they meet the four requirements *on the same level* is crucial. As has been mentioned, a good world-view expresses our historical consciousness in a radical and coherent manner and a good theory is the theory of a good world-view. To put it bluntly, such a theory is a philosophical theory. The explanation of historical events is related in this case to a general conception, including the understanding of human nature, of social structure, of morality, of socializing processes, etc. If such a theory questions the witnesses, both the questions and the answers will be original. The interrogation will become more all-embracing and profound, for the witnesses are supposed to react to our grievances, hopes and fears by recounting theirs. The balance of objectivity will be regained since the acts deepening and widening the interrogation occur both from the standpoint of our historical consciousness and from that of our interlocutors from the past. A good theory is not necessarily characterized by its encompassing more facts, but primarily by gaining *more meaning* out of the past. Hence the better a theory is, the truer the historical reconstruction becomes, provided that all other preconditions of a true historical theory are met. If a good theory is applied but the other conditions of a true historical theory are not met, we do not have to deal with a historiographical theory any longer, but either with a philosophy or with a theory of history, related not to the past but to the present.

However, at least in one respect it does not make any difference whether a good or a less good theory is applied: all theories are committed to reconstruct how an event really happened and no theory can accomplish this. More precisely, we shall never know whether any of them did, which amounts to the same thing. This statement is far from being a sceptical one. True knowledge in historiography is the absorption of the utmost possibilities of true knowledge in general. It changes according to our historical consciousness, and our reading of messages, according to our way of interrogating, and to the world-views capable of raising the questions. This is just that process that resurrects the dead. We turn them into our contemporaries, because their story is ours and we recount this story again and again. Once upon a time there was a man. He was, since he is, he is as long as we recount his story. His stories are our stories and they are true, in that they are true for us.

Chapter Nine

Theory and method in historiography

The sketchy remarks on theory in the foregoing served one purpose: to show in what way Ranke's norm can be met. Now the problem has to be debated again, not just from one standpoint, but in its complexity. Obviously, some repetition cannot be avoided.

The reconstruction of historical events seems to run through the following stages: receiving the messages (information), interpreting the messages (the testimonies of witnesses), and providing the different testimonies with meaning by connecting them within a theory. The actual procedure is, however, not so simple. World-view is, not in all historiographical works but at least in historiography as a general undertaking, the world-view existing prior to the reception of a message. The world-view is the 'readiness-for-the-message'; it is the 'receiver'; it induces us to see what has not been seen before, even though it was there, and it makes us look for a message – and for a *definite* kind of a message. What is recognized as testimony today was not identified as such yesterday, what serves as testimony for one world-view is not testimony for another. The function of a world-view does not start at the moment when the historian builds up a theory but when he or she embarks upon the ocean of the past. The better a world-view is, the more it may provide us with new items of information. A 'new item of information' is not necessarily an unknown testimony even though it can be. The testimony is new only if it is read in a way which tells us quite different stories from beforehand. The imagination inherent in, and triggered off by, a world-view is a *creative* one. If a testimony is accepted as true by the scientific community, a good world-view is able to gain more items of information out of it than a less good one. The world-view is a shaft of light sweeping over the dark spots of the past.

One may argue that the priority of the world-view can impede us in conducting proper investigation about the reliability of witnesses. No doubt, this can be true. The investigation based on the priority of a world-view is a venture, whereas to stick to the body of knowledge already existing and to the interpretations of previous historians seems to be erring on the safe side. In actual fact, there is nothing in the attempt to obtain different (and new) items of information from witnesses which departs from a different world-view that would, in principle, contradict the norm of objectivity. In the worst case, the reliability of witnesses has to be proved from another aspect as well. Complete 'scientific' safety can only be attained at the cost of *not* living up to the maximum level of our historical consciousness.

Meaning is provided by theory; witnesses make their statements in terms of a theory. The better the theory is, the more *evocative* the narrative becomes: it evokes our interests, feelings, makes us involved in the historical event. We become involved as whole persons in the whole story.

There are different kind of theories: more particularistic and more general ones. Historians can offer a theory regarding a particular event, a series of events, a period, the development of institutions in a cross-cultural manner, and the like. Good or better theories can neither be distinguished on the ground of being 'specific' or 'general' ones, nor by the quantity of facts they comprise of. If the 'higher' theory is a philosophical one, the applied theory may grasp only one particular event and this will prove 'better' than the case in which a historian describes the history of a nation without being led by a philosophical theory. Despite this, in what follows, I have to temporarily ignore the problem of 'good' theories and discuss the internal problems of historiographical theories irrespective of the question whether they are good or better ones.

If the world-view interrogates witnesses and the theory is constructed as an outcome of several interrogations, it is obvious that the procedure of 'giving a meaning' to an event or to a series of events presupposes that the same questions (or at least that the same questions, *too*) have to be asked of all witnesses. To ask the same questions too involves a methodological procedure. One cannot ask the same (or even similar) questions without asking them *in the same way*. Theories imply specific *methods*; and all theories have their own methods. The selection between relevant and irrelevant confessions is accomplished by the theory and the method simultaneously. More precisely, in this case method and theory cannot be distinguished at all. Should the theorist fail to work out a firm and conclusive principle for selection, the theory will be incoherent or curtailed.

The differentiation between 'higher' and applied theory has already been hinted at. The world-view is the kernel of all 'higher' theories, whether they are philosophical or not. What we ask from witnesses and how we ask it, is equally determined by the 'higher' theory. The 'higher' theory is always decisive in the very choice of the historical problem the historian wants to solve. Non-discriminative and reflective values are worked out in the higher theory before their application to the historical material. (And if it does not always happen this way, at least it should.) There are no applied theories without higher theories, be they ever so sketchy. The same higher theories can be conjuncts of various applied theories (for example, the same higher theory can be applied to the Peloponnesian and the Napoleonic wars). The main categories of historiographical undertaking have to be clarified by the higher theory, even though applied theories can modify the meaning of the concept and hence the higher theory itself, at least partially. (For instance, if one writes a study on the industrial revolution, one has to have a concept of 'revolution' and of 'industry' in mind defined by the higher theory: of course, it may happen that while elaborating one's theory on the industrial revolution, one will be obliged to modify the meaning of these concepts.)

Although there can be no historiography without 'higher' theory, the historiographical work is an objectivation on the level of applied theory (or theories); only applied theories can be legitimately called the theories of historiography proper. Obviously, the clarification of the concepts of 'revolution' or 'industry' is *not* in itself historiography, even if we 'exemplify' the relevance of the definitions by historical references. Historical 'examples' may be of great use in a theory of history, in sociology or in political sciences, but they have nothing to do with historiography. They do not fulfil the function of making the dead live, they do not tell us stories, they do not provide meanings for past events. Thus real historiography is applied theory, even if the meaning we gain from the past depends very much on the higher theory. 'Higher' theory has to become a faithful servant of a sovereign past.

Historiographical theories compete with each other; there is no consensus regarding theories. Consequently, it would be easy to conclude, that – unlike the state of affairs regarding facts – there is absolutely no body of knowledge concerning historiographical theories and so they cannot be regarded as cumulative. But this conclusion would be hasty and not fully applicable. From the aspect of cumulation, historiography resembles philosophy rather than art. Each philosophical theory is a new one but it should not fail to rethink and reformulate certain basic problems raised by older philosophies and to try to refute previous solutions as irrelevant, one-sided or incomplete. The philosopher is not obliged to be acquainted with all preceding philosophies, but he undoubtedly needs to be with some. The philosopher cannot start from zero without running the risk of dilettantism. The same holds true for historiography. The theory should be a new one, but it cannot be formulated without the historian's knowledge of at least certain older historiographical theories concerned with the same events or similar problems. No fact is cumulated in a 'naked' form, facts are always embedded in theories. If the historian works out a new theory and transforms the facts into the facts of this very theory, he or she has to possess a certain amount of knowledge of previous theorizing and is more or less obliged to refute older theoretical solutions. If the problems of preceding solutions seem completely irrelevant to the historian, he or she has to understand them as the expressions of the stages of historical consciousness that older theories have been imputed to. Thus former theories can be transformed into the subject matter of later ones. Furthermore, even though theories are competitive and at the same time individual, they are more than this. There are theories which complement each other, others which take similar stands, there are tendencies, schools, trends in historiography. The number of possible imputed world-views of a historical consciousness is undoubtedly restricted, for there is never an infinite amount of variation of imputed consciousness. The closer we come to our times, the more often we are confronted with theoretical solutions the tendencies of which we share. Older theories can be understood as allies or enemies; references to them have to be made. As mentioned, historiography which undertakes temporary disconnection from practice and from pragmatism is a fairly modern phenomenon. Allies and enemies are numerous and we not only make use of their facts, but also incorporate or refute their theoretical solutions. Even though we cannot speak of a body of knowledge of historiographical theories in the strict sense of the word, the cumulativity of theoretical reconstructions cannot be wholly excluded either.

All theories suggest to the reader an answer to the question of how and why something really happened. All the same, their competitive or complementary character is not due to the applied theory, but to the 'higher' one. If 'higher' theories are similar (if they belong to the same trend or tendency), the various applied theories regarding the same historical event or about the same structure of mores can be complementary ones as well (the difference of approach may be attributed to the specificity of individual interest). If 'higher' theories are competitive ones, the various derivative theories, even if applied to completely *different* historical events, will be competitive ones as well.

The thesis that all objective theories which meet the four requirements of a true theory have to be considered as equally true, if elaborated on the same level, would hardly be accepted by practising historians at its face value. Historians offer their theory as *the* true explanation, otherwise they would not offer it. All historians intend to refute the theory of other historians. They attempt to falsify the facts of their competitors or to prove that their explanations are the better ones or both. However, should the game end in a draw, they should accept that the competitive theory is equally true. But usually even then they will not admit this. So only one course of action is left, namely, to take recourse to the values themselves and to continue the dispute, not about theories, but about the set of values upon which the given theory rests and to find out whether the values were true ones.

All theories have different components interrelated with one another. Not all these components are present in every theory, even if they usually are. During the analysis of Ranke's norm, I suggested its understanding as a regulative idea of theorizing. In what follows I am going to discuss the constitutive ideas of the historiographical theory. They are constitutive in that they organize the factual material and it is in this sense that they constitute the applied theories.

The constitutive ideas of the historiographical theory are:

(a)   the organizing principles;
(b)   the explanatory principles;
(c)   the orientative principles;
(d)   the preconceptions (theoretical-philosophical ones).

Chapter Ten

The organizing principles of historiography

All histories appear as unbroken chains of events, occurrences, mores, institutions: they appear as a 'flow'. The organization of historical material requires 'cutting out' certain loops of the chain in order to enlarge them. Different historiographical works use different (stronger or weaker) magnifying glasses, but all use some. The loops not magnified are the 'before' and the 'after' of the subject matter of a historiographical work. 'Before' and 'after' are taken into consideration in proportion to their 'size': the stronger the magnifying glass is, the less relative importance is assigned to them.

'Cutting out' means to distinguish between the 'present' of a past age, event, institution, and its *own* past and future respectively. What has been 'cut out' is always the 'present of the past'. Different theories cut out different presents from the unbroken chain of events, thus 'cutting out' seems to be an arbitrary act. But the theory has to persuade us that it is quite the contrary – it has to show the relevance of the enlargement in question. The evocative character of a historiographical work induces the reader to accept the cutting as an *evident* one. I use the word 'showing' instead of 'arguing' because the historian may bring up arguments for his or her 'cutting' even though this is not a precondition for the justified existence of a historiographical work. 'Cutting' can hit us as evident without being argued for.

What I call 'cutting', what is, in other words, grasping discontinuity in continuity, is the organizing principle of every historiographical work, and so it is a universal constitutive idea in historiography. This holds true even if the procedure of enlargement takes a different course from that described above. It is possible to magnify the same (or similar) institutions, motivations, etc. in *subsequent* historical ages. If this happens, all past periods become the presents of the past subsequently and nothing else is magnified but the institution in question. But if the historian cuts out subsequent present ages while magnifying the same or similar institution, an account must be given of the transformation of this very institution in the subsequent present ages; that is to say, he/she must grasp again discontinuity in continuity.

In the latter case it is *periodization* that functions as the constitutive idea in the historiographical work. To be more correct, it is here that periodization as the organizing principle of historiography becomes explicit, although it is present in a latent way if even only one link in the chain of events is enlarged. By suggesting that one enlarged past happening had its own past and its own future which should not be enlarged, the historian makes us accept that something decisive happened in this 'cutting' which transformed another happening or a series of other happenings into 'past ones', and triggered off, again, some other events as 'future ones'. In this way, the cutting separates periods, it becomes a real division, relevant and not arbitrary, precisely because it is reconstructed as a 'milestone' or a 'watershed'. If the writer cannot persuade us that this is the case, the theory will prove inconsistent or at least uninteresting. Hence periodization is one of the basic organizing principles in historiography.

If a society is characterized by *sensus communis* and by a commonly shared basic set of values, the periodization is an expression of the same *sensus communis*. The more the dissolution of the *sensus communis* proceeds, the more heterogeneous the set of values becomes, the less the historian can rely upon the collectively shared periodizations. It is obvious that periodization is rooted in world-views. Heterogeneous world-views have to periodize history in different ways, the 'cutting' itself expresses the world-view of the writer. In times of rapidly changing world-views (such as ours) periodization itself changes rapidly. The answer to the question of where the turning points are is related to another question: 'The change of *what* can be conceived of as a turning point?' It is well-known that it was Celarius who invented the 'Middle Ages', and since his time historiography has had to accept 'antiquity' as a previous period and as the 'new' or 'newest' ages the ones which followed the 'middle' ones. And it is far from being indifferent from the viewpoint of periodization and of the theory as a whole whether one defines these stages as 'antiquity, feudalism, capitalism' or as 'Mediterranean, European, Atlantic'. It suffices to glance at these two periodizations to fully realize that the line of demarcation dividing the first and the second epoch is temporalized in the same way, even though the barrier between the second and the third epoch is not only interpreted in two different ways, but the 'cuttings' themselves are made according to divergent principles. All periodizations can be compared from two aspects: from the aspect of temporalization of the lines of demarcation between the various epochs and from the aspect of the interpretation of junctures. The first can be quite identical in different theories, even though the second may be different. Periodization as a whole will be different even if only the second aspect differs. Diverging world-views usually work with divergent periodizations.

No theory can live up to its task of endowing an event or a series of events with meaning without the application of meaningful organizing principles. Periodization is meaningful if (a) the fundamental principle of the division is identical in all periods under discussion; (b) the testimonies that the fundamental principle rests upon and refers to are accepted as objective and true by the scientific community of the historian's own time, and if they really testify to the *existence* of the criteria that the fundamental principle is based upon. Whether these criteria were 'important' or 'unimportant', decisive or indecisive ones, according to the witnesses in question, has nothing to do with the precondition described. All theories are designed in order to render items of information of accepted testimonies into important, and essential, or into unimportant and inessential ones. If this is properly done and if the same fundamental principle can be applied to all epochs that these theories divide, the periodization is meaningful and can become a constitutive idea of a meaningful theory.

I have argued that the witnesses have to testify to the existence of the criteria on which the principle of periodization rests. The question of to what extent they have to do this is a delicate one and cannot be answered in general terms. Each case is a matter for particular consideration. We have far fewer direct witnesses from the periods of oral culture than we have regarding a nineteenth-century event, and the reading of testimonies itself faces incomparably greater difficulties in the former case than in the latter. Moreover, even if we can obtain sufficient testimonies, it may be important whether they simply testify to the presence of the criteria on which the periodization rests or whether they were widespread or even general. However, it is far from obligatory to accept as criteria those which were supposed to be general phenomena. The historian asks the proper questions of the witnesses and may ask different ones; he or she may adopt the position that certain basic criteria were not mentioned by witnesses often enough because they were accepted as 'natural' ones not needing a mention. If the historian argues properly on behalf of his or her hypothesis, the theory can be accepted as a meaningful one. To refer to the most extreme case, psychoanalytical theories assume that testimonies have to be read via their *covert* message. A testimony should not be taken at its face value, it is only a symbol of the hidden meaning. If similar testimonies can be read as symbols of a different but equally similar meaning, the criteria of the principle of periodization (for instance, parricidal and matricidal epochs) can be recognized as meaningful as well. In periodizing the *mores* of a given society, Lévi-Strauss made the theoretical proposition that even if only 20 per cent of a population observe a rule, then this very rule becomes a basic characteristic of the mores of the society in question. If other rules start to be observed by 20 per cent or more of the total population, one is obliged to speak of a different (new) period. Lévi-Strauss argues properly for his hypothesis and that is why it has to be accepted as a meaningful one. How great the percentage of those observing a rule needs to be for the proposition to be regarded as the expression of the validity of customs is always a matter of personal consideration, but there are limits to this. There is no society in which the rules would be observed by 100 per cent of the population and it can be assumed that if they are observed by only 10 per cent or less, other rules may be adopted and internalized by far more. (In such a case, one might even presume that the society is in a state of decomposition and as such, it is irrelevant from the standpoint of periodization.)

In principle, periodization can be *mechanical* or *organic*. But in actual fact, mechanical periodization characterizes *chronicle*, not historiography. The mere description of the facts that King Y succeeded King X on the throne, in other words, that Y's rule took place *after* X's rule, is temporalization without any kind of interpretation. Selection is, naturally enough, present in chronicle as well (as Collingwood pointed out, there is no ideal chronicle), but without any kind of enlargement. Periodization in historiography is, however, always organic. 'Cutting out' and magnifying an event or a period as the decisive one means to emphasize that there are junctures in the *life* of a society like those in the *life* of an individual. 'Before' and 'after' are matters of life and death, flourishment or peril, grandeur or decline, strength or weakness. At the same time, 'cutting out' is not identical with 'cutting off...'. The past-present age is a present age because it has its *own* past and future; it grows out of the past and into the future. Hence periodization in historiography is genetic, like all organic types of explanation.

Every historiographical periodization involves the evocation of a *tendency*. There are different tendencies, or, more precisely, the meaning suggested by the theory suggests one or more particular kinds of tendency, such as widening or narrowing down, growth or decay (progress or regress), recurrent ups and downs, etc. As periodization is a constitutive idea and an organizing principle in historiography, the tendencies suggested by periodization have to become constitutive ideas as well.

In contrast with the chronicle, the distinctive feature of historiographical periodization has been characterized as being organic. But it is not only historiography which works with organic periodization: the philosophy of history does so as well. What is more, the philosophy of history universalizes organic periodizations. It never operates with mere 'before' and 'after', but grasps history as a sequence of periods embodying progress or regress, or expressing the universal pattern of *corsi e ricorsi*. Although the philosophy of history will be discussed later, one basic difference between the function of periodization in historiography and in the philosophy of history has to be pointed out here: periodization in the philosophy of history does not function as a constitutive but as a *regulative* idea (in its theoretical and practical use). That is why the future is incorporated into periodization which never occurs in historiography. Of course, a philosopher of history may also happen to be an historian. In his second role, the philosopher/historian has to apply periodization as a constitutive idea too. It is worth mentioning that in his capacity as an historian he might apply different organizing principles than he would in his capacity as a philosopher of history (or at least certain different ones, while eliminating those others which are irrelevant for the constitutive use of periodization). This has often been pointed out with regard to Marx, and could also be examined in the cases of Dilthey, Croce or Cassirer.

Periodization can be called the 'dyachronic pattern' in historiography. It becomes an organic, that is, a proper one if applied simultaneously with 'synchronic patterns'. Although synchronic patterns never fulfil the task of periodization, there can be no dyachronic pattern without them, the criteria of the organizing principles of periodization being but the varying contents of social phenomena grasped and understood by the use of synchronic patterns.

Synchronic patterns organize historical material from a *structural* or a *functional* aspect, or from both. They are categories of theory and so vary according to theories. Even though some among them are embedded in everyday patterns of understanding, they have to be defined and redefined by different theories.

Patterns are worked out on the grounds of similarity, regularity and repetition. A historiographical category is used as a synchronic pattern only if it can grasp a series of similar phenomena not only in the reconstruction of one event, but in the reconstruction of many events, assuming that the phenomena in question occur repeatedly and with some regularity. All synchronic patterns are *analogical* in character.

Thus a synchronic pattern is a *cluster* which encompasses functionally or structurally similar phenomena on the grounds of their being repeated and/or occurring with a certain kind of regularity. Yet a certain cluster can only be used as an organizing principle if it is contrasted with one or more others. There is no synchronic pattern in the singular, there are only interconnected and contrasted synchronic patterns in the plural. One cluster encompasses phenomena similar in nature and is contrasted with another encompassing phenomena again similar to each other but different or even contradictory to those embraced by the first cluster. The minimum number of the interconnected and contrasted clusters is, obviously, two. The maximum number is fluid, but it cannot be too big (in fact, it is around five or six), for too many interconnected patterns contradict the meaningful application of the division: they could not organize the heterogeneous material of history. The most frequent constellation of synchronic patterns is the *triad*.

It was observed earlier that synchronic patterns are related to structures or functions or both. If one uses the patterns of 'economics, politics and culture', it is basically a structural use of patterns (even in the framework of a functionalist theory), in that it distinguishes phenomena similar to each other by putting them into one cluster and detaching them from others (again similar to each other) which are themselves embraced by other clusters, and all this activity occurring inside a social structure as a totality. The same can be stated of patterns which distinguish elements dissimilar from one another within the abovementioned clusters (as in the realm of economics: production, consumption and distribution). To sum it up roughly, all patterns (not used as alternatives) refer basically, even if not totally, to structures. And the other way round, all patterns which can be used as alternatives (or are exclusively used as alternatives) are basically functional ones even if they are applied by a structuralist theory. To mention one example: for Aristotle, a state can be monarchical or aristocratic or democratic; for Weber, domination can be legitimated by tradition or by charisma or by law. In the case of alternative patterns, the set of patterns can be (and often is) called a *typology*.

The dyachronic organizing principle separates the new from the old. It organizes history from the standpoint of change; it grasps the juncture; it comprehends all periods and events in their individuality. Its message is that everything under the sun is new. On the other hand, the synchronic organizing principle distinguishes between similar and dissimilar phenomena as *repetitive* occurrences. It suggests that the variations of institutions are basically limited in number. Work, for instance, can be (a) the mere use of the products of nature (hunting, gathering, fishing); (b) agriculture and husbandry; or (c) industry – and nothing else. Integration can be instituted (a) according to blood-ties, (b) according to locality, (c) by a dominating power centre, or (d) as an ideal community – and nothing else. Society can be ruled (a) by one person, (b) by some people, or, (c) by everyone – there are no other possibilities. Exploitation can (a) be non-existent or it can occur in the form of (b) tribute, (c) service, (d) slavery, (e) contract – and no other possibility remains. The 'message' of the synchronic organizing principles is that there is nothing new under the sun, or at least not much or no more.

But just as the dyachronic organizing principle has to grasp discontinuity as continuity, so has the synchronic organizing principle to grasp the *repetition as non-repetition*, as a distinct phenomenon which stands for itself and must be understood as such.

Naturally, historiography has to apply synchronic patterns as constitutive ideas to the same extent as dyachronic ones. Even more, the synchronic patterns have to be conceived of and designed for constitutive use. How this can be achieved was brilliantly worked out in Weber's concept of the ideal type; there is no need to add anything to this. However, something does have to be added to the theoretical proposal that ideal types should be value-free. Since ideal-types are only the organizing patterns of particular theories, which express particular world-views and the set of values inherent in them, values become co-constitutive in the interpretation of patterns. If traditional patterns are simply taken over by historians, it is still a matter of evaluation on their part as to *which*, from among many, are taken over, and *what importance* is ascribed to them (for example, monarchy-aristocracy-democracy *or* monarchy-republic, *or* despotism-liberalism-democracy *or* absolutist state-constitutional state and so on. These are the historian's alternatives). Yet, once the patterns are chosen and defined in a manner consistent with the world-view, then they have to be used in a non-discriminative way, irrespective of the attachment of the author, and in this single respect, they ought indeed to be value-free.

Without applying organizing principles there is no historiography. *But organizing principles should not be used in an explanatory function at all.* Typology does not explain one single historical phenomenon. To describe Nero's or Stalin's rule as despotism is appropriate, but no one can explain or understand Nero's or Stalin's rule by stating that both were of despotic character. Unfortunately, typology often runs the risk of being misused. Historians are sometimes attracted by the easy solution of grasping one single event or organization as a 'mixture' of types, assuming that thereby they have accounted for the concrete event or organization. Working with 'mixed types' is unclear and is often a sign that something is basically wrong with the typology and that it is misused for explanatory purposes. The same holds true of 'transitory periods' frequently employed within the framework of dyachronic organization. 'Transitory periods', like 'mixed types', raise the suspicion that certain organizing principles are being used as explanatory ones.

The distinction between organizing and explanatory principles does not mean that organizing principles do not participate at all in the process of understanding or explanation. When a historian identifies a particular organization or an event with a pattern of a coherent typology, the upshot of the identification is a *statement*, that is to say, a fact. Should the statement be argued for and thus established as evidence inside a theory, the explanation can be grounded on the statement to the same extent as can the testimony of an objective witness. If a set of dyachronic or synchronic patterns is accepted by a scientific community and if it is applied coherently by at least one basic school of historians of one period, everyone who belongs to the same school and who deals with the same problems can refer to those organizing patterns as to facts.

Chapter Eleven

The explanatory principles of historiography

I am going to use the concept of 'explanation' in its broadest meaning: explanation is identical here with making something understood. Historical explanation makes us understand social issues within space-time-dimensions, in other words, the spatial-temporal changes of a social issue. The explanation is complete if it makes us understand both the social issue and its change. Once accomplished, it evokes the rational feeling of 'Now I've got it.' Explanation is *need-satisfaction*: it fills in the blank spots in our image of the world we want to be filled, and so reduces tensions. If the system of needs is basically static, the need for explanation is no less static, while in a basically dynamic world like ours, satisfied needs always create new ones, and the need for explanation follows this general pattern. Explanations are not usually accepted as complete. Even if a particular issue is completely understood at this moment by some persons, the same explanation can be conceived of by others in another time as unsatisfactory. The insatiable need for explanation can urge us to extend our knowledge, although this does not happen of necessity. It is a mundane fact that even in modernity, people are often ready to accept the pseudo-explanations of irrational myth instead of the real insights provided by some kind of true knowledge. In one respect, conspiracy theories of various sorts, occultism, and the like, fulfil the same function as theories based on true knowledge; the function of evoking the feeling of 'Now I've got it.' Apart from this, a new explanation does not offer necessarily *more* knowledge to us, but *different* knowledge by simply rearranging already existing knowledge without adding even one single bit of new information to it. If the first arrangement does not fulfil the function of explanation and the second does, we feel that we know something *better* even though we do not know *more*. If, for example, someone has an unhappy love-affair and

159

wants to fathom how and why it failed, he or she usually repeatedly re-arranges the items of the story; in other words, tries to explain how it really happened in quite different ways. There are always blank spots left as long as the need for explanation prevails. The feeling of 'I've got it' arises when the need to explain this particular happening is gone.

The same holds true of historical explanations. Our basic motivation is the need for explanation. The 'blank spots' are provided by our historical consciousness. The historian intends the understanding of something when this understanding has an affinity to the need-for-understanding of a particular group with which the historian shares a historical togetherness. New knowledge and new information are provided in order to satisfy this need. More correctly, new knowledge (information) is not a goal in itself. It is a means which serves the rearrangement of items in the space-time co-ordinate until the intellectual feeling of 'I've got it' is aroused in the historian and in the recipients of historiographical works. It may even happen that the need of some is satisfied while that of others is not. In the latter case, another historian rearranges the same items in a different way and arouses in himself and in the remaining unsatisfied recipients the same feeling: that 'Now I understand, now I've got it.' It is perhaps superfluous to state again that historiography is justified in satisfying the need for understanding only if it meets the norm formulated by Ranke: it ought to fill the blank spots and arouse the feeling of 'I've got it' only by following the regulative idea of true knowledge.

Nowadays it is generally accepted that there are two basic forms or methods of understanding: interpretation (*Verstehen*) and explanation in a narrower sense of the word (*Erklären*). In what follows, I shall analyse both types of understanding separately. I should stress at the beginning that interpretation is also a subspecies of explanation. Both interpretation and explanation (in the narrower sense of the word) intend to arouse the intellectual feeling of 'I've got it.' Both approaches claim a *truer* reconstruction of history and a *better* one too. That is to say, both claim to observe Ranke's norm in a more adequate way, and both claim to use a philosophical 'higher' theory more adequate to our historical consciousness than the other approach.

Both claims to a 'greater truth' are basically false. If both approaches follow Ranke's norm as a regulative idea they can both offer true historiographical theories, even equally true. If the approaches are related to any philosophical 'higher' theory, the applied theories stemming from them can be good, even equally good.

Whether the two approaches express the imputed consciousness of our historicity equally, can be decided very easily. If an approach exhibits longevity and it is absorbed by its recipients, it has to be recognized as the imputed consciousness of our historicity. Because both approaches displayed endurance and were widely absorbed by recipients, even though by different ones, both have to be recognized as expressions of the imputed consciousness of our historicity. It has to be added that both theories have been repeatedly altered since their first formulation. The notion of interpretation in Gadamer differs no less from the notion of interpretation in Droysen than the notion of explanation in Hempel from the notion of explanation in Buckle. The change in historical consciousness is reflected internally by both approaches, only the bifurcation and the competition remained. The conclusion lies at hand: the coexistence and the competition of the two approaches are also expressions of our historical consciousness. Their contradiction is derivative of the contradiction of the higher theories, of philosophies. When choosing between the two approaches, one chooses between two philosophies.

Historians who did not adopt the two philosophies mentioned above usually applied both interpretation and explanation (in the narrower sense of the word) simultaneously. Their method of explanation followed the procedure of everyday life and thinking spontaneously, even though in a reflected way. In the first part of this book, the combination of interpretation and explanation in everyday thinking was exemplified; it suffices then to simply refer back to it. On my part, I would argue on behalf of a 'higher' (philosophical) theory which is capable of justifying the spontaneous procedure in historiography. One argument – and a plausible one – seems to support this option: that in spite of the claims of hermeneutics on the one hand, and those of positivism on the other, no historiographical work *can* be written at all by employing only the method of interpretation or only that of explanation. Simmel's formulation is very clear: 'Our relation to a spiritual content can be that of equality between subject and object; but the relation to the *historical* emergence of this content, to it as something historical, destroys this equality, in order to oppose a spiritual reproduction *a posteriori* through causal hypotheses to the actual occurrence.'* Simmel's argument against the absolute claim of hermeneutics can be repeated against the absolute claim of positivism

* G. Simmel, *Die Probleme der Geschichtsphilosophie*, Dunker and Humboldt, Leipzig, 1907, p. 30.

as well: a historiography which refuses to understand the 'spiritual content' of historical objectivations, that is to say, the general motivations and goals of actors in past-present ages, will not bring about any kind of communication between us and our past, will cut the umbilical cord which binds us to our past, and thereby destroy our interest in it.

The analysis that follows serves to show how both explanation (in the narrower sense of the word) and interpretation have to be employed in historiography if it wants to live up to its task, but employed in different aspects so that they *cannot be replaced* by each other.

(a)   Interpretation (reading testimonies)

It has been argued that interpretation is a form of explanation proper. *If the message is self-explanatory, the only adequate explanation is interpretation,* since the message can be understood in this case only from *within.* Completely self-explanatory totalities are the works of art of transcultural validity. If one aims at the understanding of an *individual* work of art as a work of art and not as a historical document, one has to disregard everything – every piece of know-ledge, every bit of information – about it and exploit the meaning of the individual work of art from the work alone. If the interpreter interprets *Hamlet, Hamlet* is the *sole interpretandum,* and not Shake-speare, not even Shakespeare's other tragedies, not the time in which *Hamlet* was conceived, not Elizabethan theatre. *Hamlet* as a work of art is self-explanatory; it is precisely a work of art of transcultural validity, because it is self-explanatory. It is a closed *interpretandum* for *virtual infinite* interpreters. Everyone can communicate with it, everyone can mediate its message to his or her own time, his or her own world-view and individuality, and everyone can do it in different ways. The interpretations are not cumulative, but again they are virtually infinite. Because it can be interpreted in infinite ways, the *interpretandum* stands higher than the interpreter, and this is why it can be called 'intensive totality' (as Lukács characterized the 'inner world' of the works of art). But the interpreter, too, can stand higher than the *interpretandum* by exploiting answers to our questions from the *interpretandum,* answers to questions which were not raised when *Hamlet* was written. All this means that the work of art as *interpretandum* is *timeless;* what is interpreted is not its being created in time and space, but its timeless validity, *sub specie aeternitatis*. Each self-explanatory objectivation becomes timeless, thus interpretation is the only adequate explanation if the object of the explanation is timeless. Interpretation temporalizes the timeless objectivation, and all interpretations do this equally. Consequently, interpretation translates the timeless objectivation into the time and space of the interpreter. A subject being in time recognizes himself or herself in the timelessness of the object while deciphering its meaning in itself as its meaning for the subject in time. Deciphering the meaning *is* the identity of the meaning in itself and the meaning for the subject, it is subject-object identity accomplished. That is why all understanding is also a misunderstanding. As Lukács pointed out in his early Heidelberg *Aesthetics*, the explanation of a self-explanatory objectivation is only possible as a 'misunderstanding understanding'. Subject-object identity comes about only in both together.

Hence being timeless means being temporalized in and through the reception. If a work is no longer temporalized in the reception, it is no longer timeless; it 'falls back' into time. 'Falling back into time' means that, being no longer self-explanatory, it has to be explained (in the narrower sense of the word). If a work of art which was not temporalized by the reception earlier, is later on temporalized repeatedly, then it 'falls out' of time, in other words, it can be explained by interpretation

No doubt, all works of art are historical products. They were created in time and space, and, as a result, they can be explained in the space-time dimension. But, should a work of art temporalized by reception be explained in terms of the space-time dimension, it is not explained as a work of art (as a self-explanatory individual objectivation), but as a historical document. Thus all works of art can be explained too (in the narrower sense of the word), but in this case they are explained as historical, not as timeless objects. Moreover, if one intends to understand the 'works of Shakespeare' or 'the Elizabethan theatre', or 'Shakespeare', one has to have recourse to explanation, for none of these objects is an intensive totality, none of them is self-explanatory in itself. In all above-mentioned cases, interpretation and explanation (in the narrower sense of the word) have to be combined; the method of understanding has to switch from the space-time dimension to the temporalization of the timeless, and, in due course, from there switch back again to the former.

The statement that from the standpoint of temporalization a work of art is timeless, is formulated from one aspect only: it emphasizes that the interpretation abstracts from the space-time dimension of the historical object as *interpretanda.* Yet works of art have their own *time and space.* Misunderstanding can become part of understanding only if the time and space inherent in all works of art is grasped. This is obvious, for it is exactly its own time and space that makes the work of art self-explanatory. No interpreter can arbitrarily decide when and where a drama starts and ends. Any interpreter of *Hamlet* for whom in the reconstruction the play starts with the scene in the cemetery and ends with the death of Fortinbras's grandson, is not interpreting *Hamlet*; any interpreter who interprets one movement of a symphony as if it were the whole, is not interpreting the symphony.

The work of art is, as Spinoza's substance, *causa sui.* It is the only *causa sui*, not even works of philosophy can *completely* be understood as such. What is '*causa sui*' can only be timeless, even if it is created in time, since creator and created are united in time; its own time and own space is the bearer of subject-object identity. The work of art is, unlike Spinoza's substance, a *causa sui* of teleological provenance. The historical subject who created it in time gave a meaning to his or her creation. It was this meaning that constituted the timeless form. No other subjects could interfere with the outcome of the enterprise, none of them could either hinder or promote it. The only way in which other subjects could (and can) co-create or recreate this subject-object identity is reception, interpretation, in the form of a new subject-identity led by the timeless objectivation.

Why interpretation cannot become the exclusive form of historical understanding, was made clear in the foregoing analysis.

Historiography reconstructs past-present ages in a space-time dimension. It is engaged in the enterprise of fathoming what 'was there', what 'is not here', what was 'then', what 'is not now', and vice versa. Its object is change in social life. That which is changing is, however, *not causa sui.* At this point, I have to refer back to the analysis of the organizing principles in historiography: although the dyachronic organizing principles 'cut out' and 'enlarge' one historical event, happening, structure, this 'cutting' is still never absolute because discontinuity is grasped by the historian within continuity. The 'cutting' cannot be completely understood in itself without taking account of its 'before' and 'after'. Both 'before' and 'after' belong to the 'cutting' (they are *its* 'before' and *its* 'after'), but at the same time they do not belong to it (they are *not within* the cutting). Every single moment of the 'before' can have an explanatory value for what is after the 'cutting'. Conceived of as the components of 'cutting', 'before' and 'after' could, in principle, be understood by interpretation, but, as they do *not* belong to the 'cutting' at the same point in time, they have to be related to it in a meaningful way *via* explanation in the narrower sense of the word. Thus the dyachronic organizing principles call for explanation, as do the synchronic ones. The typological patterns suggest the limitedness of the possible variations in all fields of social life. Human volition and purpose can re-install one or the other of these variations, but they cannot go beyond them. Moreover, one particular pattern cannot be replaced by any other given one. Certain patterns develop according to an 'internal logic' of their own, often connected with the internal logic of other patterns. The sequence of patterns basically follows these logics (e.g. hunting and gathering cannot be followed by industrial production in an 'organic' way). It has, however, been stated that organizing principles cannot be used in a justifiable way as explanatory ones. This holds equally true of the comprehension of their sequence. (Hunting and gathering do not 'explain' husbandry and agriculture.) But it is their very lack of explanatory value that makes them call for explanation.

If a combination of patterns (a social structure) has to be explained, this can seemingly be undertaken by mere interpretation; by comprehending how people purposively observed social rules and how they maintained them by this very act, even how they tried to (and in fact did eventually) transform them. But if synchronic organizing patterns are accepted – and they have to be accepted since social structures cannot be grasped without the application of synchronic organizing patterns – the concrete mode of transformation of a society cannot merely be ascribed to human volition and purpose: the internal logic of institutions has to be considered as well. In this case *interpretation does not function as interpretation proper*, but as a kind of *explanation* in the narrower sense of the word, since the *interpretandum* is taken into account as the *cause* of an occurrence outside (after) the *interpretandum*.

What holds true for the structural analysis of a historical period (understanding of the combinations of patterns, of observing rules and of the effort to change them) is even more relevant if the historian reconstructs a particular event or a series of events. Contrary to a work of art, created as a meaningful object, and so being the bearer of meaning, an historical event has different meanings or no meaning at all from the standpoint of the different subjects who participated in it. The same event occurs as the realization of one particular subject's will and appears as blind fate for another; it may even be comprehended as the upshot of different and conflicting purposes, fulfilling no one's aim. One has to posit history as the working of supreme reason, as Hegel did, in order to comprehend historical events as bearers of meaning. In this case, history is understood in the same way as a work of art: as the creature of the Creator, thus as a subject-object-identity. Conceived of as subject-object-identity, history can be interpreted but only as a whole, as totality. All events in it may be grasped as the scenes of an immense and incommensurable drama written up to its logical end. Anyone who interprets a drama ceases to be one of its actors. The drama is timeless, whereas the interpreter temporalizes it. But how can we temporalize *this* particular drama once it is finished? Outside history, there is no more temporalization. Interpretation becomes absolute, and so timeless. But timeless interpretation is no longer an interpretation, it does not mediate to different presents. Its object is dead. Being the actors of history, we cannot be its mere recipients. But if we refuse to interpret history as the purposeful creation of a creator, then we have to recognize that no particular event is the bearer of one single meaning which merely has to be unveiled by the recipient. The interpreter may adopt the position of those having given a definite meaning to the event in question as the actors of the same event. But different actors give different meanings to it, or perhaps no meaning at all. Thus the historian has to adopt the position of those having given one definite meaning to this event and thereby *explain* the attitudes of others, or he/she has to reconstruct different meanings (parallel interpretations) and so understand the event by connecting divergent interpretations, via explanation (in the narrower sense of the word). As a result, no meaning can be given to any kind of historical event without the combination of explanation and interpretation, unless the historian considers every occurrence in history to be the realization of God's (or some quasi-God's) design.

To sum up: historical events (and structures) are not bearers of meaning; their meanings (in the plural) are relayed by the actors of the events or of the structure. Events and structures have to be grasped in the space-time dimension, they do not have a time and space of their own as works of art do. 'Own time' and 'own space' are carried by meaning and vice versa. It is for this very reason that 'cutting' becomes possible and indispensable in historiography. The recipient does not 'cut out' the work of art, for the latter is a closed world which can (and should) be understood without 'before' and 'after'. The historian has perforce to cut out the period or event to be understood. The historian is free to decide where the story starts and where it ends, when it starts and when it ends. Freedom means, in this respect, that the theorist can select the beginning and the end according to his or her own theory. It is the meaning alone rendered to the epoch or to the event by the theory that decides the beginning and end of the epoch or event in question, although both beginning and end are regarded as only relative. Also, even the most coherent historiographical theory is *open to new facts (testimonies)* and it should be equally open to the possible falsification of a fact of the theory. As has been demonstrated, this is out of question in interpretation proper: no new 'facts' can be discovered *in the Jupiter Symphony* only *in regard* to it. However, the latter possibility does not concern the interpretation. Within the interpretation of a work of art there are no mistakes (apart from mere mistakes of 'reading').

Further, a social theory is always *a quest for meaning*. If a cultural objectivation is a *bearer of meaning*, the quest for meaning is irrelevant. Even though the inherent meaning of a work of art is mediated to the subjects of the present by that same subject, it was already posited before the interpretation started. Yet the quest for meaning does not posit an inherent meaning; this is why it is a quest. In brief, mere interpretation *is not theory*. There are no theories of *Tristan and Isolde* or of *Antigone*, although there are theories regarding the art of Wagner and Sophocles; even so, in the latter case, interpretation is always combined with explanation (in the narrower sense of the word) – in other words, the theory resorts to facts, and becomes a quest for meaning.

Although historiographical theories cannot be based on interpretation (because interpretation is never a theory), they cannot be based merely on explanation either. All historical events and structures have had different meanings according to the different agents of the past, who posited different goals, aimed at the realization of different ideas, and *meant* different things, all whilst acting according to social rules or against them. Without the reconstruction of these meanings, the quest for meaning (the task of theory) cannot be fulfilled. Both the reconstruction of the mores of a past-present age and the communication with its actors presupposes an understanding of 'what these actors really meant'. No explanation can answer this question. It has often been noted that mere explanation treats human beings not as subjects, but as objects of nature, whose actions can be deduced from various general laws. This is very true but is only half the truth. The belief that one can understand history exclusively *via* explanation is sheer self-deception. The facts of historiography are mainly provided by testimonies. A theory has to be based upon facts. The sources of historical facts, namely, testimonies, *have to be read.* 'Reading a testimony' implies finding out exactly what was *meant* by those who wrote it. However, 'what was meant by someone' cannot be explained (in the narrower sense of the word), but only interpreted. Comparing testimonies, linking them with each other, testing them according to their objectivity, is accomplished by explanation. But one cannot compare or link or test testimonies which have not yet been read. Thus theories, based on mere explanation, simply take the reading of testimonies (accomplished by other historians) for granted, and in doing so they claim to have nothing to do with interpretation.

Reading testimonies is therefore the focal point of all historical theories. It implies the fathoming of *the sense of statements, the signification of signs and symbols.* It has to be assumed that *all testimonies carry a cognitive claim to truth.* That is why when reading testimonies *explanation must be temporarily suspended.* If the reader of testimonies does not temporarily suspend explanation, he or she will not be able to assume that all of them carry a cognitive claim to truth, irrespective of whether they are messages of individual or collective subjects. The claim can be questioned only *after* the message has been deciphered. Of course, no one reads a message with a blank mind. 'Readiness for the message' is prior to the reading of the message. If someone starts reading a testimony, he or she already assumes that the statements make sense (or at least might make sense) and that something in the message (or the message in itself) *is* (or might be) a sign or symbol the significance of which can be deciphered. Someone who is not ready to read the message will not be able to recognize the sign or the symbol at all. Thus the readiness for the message involves the assumption that the testimony may be a *decisive clue* for something (an event, a structure, etc.) – in other words, it may have an *explanatory* value after having been read properly. Previous readings of similar testimonies and the way they were related to each other in and through explanations enter the mind equally when one starts on a new reading. No one can keep reading testimonies without having a certain kind of explanatory framework *prior* to the process of reading, but this framework has to be temporarily suspended during the process of reading.

That the explanation can only be temporarily suspended during the reading of testimonies points to the difference between the interpretation of testimonies and that of works of art. The readiness for the reception of a work of art is a readiness for subject-object identity, while the readiness to read testimonies consists of two, *very distinct*, attitudes. The first is similarly a readiness for subject-object identity; the second is just the opposite; it is a readiness to *alienate* the object from the reader of the testimony in question. The space-time dimension does not disappear during the reading of testimonies - the testimony should not be regarded, not even for a minute, as being timeless. When the reader of testimonies is involved in fathoming and deciphering the sense of statements and the significance of their signs and symbols, he has to posit that the statements may have a different sense in space-time dimension to the one obtained by the reader of the message in the present and that the signs and symbols may have had a different significance for their author from what they have in the present and within the world-view of the historian. While the self-surrender of the recipient is a self-surrender to the timeless, the self-surrender of the readers of testimonies is a self-surrender to a past present age. The attitude of subject-object identity is, in the latter case, a dialogue with the agents (authors) of the past. The assumption that the statements had a sense which we are able to fathom and that the signs and symbols had a significance we are *able* to decipher *is a dialogue* in itself substantiated by the norm of mutual understanding of equally human beings. Without the process of alienation, however, our misunderstanding would not involve understanding at all and it could not be regarded as proper interpretation. This can be illustrated by the case of the traveller who asked someone in Sofia, Bulgaria, whether the train he was going to take was leaving for Tirana, Albania, and seeing the others nodding, felt himself reassured until he arrived at the Bulgarian seashore, only to realize that nodding in Bulgaria is the sign of negation and not affirmation. It has to be added that historical testimonies are very rarely self-explanatory in character, and never self-explanatory in the same way that works of art are. Not everything that is referred to in the testimony can be explained by the text of that same testimony; there are always statements which point outwards. If the text is interpreted, everything that points outwards has to be neglected for the time being; the testimony has to be read as if it were self-explanatory but with the constant awareness that it is not. It is appropriate to turn back again to the allegorical interpretation of *The Children of Captain Grant*. The reading of the documents was an example of historiographical interpretation. As a result of historiographical interpretation it was established that a ship called *Britannia* sank somewhere. The question of *why* was not raised at all. The finding that a sound ship had sunk pointed to something 'outside' the text. No answer could be found to this question from within the text, and this is why the interpreters of the testimony *suspended* their interest in this highly important matter. That this self-limitation in the inquiry was only a suspension of interest became clear later in the story when the *Duncan* group met a sailor, a survivor of the catastrophe, that is to say, *another witness*, and one of the first questions they asked was precisely *why* the *Britannia* sank. As the story has it, they got a false testimony then, but even when it was proved false the question of *why* did not cease to bother them. They wanted to find a satisfactory explanation and, in the end, they got it.

(b)   Explanation (arrangement of testimonies)

'Why' is *the* elementary question, the first real question of a child. 'How' is more sophisticated; it is a diffident 'why'. 'Just because it has happened like that' is no answer at all; the only proper answer is, 'It happened because of this or that.'

Explanation begins with history; genesis is an explanation.

The distinction between interpretation and explanation (in the narrower sense of the word) is a modern development. But even if no distinction could be drawn between the two procedures in previous times, I would risk assuming that the methods of historical explanation in ancient times more closely resembled explanation in the narrower sense of the word than interpretation. *The principles* of explanation did change, but *in principle* nothing changed; everything which exists or once existed, happens or once happened, is supposed to have (had) a cause (or causes). The method which raises the claim of highest scientificity is at the same time the oldest and the most naive. It is indispensable.

In what follows I am going to employ the notion of 'explanation' always in the narrower sense of the word.

Explanation with causa efficiens

The naïveté displayed in the quest for the *causa efficiens* is not that of the metaphysical creed. Even if causality (in the wake of Hume and Kant) is conceived of as a mental product, the search for causes persists. Just because we cannot understand a phenomenon without getting an answer concerning its genesis, we shall not renounce the inquiry into its causes so long as we want to understand it. In historiography, we have one more reason to do so: history is the product of human beings, of our historicity. The product is the effect, the producer is the cause. However, individuals are born into a world which is 'outside' them at the moment of their birth. They have to appropriate its norms in order to survive. Hence the world (the product of preceding generations) is the producer, and the individual is its product. This mutual causation is an *elementary human experience* that everyone has to cope with. Coping with our world *is* coping with causality. Although causality is the product of the mind, we are beings endowed with mind and this is why causality is our being, our existence. It is a constituent of our being historicity. Understanding history in terms of causes and effects is, then, not an end product of our mind. As a product of the mind, it is the expression of our being-in-itself. In consequence, when pointing out that the search for the *causa efficiens* involves naïveté, it has been said (although in other words) that this search expresses the elementary human experience of our being both cause and effect at the same time.

Ryle holds that there are two model statements of explanation: 'The glass broke because the stone hit it' and 'The glass broke when the stone hit it because it was brittle.' These model statements are usually applied in historiography in all cases when a single occurrence or a chain of occurrences have to be explained. For instance, Rome perished because of the barbarian invasion, or Rome succumbed to the barbarian invasion because of the disintegration of its social structure. In the first statement, the external force is grasped as the cause; in the second, the external force is seen as the occasion (or trigger) and the internal decay as the cause. There are also two other models used in historiography. Both internal and external occurrences can be understood as equally relevant causes, or, on the other hand, the internal changes as the occasion, and the external forces as the cause proper of the effects. Yet if a historical theory explains an event by both external and internal causes, the *specificity* of the theory lies more in the rearrangement of the internal causes than in the rearrangement of the external ones. That the barbarian invasion was the external cause of the fall of Rome is an accepted statement in all historiographical theories about that event. The basic theoretical differences come to the fore in the explanation using internal causes.

Explanation with *causa efficiens* can be done in an overt and a covert way. In the latter case it is hidden in the narrative. Even the mere description of how something happened implies the answer to the question of *why* it happened. Danto puts it this way: 'The narrative is already a form of explanation'.'*

In narratives it is usually the *occasion* that figures as *causa efficiens*. The explanation with narratives may be regarded as an incomplete one; nevertheless, it is its most general form.

An event or a sequence of events is explained when *the quest for meaning comes to rest*, in other words, when the feeling of 'I've got it' is aroused in the historian and in those who share the world-view of the historian both in the scientific community and outside it. The 'standstill' of the quest for meaning is, no doubt, only relative and temporary. It gives way to a new quest, although a certain kind of cumulative process is not excluded. The quest for meaning comes to rest if the historian makes us accept as plausible that x *could have happened because a, b, and c happened*; in other words, that the events a, b and c have to be accepted as sufficient grounds for the event x. The statement that *because events a, b and c happened, x should happen*, the deterministic understanding of causality, does not offer anything *more* than the former one, as far as the *function* of explanation is concerned. It does not arouse the feeling of 'I've got it' to a greater extent, it does not bring the quest for meaning to *more* of a standstill. Deterministic causation is always an *overdetermination* in regard of the satisfaction of the *need for explanation*. Moreover, the suggestion that nothing at all could happen in any way different from how it actually happened arouses a *protest* in our minds because it contradicts *elementary human experience*, the very source of the need for explanation, namely, the experience of our being causes and effects at the same time. Determinism transforms us into mere effects. It is appropriate to state that deterministic explanation offers not only nothing 'more' but indeed offers less than an explanation with sufficient grounds.

In historiography, *unique* events, occurrences (or chains of events) have to be explained. What happened, happened only *once*. Similar things happened, but not *the same* things. The events can be explained by similar causes, but not the same ones. All events 'have' their own causes, in other words, the explanation transforms certain events into the causes of another, distinct, event (or some other equally distinct ones) which, in their turn, are transformed into the effects of their own of previous events. The similar causes are similar only from one or another aspect. The historian is entitled to gather

---

* Arthur C. Danto, *Analytical Philosophy of History*, Cambridge University Press, 1965, p. 141.

together all the concrete causes which are similar from *one aspect* into one cluster, whereas all other ones which are again similar in one aspect, although dissimilar from those encompassed by the first cluster, into a second, third, and so on. The upshot of this procedure is a *typology* of causation. For example, for Humboldt, the cause of everything which happens is either 'the nature of things' or 'the freedom of man' or 'contingency'. This typology of causation is, however, no less an *organizing principle* of historiography than any other typology. As a result, the types of causation have no more explanatory value than any other organizing pattern. No historical event can be explained simply by 'the freedom of man' or 'the nature of things' or 'contingency'. Only if they *have already been explained* can they be placed into one or another cluster of causation.

Advocates of explanation as the sole legitimate approach in the social sciences usually propose the application of general historical *laws* in historiography (of an 'if *a, b, c* . . . then *x*' character). None the less, this deductive method in historiography involves a fallacy, and leads to a serious cognitive pitfall. The propositions of deductions can only be typological clusters transformed into statements. I have already argued for the fact that organizing principles have no explanatory value whatsoever. If propositions *a-b-c* are typological clusters formulated as statements, none of them has explanatory value in respect of any historical occurrence, and any conclusion drawn from them will not have any either. (For example, Aristotle's statement that *every* extreme democracy leads to tyranny was based on the similarity of certain sequels of events in different city-states.) General historical laws belong to 'higher theory' (they are philosophical in nature) and can be used by applied theory (historiographical theory proper) only as theoretical ideas. As Collingwood pointed out, they can lead the historian into explaining historical occurrences in a deterministic manner ('because *a-b-c* happened, *x* should happen'). To be sure, deterministic explanation is not less inductive in character than explanation with efficient grounds. (Aristotle had to observe several city-states in order to formulate his statement.) But here I want to refer to a problem already hinted at in the preceding analysis, namely, to the inferiority of deterministic explanation to that obtained through efficient grounds. If 'higher theory' assumes the existence of general historical laws, this implies applied theories operating with deterministic causation, that is to say, with an inferior type of explanation. As a result, a 'higher theory' of this kind is undesirable for historical research and theorizing.

This is why I would argue on behalf of 'higher theories' which can be applied in '*x* could happen because *a-b-c* happened' statements, which can provide complete theories regarding historical occurrences and structures while at the same time evoking the feeling of 'I've got it' in such a way that the quest for meaning can come to a temporary rest. Theories are, to quote Collingwood again, 'permissions', because they authorize us to view several things in the same way if we wish to do so. And permission, Collingwood continues, is a perfectly legitimate meaning of the word 'prove'.

Explanation with final nexus
The methodological distinction of *causa efficiens* from final nexus begins with philosophy itself, and equally with the insight that the understanding of social issues requires them to be used simultaneously. The elementary human experience to which I referred is the experience of both causes. In Humboldt's aforementioned typology, the first cluster is that of *causa efficiens* and the second that of *causa finalis*. As is well known, the final nexus is but a form of *causa efficiens* and can be described in the same way as the latter. The formula would be, then, the following: *x* could happen because *a-b-c* did happen. In this case, *x* is understood as the goal of *a-b-c*, as the upshot of volition of *a-b-c*, mediated by means of *a'-b'-c'*. In order to avoid misunderstandings, I would like to state this: although explanation with final nexus reconstructs human volitions, motivations, ideas as the very causes of the effect, it must not be confused with interpretation. Interpretation obtains meaning from the text. It reconstructs the significance of signs and symbols and the sense of statements, it understands historical subjects (individual or collective ones), their wants, desires, ideas and goals, but it does not answer the question as to why a particular change came about. If someone makes a theoretical proposal that a change came about because people wanted it, desired it, promoted it, and used this or that kind of means in order to realize their goals, he or she was not simply reading testimonies, but had connected several testimonies by an explanatory theory. It has to be added that although explanation with final nexus is entirely different from interpretation, the 'higher theories' which emphasize final nexus as the sole or the main way of explanation, usually promote interpretative understanding as well. If someone considers human volition as the basic motive force in history, he or she has to fathom in every case investigated *what* people wanted, *how* they thought, *what* they really meant.

Occasionally, the deterministic form of explanation can also be employed in the form of final nexus. In such a case, an *appeal to the present* is transformed into the explanatory principle of the past. For example, the statement: 'if we are resolute, victory will inevitably be ours', may be transformed into the following: 'because they fought resolutely, their victory was inevitable.' The transformation of the appeal into an explanatory principle is, however, far from being justified even from the standpoint of common sense. The appeal itself is overdetermined, since its real message can be translated into this statement: 'Fight with such a resolve *as if* victory depended exclusively on your stance.' It stands to reason that the transformation of the appeal into an explanatory principle carries overdetermination to an even far greater extent. Overdetermination as implied here is even more transparent than in the case of deterministic explanations with *causa efficiens* or with both forms of causations. It is obvious that although all parties can follow the appeal to fight with resolve, not all of them can be victorious, hence the resolution to win (*causa finalis a*), even together with *causa finalis b* (for instance, uplifting ideals), or *causa finalis c* (for instance, commitment) plus the adequate means (for instance, good strategy) cannot prove the *unconditional necessity* of the outcome, even if they can explain it. This very pitfall can be avoided only in a theory of universal teleology, assuming that everything happened as it did because it had to happen according to the design of a supreme reason (and not according to the reasoning of the actors themselves). Universal teleology has, however, not one iota more of explanatory value for the understanding of a single historical event and/or structure than does the application of universal historical laws. It is again the constituent of a 'higher theory' without explanatory value in the applied. If *every* event is explained as the consequence of a supreme design, no event is explained.

Simmel suggested a differentiation between *causa efficiens* and *causa finalis* as '*Realgrund*' and '*Erkenntnisgrund*'. The latter could be constructed if it is assumed that 'the events occur as if that motive governed men.'* Apart from the questionable relevance of the distinction between '*Realgrund*' and '*Erkenntnisgrund*', one has to add that enquiry into the possible and general motivations of action in the framework of social structure is far from being identical with explanation via final nexus. In this case, events are not explained by

---

* G. Simmel, *Die Probleme der Geschichtsphilosophie,* Dunker and Humboldt, Leipzig, 1907, p. 166.

the motivations of actors, but it is the interconnection of specific events and specific motivations that is argued for, and both may be explained by a common cause, namely, by the structure itself, which triggers certain typical events together with their underlying motivations. This is a form of explanation via the *causa formalis*.

Explanation with causa formalis

Causa formalis explains historical events and the motivations of these events by the *social structure* in the framework of which they occur. The cause is conceived of as a relative totality: as a structure of total rules, as an institution, as an economic or political system, or even as a system of interrelated subsystems. *Causa formalis* accounts for changes not by events, but by the internal logic of systems which are only *expressed* by the events and the volitions of the actors in these events. Explanation using *causa formalis* has both a permissive and a deterministic form, similar to explanation with *causa efficiens* or *causa finalis*. These are the respective formulae that '*x* could happen because *a* was the case' and '*x* had to happen because *a* was the case.' For example, the Second World War can be explained as the necessary outcome of the interplay of different and hostile social structures, or it can be explained by these structures *without* the assumption of the necessary outcome.

Explanation with *causa formalis* implies deduction, but not in the same way as explanation with general historical laws does. Cause is regarded as specific and individual, occurring at a particular time, triggering off various actions of similar (or even of completely different) provenance, although all of them can be explained by an individual identity. Deduction has no explanatory value here either; the explanatory force lies in the *inherence*. All actions, events and volitions are explained by *causa formalis* if it is proved that they were inherent in the very social structure serving as *causa formalis* in the theory.

I have already mentioned that *causa formalis* explains change by the internal logic of the structures (social forms). It is appropriate here to refer back to Aristotle: all explanations through the *dynamis* of a social structure are explanations with *causa formalis*, he remarked. It may be reasonably assumed that once an institution has already been established it 'lives' a life of its own, even though only relatively. Its later development is but the unfolding of all potentialities inherent in it from the beginning. It may be assumed, further, that interplay with other structures may only hinder or accelerate this inherent process.

As long as the basic structure preserves its identity, every change can be accounted for as the effect of the original establishment, be it an institution or a social form. Thus the *dynamis* functions as *causa formalis*.

Both *causa efficiens* and final nexus have been described as 'naive' explanatory principles. Even if applied on the level of *episthémé*, they are deeply rooted in elementary human experience and thus in opinion (*doxa*) as well. In contrast, explanation with *causa formalis* is not a naive procedure. Everyday thinking usually takes the existing social structures for granted. These very structures appear to the inquisitive mind as quasi-natural entities. If human behaviour is explained by them, they are taken as *causa efficiens*. Hence, to explain events and attitudes with *causa formalis* is the *sole genuinely scientific* type of explanation in social theories. Undoubtedly, theories based on explanations with *causa formalis* can be grasped and applied by everyday thinking too. Even if everyday thinking does not generate them, it can repeat and make use of them.

The assumption that *causa formalis* is the only genuinely scientific principle of explanation in historiography implies two further state-ments. The first is obvious: no historiographical work as *episthémé* can accomplish its task without the use of explanation with *causa formalis*. The second statement is less obvious: if an event is explained solely by *causa formalis*, the quest for meaning *cannot come to a standstill*. This kind of explanation never arouses the feeling of 'I've got it.' All theories are incomplete if they fail to apply both *causa efficiens* and *causa finalis*. Human beings cannot recognize their life-experiences in these incomplete theories. Historical theories which only apply *causa formalis* are empty. They offer the skeleton of a history which has not yet been written. Of course, without this skeleton no true history can ever be written.

To sum up: in the quest for meaning, historiography has to operate with all three types of causation and has to account for the events and structures of past-present ages by explaining them in a 'permissive' way, suggested by the following formula: 'x could happen because a-b-c was the case, and because a'-b'-c' wanted x to happen, and because a''-b''-c'' did happen.' Historiographical theory has to invite us to satisfy our need for explanation by offering an explanation which can satisfy it if we are ready to accept it, that is to say, if we wish to do so.

Chapter Twelve

The orientative principles of historiography

Generalizations are the orientative principles of historiography. I have already argued in the first part of this book that generalized statements have an orientative function in everyday life and thinking as well. Let me refer to the analysis of proverbs, the generalized statements of popular wisdom. The reader may remember that proverbs are usually conditional assertions (if this happens, that will happen) and therefore occasionally suggest a causal relation (because this happens, that will happen). In spite of this, proverbs have no explanatory value of their own. They do not explain anything, but they do orient us in our explanations in a well-known way. If we are confronted with an occurrence that is regarded as a result of something, we use the proverb as *an analogy* in order to find out the cause of this very occurrence. The function of generalized statements in historiography is basically the same: they are used as analogies. I would defend the standpoint that *all analogies employed in historiography are generalized statements in an overt or covert way and that all generalized statements, formulated in historiography, are analogies, again, in an overt or covert way.*

The underlying idea of the analogical orientation is the assumption that nothing is new under the sun, or, at least, that no event is unprecedented. This is one of the most ancient ideas of historiography, and has been able to survive two and a half thousand years of its history. Generalized statements can be applied, with varying degrees of criticalness, but they have always been used. The norm of their critical usage requires that they should never be used either as explanatory or as organizing principles. The reason for the first requirement is obvious, the reason for the second is less so, at least as far as synchronic organizing principles are concerned. Synchronic organizing principles are typologies based on the similarity of certain phenomena in the same cluster. Should the historian apply the same cluster in different cases, he implies that the *types* of social phenomena are in those cases *identical*. In a manner of speaking, he can put his finger on them: *this* is democracy, *this* is autocracy. If orientative principles are applied, no identity ought to be established at all. If it comes to open generalizations, establishing identity concludes in mere tautology, for one would identify with one another two phenomena which were anyhow supposed to be identical. If the generalization is covert or incomplete (as in the case of precedents), the organizing usage of orientative principles hinders the historian in his working out of the specificity of a particular historical event – and precisely for that reason it is a misuse.

Precedent is a simile. In the process of analysis of a particular historical event or social structure, the historian refers to a preceding or a subsequent one, similar in some aspects to the event or structure in question. Thus the preceding case (the precedent) serves as a crutch that the *hypothesis* can lean on. If there are plenty of testimonies available about the preceding (or subsequent) cases which are supposed to be similar to the one in question, it is analogy which orients the historian's readiness for the message no less than his or her arrangement of facts within a theory. If this arrangement is based solely or mainly on a preceding case, it can only serve as a pre-arrangement; the hypothesis can be proven as irrelevant in a later phase of the research. Moreover, if the historian becomes able to give a meaningful account of the particular event or social structure that he/she was investigating, the crutch can be thrown away, it is needed no longer, and the preceding case (or cases) lose their orientative functions. Even if it is proved that two or more events or structures were, in fact, very much alike, the preceding cases will no longer be regarded as orientative principles: a comparison does not involve precedent and is not orientative in character. If the crutch is not thrown away and if the preceding case serves as a complete *model* for the understanding of the new event or structure through identification, then precedent is used as an organizing principle, and not as an orientative one. For example, Trotsky used the preceding case of the French Revolution for the purposes of understanding the Russian Revolution *not* as an orientative principle, but as an organizing one, not only in order to work out a hypothesis, but in order to identify the basic patterns of two different events. Because of this it was a misuse and proved to be irrelevant.

Generalized descriptions are no less analogical than precedents are.

If someone makes the following statement: 'External aggressions are always internal ones that have been redirected', he or she is drawing an analogy from the same aspect not between two or three, but between all possible cases. Obviously, such a generalized statement is of absolutely no value whenever any particular war has to be explained. Should, though, the historian accept this general statement as the starting point of an enquiry concerning the causes of a war, the general analogy might orient him or her in a reasonable way. The historian might look for internal tensions and aggressions when studying a body politic involved in (or responsible for) waging wars repeatedly, or he or she might look for witnesses who support the hypothesis by their testimonies that some basic inner tensions and aggressions were, in fact, present in the society in question. Should one accept Marx's generalized statement that 'the history of all societies is a history of class struggle', he or she will look for *special tensions* of class antagonism and for testimonies confirming these particular tensions in every society. Should the historian find the relevant testimonies and be able to arrange them into a meaningful theory, the generalized statement has to lose its orientative function, and might not even be restated in the accomplished work.

Each and every analogical hypothesis is an injunction. It can be translated into this: 'look for this!', 'have this in mind!', or 'never look for this!', 'exclude this!' This should be obvious, for generalized sentences are always rooted in the understanding of their authors' present world and are meant to lead his or her contemporaries theoretically and practically. They can be philosophical sentences or common-sense statements of everyday thinking, but in both cases they express our world-view, that is to say, our 'higher theory'. Which of the selectable cases is chosen as a precedent is something determined by this world-view.

It has to be emphasized, however, that although all generalized descriptions are hidden injunctions and that all of them are embedded in present-day world-views, not every type of generalization is accepted by the adherents of one or another world-view. To put this more clearly, there are types of generalized sentences which may be *cumulative* and thus accepted as orientative principles by the *whole scientific community* of a period or some subsequent periods. They are mostly *conditional generalizations* or statements concerning *general correlations*. The following statements are reasonable examples of them: '*x* usually occurs together with *y*' (for example, a sedentary way of life with higher population density as compared to a nomadic one), or; 'provided that all components are similar, *a* can be achieved quicker (or easier or in a better way) by *x* than by *y*' (for example, democracies are always slower in preparing for war than tyrannnies). There are several conditional generalizations or statements regarding general correlations related exclusively to one historical period, or one type of society or one territory, (such as the correlation between cotton prices and lynching in the Southern states of the USA, at least for half a century). Plainly, no concrete event can be accounted for by these correlations via deduction, though this does not detract from their merits in orienting historiographical enquiry. General correlations provide the historian not only with hypothetical sketches but also with a certain amount of *information*, suggesting a *probability* of an occurrence in some of the studied cases.

Orientative principles have an undeservedly bad reputation in various present-day philosophical theories, although for different reasons. For example, Hempel criticizes their shortcomings in their capacity as explanatory principles. Generalized sentences are not real historical laws, only sketches of laws, he argues, and this is why their application cannot establish scientific historiography. As adequate explanation must include at least one general law, at least one of the sketches has to be transformed into a proper general law with explanatory force. On the other hand, Popper rejects the use of generalized sentences in an offhand manner. He considers orientative principles to be empty, tautological, platitudinous. What seems even worse to him, their use belongs to historicism, to the holistic approach, and they are thus ideological, dangerous, the main obstacle in the way of true historical knowledge. Still, it is not without significance that Popper himself applies at least one orientative principle to history when stating that *all* historical events are upshots of individual actions. Even the most ardent enemy of orientative principles cannot escape them, if he wants to state *anything at all* about history.

An historian who rejects the use of orientative principles is like a sailor who decides to navigate without map or compass, or even without listening to the narratives of other sailors about their experiences upon other oceans and seas. As long as we were ignorant of many parts of our earth, all maps were repeatedly corrected and the blank spots were gradually filled in. Certain generalized statements proved to be mistaken, others not; certain valued generalized experiences proved not to be general at all, others were reconfirmed. But only a fool would have embarked for the unknown without being equipped with all available tools of orientation. And no historian is such a fool.

The bad reputation of orientative principles is undeserved but understandable. It is due to the frequent misuse of these same principles. The cure suggested by Hempel would, however, kill the patient, for it is exactly the explanatory use of orientative principles which is the pitfall that has to be avoided. The cure suggested by Popper would kill the doctor, and the patient. Historiography as an undertaking is impossible without the employment of orientative principles. If someone does not know what has to be looked for, he or she will either not look for anything at all, or perish on the infinite ocean of historical facts without the slightest hope of ever again setting foot on solid ground.

Chapter Thirteen

The 'higher' and the applied theory

Organizing, explanatory and orientative principles are generated in a world-view, in other words, in a 'higher' theory. As applied theory has to make use of these principles in order to arrange (or rearrange) testimonies in a coherent way, so has the 'higher' theory in order to arrange (and rearrange) the different principles themselves, in an equally coherent way. Historians who accept different 'higher' theories may occasionally apply similar principles (for example, the same periodization or certain generalized sentences in common or the same explanatory principles), but their arrangement has to be different. Should the arrangement of principles be basically the same, the 'higher' theories are basically identical too, irrespective of the 'range' of their application. It is obvious that the same historian usually also applies his or her 'higher' theory to quite different historical events or structures. Thus all applied theories are *distinct* and non-recurrent, even if 'higher' theories are the same. 'Higher' theories which do not express the imputed consciousness of our historicity any longer will not produce good theories when applied, even though they can produce new ones.

In the foregoing analysis the 'quest for meaning' was exclusively attributed to *explanation* (both to interpretation and to explanation in the narrower sense of the word). It has been noted that it is precisely explanation which evokes the feeling of 'I've got it.' Although *explanatory principles* are embedded in the 'higher theory' to the same extent as the organizing or orientative ones with which they are interconnected, the *process of explanation* takes place in applied theory. More properly, applied theory *is* the accomplished process of explanation. Accordingly, *the quest for meaning in historiography is pursued only in applied theory.* 'Higher' theories in themselves are never historiographical theories, they are theories *about* history.

Applied theory *is* historiography, and it is the resurrection of the dead, the reconstruction of past-present ages, it is the interconnection of deciphered messages – things accomplished by no other theoretical undertaking.

'Higher' theories do not accomplish the quest for meaning, but without them such a quest cannot be undertaken at all.

All the same (and I have argued this in detail), 'higher' theories are *meaningful* world-views. And then the pertinent question arises as to why the quest for something which is already there should be undertaken. Our meaningful world-views express *our* historical consciousness, together with the readiness for the message (for one or another particular message). To obtain meaning from the past is a procedure triggered off by this readiness, but the meaning can be obtained from the past only in the course of this procedure. Just because historiography deals with the past and not with the present, the quest for meaning is a quest for meaning in the past from the viewpoint of the present and for the present. To sum up: there are no meaningful historiographical theories (that is to say, theories at all) without meaningful higher theories, but the *historiographical* quest for meaning is accomplished in the applied theories.

It is well known that all world-views imply definite sets of values. Thus all components of the higher theories more or less express the same sets of values. The more coherent the theory is, the more they do so. Organizing, explanatory and orientative principles are arranged within the framework of higher theories. As a result, they express values. The more coherently they are interconnected, the more coherently they express these values.

Not every meaningful world-view contains these three principles of historiography or arranges them in a coherent way. Only theories of history can serve as 'higher theory' for historiography and they have to be made appropriate for historiographical application as well. It is this very clarification of the principles discussed and their coherent arrangement which can accomplish this task. In the procedure of arrangement, the values provided by the world-view not only have to be reflected upon, but the historian has to eliminate all contradictions of value as well, contradictions which may occur in the process of the arrangement of various principles. A theory of history only becomes a theory for historiography if these requirements are met.

The organizing, explanatory, and orientative principles of histor-iography *mediate* the 'higher' theory to the applied one. Through them, an applied theory becomes the applied theory of a particular 'higher' theory. This is why the coherence of principles and the elimination of their possible value-contradictions are matters of the highest importance. If mediation is performed in a coherent way, the values of the 'higher' theory will reappear in the applied theories as *intrinsic* ones; they will be absorbed by the applied theory. In this case, applied theories may *seem* to be value-free. If mediation fails to perform this task properly, evaluation will not be absorbed by the applied theory, but rather figure as an 'appendix', a label glued on to a bottle which does not contain what it says it does.

The mediation performed by the three basic principles of historiography implies a *selection* from a particular viewpoint (the 'higher' theory). Selection is aimed at what is essential (once again, from the viewpoint of the 'higher' theory). Essential periods or events or structures are selected from among numerous others (often infinite in number), essential testimonies are selected from among several others, essential messages are distinguished from those of secondary importance, and so on. What is thought to be essential from the viewpoint of one 'higher' theory may prove inessential from another, and vice versa. Or, in a more exact formulation, the three principles *render* some things essential and other things inessential. For Bloch, the slight differences between French and English serfdom were essential; for Mommsen all details of political events and deliberation; for Tillich the nuances of religious consciousness. What was essential for one of three historians was definitely not essential for the other two. It is precisely what is thought to be essential which becomes central in the quest for meaning. However, the quest for meaning only comes to a standstill when the 'essential' is *proved* to be the essential, and this happens in applied theories powered by explanation.

Historians can either work out their philosophical 'higher' theories themselves, in which case they are philosophers and historians in one, or they become *recipients* of a philosophical theory elaborated by someone else. Due the specialization of talents and interests, the first case is the exception rather than the rule, even though it does happen occasionally. But even if it does, one or the other type of the two talents is predominant. Obviously, Hegel is more a philosopher and Ranke more an historian. To simplify the problem, historians are going to be discussed as recipients of philosophical theories, and if they are both philosophers and historians, as the recipients of their own philosophy.

All philosophies contrast Ought with Is. Ought is the unity of two ideals: that of the good and that of the true (occasionally even that of a third one: the beautiful). The identity (unity) of good and true is *the truth* (the identity of true knowledge and good morality, theory and practice). Ought being contrasted to Is is also inferred from Is rationally. Philosophy enjoins all human beings to do the same: to come to know truth rationally. Thus philosophy enjoins us to carry out three tasks simultaneously: 'Reflect on how you should think, how you should act, how you should live.' The answers to all three injunctions are offered by all philosophies. They are interwoven. The answer to one question implies the answers to the others to a no lesser degree. They all offer a solution to the problem of the sense of human existence. It should be mentioned in advance that the 'sense of human existence' is not identical to the meaning of history. The two are merged only by a special kind of philosophy: the philosophy of history.

There are two types of reception of philosophies: the total and the partial. In the case of total reception, the recipient lives up to all three invitations equally, in partial reception only to one of the three. The total recipient commits himself/herself to think, to act and to live by the philosophy received – this is the philosophical reception which implies the unity of theory and practice. The partial recipient commits himself/herself either to think, or to act, or to live according to the philosophy received. One lives and acts in the present and for the future. Consequently, whether the reception is total or partial, the recipient is committed to the 'future in the present'. Historiography deals, though, with the past. Moreover, it has to disconnect its search for true knowledge from pragmatism and direct practical involvement: thus historians cannot be the total recipients of just any philosophy. They have to be (because they *can* only be) recipients of the first injunction of philosophy: 'Reflect on how you should think.'

The historian *views* the world from the aspect of the sense of human existence but it is not the sense of human existence that is seen by him. Since we see with our eyes, we cannot see our eyes. The 'sense of human existence' is not operational with regard to historiography, it cannot be 'applied'. It is the beam which projects light into the darkness of the past, but it throws light on actors, fates, institutions, joys and suffering – everything but itself.

The simile may suggest that the 'sense of existence' is like an 'abstract framework', whereas objects as subjects illuminated by it are the 'concrete'. But this is far from being so. Nothing is more concrete than the answer to the *Sinnfrage* (the question of the sense of existence). Not only do all philosophies answer it differently, but also all recipients of philosophies modify it individually. Let me exemplify this on three formulations of the *Sinnfrage*, all similar to each other in certain important aspects.

(1) Ranke: 'Individual life only counts because man dies. All moments of the life of nations have to be considered as independent developments, not only to the extent they serve a certain final development.'*

(2) Rickert: 'An object of history attains to sense and meaning by the fact that it is related to a general value to whose realization it contributes through its individual structure'.**

(3) Troeltsch: 'History cannot be transcended within its own boundaries and knows no other salvation but that in the form of religious anticipation of the other world or that in the form of exalted magnification of partial salvations. God's realm and Nirvana are beyond any history; in history itself there are only relative transcendings'.***

All these answers to the *Sinnfrage* reject a philosophy of history. In their conception, history has no goals, no universal tendency of progress, the idea of history is *not* 'the education of the human race' (Herder). Besides this, Troeltsch is a recipient of Ranke, he follows in the footsteps of historicist tradition. But despite all common endeavours, the answers to the *Sinnfrage* are not only different in all three cases, it is even impossible to compare them in any reasonable way. In order to do so, one needs to refer to the complete philosophical framework they express, and to *interpret* all of them, not only to explain them. It is obvious that this task cannot be undertaken here and it is exactly this that proves the individuality and the concrete character of all 'higher' theories as far as the answer to the *Sinnfrage* is concerned.

The answer to the question about the meaning of human existence is the hidden starting point and the explicit end result of all philosophies. This answer is embedded in all three injunctions transformed into the three commitments. I have already argued for the assertion

---

* Quoted in Ernst Schulin, *Die weltgeschichtliche Orients des Erfassung bei Hegel und Ranke*, Vandenhoeck and Ruprecht, Göttingen, 1958, p. 168.
** H. Rickert, *Die Probleme der Geschichtsphilosophie*, Carl Winters Universitätsbuchhandlung, Heidelberg, 1924, p. 129.
*** E. Troeltsch, *Der Historismus und seine Überwindung*, Scientia-Verlag, Aachen, 1966, p. 160.

that even though historiography accepts only one of the three injunctions and so is committed only to this one, the other two commitments are intrinsic in this one as well.

The *Sinnfrage* is always raised from the standpoint of its supposed solution; the answer is already inherent in the very question. Nevertheless, it has to be inferred rationally and this inference is the true knowledge of philosophy. If this true knowledge is knowledge about history, or if it can be translated into the language of history, philosophy becomes in all its forms the 'higher' theory of historiography. It is appropriate that these forms be discussed now.

It is commonplace that every philosophy is an anthropology in the broader sense of the word. Granted this, a philosophy can become a 'higher' theory of historiography only if its basic paradigm offers an answer to the questions directly dealing with human essence and existence, such as: what is the relation and proportion of 'nature' and 'culture' in human existence? What propensities and powers distinguish human beings from the animal world? Which are the basic and which are the secondary human powers? To what extent are human beings autonomous? To what extent are they rational? Which are the decisive human motivations, and, are these stagnant or changing, and if the latter is the case, how, when and why do the changes come about? To what extent can human beings master their motivations, why should they do so, and what may be the possible consequences of their self-control? Which are the minimum and maximum possibilities of human nature, or, in ethical terms, what is the best and the worst that human beings are capable of? Is humankind self-creating or created or both? Which are the basic human cognitive abilities; which are the basic human practical abilities? Which are (if any) the basic human values? And so on.

The image of man and the image of society cannot be separated, and indeed they have never been. Therefore, the paradigm of the 'higher' theory of historiography must also offer answers to questions such as whether man is created by society or vice versa; whether or not an ideal (perfect) society is possible, and if the answer is in the affirmative, how it has to be conceived, and if it is in the negative, what is the reason for the negative decision? Which are the basic social integrations? Are they the same in every society or different? Are humans especially socialized by one type of integration, and if so, by which one, if not so which are the integrations participating in the socialization process? Does the development of the human character depend on socializing integration, and if so, to what extent and in which direction it can be influenced? Are human beings equal or unequal, and if they are unequal in which respects? Are all societies based on inequality and to the same degree? Is society identical to the state or not? What has the state (the society) to offer to its subjects (citizens) and vice versa? Which basic social conflicts exist in our present society and in various other ones? And the like.

Images of society and images of man always answer the question about the meaning of human existence in concert, since they are *unified* when it comes to the two basic issues on which the answer to the *Sinnfrage* rests. These are the issues of *happiness* and *freedom*.

And so all philosophical theories which raise the issues of human existence and essence directly from the aspect of happiness and freedom (or both) can become 'higher' theories of historiography. But I hardly need to add that the solution of the *Sinnfrage*, even though crucial, is not in itself a sufficient criterion for the historiographical applicability of a 'higher' theory. Although the 'higher' theory of historiography has to be applied, the answer to the *Sinnfrage* cannot be. More precisely, the answer to the *Sinnfrage* can only *seemingly* be applied, but never in fact, since the meaning to be obtained from its application is already posited before the application itself. There is only one single segment of philosophical 'higher' theory which has a real 'say' in the application, namely, its *method*.

The historian as a recipient of a philosophical theory has to work out a categorical framework which mediates between philosophy and its application. This categorical framework belongs to 'higher' theory to the same extent as the answer to the *Sinnfrage*; moreover, the latter has to penetrate the whole categorical framework to be applied. It has to be added that several philosophies provide a categorical framework for historiographical application, philosophies of history do this frequently. Still, the historian has to use the utmost caution in taking them over without further reflection. Even though philosophies of history do offer explanatory, organizing, and orientative principles, the latter are usually only apparently appropriate tools for this task, being mixtures of the *Sinnfrage* and the framework for mediation. The actual applicability of the principles has to be reconsidered by the historian even if he or she completely accepts the philosophy in question.

It is obvious that the philosophical theory chosen by the historian need not necessarily be a philosophy of history. For example, both Voltaire and Hume were historians to the same extent as they were philosophers, and in their first capacity they were recipients of their own philosophy, but their philosophies were by no means philosophies of history. It is, in fact, a matter of great importance for historians whether the problems of history are raised by the philosophy they adhere to. No wonder historians usually adhere to philosophies which answer the question about the sense of human existence historically. In all other cases, historians have to raise the same basic issues themselves within the framework of a mediating theory.

The reception of a philosophy in itself is a kind of interpretation. All philosophies can be received (and so interpreted) in entirely different ways within given, but mostly indefinable, limits. The same philosophical 'higher' theory can illuminate not only different dark spots but also the same spot from different aspects. While applying philosophical theories to historiographical ones, the historian re-creates the philosophical theory as well. The latter is preserved as well as transformed by historiographical theories.

In summing up the basic levels of theorizing in historiography, we obtain a chain of different kind of theories, all accomplishing different tasks. At first sight, it looks like a cable-chain deeply anchored in the ocean of the past. The ship can be the philosophical theory (the answer to the question about the *sense* of human existence), the chain is fastened to the ship by the orientative, organizing and explanatory principles interconnected with, and penetrated by, the philosophical theory. The consecutive links of the chain are the process of selection, the quest for the *essential*, the explanation, the quest for meaning, which concludes in offering meaningful theories about the events and structures of the past anchored in the bottom of the ocean. But, in actual fact, the simile of the cable-chain and the anchor is misleading. The chain of historiographical theories is a spiral. Historiographical theories are received by historicity and by the various types of its imputed consciousness, the philosophical theories. The ever-new answers to the question about the sense of human (historical) existence are not only the starting points of historiographical theories, they are their destination as well. Philosophical theories of history *presuppose* the knowledge of history (histories). There is, however, no knowledge of history other than the one offered by historiographical theories. We do not know history except in and through historiography. We have no other past than the one presented by historiography.

For all of this, historiography does not offer us one past but many. Historiographical theories are conflicting and competing ones. As a result, we are confronted by competing *meanings* and can choose from among them the one which satisfies *our* need for explanation, which, on its part, is deeply rooted in our world-view and practice. Through this very choice, historiography is reintroduced into practice. The disconnection from practice proved to be temporary indeed. The reflux of historiography into practice takes place again in two, even if interconnected, ways: back to philosophy, to the solution of the *Sinnfrage, to the identity of the good and the true,* and back to our social practice, *to historical consciousness in action.*

How can we learn from history?

According to Hegel's well-known aperçu, 'That which is taught, however, by experience and history is that peoples and governments have never learnt anything from history and have never acted according to doctrines that could have been inferred from them.'* Paradoxical as it is, the statement confirms the Hegelian philosophical system as a whole. Out of this context, it is but the summary of a common-sensical 'unwisdom.' People and nations are not obedient children who would not commit a mistake anew for which they had already been scolded by the Big Schoolmaster, History. Neither are they naughty children who refuse to pay attention to the warnings of that same schoolmaster. Nor are they stupid children who burn their fingers twice at the *same* fire. They are not children at all, and there is no schoolmaster called History for them. 'History' as such does not teach us anything; as a result, there is not even the lesson to draw from it that we remain ignorant of its lessons.

We are history. The history of each people is their own past, present and future, and the present itself is at the same time the past of present and the future of present. When we learn, we learn history; we can only learn history. Not to learn history would mean not to learn at all. But Hegel's problem is not solved by this simple statement. The question has to be formulated in the following way: does learning histories imply, or at least allow for, learning *from* history as well?

The question reformulates Hegel's statement while substituting 'histories' for 'History'. Obviously, no one learns from 'History' (with a capital H) because 'History' is only a mental construction of the

*G.W.F. Hegel, *Vernunft in der Geschichte (Vorlesungen über die Philosophie der Weltgeschichte I)*, Akademie-Verlag, Berlin, 1970, p. 19.

philosophies of history. This problem will be discussed later. For the time being, it suffices to point out that 'learning from history' is meant as learning from histories.

There are different types of learning. Having once learnt the elements of arithmetic, we will later apply them spontaneously, and in all cases they have to be applied in order for a task to be accomplished. Having once learnt geography, we may subsequently forget certain bits of information, but we still know just where to turn to when in need of those bits of information. Both types of learning belong to 'learning history', but they have nothing to do with 'learning from history'. 'Learning from history' is roughly akin to learning from our own particular life-experiences. In the case of life-experiences, the cognitive and emotional interpretation of an event belongs to the very event. The testimonies of others (who participated in the event, witnessed it, or were informed about it) and their emotional and cognitive interpretations of that same event can be constitutive in the emotional and cognitive interpretation of the event by the individual concerned, even more so in the recollection and reinterpretation of that same event by the same individual in a later period of his or her life. The coalescence of these interpreted experiences can alter the individual's general attitude to a greater or lesser degree. Whether it alters one's behaviour depends mainly on one's other life experiences in relation to which the *interpretandum* can be considered as a decisive or indecisive experience.

Apart from a possible change of attitude there are other forms of learning from personal experience based chiefly on analogy. If a new situation is considered to be analogical to a previous one, the actor will tend to avoid the *same* type of behaviour, choice or action which was interpreted by him or her as a 'pitfall', a failure, or a misunderstanding in the preceding case. In other words, the former experience will serve as an *orientative model* for the later one. This is a relatively simple story: should a friend betray you, you will be more cautious in making friends later, or, more correctly, in making friends with similar individuals under similar circumstances. Yet this does not necessarily mean that you will not make friends at all. You may take into consideration that the differences are greater than the similarities; you may decide to approach the would-be friend in a different way; you may even consider taking the same risk being aware of its being a risk. But even in the last case, one has learned from one's own history. Thus learning from something does not necessarily mean avoiding similar experiences; it may also mean re-experiencing them with the awareness of the risk involved. Furthermore, we learn not only from our own life-experiences, but also from experiences of others that we were witness to, and again we do this through *analogy*. To learn to *judge human nature*, a knowledge indispensable for our survival and even more so for our capability of leading a 'good life', is in itself an analogical process. We work out a *typology* of human characters and attribute different typical attitudes and motivations to different types. The types function as *orientative* principles (not as organizing ones) called *expectations*. Of course, the interpretation of life-experiences (of one's own and of others) is not merely a cognitive process, it is emotional learning as well. Its product can be a certain kind of 'acquired instinct' (we 'smell' that something is 'rotten' in the behaviour of somebody, or we 'feel' that the person in question can be trusted).

Only what has been learned can be forgotten. Our life-experiences can also be forgotten. They can be forgotten either because we are unable to face them, or because they become irrelevant. Learning to forget can also reasonably be called a learning process. If we cannot forget any of our life-experiences, we will fail to grasp the entirely *new* situations or the new factors in a situation and will handle them according to mere analogy: we will no longer be open to learn something in a *different* way.

Let us approach the problem from a new angle. While sitting at the breakfast table each day we read the newspaper: reports of correspondents, commentaries on political events. While listening to the news on the radio or watching similar programmes on the TV, we do the same. What are we doing in all these cases? We are reading testimonies, testimonies of the past of present. Thus we learn history, which, it should be noted, does not mean that we learn *from* history.

But obviously not everyone reads the same papers, not everyone reads the same reports or commentaries. There are options rooted in interests. If we disregard murder cases or sports news or art criticism and we have only reports on social and economic and political events, it can be assumed that the ratio of personal options will reflect the ratio of personal involvements in the different events the testimonies bear witness to. That which concerns our life directly has a primary option; that which concerns us indirectly or incidentally comes second in the rank; and that which concerns us not at all will come the last (if it appears on the list at all). The question is, however, what the events are that we consider as those 'concerning our lives'. If a reader of these testimonies comes across a report on an event which does not directly affect his/her life, wellbeing or voting behaviour, and considers it to be a testimony which does (or at least might) concern people's lives to a great extent, in the present or in the futre, one is entitled to say that the person in question has learned from history.

In addition to this, there are always quite different commentaries on the same political event: different witnesses give different, often contradicting, testimonies. The reader of the testimonies regarding the past of present has to test the *credibility* of witnesses. We usually have more confidence in witnesses who express *our* world-view to some extent. But our world-view, like all others, is an upshot of learning processes, and one of these processes is that of learning from history. In this case, learning from history occurs prior to the selection of witnesses according to their greater credibility. If, though, our confidence is only founded on the similarity of world-views we run the risk of confiding in biased witnesses. Obviously, biased witnesses cannot promote learning processes for relevant action. But it goes without saying that the fact that a testimony is written that departs from a particular world-view is not evidence of its being biased.

It has to be emphasized that 'learning from history' does not only mean learning 'something good'; one can also learn 'something wrong' from history. Histories are not repositories of exemplary behaviour. However, in accord with the stated project of this book, a particular emphasis will be laid on 'learning something good'.

As mentioned, 'learning from history' is also present in the most trivial cases, namely, in our options of reading testimonies about the past of present. Usually here too we not only read testimonies and test them according to their credibility, but we also work out a theory of our own (even though it is mostly sketchy) by *explaining* events through the arrangement of different testimonies. If this quest for meaning comes to a relative standstill, the new knowledge enriches the world-views and might be implemented in social action. 'Learning from history' means just this kind of feedback, or more precisely, feedback is the accomplishment of learning.

In our epoch, the information pool of the past of present is enormous and that alone would allow for a great variety of theories competing for feedback into various world-views and practices. Manipulation of opinion tries to block the channels of this 'flux to and fro' (world-view-applied-theory-action-world-view) with greater or lesser, but never complete, success. The interest in testimonies is lost if testimonies are neutralized. I would refer back to Bloch once again:

the most trustworthy historical witnesses are the ones who give divergent, but not completely contradictory, testimonies about the same event. If public opinion is fed with the testimonies of witnesses who either relate only the same thing or only the contrary things about one and the same event, the credibility of witnesses is destroyed. The information becomes distorted if the public is kept informed in a completely discontinuous way, if an event which made the headline yesterday disappears from the press today. But not all testimonies can be neutralized and not all interests destroyed. Testing witnesses by their credibility and by the *unbiased* presentation of the chosen world-view becomes difficult in our times, but not impossible. Even though feedback to world-views and actions becomes even more difficult, it will not be impossible. All world-views which cannot be reinforced and modified by such feedback are in a serious danger of losing their meaning.

Should a world-view impede the quest for meaning, that is to say the continuous explanation of the events of the past of present, or should the feedback of applied theories be arbitrary or occasional, 'learning from history' becomes 'overlearning' or 'underlearning'. In the case of overlearning, even the sketchiest theory comprising a few facts regarding social events can query and undermine the meaning of the world-view, every feedback changes its very structure. The world-view becomes fluid, malleable and unfit to lead to further quests for meaning. In case of underlearning, the world-view resists all manner of feedback of applied theories; it becomes rigid and equally unfit to lead any further quests for meaning. World-views are insured against loss of meaning only if they are open systems; open to learn from history, but capable of building new learning processes into their systems without the loss of their coherence, since only a coherent world-view can lead to a further quest for meaning. Learning implies here too the ability to forget theories which were challenged, undermined, and replaced by others.

One could argue against this hypothesis and say that world-views change or resist changes not because of distorted feedback of applied theories or 'theory-sketches', but because of the changing experiences of their adherents. Undoubtedly, the personal experiences (of individuals and groups) have a say in the eventual loss of meaning of world-views. But personal socio-political experiences are also interpreted experiences, and world-views participate in their interpretation. Thus personal experience is not only a source but also a result of world-views. It has been observed that if we only learned from our own lives, we should also rely upon the interpretation of the co-actors and witnesses of the events. But our personal experiences in the socio-political field are mostly very restricted. Even if we believe that the main sources of our 'theory-sketches' arise from our personal experience, this is far from being the case. Items of information procured from other witnesses, interpreted by them, interplay with our own experience in all cases. 'To have a gut feeling' makes us ready to receive special kinds of messages and accept special kinds of theories regarding the experienced event, but the former never replaces the latter. One could rather say that the more confined to our personal experiences we are, the less we can theorize them, for then we have no world-view at all. Of course, learning a world-view is always learning from the human beings who share the world-view. But a world-view is an objectivation that guides the understanding and the actions of all those sharing it and enables them to build *all their interpreted experiences* which are *not shared* by every adherent of the world-view into their common framework of understanding. Arbitrary feedback is the feedback of some experiences and the inability to learn from others. If the world-view becomes rigid, the only experiences which get fed back are those which reinforce previous learning processes, and this is why new learning is impeded.

The learning process of world-views *is not based on analogy.* 'Learning from history' is accomplished in this case by a progressive incorporation of applied theories or 'theory sketches' or even mere testimonies (interpreted experiences) by the world-view in question. The viability of a particular world-view depends on its readiness for learning from history, on its elasticity for incorporation. If the elasticity turns to malleability, the world-view pays with its loss of meaning and progressively ceases to be a world-view.*

Learning from the history of the past of present can also be a *learning for action.* 'Learning for action' can either mean learning to undertake a particular action (or series of actions) or learning *not* to undertake a particular action (or series of actions). This learning process comes about as the result of the combination of three factors. One learns from the interpretation of previous actions undertaken by

---

* The problem of world-views is discussed here only from the aspect of how far they can learn from history. Needless to say, not all world-views are interconnected with the same learning processes, not all world-views claim generality, and different world-views can be combined with each other from different aspects (for example, Catholicism becoming a world-view from the Renaissance onwards can be combined with conservatism, liberalism, romanticism, socialism, etc.).

the same group of people; one learns from the world-view of the group in question; and one learns from the testimonies given and the applied theories presented about actions of other (but similar) groups. The learning process of world-views having already been discussed, the two other components of learning for action have to be briefly looked at.

To learn from the previous experiences of the same group is not as simple as it seems to be, and this is so, first of all, because the identity of a group involves non-identity as well, and does so from different aspects. If the group is institutionalized on the ground of shared interests and/or needs and some common goals, it always has a history of its own; in other words, the history of the group is not identical to the experience of the individuals who comprise it. For those members of the group who have not shared all the experiences, several experiences are only available through testimonies of witnesses. These testimonies are historiographical ones and have to be read in the right way: their credibility has to be tested. This is also true of cases in which testimonies are orally mediated (for instance, old people tell their own stories). If the group is not institutionalized, one has to consider a very wide range of different proportions of identity and non-identity. On the other extreme, the 'past experience' of each member of the group is different and varies individually. Certain similarities between the interpretation of various past experiences constitute the very vague 'common past experience' of the group. But without *any kind* of previous (interpreted) experiences transformed into a vague common experience of a group, there can be no group-action at all. Undertaking a common action presupposes at least some learning from previous personal experiences, whereas not to participate in group action might only be the result of learning from the experiences of previous group actions. Also, as no two situations are identical, 'learning from previous experience' is based on *analogy*. The previous experience, whatever it has been, functions as an *orientative principle* in the new undertaking. If the typology of actions is applied to a new undertaking not in an orientative, but in an organizing way, the action is usually doomed to failure. Here again, we have to reckon with the possibility of 'overlearning' and 'under-learning' from history. Overlearning comes about if one forces the analogy and thereby impedes readiness for the perception of the novel aspects in the situaton; it hampers the actors' ability to relearn. Underlearning comes about if one refuses to learn anything from previous experiences. It concludes in action without orientation. It is obvious that overlearning from past experiences and underlearning with regard to world-views are usually combined, as are underlearning from past experiences and overlearning with regard to world-views. The third component of 'learning for action' from the past of present is learning from the testimonies of witnesses concerning the actions of *other* groups and from theories applied to those actions. The larger the pool of interpreted and theorized items of information, the bigger is the chance for 'epidemic' actions. If an action was undertaken somewhere in the world, different people at another part of the world might get the idea of copying it. The first aeroplane hijacking was the action of a single fool, but the idea of blackmailing governments through hijacking planes very soon became an epidemic, undertaken by various terrorist groups. *Samizdat* was invented by certain courageous intellectuals in the Soviet Union for a particular purpose, but the idea of regularly distributing an opposition 'newsletter' became an epidemic: it has been done not only in Eastern European societies, but in China as well. The student movements of the 1960s originated in the United States and France but they became epidemic throughout almost the whole of the industrialized world. Obviously, the undertaking of a similar action by similar people in a different part of the world is the application of interpreted testimonies as *analogies* for new action. The idea of action procured from the interpreted information and its various theories have an orientative value for all further actions in similar situations and undertaken by similar actors. The possibilities of underlearning and overlearning are at hand here too. Epidemics are always signs of overlearning.

'Learning for action' from the past of present can be multifarious. One can learn tactical or strategical techniques, ethical behaviourial patterns and abilities or ideas of a new approach. But all learning processes can be subdivided into two basic clusters; they can be either of a *pragmatic* or of a *practical* kind. In the first case, the group acquires certain means to increase its power; in the second, it learns to pursue a valuable enterprise appropriate to an equally valuable goal. If learning is practical, success (increase in power, attaining the goal) should be equally practical, but since the action is regarded as being valuable in itself, it can be undertaken even without the hope of success. Learning from history involves differentiating between the practical and pragmatic ways of learning without succumbing to self-deception. If pragmatic learning pretends to be practical, moral transgression may be the result. It has to be added that in the present this substitution does not pay in the long run. If, on the other hand, practical learning pretends to be pragmatic, disillusionment and despair may be the result.

Underlearning and overlearning from the past of present are *wrong options*. Proper orientation leads to right options, and if action is undertaken, to right actions. The *norm* of learning from history (of the past of present) is as follows: *whether you undertake an action or you refuse to undertake it, practical learning should have primacy over the pragmatic.*

Up until this point, Hegel's statement has been reconsidered only in one respect: how *peoples* can and do learn from the history of the past of present. The question of whether governments can and do learn from it, has been deliberately neglected.

The learning process of governments can be clearly distinguished from that of peoples only if we have in mind absolutist states and their equivalents: non-traditional autocracies. In traditional societies, on the one hand, and in democratic-legal states, on the other, no clear line of demarcation can be reasonably drawn. More correctly, the distinction is only clear from the viewpoint of a romantic-elitist world-view. Even though the majority of societies today are only various combinations of traditionalism and autocracy, and this is why the former distinction is far from being outdated, it still seems to be reasonable to restrict the analysis to democratic-legal states, in order to give a basic account of the main question discussed. I am going to disregard models such as tyrant-subject, bellicose elite-obedient folk, hero-followers, etc., and I will only consider more 'prosaic', but at the same time more relevant, models.

It is a mundane fact that the learning of 'peoples' is in itself derivative of the learning processes of different (and often conflicting) interest groups, classes, strata, occupations, etc. The government participates in these learning processes in two ways: on the one hand, it expresses them, and, on the other, it interferes with them. If the 'people' do not learn from history (or if it becomes unable to forget which amounts to the same), the government will not learn from it either. A government unfit to learn anything from history becomes weak and impotent, even if it gives a pretence of strength. One may assume that in a democratic-legal state the decrease of the learning ability of a government indicates a decrease of the learning ability of the population. The Bourbons, who proverbially did not learn or forget anything, were swept away by the 'people' for just this reason. This is often the case with absolutist governments, but very rarely with democratic states, since in the latter the learning process of government and population are very similar in nature.

Learning from the history of the past of present has its *milestones*, the *establishment of new institutions*. New institutions (especially directly political ones) are established in order to prevent certain undesirable past events from recurring and to promote patterns of action and behaviour deemed as more satisfactory or fruitful. From Solon's reform (which put an end to the enslavement of debtors) to the modern constitutions and their different (French, American, etc.) models (which block the restoration of feudalism), the establishment of a new institution always results from a determination to take the lessons of history seriously. Of course, new institutions undergo new learning processes (as, for example, the trade unions have). They can also fail in these processes if they become successively unable to persevere in guiding action in their 'behaviourial patterns' corresponding to new rules (for example, it was in this way that the anti-trust legislation in the United States and almost all international organizations in the twentieth century failed). Trial and error is, however, a learning process by definition. Even a failure can provide us with new knowledge which can be turned into practice (even if it is not necessarily turned into practice) in the establishment of new institutions.

As noted, the milestones of learning from history are not singular actions, but the establishment of new social rules for action that are practically infinite in number. The learning process crystallized in institutions is more like the learning process of world-views than 'learning for action'. Learning is *incorporated* in novel institutions and does not imply analogies. Different lessons drawn from various events are incorporated into the learning processes of world-views; should these world-views be shared on their part by a significant part of the population, they are again incorporated into the new institution. The expression, 'a significant part of the population' is deliberately vague, for it depends to a great extent on the scope and the particular aims of the new institution whether a 'significant part' is the majority of a nation, a class, or an interest group. At the other extreme, one can say that if it is ten people who decide to live and act in compliance with new social rules, their learning will not result in a new 'milestone' of historical learning processes, unless the same new rules become successively accepted and institutionalized by 'a significant part of the population', a portion which will vary in number subject to the character of the institution in question.

Although the 'milestones' of learning from history presuppose mainly 'incorporative' learning processes, *analogy* is not excluded in this case either. Institutions can become 'epidemic' too, even though to a lesser extent than actions. If a new institution is established in a country it can serve as a 'model' for other countries: it may mobilize part of the population of a country with different institutions to introduce this new institution. If it is about single actions, the 'model' can function only in an orientative way, otherwise the action will fail. Yet if it is about institutions as 'milestones' of historical learning processes, the model *can* function in a constitutive way as well; that is to say, the same institution can be established even if with certain modifications (for instance, the institution of civil marriage).

I have stated that learning from the history of the past of present can be learning world-views, learning for action and learning to institutionalize new social rules for behaviour and actions. All three are part of the learning process as a whole.

Up to this point, learning from history has only been discussed as learning from the past of present. However, the more conscious we become of our past, the more our readiness for the messages of the past develops, the less our learning from the past of present can be accomplished without learning from the past. Even a 'pure' interest in the past is in itself the result of learning. Hegel said that no government or people have ever learned from history. But have we got a history at all except in our reconstruction? Is the reconstruction of the past not part and parcel of learning from the past of present?

What is our past? The past of our present *lives* in our experiences and in those of our contemporaries, in other words, in our Togetherness. Even though the historical past continues to live in our gestures, behaviour, language, rules, institutions, in all our objectivations, it does not appear for us as the past, but as our present, unless we *know* it to be otherwise. How can we know it to be otherwise? How *do* we know it to be otherwise? How can the past absorbed in the fabric of our present be recognized as past at all?

The past lives in images, myths and narratives about the past, in the myths, images and narratives which embody the answer to the eternal problem of 'where we came from'. Genesis stories have always provided human beings with *analogies*. According to the ceremony of the myth, whatever happened once will always be repeated, what is ancient serves as a model for repetition; thus the ancient and the present are not distinct. Anyone who repeats the ancient *is* ancient.

Ever since the emergence of the consciousness of history, the past has become partially alienated. It is reconstructed as a model, but at the same time as a story which cannot be repeated any more. A no longer mythical, but genuinely historical, past always implies this double significance. No wonder, therefore, that it can serve both as an analogy and as a contrast with the present.

Our past lives, to the same extent as that of our ancestors, in images, narratives and myths about the past. It is equally an analogy and a contrast and can serve for the present in both of these capacities, although in a more complicated and manifold manner.

Our past lives in the testimonies of dead witnesses, in their interpretations, in the explanations of historical events and social structure. Testimonies can either be signs or symbols (the significance of which may be discovered) or *objectivations that were created in the past and which embody an intrinsic meaning,* like works of art or philosophy. Historiographical works created in the past can be understood as testimonies of their present and as interpretations and explanations of their past. If an ancient work of history offers interpretations which do belong to our body of knowledge, it is its explanatory value that becomes predominant. If not, the work is regarded as the testimony of a past-present age.

Still, witnesses can become witnesses of the past if the present understands them as such. It has already been argued that the pure interpretation of works of art (the reception of the work of art) is accomplished by means of a process in which subject-object identity comes about via temporalizing the eternally valid. This holds true even in the case of merely interpretative receptions of works of philosophy. Works of art and works of philosophy are witnesses of the past only if they are dealt with as such; if they are explained in a space-time dimension. Again, this is undertaken by historiography. Thus no other objectivation but historiography deals with the past, and a witness becomes a witness of the past only within the framework of historiography.

The question of what our past is can therefore be answered as follows: *our past is historiography;* we have not got any other past but the one embodied in the sum total of historiographical works. The question of whether people or governments learn anything from the history of the past is identical to the other of whether they learn anything from historiography. The statement that peoples and governments never learn anything from history suggests that although clever historians discover, explain and interpret our past, foolish or wilful peoples and governments never learn anything from them. Yet historians belong to those same 'peoples and governments' who allegedly learn nothing from history. In so far as they keep writing historiography, they express only the imputed consciousness of their own times. Their achievements belong to the learning process of 'peoples' as part and parcel of the learning process of that very present in and for which the past is constructed. Hence the Hegelian question has to be reformulated. The problem is not *whether* peoples and governments learn anything from 'history', but *how* our learning through historiography, our actual learning from the past, can become practical.

The problem has to be divided into two components: first, historiography as learning process; second, its possibilities of being fed back into practice.

Our age is characterized by a heterogeneity of value systems. All world-views have to be understood via *their* intrinsic set of values, even though they *can* only be understood from the standpoint of one particular world-view, encompassing another particular set of values. This is the paradoxical norm of our practice and this is why it is the paradoxical norm of our historiography as well. The norm of *objectivity* in modern historiography, in other words, the postulate of a proper balance between analogy and alienation in the present-past relation, is due to our human condition. We have learnt to reconstruct histories from our standpoint as being *different* from ours.

Although the historiographical undertaking is in itself a result of a historical learning process, historiographical research endows us with new knowledge and enriches human experience. Going by the norm of true knowledge, historians are committed to the attempt to grasp how something actually happened. While so doing, they have 'to induce the past to speak'. For Burckhardt, the resurrection of the past triggered off by present human effort endows us with *wisdom* from different aspects. 'The wisdom of the ancients' (Bacon) becomes an integral part of our knowledge. Knowledge of ancient histories relativizes our culture. By comparing different histories, we become more able to measure up the gains of humankind against the losses. It widens our horizons. Last but not least, it offers an up-to-date answer to the eternal question of 'where we came from'. In confronting us with different histories of humankind, historiography offers several of humankind's possible autobiographies. It is in this way that the ancient command of 'know thyself' is fulfilled. While writing and reading historiography, while delving into our own past, we acquire a self-knowledge adequate to the requirements of the present. Since the emergence of historical consciousness, and even more since the emergence of world-historical consciousness, the learning process involves learning from history. Our world is four-dimensional; the fourth dimension encompasses the past. What has been learned from history enriches and reinforces the fourth dimension of our human existence.

We learn from history even if we do not draw so-called 'lessons' from it. Historical parallels and contrasts are co-constitutive in our actions. The knowledge that there are no eternal forms of political bodies and social structures, that everything which exists has been developed, and can be developed further or substituted for something else, is present in all endeavours aimed at change. When faced with a new tyranny, stories about ancient ones are lurking at the back of our mind; when participating in a revolution, stories of bygone revolts are recalled. In mortal danger, a nation usually recalls memories of past mortal dangers which were overcome; a vanquished nation remembers past humiliations endured in a manly way; a victorious nation recalls past victories. In all these cases, the events of the past carry momentum for the new events without necessarily figuring as models for any kind of concrete actions.

But the past can play the role of an orientative principle as well if it not only reinforces present actions, but also serves as a model for action. In this case, the various applied theories of historiography (explanations of events of the past) lead the actors of the present to act in a way similar to the way in which the actors of the past allegedly did. Should past events serve as orientative principles for our present actions, we have to avoid overlearning and underlearning even more than in case of learning from the past of present. One cannot solve new problems simply by drawing a lesson from the past; should one try, one would be doomed to failure. Nevertheless, one can solve a new problem, avoiding, at the same time, *typical* mistakes committed beforehand in similar situations, if one is guided by the historiographical reconstruction of the past. If both pitfalls are avoided, we have learned from history, even if we make a *new mistake* from which future actors may learn again.

As mentioned, there are two clusters of feedback in the case of learning from the past of present: the pragmatic and the practical ones. I argued on behalf of the primacy of practical feedback. With regard to learning from the past (from historiographical theories) the same distinction has to be made.

In an earlier chapter I stated that historiography as true knowledge has to be divorced from every kind of pragmatic motivation. Historiography should not be written in order to justify a goal or an action. If an historiographical work does not observe this norm, it does not offer true knowledge, but functions as mere ideology. But even historiographical works which have observed this norm of true knowledge can be used in a pragmatic way and are frequently used in their capacity as ideology. When the wolf wanted to devour the lamb, he justified his goal with an 'historiographical theory': the lamb's mother had allegedly slandered him (at some time in the past). Sometimes, hungry wolves justify their murderous appetites with true historiographical theories (it may have happened that the lamb's mother did slander the wolf, but this was not the real reason for the wolf's devouring the lamb). And because anyone can invent a story, and do so for all kinds of purposes, this is why no one should use this story for any pragmatic purpose. Historiography provides an arsenal of weapons which can be used against our fellow-creatures. History is the history of murder, suffering, looting, oppression. Should these stories be used as means of justification, they cannot but be used as means for further murders, looting, suffering and oppression. This is why the norm that *they should not be used as means* has to be posited.

Historiography can be used in a pragmatic way only if human beings use it against other human beings as a weapon, and it is precisely for that reason that it should not be used in a pragmatic way. Despite this, humankind is now divided into hostile nations, groups, parties, and classes, and this is why historiography is in fact used in a pragmatic way. This is the antinomy of the feedback of historiography. Historiography needs to be used pragmatically as long as there are hostile nations, classes, etc., even though it should not be.

The circularity of 'Is' and 'Ought' intrinsic in pragmatic feedback of historiography can only be overcome by *practical* feedback.

The statement that historiography as true knowledge has to be divorced from practice only temporarily has to be understood in the way that it has to be divorced only from *direct* practice. Were it not disconnected from direct practice, historiography would simply offer stories for moral edification. The practical involvement of historiography is intrinsic in the set of values it operates with, while, on their part, the set of values in question are intrinsic in the philosophical 'higher' theories. Philosophies contrast 'Ought' with 'Is'; they raise the question of human existence, and find the answer to it in the unity of the True and the Good, that is, in Truth, in the highest identification of theory with practice. As the identification of theory with practice, truth leads historiography in its quest for meaning, in all its applied theories about the past. And this is why the feedback of these theories can be practical. They are mediated back to practice by the world-views and philosophies that they have enriched through greater insight into the past. True historiographical theories not only tell us stories which can be used as means, but they endow us first of all with *attitudes, behavioural patterns,* if we are, as free persons, ready to reflect upon our fourth dimension. As a result, were historiographical theories motivated by *a partiality for those who suffered most,* practical feedback would 'perforce' be an attitude of partiality for those who suffer most here and now. The kinds and ways of suffering have always been innumerable; thus historiographies motivated by partiality for those who suffered the most can be practically innumerable as well. The same story can be told in various ways too, since suffering has always been multifarious. Historiographies based on the above principles can break through the vicious circle of pragmatic feedback. In order for an end to suffering, no suffering can be justified any more.

But whatever the practical intent may be, all practical feedback of historiography concludes with 'making sense of history' (Sinngebung). Meaningful historiographical theories suggest to us that we order our present experiences and act upon them according to a sense which is not 'there', but which can be introduced and maintained by and through our world-views and actions. And so historiography leads us back to the unity of theory and practice from which it departed, from which it was separated by its deep dive into the past. And this is the most sublime form of learning from history.

The foregoing analysis seems to have contradicted the previous statements about the possible orientative functions of past events and structures for making us capable of coping with the present. If 'overlearning' and 'underlearning' can be contrasted with proper balanced learning in both practical and pragmatic aspects, how can the thesis possibly be supported that pragmatic learning, being ideological, leads, by definition, to circularity and should be avoided?

In analysing the orientative application of the models of the past of present, I have already emphasized the primacy of practical learning as a postulate for all learning processes. In learning from the past of present, the two forms of learning (the practical and the pragmatic ones) cannot be easily distinguished from one another and this is why they *should* be distinguished and hierarchized. Obviously, all present actions and structures are 'open' ones. In the moment in which actions are undertaken, their consequences are not yet present, and anticipatory intellect is not far-sighted enough even to know whether they will be fruitful from one or the other aspect in the long run. Whether or not they will introduce new values is no less uncertain than whether they will increase the power of the actors. People involved in actions may think as follows: actions which may have beneficial results for others in the long run, *will* have beneficial results in our case as well, and this is why they should be imitated or at least used for orientation. The norm of the primacy of practical orientation is observed if the actor accepts as models only those actions or structures which *maintain* and reinforce relevant and valid values *now* (of course those relevant from the viewpoint of the actors' set of values), irrespective even of the possible and still unknown outcome of the enterprise.

The problem discussed here does not occur if the historical past (not the past of present) is to serve as a model for action. In this case, the actor is confronted with historical events and structures the consequences of which are well-known. It is known what kind of values were developed and what kind of devaluations were triggered through bygone events and structures, with all the consequences they implied. If we use past events as orientative principles, learning cannot serve as a *norm*. Which historical actions and structures of the past can serve us in their capacity of orientative principles, has already been established by true historiographical theories led by the 'higher' theory of historiography. The latter is, as we know, already the unity of theory and practice. As a result, only those actions and structures which have *already been accepted from practical aspect* in terms of our world-view can serve us for the orientation in *pragmatic* aspect. For example, no zealot of the Enlightenment would have chosen the system of Chinese despotism for a model of legislation or would have suggested accepting Nero as the model of a sovereign. But they were mostly unable to avoid cherishing illusions about the so-called 'enlightened monarchs' of their present and acting accordingly, at least until proved to be wrong (as, for instance, Voltaire did in the case of Frederick the Great). If one uses the actions or institutions of the past as orientative principles, *no disillusionment can result.* Anyone who regarded Roman law as the model for the establishment of new legal systems has been perfectly aware of his own intentions. The only ones who suggested the reintroduction of Roman law were those who considered its results desirable. The implications of its reintroduction were well-known, as were their actual effect. However, the acceptance of the institutional patterns of the Leninist party could, and in fact did, lead to disillusionment on the part of several of our contemporaries: they have not observed the norm of the primacy of practical learning from the history of the past of present over pragmatic learning. Rosa Luxemburg's personality was brilliant not only because of the superiority of her anticipatory intellect, but also because she never failed to observe the norm of the primacy of practical orientation.

To sum up: if we learn from the history of the past (that is to say from historiography) via analogical orientation, the feedback of our learning is practical. Even though pragmatic learning may also be involved, pragmatic use is in fact always subordinated to practical use. Only if we accept the practical message of a past event or social structure, can pragmatic learning have any relevance for us. Stalin could (and in fact did) learn from Ivan the Terrible certain techniques of despotic rule; but a democratic leader could learn no techniques at all from Ivan. Yet if someone tries to learn socio-political techniques from the past which have no bearing on his or her worldview and which are thus out of context, he or she does *not* learn from history. We can only learn from history because we are able *not* to learn from it.

We do learn from history because we forget and recall. We can learn both good and bad or we may learn nothing at all. Learning from history involves effort, the concentration of our mental forces, as with all learning. It is painstaking and rewarding, as all learning is. We can make mistakes as we can do in every form of learning. We often have to start again as can happen in all types of learning processes. But we learn just the same, and we learn all the time.

History does not teach us anything – it is in learning from it that we teach ourselves. We are historicity, we are history. We are the teachers and the pupils in the school which is our planet. We only cease to learn when we cease to exist. (We can also learn how we may cease to exist.) The question is not whether, but *what* we learn from history.

History does not 'march forward', because it does not march at all. We march, walk, or crawl in a self-created world. A world created by us can be understood by us, as Vico said. We are not simply groping in the darkness. The beam which illuminates the dark spots of our past is the reflector of our consciousness.

We learn the good and we learn the bad. Indeed, we have to make every effort to learn the good, so that we can follow it, and the bad (wrong), so that we can avoid it. We know that we have not done what we ought to have done and that we are not doing it now either, but we also know that we ought to do it.

We are the past of our future. Our stories will become the stories of future historians and future generations will learn from our stories. They will learn that although we knew what we ought to have done, we failed to do it. For them, all our deeds will be regarded as one 'sample' of the past from among many. For all of this, we are confined to our Togetherness, the absolute present, a limited enterprise. Our resurrection in and through the historiography of the future is no consolation for us. The best we can do is not to look for any consolation. We have our norm and our reinforcement: the norm of true knowledge and good action and the reinforcement that, as far as suffering is concerned, all historical periods are equally close to humankind. We have learned both these things from history.

Let us listen to historiography:

> .... so shall you hear
> Of carnal, bloody, and unnatural acts,
> Of accidental judgments, casual slaughters;
> Of deaths put on by cunning and forc'd cause,
> And, in this upshot, purposes mistook
> Fall'n on the inventors' heads; all this can I
> Truly deliver.

Historiography starts to speak when *one* tragedy is over and all the protagonists have left the scene. It presents *truly* the criminal case wherein the actors do not murder or suffer any more. What happened cannot be changed, only the beam which illuminates the scene of the events can be changed. The beam is changed in every 'here' and 'now', in the past, the present, and the unseeable future. But when the stories are told, the *empathy* of the narrators and that of the audience is aroused. So future narratives will arouse empathy with us. The reinforcement that mortals living in the present can procure is not our resurrection, but it is rather the empathy of future narrators who will truly deliver our story to all those who will listen to it. Historiography passes moral judgments only on historical monsters. It explains human achievements and failures in their space-time dimensions. The future will nail us to the cross of our times where we so rightly belong, and it will do this while sympathizing with our misfortunes and ridiculing our foolishness.

Goethe compared history to a gallery: 'What commotion in this hall of past. One could even call it the hall of the past and the future.... Nothing is passing in it but the one who enjoys and watches.' Only the viewers are mortal, it is true. But we shall very soon become exhibits ourselves.

Part III

Sense and truth in history or philosophy of history

Chapter Fourteen

The specificity of philosophy of history

Historiography is subject to change in our historicity, in other words, to change in its own subject, but historiography has been a continuous undertaking for about 2,500 years. The philosophy of history is no less subject to change in our historicity, in other words, its own subject matter, but it emerged only at a fairly recent stage of historical consciousness. The function of historiography cannot be replaced by any other kind of objectivation, whereas the philosophy of history is only a subspecies of philosophy, not an independent objectivation; it can be replaced by other kinds of philosophies. Consequently, the discussion of the philosophy of history requires a different approach than the analysis of historiography. In the earlier discussion of historiography descriptive and prescriptive elements were always combined. The norm of historiography was suggested as needing to be met by historiographical works in order to live up to the ideal type of historiography. It was assumed that this very norm is, in fact, met by several historiographical works, although not by others. In discussing the philosophy of history, factual and normative aspects cannot be distinguished. First, I am going to discuss its constituents and its message, and later I will make a theoretical proposal for its eventual replacement by a different kind of philosophy, by a philosophy about history, and not *of* history, by a *theory* of history.

In philosophy, the genesis of our existence has always been reflected upon. Thus the reflection upon the genesis of our existence is *not* specific to the philosophy of history.

In philosophy, the emergence of different (particular) social institutions has always been a matter of speculation. Questions like how the state (or *this* state) emerged, how property (or *this particular* type of property) came about have always been raised by philosophers.

Hence reflection upon the development of social institutions is *not* specific to the philosophy of history.

Philosophers have always made statements about the *regularities* of social life. They postulated *causal interconnections* of different kinds and applied them to the social phenomena of their times. They have always formulated *generalized statements* about society. Thus the generation of social *laws*, the application of typologies and the generalization of certain structural and temporal interconnection of social patterns is *not* confined to the philosophy of history.

There have always been philosophers who contrasted the 'ideal' of society with its existing state. Therefore, the designing of 'models' or 'Utopias' of a perfect society is, again, an activity not confined to the philosophy of history.

Before summarizing what is really specific to the philosophy of history, it must be mentioned that these things can be regarded as 'specific' to this undertaking only if they are not present in other types of philosophies. It will be argued later that some of the procedures and theoretical proposals first suggested by philosophies of history belong exclusively to this particular form of philosphy, though some others can be taken over in a reasonable way by philosophies about history, in other words, by theories of history. It is obvious that only the former constituents can be accounted for as 'specific' to the philosophy of history. They are as follows:

1   The central category of the philosophy of history is History with a capital H. All particular human histories are subjected to this particular one. They are supposed to be branches of the tree called History; or are regarded as manifestations of the same essence called History.

2   History with a capital H is comprehended as change. This change has a general *tendency*, realized by the particular tendencies inherent in the different branches or manifestations of History. The general tendency is conceived of as progress or regress or as the repetition of the same developmental patterns (progress = regress) in all branches of History.

3   General statements are formulated regarding History as a *whole*. Even the statement 'there are no general laws in history' is a general statement about History.

4   Causal explanations do not lead us to an understanding of particular events, structures, or particular societies: History as such is explained by them (by causal nexus, final nexus, or both). The

statements that history is the outcome of individual decisions and that
historical development is the outcome of merely contingent factors are
no less explanations of History than the statement that History is the
self-development of the world-spirit.

5   The genesis of existence is identified with the genesis of history.
The universe is either not thematized at all, or it is thematized only
as the prehistory of history, and often simply as its precondition and
limit. The emergence of the philosophy of history was coeval with the
'disenchantment of the world', with the emancipation of the natural
sciences from philosophy, with the tendency to construct nature as a
mere object. The attempt to apply the procedures of natural science to
'History', in order to make social theories 'scientific', is but one
conclusion drawn from the abovementioned tendency.

6   The philosophy of history comprehends the present as the product
of past history. In this way human nature is also conceived of as the
product of 'History'. The historicity of human existence is the focal
point of the anthropology of the philosophy of history, even though
explained in quite different and often contradictory ways.

7   The philosophy of history is only a special branch of philosophy
– it follows the general pattern of all philosophies. It contrasts *Ought*
with *Is*, it infers *Ought* from *Is*. *Is* in this case is history and
historicity, *Ought* is either both, or only historicity. Thus *Ought* can
be conceived of as a new (future) 'step' in the historical progress, or as
a self-awareness of historicity. *Ought* is comprehended here, as in all
philosophies, as the unity of the True and the Good, of theory and
practice, and so as *Truth*. But if existence is understood as historicity
and the human condition as history, truth can be identified with
'truth-in-history' or 'the truth of history'. As Hegel put it: *'die
Wahrheit in der Geschichte'* (truth in history) is constituted by the
philosophy of history. The ideals of philosophy are always the
supreme values; *Is* is measured by the yardstick of supreme values. In
the philosophy of history, supreme values are projected into the future
or the past of History or of historicity. In this case both truth and
supreme values are equally temporalized.

8   In the philosophy of history, the truth of history reveals itself in
the future: in the future of history, of historicity, or of both. It reveals
itself in the future even if it is projected into the past. In this case, the
future is what ought not to be, History itself is constituted from the
standpoint of the ideals (of truth). History with a capital H is not the
past. It is the present which *contains* the past and the future of History
or of historicity. To quote Hegel again: history *'ist im Sinne der*

absoluten Gegenwart' (history stands in the sense of the absolute present).

9   If the absolute present contains the *Is* and *Ought* of history and not just of historicity, the present is regarded as a *turning point.* The present embodies the historical past and is also the cradle of the future. It is the very moment in which all the conclusions of history have to be drawn according to the 'truth-in-history'. 'Here is the time', 'now is the time'; the historical Doomsday is embedded in our very present. The same present which contains the past and the future, is the 'caesura-in-history'. The end of world history is on the agenda unless 'true' history (in contrast to prehistory) is realized 'here and now'. As Saint-Simon put it: 'The golden age of the human species is not behind us, it lies ahead of us... Our fathers did not see it, our children will reach it one day, it is our duty to clear the road for them.'*

The philosophy of history and modern historiography differ from one another in the following aspects:

1   History with a capital H can only be contrasted with Nature (with a capital N). The philosophy of history distinguishes Culture from Nature. This distinction is, however, not basic to historiography: the essential undertaking and commitment of the latter is to grasp a particular culture and contrast it with another.

2   As has already been argued, the philosophy of history does not deal with the past, but with the present. History (with a capital H) is not the past, it is the past and the future in the present. Accordingly, the philosophy of history does not supply us with new items of information about the past. It rearranges the items of information offered by other objectivations – the sciences, art, religion, and, primarily, historiography – from the standpoint of its supreme values, its own truth. Historiography, on the other hand, deals with the past and supplies us with new items of information and theories about the past.

3   The philosophy of history does not 'tell stories'; it does not satisfy our curiosity as historiography does. It does not lead us into communication with the past. Thus the two criteria of objectivity that are relevant for historiography are not relevant for the philosophy of history.

4   The philosophy of history does not imply disconnection from practice. It is formulated with a practical intent. The total reception of

---

* C. H. de Saint-Simon, *La physiologie sociale, Oeuvres choisis,* Presses Universitaires de France, Paris, 1965, p. 69.

the philosophy of history is a commitment to act, to live, and to think according to the supreme values embedded in it. The reception of historiographical theories is, however, accomplished only if the feeling of 'I've got it' can be evoked, if we are persuaded that something really happened in the way suggested by a historiographical theory.

5   In historiography, the present is not regarded as a 'turning point'. More precisely, no historiographical work can *prove* that the present *is* such a turning point and it should not try to. (Though it can suggest it as a hypothesis provided that it makes clear that proving it is beyond its reach.)

6   The philosophy of history may serve as the 'higher theory' of historiography if the historian accepts it as the relevant answer to the question raised regarding the sense of historical existence. But even in this case, historiography has to observe the rules of its own discipline. An historian can accept the notion of History, but cannot study it: he/she can accept the notion of universal progress, but cannot argue for it, let alone prove it. He/she can only work out particular historiographical theories from the *standpoint* of progress. Historiographical theories, on the other hand, may 'flow back' into philosophies of history. Moreover, the historiographical theories which can be 'fed back' into philosophies of history are not only those which were meant as the application of the same philosophy, but also ones which fit into their theoretical framework as items of verification. Historiographical theories have to be 'fitted into' the usual procedure of inference, into the deduction of *Ought* from *Is,* to verify thereby the truth of philosophy. Any historiographical theory can be falsified if the facts which it interconnects and explains are falsified and cannot be replaced by functionally equivalent ones. However, the philosophy of history is not falsified, even if certain historiographical theories used for its verification are. There are always several other theories at hand which can be used in the same way as the falsified ones, in order to prove the 'truth' of the philosophy of history in question. Precisely because the philosophy of history does not deal with the past, but with the present, changing knowledge of the past has no bearing on it whatsoever, but changing knowledge of the present does. If the people no longer acknowledge the validity of the supreme values which make up a philosophy of history, they will turn away from it, even if none of the historiographical theories used by it is falsified.

It has been stated that the philosophy of history does not satisfy our curiosity. But as an expression of our historical consciousness, it satisfies other needs deeply rooted in it. Which kinds of needs? Philosophies of history raise *simple* questions, even though the answers to these questions are far from being simple. The simple questions raised by them are also formulated by the man in the street, by practically everyone who reflects upon his/her life experiences in our world. We experience change in values and institutions, we experience our fate and the fate of others, even of remote peoples, as being interwoven. New events and experiences happen to us, and we participate in new undertakings or we suffer because established ones are shaken. We are the victims of world-catastrophes and we turn our faces towards the first glimmers of the dawn. We cherish hopes concerning the years to come and we despair when they betray our expectations. We ask: what is the sense of all this? We ask whether or not our lives and struggles are vain and fruitless. We ask whether our children will live in a different world, in one better or worse than ours. We ask whether a better future is possible at all; and if the answer is in the affirmative, what we can do for it, if in the negative, when and how we 'missed the bus'. These are questions asked every day and by everyone. We need to get an answer, we need to get answers. The philosophy of history is badly needed because it is exactly these questions which are answered by it.

All philosophies raise the question of the sense of human existence. Human existence over the last two hundred years is experienced as historical existence. Philosophies of history answer the questions about the *sense of historical existence* and so they satisfy the needs of our times. But they claim to answer another question as well, a question about the *sense of history*. In this claim resides the *ambiguity* of all philosophies of history: they equate the sense of historical existence with the 'sense of history'.

'Sense' can be attributed either to statements or to actions.

History (with a capital H) cannot be comprehended as a statement. If we state that 'history has a hidden sense', our *statement* makes sense. It means that *we* attribute a hidden sense to history. One cannot jump, however, from the acceptance of the sense of this statement to the conclusion that history *as such* 'has a hidden sense'. History existed before this statement was formulated. It is nonsensical to assume that history has a 'hidden sense' except in this statement about it, which is a very recent one. Hence the statement that 'history has a hidden sense' is one which makes sense, but which is *false*.

An action 'makes sense' if it is taken in keeping with norms, rules, values, or if it aims at the realization of goals according to the will and design of the actor. We can rule out the first conception because no philosophy of history has ever stated that the 'sense of history' could be grasped and described as a chain of actions undertaken by a certain mystical subject called 'History', and undertaken according to values, norms and rules. The second conception has, none the less, played a certain part in various philosophies of history. It has been assumed that God or some world-spirit set the goal, and human beings realized it. But unless one posits a higher intelligence whose goal is realized by the actors of history, the thesis of the 'sense of history' cannot be supported in this case either.

The only philosophy of history in which the 'sense of history' was well-established was that of Hegel, who succeeded in combining the sense of a statement and the sense of an action. He construed history as a subject which sets and realizes its own goals and at the same time as logical deduction. Various other philosophies of history have only been able to accomplish this task in an inconclusive way.

This explains the alternative suggestion that the statement 'history has a hidden sense' be replaced by another, that 'we make sense of history'. The concept that one 'makes sense of history' implies the idea of a condition: 'We are able to make sense of history if....' (For instance, *if* humankind acts according to some particular values and *if* it controls the outcome of its own actions, then it will make sense of its own history and thus of History.)

This 'weak version' of the theory of the 'sense of history' is by no means less problematic than the 'strong' (Hegelian) formulation. Moreover, it is particularly clear in this case that the question concerning the 'sense of history' has merely been substituted for another concerning the sense of historical existence. In fact, the theory implies an inadmissible extension of individual life-experiences to the 'life of humankind'. If one has lived up to one's commitments in a consistent way, one can state: 'my life had a sense because I made sense of my life'. If one's life has a positive outcome, one can truly state when looking back on numerous sufferings: 'everything makes sense now because I succeeded in making sense of my life.' Even collective subjects are entitled to make similar statements. I repeat: only actions and statements can 'have' sense. How can I make sense of the lives of past generations with *my actions* more than I can with *my statements?* Even if a collective subject succeeds in making sense of its own actions, how can it 'make sense of History' thereby? How can the actors of the past obtain any sense at all from our actions? Do we diminish their sufferings? Do we alter their fate once lived and suffered? The concept of 'making sense of history' is 'bashful' Hegelianism. It is bashful because it lacks the straightforwardness and consistency of the original. It is Hegelianism because it assumes, even though only conditionally, that we can prove that we are the goal and outcome of history and thereby justify retrospectively everything that has happened. But to suggest that if we make sense of our lives, we make sense of history as well is blasphemy.

History has no hidden sense and we cannot make sense of 'History'. The statement that History is senseless suffers from the same ills. What cannot have sense, cannot be senseless either. There are statements and actions without sense, but there is no 'senseless history'. Moreover, the notion of history without sense may suggest that no historical actors (whether individual or collective) can make sense of any of their actions. This is an untrue statement simply because all those attributing sense to history have made sense of their understanding of history and of their actions.

It has been noted that in all philosophies the supreme values (the truth) bear the sense of human existence. In the philosophy of history, the supreme values (the truth) are either comprehended as historical ones or as embodiments of the only worthy relation to our environment as a historical product. Therefore, in the philosophy of history the supreme values are the truth of the human existence as historicity, that is to say, of our *historical existence*. The sense of human existence is understood as the sense of historical existence. In transforming the question about the sense of human existence into the question about the sense of historical existence, philosophies of history express the historical consciousness of an age in which human beings have become *self-conscious* about the historicity of their existence as individuals and as a species. Of course, all stages of historical consciousness have expressed historicity, but it is only the consciousness of reflected universality which encompasses the total self-reflection of the same. The philosophy of history is the philosophy of reflected universality. It was born around the time of the French Revolution, and has taken many shapes and forms, but all of them conceived of the sense of human existence as the sense of historical existence. In so doing, philosophies of history met and still meet the needs of the past or present and, equally, those of our present, since they answer precisely the 'simple' questions raised by everyone who has wanted and still wants to make sense of his/her life over the last two centuries. This is why one is entitled to say that there is a need for the philosophy of history.

Philosophers of history feel this need the same as anyone else and they ask the same questions, but they also undertake to satisfy the need and to answer the questions. They try to make a good case for the sense of historical existence by presenting a powerful answer. However, the subject who answers is historicity as well. His/her *Ought* can only be a historical *Ought*, since the answer to the question about the sense of historical existence can only be formulated as an answer of historicity, an answer-in-history: thus an answer in time-space and not an answer *sub specie aeternitatis*. Each and all of Mannheim's remarks regarding Marx can be applied to all philosophies of history, even if the same problem is less evident in certain other cases. Anyone who reflects on his or her *Is historically*, cannot formulate his or her *Ought* as *universal truth*. In making a good case for their *Ought*, however, philosophers of history feel compelled to present it as 'Universal Truth'. In so doing, they formulate their answers to the question about the sense of historical existence as if they were the answers to the question about the 'sense of history', or 'lack of sense in history', which amounts to the same thing. They infer the future from the present and the present from the past. From this viewpoint, it really does not matter whether the future inferred is thought of as salvation, doomsday or eternal repetition. In all cases, it appears as the 'riddle of history solved', either in an overt or in a covert way. And all this implies an overdetermination in order to solve a problem which cannot be solved by philosophy at all.

It is obvious from this description that the philosophy of history is defined here in a broader than usual sense. There are several conceptions restricting the application of this notion only to those philosophies which plead for universal progress. Even so, I wish to argue that philosophies which waged war against doctrines of progress and denounced them as 'philosophies of history *sui generis*' were of the same provenance in all basic aspects. The philosophy of history is not an episodic undertaking starting with Hegel and (probably) ending with Marx, but a general trend in the philosophy of the past two centuries. It is the rule rather than the exception. Even if one agrees with the assertion that Hegel's philosophy represents the 'model case', the 'ideal type' of a consistent philosophy of history, it is far from being the only representative example. Obviously, *not all* aspects and characteristics of the philosophy of history can be pointed out in *all* philosophies of history. It would be a vain effort even to try to do this.

But the majority of these characteristics are constitutive in all philosophies of history, even though their combination may vary.

Watkins wrote: 'Philosophies of history attempt to capture future without realizing that if we knew future, we could control the present and so such discoveries would be useless.'* In this statement, Watkins takes the false consciousness of the philosophy of history at its face value. Although the philosophy of history attempts to 'capture the future', it never in fact does so, because this cannot be accomplished. The philosophy of history tries to do this because it wants to make a good case, and because it wants to answer the questions raised, the questions about the sense of historical existence. In so doing, it overdetermines its task. It confronts us with our future in the form of a paradise lost or paradise regained, as light or darkness, as everything or nothingness come to realization, but in all its variations it confronts us as the 'plenitude of times'. Yet this is far from being a futile undertaking. It implies promise and warning. It is a function of the philosophy of history to promise and to warn. Overdetermination makes promise and warning powerful, and both promise and warning are badly needed.

If philosophy only undertook to answer the question about the sense of historical existence, it would overcome false consciousness and overdetermination. It would not provide us with false promises and warnings either. It would renounce attempts to ponder on the 'sense of history'. Yet it would become thereby unable to deduce *Ought* from *Is;* it would become an 'incomplete' philosophy. Instead of a philosophy of history, it would be transformed into a theory of history.

A theory of history could, in principle, replace the philosophy of history, and all sorts of arguments can be mobilized in order to justify this replacement.

But it is better to insist on the 'sense of history' and on 'making sense of history' than to renounce the quest of making sense of our actions and lives altogether. It is better to insist on the 'truth in history' than to renounce the quest for truth. It is better to overdetermine and to produce thereby forceful promise and warning than to give up the attempt to promise and warn altogether.

This is why - despite severe criticism of the false consciousness of the philosophy of history, despite all scepticism in regard to its

---

*Quoted in: Arthur C. Danto, *Analytical Philosophy of History,* Cambridge University Press, 1965, p. 284.

achievement, despite awareness of the dangers inherent in this undertaking, both theoretical and practical – one has to repeat with Herder: *'Auch eine Philosophie der Geschichte zur Bildung der Menschheit'* (a philosophy of history, too, is needed for the education of mankind).

Chapter Fifteen

The notion of universal development as the basic category of the philosophy of history

The developmental tendencies of particular civilizations or political bodies were consistently scrutinized by philosophers and historians long before the emergence of the philosophy of history. The main concern of the philosophy of history is, however, a wholly different problem, namely the cognitive establishment of a developmental scheme in 'History' (with a capital H) as a whole. All theories of development, be they particularistic or universalistic, have to arrange all events and structures understood by them as elements of one and the same social process, and have to evaluate them according to the 'place' they occupy in the temporal sequence, that is to say, in the life of the social entity in question. If one reconstructs the life of the social entity called 'ancient Rome', one has to 'cut out' events and structures which can be grasped as belonging to 'Rome', in order to establish a developmental scheme of 'Rome'. In this case, the 'one and the same social process' (Rome) is grasped as a continuity, and the developmental sequences of events and structures have to be understood as discontinuous stages of this very continuity. These stages are equally amenable to evaluation as periods of progress, as golden ages, as decline, and the like, and as the sequence of stages interpreted as a chain of changes following an internal developmental tendency. The philosophy of history uses the same method: all the same, it does not apply it to one or another particular civilization or political body, but to 'History' as a whole. In so doing, however, it has to construct a 'unit' which cannot be cut out of human structures or events because it encompasses all human structures and events. The 'unit' so chosen is not a 'closed' but an open one, and its logic cannot be reconstructed from its *end result* since this result is not yet given. As a consequence, the logic inherent in the 'unit' cannot be reconstructed at all, it is (and remains) *unknown*. And this is why philosophies of history, in order to be consistent, have to include the *future* in the logic of their unit as well, as if it were (or could be) known. The developmental logic has to be established from assumed knowledge of the future. In this regard, it does not matter whether the philosophy of history operates with a strong or a weak argument. It can suggest: this *will* be the future, because this *will* be the outcome of the logic of 'History'; or it can suggest: if there is any future, *this* is what it will be like. The alternative formulation (either–or), the permissive formulation (if–then), and the apodictic formulation (of necessity) do not differ on this main point: they all suggest the acceptance of a developmental logic inherent in the undertaking called the life of humankind. Thus the philosophy of history, in order to grasp 'History' as a unit, a continuity characterized by *one* logic, *one* developmental tendency, is compelled to arrange *all* human cultures in one single line, and evaluate these different cultures according to the place they supposedly occupied in the life of humanity. The application of the same method to particular entities and to 'History' as a whole leads to completely different theoretical consequences. As Barraclough put it, 'It is one thing to talk of progress of one civilization, another to talk of progress from one civilization to another – by which we affirm that the spirit of one civilization is more "advanced".'* One only has to add this: even if no civilization is considered as 'more advanced' than others, the *arrangement of all civilizations* is nevertheless accomplished in exactly the same way. When Ranke stated that *every* civilization is equally close to God, he was also making a statement regarding 'History' with a capital H (history as a whole), and equally arranged *all* civilizations in a circle (around God). He assumed that the future, too, will again be another link in that same chain (or circle), and a link not better or worse than the anterior ones, but one equally close to God. It has to be added that the older Ranke changed his mind in this regard, and viewed the future as a progressive period (in a permissive way).

If 'History' is continuity as such, discontinuity is regarded as the life of different cultures. These cultures are usually classified as 'advanced' or 'less advanced', 'progressive' or 'regressive' ones, according to their contribution to the basic tendency or logic of 'History'. Only very rarely does it happen that the arrangement exactly follows the temporal sequence of particular cultures, and even

---

* Geoffrey Barraclough, *History in a Changing World*, Blackwell, Oxford, 1957, p. 230.

if it does, only in conditional terms. Philosophies of history mostly arrange cultures in a very sovereign manner: they combine temporality with an emphasis on 'representative'. Some nations are evaluated as 'world-historical' as against others, and thus – irrespective of temporal sequence – are understood in principle as 'more advanced' just as some others are evaluated as 'regressive', 'primitive', again irrespective of temporal sequence. Such ordering is obviously determined by evaluation. Philosophers of history imagine the *future*, and also have preferences for actions and types of behaviour in the *present*, and because the images present the *value* for the periodization and thereby its *criteria*, they *define completely* the way in which these philosophers arrange different cultures. Should Superman and his culture be conceived of as the only future worth living, bourgeois democracies obviously could not be understood as the embodiment of 'advanced' civilization. It is equally obvious that if one opts for 'piecemeal engineering' based on the increase of knowledge, the same bourgeois democracies will be comprehended as the most advanced forms of history. Thus the periodizations of history are not historiographical in nature. They always have to be 'corrected' if applied by those historians who accept one or another philosophy of history as their 'higher' theory. The function of the arrangement of different cultures from the viewpoint of 'History' in philosophies of history is not primarily the periodization of the past, but the *ensuring* of overdetermination, in order to make promise and warning forceful. In the philosophy of history, 'periodization' has to be *evocative* precisely from the angle of promise and/or warning. The possibility of variation in the process of arranging cultures is theoretically infinite but representative world-views and their respective sets of values are limited in number, and this is why the variations are equally limited. The only arrangements which make sense (that is to say, the only ones which appeal to our historicity) are those which imply answers raised by this historicity.

The philosophy of history is the expression of the consciousness of reflected universality, and 'reflected' has to be emphasized here. Christianity, following on in the wake of Judaism, also made promise and warning forceful. Promise and warning were here equally backed, but not made forceful, by 'periodization'. Just the opposite was the case: it was promise and warning, based on belief in a deity, in a divine design, that made periodization forceful. The philosophy of history cannot simply be understood as secularized Christianity, mainly because of the switch of paradigm. The paradigm is completely switched, not only in the case of those philosophers who attempted to verify their promise and warning through science, but also by those who constructed a new (individual) mythology. No Christian philosopher was compelled 'to argue for' the Last Judgment, but Sorel, to mention one example, had to argue for the myth of the general strike, and he did argue: he argued with history. His nostalgic description of a 'bellicose' bourgeoisie, followed by a period of decadence represented by peace-loving politicos ready to compromise, was viewed as a rearrangement of cultures in order to *prove* the relevance of the promise embodied in the myth. Even in this extreme case, it was history that made the promise forceful and not vice versa. The fruitful inconsistency of philosophy as a whole, contrary to the intentions of its authors, cannot happen with quasi-prophetic philosophies of history, though it does happen occasionally with philosophers who buttress their promises with science. This is the fallacy involved in the genuine attempt to avoid arbitrary periodizations as far as possible, the most praiseworthy fallacy in that it generates a self-reflection of the theory, together with a self-reflection on the promise contained in this very theory. If this kind of self-reflection hinders the reinforcement of the original promise, the undertaking collapses. If the opposite is the case, the philosophy of history completes itself by exhausting its ultimate possibilities.

It has been argued that the consensual value-idea of our modern age is that of freedom. No wonder, then, that freedom is the consensual value-idea of all philosophies of history. This is the second reason why philosophies of history cannot simply be denounced as secularized forms of religion. Neither in Judaism nor in Christianity was freedom regarded as the Supreme Value as it is in philosophies of history. Even the value of happiness is either subordinated to that of freedom or, at least, identified with the latter. The basic differences and contradictions between the various philosophies of history are due to their different and contradictory *interpretations* of the value of freedom. Not only does the answer to the question of 'what is freedom?' vary, but the sphere of objectivation to which freedom has to be attributed also displays the greatest diversity. But in each case progress is regarded as an increase in freedom, regress as decrease in freedom, and 'eternal repetition' as an equal amount of freedom or unfreedom or the eternal repetition of increases and decreases in freedom. If industry is regarded as the repository of freedom, the increase in industrialization will be seen as progress. (As Saint-Simon put it: *'L'industrie libérera l'humanité du joug de l'Etat'* – 'industry will liberate humankind from the yoke of the state'). If industry is understood as the repository of unfreedom, an increase of industrialization will be comprehended in terms of regress (see, for example, Ferguson: industry, the child of ignorance, makes slaves of all of us). If freedom is understood as a power of an heroic elite, the periods regarded as exemplary will be those that ensured the power of an heroic elite. If freedom is understood as the equality of all, the periods that ensured (or almost ensured) equality to all will be regarded as exemplary. If freedom is localized exclusively in the human will, there is no progress or regress, because we either are (were) always free or never. But promise and warning are unmistakably present even in the last case: we are promised that nothing except ourselves can do any harm to us, and we are warned to never believe in any kind of promise.

As all philosophies of history are different, so the theories of development of 'History' constituted by them are different. The typology of these theories that I am going to work out in the following section will therefore not denote any particular philosophy, but only certain basic tendencies common to the variations of the undertaking.

Theories of progression

Going by this conception, 'History' has a tendency to progress, in other words, the *continuity* of the unit called 'History' has to be grasped as a development from a 'low' stage to a 'high' one. The frame of reference is the *present* as a *turning point* to the 'much higher' or the 'highest'. Hence theories of progress adopt the stance that 'here is the time' and 'now is the time' to undertake the final step in the chain of progress, to recognize that our present embodies the outcome of history, to choose 'progress' as our value, to mobilize our energies for times to come, and so forth. Of course, these are different conceptions bound together by the emphasis on progress and on the present as a 'watershed' in historical development. From this aspect it is of secondary importance whether or not progress is understood as unilinear, whether it is mainly related to one objectivation or conceived of as an all-embracing development, whether it involves the concept of 'perfection', whether it is formulated ontologically. Progress can be posited as absolute or conditional, and the question whether the notion of 'progress' can be applied as an evaluative category or as a seemingly value-free notion is of no importance: all the various philosophies of progress belong to the same cluster. Philosophers such as Kant, Hegel, Marx, Husserl, Bloch, Lukács and Sartre have almost nothing in common except this emphasis on one kind of progress in 'History', as progress towards freedom. It is an altogether different and separate problem that the interpretation of freedom varies in different philosophies (indeed certain interpretations may even contradict one another).

Theories of regression

This perspective holds that 'History' has a tendency to regress: the continuity of the unit called 'History' is grasped as a development from a 'high' to a 'low' stage. History is the story of a decrease in freedom. In terms of the theory of regress the norm of 'developing' our present society is not relevant because 'further development' can only mean a further decrease in freedom, and the self-destruction of our species. We have lost, 'here' and 'now', the possibility of any kind of 'free' future. It is of secondary importance to which objectivation, to which 'historical moment', the process of regress is related. It is usually the so-called 'primitive societies' that are regarded as the embodiments of 'golden ages', but occasionally antiquity or medieval periods have been conceptualized as the starting points of the 'decline'. All versions of romanticism belong to this cluster; its greatest philosophical representative in modernity is undoubtedly Heidegger.

Theories of eternal repetition

According to this conception, 'History' can be grasped as the repetition of the same developmental sequences (progress–regress) or as a varying combination of the same basic patterns. Either human freedom and/or unfreedom does not increase or decrease, *or* the increase and decrease in freedom repeats itself again and again in the same manner. The present can be grasped as a turning point towards 'betterment' (even though only temporarily) or as a futureless period (dependent on the whole philosophical conception). But usually, the idea of eternal repetition is more akin to theories of regression, especially in our century (as, for instance, Toynbee or Lévi-Strauss), or is at least of a highly pessimistic character, as was Freud's philosophy of history.

A theory of history that may replace the philosophy of history involves the *value* of progress but, in contrast to various philosophies of history, it does not *ontologize* progress. On the other hand, all philosophies of history ontologize 'progress', 'regress', and 'eternal repetition'. The 'trends' of history are comprehended in them as *factual* ones. In order to distinguish theories of history from the philosophy of history, the different types of ontological interpretation of progress have to be briefly looked at.

1   The modern (bourgeois) society and state is both the *culmination* of historical progress, and the point of departure of a linear progression. Progress in the past is interpreted as qualitative, progress projected into the future as quantitative, as further increase in knowledge, accumulation in wealth, growth of complexity. Entirely different philosophies may grasp future progress in a similar way, from Kant (until 1791), through to Hegel to the theories of progress in positivism.

2   Modern (bourgeois) societies are products of progress. Their developmental tendencies lead, however, to a qualitative 'rupture' in the future, to a partial or total social revolution, hence to a new process of a practically infinite progress. The history of the past will be transcended in the future, whereas the results of the various kinds of learning processes acquired in the past will be implemented and brought to perfection. (All rationalist socialist theories belong to this cluster, from Kant's last philosophy onwards.)

3   Modern (bourgeois) societies are products of regress, and for this reason progress is viewed as a *total rupture* with the history of past (and present). The qualitatively new future has nothing to do with quantitative accumulation; it must be a 'Great Salvation', an act of redemption and self-redemption. The future is a mythological image rather than a rational Utopia or model and it is often related to the myth of the biological transformation of human beings. This theory is located on the borderline between the philosophy of history and prophecy pure and simple. In its extreme formulation (which can be found, for instance, in Sorel) it rejects the application of the notion of 'progress' altogether. Nevertheless, it has to be counted as one of the conceptions of 'progress' because there are no fixed lines of demarcation between the second and third formulations (see, for instance,

Marcuse's later work). But it is worth mentioning that this extremist version of the theory of progress can be (and in fact often is) combined with a universal theory of regress or 'eternal repetition' (as in Toynbee or Pareto). And Rousseau was the philosopher who combined almost *all* possible theories of the philosophy of history.

It has been mentioned here that philosophies of history rearrange 'History' as the basic unit and continuity, on the basis of discontinuous phases or stages defined as 'lower' or 'higher', 'less advanced' or 'more advanced', from one or another aspect. This arrangement or re-arrangement can follow a *mechanistic,* an *organistic,* or a *dialectical* pattern. It has to be stated in advance that if mechanistic or organistic arrangements are restricted to one single objectivation or social phenomenon alone, they can even perform this task without 'lining up' historical stages on a developmental scale. In this case they have nothing to do with the philosophy of history, but rather with historiography or historical sociology. Yet this self-restriction occurs very rarely, even when it is intended, because it presupposes a completely value-free operation. In contrast with mechanistic and organistic theories, dialectical conceptions of development are always seated in philosophies of history.

The mechanistic concept of development is based on the arrangement and comparison of quantifiable social data, or at least of social data which are *seemingly* open to quantification. Theories operating with this concept measure aspects of society along 'more' or 'less' lines – such as increase in population density, increase in *per capita* production, increase in scientific knowledge. They also can measure societies as 'small' or 'large' as regards actual size. It is a simple operation if the arrangement is based only on the comparison of one single factor. But if several factors are taken in consideration (and this must happen in order to undertake a line-up of *whole* societies), the mechanistic concept of progress leads to confusion and self-contradiction. Increase in one type of knowledge can go hand in hand with a decrease in another type of knowledge. If the population density decreases, an increase in *per capita* production (if it can be measured at all in past societies) can go hand in hand with a decrease in production. A larger society does not always produce more goods or greater knowledge than a smaller one. And, more importantly, an increase in freedom – the supreme value of the philosophy of history – is far from being proportional to all other types of 'increases'. This shortcoming is responsible for the fact that mechanistic conceptions of development are very rarely 'complete' theories. In the main, they are formulated in order to denote (and establish) the 'independent variable' of historical progress (or regress).

The organistic idea of development is based on the arrangement and comparison of total social entities according to their inherent *structure*. The basic elements of these theories are not 'small' and 'large' or 'less' and 'more' but 'simple' and 'complex' or 'immature' and 'mature'. Long before the discovery of systems theory, several philosophies pictured societies as organic systems. The comparison between philogenesis and ontogenesis was at hand. 'History' allegedly started with societies which could be compared to infants and children, and these were followed by adolescent societies, and later still by adult ones. The same idea can be formulated as the 'growing complexity' of social bodies. The organistic concept of development can circumvent the contradictions of its mechanistic counterpart. However, it runs the risk that no mechanistic conception ever has to face when suggesting directly the superiority of those societies regarded as 'more complex' or 'more mature'. For a mechanistic conception, an increase in one factor does not necessarily qualify a society to be ranked as 'higher' in its *totality*. The organistic theory is, however, holistic, and this is why it cannot be proved that an increase in complexity also implies an increase in freedom (or vice versa).

The dialectical concept of development is a synthesis of the mechanistic and organistic conceptions. Its specificity is not exhausted by the emphasis on possible setbacks, or even catastrophes that could block progress. Also, mechanistic and organistic theories proper can take account of 'regressive' stages in historical development. Dialectical theories 'line up' social structures or cultures in a chain as 'wholes' in the same way that organistic theories do (according to their complexity and 'immaturity'), but they also measure and compare two or more concrete objectivations or social entities inherent in the structures in question by using the yardstick of 'more or less', 'small or large', just as mechanistic theories do. They account for the discrepancy or contradiction between an increase in one respect and a decrease in the other, or between increase and stagnation. Thus progress is construed as a *contradictory* process. In Hegel's view, history marches forward at the cost of individual happiness, an epoch 'standing higher' can be less favourable for specific types of artistic creation than one 'standing lower'. Moreover, the majority of dialectical theories directly reflect on the increase or decrease in *freedom*. Freedom is precisely one of the yardsticks (though never the only one) by which progress can be measured. For Condorcet, the progress of knowledge is absolute, but not so the progress of freedom. Knowledge can produce progress at the cost of freedom. The same duality holds true of the Marxian concept of alienation. Freedom did indeed increase in one respect (in the relation of society to nature), but it did not increase in other aspects; moreover, it occasionally decreased (with respect to the freedom of the individual). Considering the fact that freedom is the consensual value-idea of philosophies of history, it is obvious that in terms of dialectical theories, progress has to be understood as *conditional.* It can be formulated as follows: provided that all contradictions of progress are abolished in the future, history can be comprehended as a progressive development. Nevertheless, dialectical theories are generally not formulated conditionally; they rather suggest that the condition inherent in them will, of necessity, be met in the future. As Condorcet put it: 'the progress of knowledge and that of liberty *must* become inseparable'.* Last but not least, precisely because the concept of freedom always involves the concept of the *individual* (and, even though subordinated to freedom, individual happiness), dialectical conceptions of development imply a tension between the standpoint of the 'whole' and the standpoint of the 'individual' human beings. They adopt the holistic and individualist approach at the same time – though with holism taking priority – on the grounds that future development will reduce or completely abolish the tension prevailing in the historical past and present.

All ontological theories of development, all theories which assume that 'History' has in fact 'unfolded' in one or the other direction, can accomplish the task of 'lining up' cultures and societies (positioning them in the 'chain of development' of History) by emphasizing one or several *indicators* of progress (or regress). Of course, the same indicator has to be applied to all societies and cultures. It is only with the guidance of the indicator that we can 'read off' whether one society is 'more developed' than another. I have already mentioned that in principle any social phenomenon can be used as an indicator, but in fact only a very limited number qualify for this task. In the last instance, all indicators ever applied by the philosophy of history can be reduced to two: knowledge (of some kind) and freedom (of some kind). But these two variables offer a very wide range of particular options. Which indicator is chosen from among many is always

---

* In *Theories of History,* ed. Patrick Gardiner, Free Press, Chicago, Illinois, 1959-60, p. 53.

dependent on the primary value (values) of the philosophers of history. This depends, first of all, on our willingness to grasp 'History' as a 'unit' of progress or regress or eternal repetition, it depends on our concept of praxis, on our image of the future, and on our image of the bearers of this future. Philosophies of history are contrasted with each other simply by applying *different* indicators or by reinterpreting the same indicator or by people evaluating an indicator differently. From one standpoint, production is the indicator of progress; since production has increased, history is making progress. From another standpoint, industry destroys happiness and livelihood, culture and freedom: if industry makes progress, humankind is regressing. From yet another standpoint, adjustment to the natural environment is the only relevant criterion by which societies can be measured, and since all societies can adjust equally well to their natural environment, there is neither progress nor regress. Yet another suggests to us that language is the criterion by which human societies can be measured, and since all languages accomplish the same function equally well, there is no progress at all – a stance to which the adherent of a different position would reply that speech acts have developed (in the sense of becoming more manifold and more equal) and as a result history has made progress. Or one can adopt the position that knowledge is the indicator of development; that we possess always more and more knowledge. And, the reply to this is that there is never a larger, only a different cluster of knowledge. The first statement implies the concept of progress, the reply does not.

The choice of the 'true' indicator depends on the answer to the question of what *true value* is. If there are *several* true values (as I assume), there are several 'true' indicators of progress as well. However, no philosophy of history can be satisfied with this answer, they all need an ontological proof of the existence of their God. They get the ontological proof by using (and misusing) the indicator of progress as its independent variable. Philosophies of history man-oeuvre themselves into great difficulties through this operation. On the one hand, they posit history as the upshot of human action, and on the other, they alienate that same human history from human action and treat it as a mere object, as natural scientists do with nature. It is obvious that if histories depend on human action, no independent variable can be ascribed to them, let alone to 'History' as such. It is worth mentioning that only once has this internal contradiction been theoretically resolved, namely, in Hegel's philosophy of history. If the development of history is identical to the development of the world-spirit towards a subject-object identity posited from the start, whereas the indicator of progress (i.e. freedom) expresses the unfolding of the independent variable (reason in history) from its state of substance to its becoming subject, the abovementioned contradiction does not even emerge. But the price paid for the coherence of the system is the elimination of the will to transcend the present, the reconciliation with reality. No other philosophers of history were willing to pay such a price. The elimination of the contradiction was conceived of by them as a project, or an *Ought*, according to their values. And this is why they could not eliminate (or only seemingly eliminate) the difficulties. They could not totally conceal or eliminate the evaluative source of ontological constitution: the procedure by which what was originally a true value was posited as the true indicator of progress, and as an independent variable as well: that a rational but subjective choice served as the objective criterion of development (a justifiable procedure as long as methodologically deliberate), but that finally the objective development thus constructed was disconnected from the subjects of development.

It has been noted that in dialectical theories of development progress is interpreted as a contradictory process. As a result, dialectical theorists (except Hegel, for whom contradictions are only the expressions of the self-development of world-spirit) have to operate with *two indicators*. But if the function of the two indicators was identical, the ontological establishment of historical progress would become impossible. As Collingwood put it: 'If there is any loss, the problem of setting loss against gain is insoluble.'* This is why dialectical theorists also have to elaborate the idea that one of the two indicators is the decisive one; that an increase of one social factor ensures an increase in the other, in the past, present and the future. It is one indicator only, not both, that indicates our arrival at the 'turning point' of history towards perfection (or in the case of theories of regress, to the Fall). Only one indicator can function as the *independent variable* of progress (or regress); the other indicator measures, however, the realization of values. Thus the first indicator serves as the principle of explanation whereas the second serves as the regulative-practical idea for human will.

There are several versions of this idea. For instance, Kant in his last period worked with three indicators and this is why he established two

---

* R. G. Collingwood, *The Idea of History*, Oxford University Press, 1963, p. 329.

different 'turning points'. The three indicators are: needs, the 'ethical world' (*Sittlichkeit*), and morality. The argument is roughly as follows. Up until now, the development of needs has preceded the development of the 'ethical world' (*Sittlichkeit*), hence progress has been achieved through evil forces. The first turning point will occur when the 'ethical world' takes priority, introducing a period of eternal peace and a process of quantitative progress during which evil will be controlled, but will not disappear. This progress can open the way for the realization of morality (the second turning point) and for the establishment of human perfection in a completely moral world, of the unification of *homo noumenon* and *homo phenomenon*, the unification of the idea and the empirical existence of humankind. Marx, who never accepted the division of human race into 'noumenon' and 'phenomenon', conceived of only one turning point. This is that the wealth of the human species (the generic essence) has developed up until now exclusively on the level of social objectivations, but it could not be appropriated by individuals. Moreover, individuals were impoverished while social wealth increased. The turning point (prepared by the progress of universal wealth on the level of societies as wholes) will occur when individuals become able to appropriate all the wealth produced. This turning point was also seen by the young Marx as a unification of individual and species.

Theoretically it is not impossible to elaborate a dialectical concept of progress without relapsing into ontology and without constructing so-called 'laws' of historical development. In this case, progress could serve as a regulative idea, though without the assumption that history actually has made progress according to this or that general historical law. Kant experimented with this conception and this is why he posited the teleological progress of history as a theoretical and practical idea. But he also regarded the development of 'the ethical world' as actual progress, and both the development of needs and of the 'ethical world' as an indicator of explanatory value. Unquestionably, promise and warning have to be made powerful enough to catch human minds. The result is that overdetermination through 'ontologization' is a great temptation, and generally speaking, philosophers of history have yielded to it.

Chapter Sixteen

Universal historical laws: goal, law and necessity

History (with a capital H) is the past, the present, and the future. An indicator of progress or regress in it is, as a result, an indicator of *future* progress or regress. In dialectical theories the second indicator (which serves as a measure of values and not as an explanatory principle of the past) is also ontologized, even if only with regard to the future. What ought to be, will be.

All philosophies of history claim to formulate true statements about the 'history' of the future. The contradiction intrinsic to the attempt to regard History as the outcome of human volition and action and the conception of that same History as a mere object become even more manifest in relation to the future than to the past. If true statements can be formulated about 'History' of the future, nothing can depend on human will, or rather, human will has to be understood as a mere manifestation of universal historical laws. History becomes quasi-nature, whether this is intended or not.

The formulation of statements about History-in-the-future that have a claim to truth is not prognosis, or even prediction. Those making prognoses always have the future of present in mind, not 'Future' (this derivative of 'History') and are restricted to one single social phenomenon or to certain interrelated phenomena. This is mostly relevant in cases of repetitive activities in which individual will has to be taken as given. (An example of this is a prediction regarding an increase in steel production.) But even unilinear prognoses often prove to be mistaken (as is the case with almost all prognoses about the present economic crisis). Prediction is of itself always hypothetical. The following assertion makes sense: if this or that condition is met, this or that will be the outcome. It is obvious that prediction can only be relevant as regards the future of present, and again, it has to be restricted to certain interconnected social phenomena alone; it cannot imply many factors for the very reason that all possible conditions have to be taken into consideration. Yet according to the philosophy of history, 'History' (historical development of the past and the present) is viewed as a 'sufficient cause' of the future, and hence the future development of History is grasped in an unconditional way.

Let us leave the sphere of history for a moment, in order to discuss similar problems in human everyday life. A shoemaker can say: 'your shoes will be ready tomorrow' and a young man can say to a young woman: 'I love you forever.' Both are statements about the future, both are commitments, both are promises. The shoemaker has committed himself to repair the shoes by the next day, he has promised it. Equally, the amorous young man has committed himself to his girlfriend for good, he also has promised it. It is a possibility that the shoes will not be ready next day and that the young man will not love his girlfriend forever. In this case the person to whom the commitment had been made will say: 'you lied.' All the same, one can only lie if one knows (and is able to tell) the truth. In the shoemaker's case (provided that his conditions did not change during the day) one is justified in saying: 'you lied.' It is reasonable to assume not only that he has not kept his promise, but also that he *knew* that he would not keep it at the moment of the commitment, or at least that he *could* have known that he might not be able to keep it. He could tell the truth, but he did not tell it (on purpose, because of negligence or simply having forgotten certain other commitments). Such statements are similar to a prognosis: they can be true or false in the moment of their uttering. If proved true or false, their being true and false *in the moment they were uttered* is proved as well (provided that conditions did not change between the time of making the statement and the time the promise was to have been kept). Should, though, the young man grow older, and cease to love the girl to whom he committed himself with the promise ('I will love you forever') and should the woman tell him, 'you lied', the following answer has to be (or at least can be) accepted as true: 'I never lied to you, I told the truth, because when I told you that I should love you forever, I really meant it, I really felt like that.' And so the commitment, the promise, is considered here to be a *report on feelings*. Whether the report is true or false depends completely on the fact of whether this feeling was the case. If the feeling existed, the statement was true; if it did not, it was untrue. But irrespective of whether it was true or untrue, the truth of the statement did not (does not) depend on the realization of the commitment. In all similar cases (for instance, in the case of the statement that 'I shall fight for my country till my last breath') the promise is an emotional or moral commitment, (or both), but not an epistemological assertion. In the realm of instrumental rationality there is such a thing as prognosis; in the realm of value rationality there is not.

The philosophy of history has to be understood as a value-rational commitment even though it is more complex than statements of the 'I will love you forever' type. The philosopher of history may claim to make true statements about future History. But because of the very fact that they are statements about future History, they are neither true nor untrue. They are value-commitments, and this is why their being true or false depends totally on the fact of whether they were 'really' meant. In the philosophy of history this can be decided without fail. The image of the future is a true commitment if the philosopher commits himself or herself to the same supreme values in life and action to which he/she was committed in theory at the time of the conception and formulation of the theory, *and* if there are no unreflected values, value-contradictions, or logical contradictions within the theory. *If these conditions are met, all statements about Future can be acknowledged as true statements about the present; if not, the statements are false.*

Naturally, the philosophy of history is not only the commitment of an individual philosopher. The image of future history is meant as a promise or a warning for everyone, or at least for the addressee of the philosophy in question. Whilst depicting the future, the philosopher of history intends to induce others to commit themselves to the same values; to the same lifestyle and activities as contained in his or her philosophy. The philosopher wants the addressee to *create* the future designed in the philosopher's imagination. The truer a philosophy of history is (in the meaning described above), the greater the possibility of its acceptance. Marx's thesis that the truth and the this-wordly character of a philosophy is proved by praxis, can properly be understood only in this way. However, the following question has to be raised: in order to make true statements about our present commitments, and to induce others to share them, do we have to overdetermine them by claiming to make true statements about the Future? In other words, is the statement 'I will love you forever' in fact *stronger,* not only more vague, than the other, 'I feel that I may love you forever'?

Although the statement 'I will love you forever' can be replaced the by the statement: 'I feel I may love you forever', it cannot be replaced with 'Next week we shall make love', or: 'We shall know each other better in the future.' Raising doubts about the claim of the philosophy of history to 'knowledge of the future' does not mean raising doubts about its *holistic* character. Should we want to get an answer to the question about the sense of human existence, about the sense of historical existence, our eyes are necessarily directed towards the whole. No piecemeal engineering, no prognosis, can replace the philosophy of history. To paraphrase Angelus Silesius: if you cannot look into the sun, it is your eyes which have to be blamed, not the great light.

The ensemble of true statements about the historical future, or, more correctly, about the knowledge of historical future, has to be well founded. Space does not permit an inventory here of all the different versions of this foundation. I can only suggest the main tendencies. They are the following: (a) theories of logical necessity; (b) of universal teleology; (c) of universal determinism; (d) of the unfolding of categories of history according to their internal logics.

(a) Operating with logical necessity was ingeniously analysed by Danto through the example of *Jacques le Fataliste*. He recapitulates the deduction of fatalism in the following way:

P is necessarily either true or false.

If p is true it is impossible that p is false.

If it is impossible that p is false then it is impossible that p is not true.

If it is impossible that p is not true, it is necessary that p is true.

If p is true then it is necessary that p is true.

Danto argues that the fallacy can be located in the first proposition. For Aristotle, all statements about the future can only be formulated in the following way: it is possible that p is true, it is possible that p is false. Hence operating with logical necessity proves nothing because the major premise of the deduction is untenable. But no philosophy of history would design an image of the future merely in order to state that it is possible that something is true and that it is possible that some other thing is false, simply for the reason that philosophy of history is a commitment for one alternative and against another, and it is precisely here that overdetermination occurs.

(b) The use of *universal teleology* has served as an explanatory theory in philosophy since Aristotle. After the emergence of the modern natural sciences, it became restricted to the philosophy of history. In Kant's thinking, history has to be allied with the idea of purposiveness. This is the 'weak' theory of teleology. Its 'strong' version posits a *telos* operating through history as a whole. Already outlined in Leibniz's '*praestabilita harmonia*', it was made absolutely conclusive by Hegel.

(c) Theories of *universal determinism* are only versions of those of universal teleology. This theory posits that each historical event is completely determined by its precursor, and so on, *ad infinitum*. Certain Marx-receptions follow exactly this pattern. Among others, Bernstein spoke of the 'necessity of all historical processes and developments'* as did Plekhanov. But the chain of determination is usually not regarded as an infinite regression of the reconstruction. Theorists construct a virtual point in the remote past as the decisive one which triggered the chain of determinism (such as progress, regress or eternal repetition). From Rousseau to Freud, this virtual point is the symbolic act that produced *civilization*. Once civilization was 'launched', human beings either lost their freedom or won it, depending on the particular theory, but the die was cast either way.

(d) The theory of an '*internal logic*' of historical development is the most widespread one. 'History' is conceived of either as a chain of cultures all repeating the same developmental patterns or as the self-unfolding of categories inherent in humankind from the beginning. All organistic theories are based on the principle of an 'internal logic' of development. History is understood as the 'life-story' of humankind based on the 'parallelism' of philogenesis and ontogenesis. For Vico, every people passes through the same phases as individuals do; for Habermas, the internal logic of the cognitive development of the child serves as a (hypothetical) analogy for the self-understanding of communicative rationality throughout human history. Marx, who experimented with various theories of historical progress, was also occasionally inclined to operate with the 'internal logic' of historical progress. Human beings can only develop the basic constituents of human essence, hence progress is the unfolding of this essence, he argued in *The Paris Manuscripts*. The theory of 'internal logic' can be formulated in a conditional manner as well: if history develops further it can only follow the internal logic of development. The theory can also account for cultures which have not unfolded precisely those constituents which were regarded as the 'essentially human ones'. These cultures are thought of as stagnating, regressing, or 'abnormal'.

---

* E. Bernstein, *Die Voraussetzungen des Sozialismus*, Dietz-Verlag, Stuttgart, 1902, p. 5.

For Marx, the 'normal childhood' of humankind was to be found in ancient Greece.

Although the theory of the 'internal logic' of History is sometimes formulated in a conditional manner, its hypothetical character is always pretended, never genuine. In this theory the Future is obviously understood as the necessary outcome of this logic, even in its weakest formulation ('if there is a future, this is what it will be like'). Despite their struggle against it, philosophers of history cannot circumvent teleology.

To sum up: *all* theories of universal development are basically teleological in character. They construct the present and the future as the outcome of the past, thus the outcome must have been 'there' in the beginning. No abnormal development, or 'regression', or 'counter-tendency', should it be emphasized as many times as the different variations allow for, can obscure their common teleological provenance. Kant was clearly aware of the implication that 'History' as such cannot be grasped except together with the idea of teleology.

The basic contradictions inherent in philosophies of history have to be repeated again here. On the one hand, history is understood as the upshot of human action, purpose, and volition; on the other, as a development occurring via a universal plan, a deterministic sequence, or the self-unfolding of an internal logic. The most viable theoretical solution of the dilemma (apart from Hegel's) is to denote certain types of human action and ways of thinking as the 'repositories' of the 'internal logic' of development (such as freedom, knowledge, universality, communicative rationality, or the will to power, aggression, etc.) But these latter are constructed by philosophers in correspondence with their own values and paradigms, thus the standpoint of the present and of *one* world-view of the present is superimposed on all historical actors. This is why all philosophies of history have to face the dilemma of 'freedom and/or necessity'. The dilemma is insoluble within the framework of philosophies of history; at the same time each of them offers a solution, not despite, but because of, this very insolubility.

I have stated that in philosophies of history, the indicator of development is applied as the *independent variable*. The indicator can be *broader* than the independent variable (one single aspect of the indicator may function as the independent variable), but never narrower. If two or more indicators are posited, only one can serve as the independent variable. The main idea underlying this procedure can roughly be summarized as follows. Throughout the whole of history, stages of progress (or regress) are triggered off by the development of *one* single factor and always by the development of the *same* single factor, thus every change can be accounted for by the change in this very factor. Reciprocity or interaction is almost never excluded, but the independent variable is understood as the decisive element of the interplay, 'in the last instance'. For example, if the 'elite' is the independent variable (as with Pareto), new epochs or cultures are always triggered off by new elites, and their decline can be explained by the exhaustion and decadence of that same elite, 'in the last instance'. Or, returning to Saint-Simon: 'scientific and political revolutions are successively... causes and effects...' but *ultimately* 'it is science which constitutes society.'* In philosophy of history, the independent variable is always considered as *cause*, and all other factors of change as *effects*. Thus all theories which operate with a general independent variable formulate a *general historical law*, although, because of the circularity of its construction, it is a *pseudo-law*. First, the image of the future is established (in keeping with values inherent in the conception); then, in keeping with this image, the indicators of progress are outlined, and finally one indicator is denoted as the independent variable whose development 'feeds back' to the future already posited at the beginning. This 'law' cannot be falsified, nor can it be replaced by a more universal one – it claims to be the ultimate truth because of its commitment to values and to one particular way of life, in its being an answer to the question about the sense of historical existence. The pseudo-law is the skeleton of this very answer. It does not prove anything, but it has its 'truth'.

Apparently, the independent variable of the philosophy of history is an independent variable of a particular kind. The following assertion makes sense: 'if a changes, b changes as well', or: 'if a changes and b is constant, c changes'. Assertions of this type operate equally well with an independent variable, but they are open to falsification. Similarly, the following assertion makes sense: 'If a increases, b increases as well (if all other elements remain constant).' The independent variables of the philosophy of history are, however, conceived of in a different way. Their formula reads as follows: '*A changed* in history and this change brought about change in *all social elements.*' All changes of all historical elements (for better or worse) are always effects of a change

---

* C. H. de Saint-Simon, *La physiologie sociale, Oeuvres choisis,* Presses Universitaires de France, Paris, 1965, pp. 78-9.

244 Sense and truth in history

of element *a* (for better or worse). And so it will be in the future. Yet it would be a mistake to propose for philosophies of history the replacement of their formula by the application of the 'if *a* changes, *b* changes as well' type of independent variable. For instance, one could say that whenever input increased and all other conditions remained constant, output increased as well, and will do so in the future. This and similar statements are totally *platitudinous*. The independent variables of philosophies of history are *not* empty and not platitudinous, they are the bearers of promise and warning. One should not suggest replacing the use of the independent variable, as a pseudo-law, by a falsifiable, but totally empty formula, but should rather renounce the idea of an independent variable of 'History' *altogether*. However, philosophies of history cannot renounce their independent variable without ceasing to exist.

Philosophies of history operate with a wide range of historical laws, but the pseudo-law of development always occupies the highest place, with all other laws being subordinate to it. Whether this subordination is total, is another question. It mostly depends on our interpretation of the philosopher and our interest in the interpretation as to how far contradictions are detected within the conception or, on the contrary, weakened to imperceptibility by the recipient. The various Kantian, Hegelian, Marxian and Freudian schools (to mention only the most important) never agreed on the interpretation of their 'fountainheads' in this respect.

Except for mythologically founded theories of universal development, philosophies of history verify their laws with science; more correctly, they formulate them as scientific laws. The spell of the natural sciences is not novel; it is inherited from the previous philosophical tradition. The novel element is the transformation of 'eternal' universal laws into historical ones and the emphasis on the specificity of particular laws in particular historical periods. In this new conception, everything changes (makes progress or regress) according to a universal law of development but each period 'has' its own structural laws which are outmoded and replaced by others in the next period. Even though the diagram of world history in Fourier strikes us as a fairy tale or as abstruse speculation, the author was convinced of its complete scientific relevance, claiming that it was scientifically proved beyond any doubt.

The concept of laws in the nineteenth century was fairly ambiguous; it is this ambiguity which 'reveals its secret' in philosophies of history. 'The laws of history' were mixtures of juridical laws and those of the natural sciences.

The notion of juridical law involves the obligation that all persons *have* to obey it. The law implies a vindicatory and/or punitive formula: it has to be observed (be it the commandment of God or the decision of a juridical power). Should someone fail to observe it, he/she has to be punished, be deprived of his/her liberty, possibly even perish: the law 'crushes' the guilty person. The concept of the law of natural sciences implies, however, an *explanatory* formula: taken in abstraction from any philosophical interpretation, we interpret it as a *model* which enables us to explain single natural phenomena. Moreover, the latter are not explained by one law, but by many. The formulation that natural objects 'obey' the laws of nature is an anthropomorphism. (Einstein's statement that space gives the 'orders' is a philosophical one.) Philosophies of history work with models and explain single phenomena with these models on the one hand, and, on the other hand, try to convince us that every human person has in each case to 'obey' the 'orders' deduced from certain models. The 'laws' of the philosophy of history are *not* formulated in the following way: 'If *x, y, z,* phenomena obtain, process *E* will be the outcome.' Their usual formulations are: 'We *must* do this or that because we are subordinated to the law, should we fail to do what we must, we will perish', or 'We can only do what we are compelled to do'; or 'Whatever we do, we "realize" the law.' It can be argued that even theories of eternal repetition proceed in a very similar way. Among others, the structuralist conception according to which all societies combine the *same* patterns in different ways, suggests that we cannot 'escape', that we cannot help continually rearranging a limited number of particular basic institutional possibilities. The law of non-development is also a law of this provenance. It is worth mentioning that Marx reflected on this ambiguity in an ambiguous way. Though he himself applied this concept of 'law' in the same way, he occasionally protested against this procedure. It was, however, the former that proved to be stronger with him, for the simple reason that the category of *necessity* (the tendency embodied in all concrete laws of different historical periods) was that which finally had to be advocated.

In the philosophy of history, the design of models of concrete structural laws is never an end in itself. The priority of the universal law of development is always established. What has to be explained is the *emergence* of particular systems of laws and their *disappearance*, or more precisely, their *replacement* by other ones. In theories of progress and regress, *necessity* stands for the unavoidable *sequence* of historical structures; in theories of eternal repetition it stands for the untranscendable *limit* of the possibilities of all social bodies. As has been mentioned, the conception of 'developmental logic' is only a weak formulation of universal theories of progress.

Although philosophies of history occasionally distinguish between causal and functional laws, when it comes to 'necessity', this distinction disappears. All types of law are transformed into mere expressions of the necessity embodied in the universal law of development, pseudo-teleology prevails. This procedure leads to the second dilemma of the philosophy of history: the contradiction of *contingency and necessity*.

Chance (contingency) can reasonably be comprehended in four ways. If I say: 'I met *X* on the street by chance', I mean that I did not *intend* to meet him. In this sense, something non-volitional or non-deliberate can be called 'contingent'. If I ask the following question: 'Do you by any chance know his adress?', I assume that the person addressed *may* or *may not* know it, thus its meaning is 'perhaps', the presence or absence of possible knowledge. (A similar statement is: 'He has a chance', i.e. 'Perhaps he can make it.') In the assertion that 'incidentally such things happen', contingency has the meaning of not being a rule or habit, of not being usual; it means an exception, the upshot of coincidence. Last but not least, in sentences like 'let chance decide', contingency does not have the meaning of 'I do not intend to', but that of 'hazard', 'good luck', or *sors bona*.

In the philosophy of history, chance (contingency) cannot be understood in any of its relevant meanings. It is ontologized. The 'momentum', the motivating force in history, is grasped either as chance, or as necessity (which is 'realized' through chance). The 'nose of Cleopatra' is the model case of the first suggestion. The inherent theorem is that in 'History' everything happened, happens, and will happen by chance. 'Chance' (contingency) is identified with the universal law of historical development in a negative sense: the universal law of history is that there are no laws in history, not even regularities, not even a typical interplay of actions. Granted this, if there is nothing but contingency in history, then there is *no* contingency in history for the perfectly simple reason that contingency has a meaning only in relation to something which is *not* chance. Moreover, with regard to human freedom, there is no difference whatsoever between total necessity and total contingency, so human freedom is apparently nil in both cases.

The other conception in terms of which necessity is 'realized' through contingency is more sophisticated but not more viable. For instance, in Hegel's work contingency is attributed particularly to the average human will. But taking the human will as *the* contingent factor contradicts the basic concept of contingency (something which is not intended). One could argue against this characterization in the following way: Hegel's theoretical effort was centred on human intentions; human beings intend to achieve certain goals, but something unintended results from their endeavours. But the 'unintended' is identified by Hegel *not* with contingency but with necessity! The meaning of 'contingency' is therefore completely reversed. What is grasped as contingency from the viewpoint of *real* subjects is conceived of as necessity from the viewpoint of a *mythical* subject – History. Hence the *real subject* of history *as such* is understood as *contingency*. Human beings will only cease to be 'contingent' factors of history when they directly intend the realization of necessity. Whilst fulfilling necessity (the universal law of development), they become free. The 'recognition' of necessity and freedom are thus identified.

After Kant, no philosophy of history could completely avoid this pitfall. Kant circumvented it by opposing moral law to the law of nature. But once 'historical law' became a mixture of the propensities of natural laws and juridical laws, and contingency (as unfreedom) was identified with the unconscious fulfilment of 'law' and freedom with 'liberating ourselves' from all contingencies while fulfilling necessity, the notion of 'freedom' lost its *moral* content. In this respect (but only in this respect), it does not make any difference whether freedom is constituted by the imputed consciousness of the proletariat or understood as 'being-to-death' *(Sein-zum-Tode)*. In both cases, it is identified with liberation from 'contingencies' and is void of the content of moral decision. Whether they realize necessity or make their choice against it, human beings stand beyond good and evil. Even if the outcome of choice is identified with good, morality has no say in the choice itself.

To sum up: the problem with philosophies of history is not their attempt to formulate social laws. Moreover, the refutation of the theory of 'general natural laws of society', this article of faith with their predecessors, was in many respects a crucial expression of a new historical consciousness. However, the priority of the 'universal law of development', conceived of as 'necessity', on the one hand, and the tendency to subject all concrete historical laws to this necessity, on the other, resulted in an ambiguous concept of 'social laws', which, on its part, led to a notion of freedom emptied of moral content. Although the best philosophers of history have expressed their partiality for value rationality and posited an ethical world in the future (such as Lukács) or defended the case of morality as against instincts (such as Freud), the shadow of 'beyond good and evil' fell heavily upon their work.

Chapter Seventeen

Holism and individualism

Holism and individualism in the philosophy of history have nothing to do with the ancient philosophical problems of 'the whole and the part' or 'the one and the many'. An all-embracing category in the philosophy of history is *substance,* irrespective of whether the notion 'substance' occurs at all in the system (though it mostly does). 'Substance' is human essence. It is either represented as unfolding historically or as being a timeless reaction to History regarded as an empty shell of meaningless change. Substance is, however, always grasped as a *totality.* This totality may be *universal* (history, humankind), *particular* (cultures, nations or one particular culture, one particular class), or *singular* (individuality, the person). Prominent philosophies of history combine all three types of totality. But in this case philosophers *make a hierarchy* of totalities, and in the main they do so from two different aspects; aspects which are not always congruent with each other. In dialectical theories of development hierarchies are usually incongruent due to the application of two or more heterogeneous indicators of progress (or regress). The different totalities are normally not related to each other as the substance is to its attributes, but either as goals to their means or as exchangeable entities which can be either goals or means. This follows from the teleological or quasi-teleological structure of philosophies of history.

(a) The absolute priority of world-history as the all-embracing whole is best represented in Hegel's philosophy of history. Particular cultural totalities (the spirit of peoples or *Volksgeist*) are only partial expressions of the world-spirit and embody 'stages' of its 'unfolding'. They are the means serving the goal: the march of world-history towards its accomplishment. All particular cultures are swept away in order to be replaced by other (higher) ones. Particular totalities work out, as it were, in anticipation, certain categories of the highest order of totality, which is, on its part, the totalization of all categories. As Hegel writes: 'The right of the world-spirit is superior to all particular legitimations.' And the same applies to individuals: 'Reason cannot be halted by the grievances of individuals; particular goals are absorbed by the general.' Should the individual suffer loss or injury, 'it is of no consequence for world-history for whom the individuals *serve as means for its development.*'* Hegel was by no means alone in this 'world-historical indifference' towards the individual. Even Goethe, for whom the individual as a totality was of much greater concern, stated 'it does not matter to me whether this or another individual dies, this or another people perishes; I would be a fool to worry about it.'** As far as *homo phenomen* was concerned, Kant, also argued on behalf of a similar conception.

(b) There are several different arguments on behalf of each particular culture as a value-in-itself, as the real (and only) repository of world-history. The two most typical versions are best exemplified by Herder's and Ranke's theories. In Herder's view: 'The research into nature does not presume any difference of levels among the creatures [the researcher] investigates: they are all equally dear and important to him. The researcher into the nature of humanity proceeds in a similar way.'*** However, for Herder the equality in value and substance *includes* an emphasis on progress. The achievements of one culture are the foundations of the achievements of the next. 'The Egyptian could not come about without Oriental man, the Greek founded his world on the former, the Roman climbed high on the shoulders of the whole world.'‡ (It is worth noting that theories of diffusion of modern ethnology apply just the same notion of the philosophy of history.) Ranke shares with Herder this emphasis on the equal value of all cultures but he refuses, except in his last period, to line them up according to a progressive continuity. He formulates strictly: 'I contend, however, that every epoch is immediate to God and its real value does not rest on what derived from it but in its very existence, in its real self.'‡‡

Philosophies of history which refused to regard particular (relative) wholes as mere stages in the development of a universal whole could,

---

* G. W. F. Hegel, *Vernunft in der Geschichte, Vorlesungen über die Philosophie der Geschichte*, Akademie Verlag, Berlin, 1970, pp. 109, 76.
** Quoted in Friedrich Meinecke, *Die Entstehung des Historismus*, Verlag von R. Oldenburg, München/Berlin, 1936, p. 556.
*** Quoted in *ibid.*, p. 474.
‡ *Ibid.*, p. 422.
‡‡ *Ibid.*, p. 644.

nevertheless, still regard individuals as means serving the realization of the 'higher' totality (in this case, of another particular culture) to the same extent as Hegel. For Ranke, the value of the individual depends completely on his identification with a higher totality: 'The greatest thing that can happen to a man is to defend the universal cause through his own. Thereby his personal Being will be expanded into a world-historical episode.'*

It is no wonder, then, that this emphasis on the totality of particular cultures has been attacked from two directions. Kant argued against Herder with a concept of humankind as the highest totality, emphasizing that 'no specimen of any race of humankind, but the species alone completely achieves its defined character.'** Almost one and a half centuries later the old Meinecke made a self-critical confession in a letter to Croce regarding the affinity of historicisms with nationalism. On the other hand, de Tocqueville denounced the concepts of both universal and particular totality as philosophical constructions 'which...more or less eradicate human beings from the history of the human species'.***

(c) The outcry against the misuse of individuals for the sake of universal or particular totalities led to various philosophical solutions, but mostly to renouncing the philosophy of history on the very basis of the philosophy of history. Feuerbach and Kierkegaard were the first great protagonists of this trend. For Feuerbach, individuality itself became the highest totality, and indeed the only one, for here the individual was conceived of as the bearer of the human species. His theory was undoubtedly a kind of philosophy of history too, because it contained the idea of the *alienation* of human essence (in religion) and advocated the abolition of alienation in the present and in the future. At the same time, it was also a renunciation of the philosophy of history, because it excluded theoretical reflection on objectivations and institutions as progressing or regressing. On the other hand, Kierkegaard replaced this optimistic radicalism by the radicalism of despair. In the second part of *Either-Or*, he followed the logic of the philosophy of history, as a quest for the possibility of the interplay or the identity of individual and species, but he realized that if the progress of institutions cannot be theoretically supported, the identity of the individual and the species cannot be defended either. This is

---

* *Ibid.*, p. 644.
** Kant, *Werke*, vol. XII, Frankfurt, 1964, p. 79.
***Quoted in *Historische Theorie und Geschichtsforschung der Gegenwart*, pp. 34-5.

why he basically renounced the philosophy of history while replacing the individual-species relationship with one between the person and God.

(d) There were certain grandiose attempts to coordinate the universal and individual totality and work out philosophies of history which would avoid the extremes of both 'holism' and 'individualism'. I will only discuss two solutions, both of them classic and extreme: those of Kant and Marx.   As has already been noted, Kant solved the problem by duplicating the notion of 'human species'. Human species as nature is historical. Its development can be understood with the aid of the idea of teleology. Individuals are means in the realization of the whole. The human species as morality, as pure Will, is, however, not historical. It obliges us to act in such a way that the use of another human being should never be viewed simply as a mere means, but also as an end in itself. In obeying the moral law, human beings should renounce their individuality and identify themselves with the idea of humankind, respecting humanity in all individual human beings. This is how, on the one hand, the empirical individual acts according to his or her individual nature (interest) *against* other individuals regarded by him as mere means for goals. On the other hand, this is how the empirical individual realizes the progress of phenomenal humankind, the progress of institutions and objectivations, whereas pure practical reason is not individual, but is related to the idea of the species. Acting in keeping with it means treating other individuals as ends in themselves. Yet there is *no progress* in this species-activity, or at least we know nothing of it. Due to the duplication of the species, the two totalities never 'meet'. (Except for Kant's last philosophy, the conception of which has already been described.) On the other hand, although Marx worked only with one notion of human essence, he argued for its actual separation into essence and existence (this is the meaning of alienation) and for its 'reunification' in the future process of de-alienation, thus he historicized *'homo noumenon'* as well. Deprivation (existence without essence) was conceived of by him as a motivational force bringing about (in the future) the identification of the species and the 'singular' *in the individual* (in *every* individual). Consequently, *real* history can be grasped as the history of institutions, objectivations, as the history of *alienated* human essence. As a result, institutions must disappear in the process of de-alienation. At the very least, it is the state and commodity production, the most crucial sources of alienation, which have to wither away. In this manner, the Kantian duplication of 'human essence' is translated into the duplication of History: a 'pre-history', 'hitherto', and a 'real' history in the future.

The result of the above analysis can be summed up in the following way: whichever form the subordination or co-ordination of the three 'wholes' of the philosophy of history may take, the outcome of the undertaking is fairly problematic. Either particular respective individual wholes are conceived of as mere means, or humankind and human persons are subordinated to particularistic cultures, or the whole civilization of institutions and objectivations is rejected, or the human species is 'duplicated' ontologically or historically. The outcome is either realism without radicalism or radicalism without realism.

Of course, there is absolutely no philosophy of history which would have denied that human beings shape history, which would not have taken into consideration the actions and sufferings of human beings in one way or another. The question is not whether men make history, but whether all or only some of them make it, whether everyone shapes it equally or some do to a greater extent than others, whether History is the outcome of human actions or whether it obeys laws, goals, or necessities, irrespective of the character of subjective goals and purposes, whether the purposes and decisions of the actors are only epiphenomena of powers acting behind them or not. The answer to these questions is apparently connected with the definition of History. Although philosophies of history consider History as the developmental process of humankind, they usually distinguish 'historical' times from 'prehistorical' ones. The question is always raised: from which time onwards can one speak about history at all; that is to say, at which time was the developmental process called History actually triggered off?

The dictum of the *Communist Manifesto*, that the history of all societies hitherto has been the history of class struggles, can only be reasonably read in the following way: only those societies characterized by class struggle were *historical ones*. History is overwhelmingly identified with the history of civilization, and basically with the history of European civilization. For Hegel or Ranke, even the history of the great oriental empires (China, the Ottoman Empire, India, Persia) served only as an analogy for, or as a contrast to occidental history (History), or served as its prehistory. Although it is common knowledge nowadays that paleolithic cultures embrace more than 90 per cent of the whole of human history and several evolutionist theories are preoccupied precisely with this longest period of humankind, philosophies of history (except the ones based on 'eternal repetition') usually neglect these new horizons of the past and keep grasping History as the story of civilization, particularly when it comes to the identification of the historical subject *par excellence*.

The 'carrier' of historical change, the actor who creates history either in keeping with his will or by realizing necessity, is termed the 'world-historical subject'. The world-historical subject or subjects can be conceived of as *individual subjects* or *collective subjects*.

(a) Philosophers can agree in regarding the 'great personality' as a world-historical subject, but disagree in selecting the characteristics of 'greatness'. The objectivation, institution or activity which is regarded by them as the decisive aspect of historical progress completely defines the content of 'greatness'.

Going by the most general view, it is the political sphere, and so political action, which shapes historical events. As a result, world-historical subjects are identified with the *most powerful* historical agents, even though power is usually regarded as only one of the prerequisites of their greatness. The only powerful actors identified as world-historical individuals are those who took advantage of their power to give a new turn to history: the great conquerors and the great statesmen. This is the philosophy of 'hero-worship'. Even if not all types of hero-worship are rooted in the concept of the world-historical individual to the same extent (for instance, the cult of genius in art and literature), the emphasis on 'greatness' as 'power', as a 'gift of nature' may rightly be added to the idolatry of political might (see, for instance, Burckhardt). The most frequent protagonists in the hero-worship perspective are Alexander the Great, Julius Caesar, Augustus Caesar and Napoleon. Hegel, for whom Napoleon was matchless, defined the world-historical subject as the Will of the world-spirit. For such subjects 'the present world is only a crust... which encompasses another in itself', 'they know best what is to be done; and what they do, is right action. Others must obey them, for they feel this', 'They have no respect for any limits.'* The ancient debate between two ways of life – *vita activa* and *vita contemplativa* – is decided here in favour of action. But this action is *void* of all moral content. Everything which is done by the 'great man' is *right*

---

* G. W. F. Hegel, *Vernunft in der Geschichte, Vorlesungen über die Philosophie der Geschichte*, Akademie Verlag, Berlin, 1970, p. 99.

because he is *righteousness* himself and no one can be right against him. Nietzche's Superman was conceived of in this way.

The age of liberalism and democracy could not follow in the footsteps of hero-worship. In the twentieth century, the great statesman and warrior was revived only in the ideologies and doctrines of totalitarian societies (and mental asylums). A new hero emerged, a new world-historical personality, more adequate to the imagination of the times: the *great natural scientist,* who changed history with his discoveries. The 'temple of science' became the new Pantheon. Galileo and Newton inherited the laurels of Caesar and Napoleon.

The new type of hero-worship was invented by Saint-Simon. Industrial progress, the prompter and repository of the future turning point in history, is bound up with the name of Newton. All different branches of positivism follow him in this crucial aspect, as do certain other philosophies. In Husserl's view, the change of attitude *(Einstellung)* in modern times is due to Galileo. Popper suggests that only the great scientists are real historical individuals. Lévi-Strauss argues that the 'Newtons' (Newton again!) of paleolithic societies invented the new family structures. To be sure, the ancient dispute between *vita contemplativa* and *vita activa* is only *apparently* solved here in favour of the former. Scientific discoveries change the world by introducing *new forms of technology* into production, management and social structure. Thus this understanding of 'world-historical individuals' is equally as void of moral content as was the more traditional hero-worship. It is taken for granted that new scientific discoveries instigate progress while increasing knowledge, or at least that new inventions are always value neutral. (The later Husserl is an exception in this respect.)

The identification of the 'world-historical personality' with the personification of *exemplary moral behaviour,* common as it was in ancient historiography, disappeared almost completely in the philosophy of history. It happens only with those philosophers who set out to destroy the philosophy of history by departing from this very same basis (philosophy of history). This attitude reconstructed History as the theatre of crimes and sufferings (and rightly so), where Good was doomed to extinction, and in any case had no say at all in change. In spite of this, the attraction of moral greatness did not go to waste. The defeated can be closer to our hearts than the triumphant but it is difficult or almost impossible to suggest that losers were the prompters of historical progress. There was only *one* defeated individual in history who could be regarded as a prompter of a decisive turning point in its 'march': the mythological figure of Jesus Christ. He is the only possible 'moral hero' of the philosophy of history. If, however, History is a continuous, steady march, there must be *more* world-historical individuals than one, and this is why the philosophy of history has to eliminate the image of 'world-historical individuals' of morality. To mention again only the greatest examples, Feuerbach and Kierkegaard suggested the 'imitation of Christ' and thereby destroyed the philosophy of history, though in different ways. (Simone Weil can serve as a prominent modern example of this trend.)

(b) The 'carrier' of social change can also be conceived of as a *collective subject*. Even conceptions based on individual world-historical subjects cannot be conclusive without presupposing a certain kind of collective subject. No conqueror can conquer without a devoted army, no statesman can transform history without subjects who realize his aims. But if one mentions collective subjects as 'carriers' of social transformation, one has in mind philosophies of history which invert this relationship by turning collective subjects of various origins into 'primary movers of History', and one is led to understanding historical personalities only as the manifestations and servants of these substantial subjects. Theories of collective subjects allow for much more variation than theories of individual historical subjects. Not only can the type of world-historical achievement vary from theory to theory, but also the social integration to which they are related.

A culture of society as a whole can be regarded as one single collective subject. In this understanding, every objectivation, institution, or action, either collective or individual, expresses equally – even if not always with equal force – the *same* pattern embodied in an undercurrent: a pattern embodied in the 'spirit of the times' or 'the spirit of the culture' in question. This spirit unfolds until it becomes exhausted and is replaced by a new culture with a different spirit (due to organic development or to force). Nations can also be regarded as collective subjects of this kind. The distinction between world-historical and 'other' cultures or between world-historical and 'other' nations is not always explicitly made. When it is, the present culture and the evaluation of the present culture serve as the only yardsticks. The cultures or nations called 'world-historical' are those which made the greatest cultural impact on posterity or which serve as examples of the highest perfection ever achieved. In regard to any particular philosophy of history, of course, it is very telling whether it is ancient or classical Greece that serves as example of the high point of world-historical culture, or whether it is Sparta or Athens that serves as this model of perfection. The temptation to differentiate world-historical and non-world-historical cultures is very great. Even those who resist it in theory, cannot resist it in practice (for instance, for Ranke the 'great nations' are the Germans and the Franks).

A culture and a society can be characterized as an entity by the conflict or the symbiosis of *several collective subjects*. Collective subjects can in this way be grasped as classes, strata, professional groups, castes and estates. No doubt, regarding societies as *stratified* wholes has in itself nothing to do with the idea of a collective subject. The collective subject is never identified only with the place occupied by a group of people in the social structure, not even with certain activities shared by the members of the same group. A group is a collective subject only in so far as it is characterized by *collective consciousness* and *collective action*. Only a group conscious of its common interests, common needs, common ethos, common way of life can be regarded as a 'carrier' of historical change or of the conservation of an existing culture and social order.

There are three typical variations on this theme, as well as various versions of the three typical variations.

According to the first variation, all collective subjects contribute *equally* to the development of societies. This conception can be best exemplified by Durkheim's idea of 'organic solidarity'. The independent variable of historical development (increase in population density) makes the occupational division of labour unavoidable. Hence the originally homogeneous *conscience collective* is particularized. Different occupational groups have a different collective consciousness (an ethos), which regulates their actions and behavioural patterns. Conflict (as a possibility) is included in this model but is not considered as being 'normal'. Normality, the 'idea' of modern society, is identical with the togetherness of various collective consciousnesses, and this is exactly what 'organic solidarity' is all about.

According to the second variation on the theme, the collective subject which contributes most to the development of cultures, the real repository of conservation and/or change, is, in all social structures, the elite. The *elite* is the motivational force, the embodiment of will and resolution. This, too, is a kind of hero-worship with the collective hero as protagonist. The 'elite' can be defined as the ruling elite (as with Pareto) but as far as modern societies are concerned, the 'ruling elite' is usually replaced by an aristocracy of scientists, revolutionary activists or the aristocracy of race. (And there is good reason for this, given that present ruling elites do not fit easily into an overall image of an 'aristocratic elite'). In this respect, there is no significant difference between Blanqui, Nietzsche and Gobineau.

According to the third variation on the theme, the collective subject, and the subject that contributes most remarkably to historical development, is always the oppressed, struggling for recognition. This is the standpoint of the *Communist Manifesto* when it emphasizes particularly the progressive role of the bourgeoisie in its struggle against feudalism. The same bourgeoisie, which is the mainspring of progress until it comes to power, immediately becomes a brake on that same progress, once in power. The torch of progress is passed on to the new oppressed class: the proletariat. The identity of the independent variable of progress (the development of the forces of production) and the collective subject of progress (the oppressed) is the upshot of History. The substance (work) becomes subject (worker), the new collective subject is *the* world-historical subject, and it brings about the total change in the course of history.

It is well known that in at least one basic way of appropriating Marx, this conception was reversed and gave way to different types of revival of elite theories.

All conceptions of the 'collective subject' as the repository of historical change and eventually that of progress, suffered, however, from the same malaise as did the theories of 'great historical personalities'. Politics, production and the economy are the great theatres, wherein conflicts are expected to be fought out. If ethos was reflected upon at all, it was in a relationship with the above prime spheres. Ethics (morality) was not thought of to any degree as a lever of progress in its own right.

This is why theories of the 'collective subject' aroused the same uneasiness as those of world-historical personalities, and did so above all in thinkers who sided with progress. The ambiguity of theories of progress which explicitly disregard morality as a motivational force was already spelt out (with the intention of overcoming this limitation) by socialist theories which combined Marx with Kant. This undertaking was, however, not very successful, for the emphasis on a collective world-historical subject constituted by the socio-economic structure of society is incompatible with the idea of individual commitment to moral values (or to values with moral content). The whole theory hinges on the concept of *justice* and is based upon the consideration that the class which suffers injustice is, when led by the value of justice, motivated to put it right, and all this brings about the 'ethical world' designed by Kant. But the problem is that if the value of justice *conforms* to the interest of the class, it does not trigger moral motivation even if the cause is right, and is only considered (as a moral issue) by *others* whose interest is *not* involved. Because of this, both Kant's and Marx's theories, if combined, are weakened and lose their plausibility. After the Second World War and the horrifying experiences of the Holocaust and the Gulag, this feeling of uneasiness grew to the level of outcry. Marquard's paraphrasing of Marx's thesis on Feuerbach summed up the feeling bluntly: 'Philosophers of history have changed the world in various ways; now their duty is to forbear.'*

This is why philosophers of our epoch started to experiment with a completely new notion of 'collective subject': a notion neither identical with the 'spirit' nor the structure of a historical period as a whole, nor grasped as a particular social class, ruling or oppressed. Also, this notion of a 'collective subject' was not constituted by occupation nor by common economic-political interest. Serious attempts were made in this direction by the ageing Ernst Bloch and Goldmann (in the last phase of his activity), but the most philosophically conclusive model was designed by Apel, who identified the collective subject as the 'community of communication' *(Kommunikationsgemeinschaft)*. The community of communication is the 'carrier' of transindividual consciousness (as all collective subjects are) and comes about through rational argumentation, both theoretical and practical. Every human being becomes a member of a *genuine* community of communication through his or her socialization process. The communicative competence achieved in this process obliges everyone 'on all occasions which affect the interests (the virtual claims) of *others* to strive for concord in order to achieve formation of Will in solidarity'. Thus solidarity becomes a norm and it is not factual as with Durkheim; interest does motivate, but it is not our own interest which is related to 'formation of Will' (as in class theories), but that of *others*. Thereby, natural law (reconsidered by Bloch as well) is *historicized*, and the real (social) community, although remaining the point of departure, is not considered to be the guarantee of a progressive historical outcome. 'Whoever really thinks

* Odo Marquard, *Schwierigkeiten mit der Geschichtsphilosophie*, Suohrkamp, Frankfurt, 1973, p. 32.

in a concrete and radical way, must be always ready to establish his or her social commitment in terms of the ever given situation, through philosophical ethics.'*

Apel's philosophy is not a philosophy of history, at least not a 'complete' one. It is Habermas who has based a philosophy of history on this novel concept of the collective subject. The collective subject constituted by rational argumentation is grasped in successive *progress*. Space does not permit here an analysis of the attempt which led Habermas to a theory of universal evolution (I have done this in detail elsewhere). As might be thought, all traditional categories of the philosophy of history recur in this undertaking: the independent variable, the indicators of progress, the general laws of 'History', and so on. Even the biological analogy is taken up once again. This ambitious theoretical undertaking is also a sign of the need for a new notion of the collective subject. It is another question whether the traditional philosophy of history *ought* to be revived in order to confront the implied challenge.

Every philosophy of history involves *anthropology*. History is the history of human beings. Anyone who makes statements about History makes statements about the 'nature' of human beings.

Everyone accepts the empirical but not very profound statement that societies are different and that they undergo change. But even such commonplace assertions inevitably imply further statements which are far from being as simple and which have to be argued for. For example, one can suggest that 'human nature' is always the same, that it is 'eternal' and 'unchangeable', and only institutions and habits change. Or one can suggest that human nature changes through the changes of institutions and habits. Particular answers to the question are normally somewhere between the two poles. The first statement usually takes the form that the *essence* of human beings never changes but that the attributes and manifestations of that essence undergo change. The second statement is usually formulated in the way that although there are biological immutables in human nature, the *essence* is social, and as a result, it changes in keeping with institutional changes. In spite of my affinity with the second standpoint, it would be improper to deny the philosophical relevance of the first. On the one hand, it can make warning and promise powerful; on the other

---

* K. O. Apel, *Transformation der Philosophie*, Frankfurt, 1973, vol. II, pp. 426, 433.

it can serve as a much-needed antidote to the arrogant ethnocentrism frequently displayed by those who advocate the case of the progressive change of human nature. Moreover, it can also defend the *unity* of the human species. For instance, Roheim argued for the Oedipus complex against the neo-Freudians precisely in order to maintain the claim to universal humanity.

Both statements, that human nature has changed, and that it has not, allow for several controversial philosophical solutions which cannot be analysed or even listed here. Theories of progress generally reconstruct change in human nature as the unfolding of human abilities towards perfection whereas theories of regress depict a process of our successive degradation and depravation. Dialectical theories usually combine the two approaches, but even here the final upshot is still a vacillation between the utmost perfection or the utmost degradation. (Marx's works and Rousseau's *Discours* exemplify these tendencies in the most characteristic way.) The concept of the 'tendency' inherent in the change is, however, only the skeleton of the anthropologies related to various philosophies of history. In both cases, the particular constituents have to be grasped. We need to be aware of whether the 'essence' is grasped as the starting point of the degradation or as the outcome of perfection. How and why the essence has either unfolded or reverted is another crucial question to be answered. Whether anthropological development precedes the progress of institutions or follows from it, or the two processes are simultaneous, is also an issue of great importance. The chicken-or-egg-dilemma of cause-effect precedence also has to be taken account of here. Anthropology is, in all its implications, the *backbone* of philosophies of history. It is directly attached to the values constituted from the standpoint of the future. It is related to *every* category of a particular philosophy of history. When Marx stated that being radical means grasping matters by their roots, and that the root of all matters is Man, he was obviously seeing philosophy as a radical undertaking. The image of 'Man' in the philosophy of history is historical man: it is the *changing essence* of humankind and individuals, of the two wholes, and this is why historical man could and should be understood as *freedom*. But the same image is that of the *changing existence* of both to a similar extent and this is why historical man has to be understood as *unfreedom* as well. History is constituted in order to grasp this common root: historical existence as freedom and unfreedom, and the sense inherent in it.

The question as to the sense of historical existence is one that has to be answered. Yet it is far from being obvious that every answer presupposes the construction of History (with a capital H), the ontologization of our values, the making of true statements about historical future, the universalization of progress, regress, eternal repetition, the universal teleology or pseudo-teleology, the ambiguous application of the notion of 'law', proposing one indicator (of universal progress or regress), the explanation of all changes and transformations by the same independent variable throughout History, the hierarchization of 'wholes', the construction of (individual or collective) 'world-historical subjects', 'lining-up' cultures according to their contributions to the 'outcome' of History, or the emphasis on the present as the 'turning point' towards Salvation or Doomsday. The question to be answered now is whether the philosophy of history can be replaced or at least supplemented by a theory of a *different kind*, less challenging perhaps as far as its construction is concerned but more realistic in its claims: a theory which would be able to answer the problem of the sense of historical existence to the same extent. Angelus Silesius is absolutely right: if we cannot look into the sun, it is our eyes which must be blamed and not the great light. But we have only got our eyes and we want to see our way.

There are two main fallacies involved in the philosophy of history which cannot be circumvented. These have to be finally summed up.

The first great fallacy was detected by Mannheim. Even though he was speaking specifically of Marx, he attacked the philosophy of history in general. The philosophy of history reflects upon human existence historically from an *ahistorical* standpoint. It does not apply its own criteria to itself. The questions can be rightly raised: why is it precisely *our* time which is the turning point in history? Why has necessity been recognized only now? Why do our projects differ from all other projects in history? What entitles us, and specifically us, to disclose the 'world-historical subject' of history? Of course, the present (and the future and the past of present) have always been the concern of philosophy, but former philosophies never raised claims like the philosophy of history *does;* that this very present is, at the same time, the focal point of the whole process called the 'history of humankind'. The philosophy of history deals with the present, but it also claims, falsely, to solve thereby the 'riddle of history' – a riddle which cannot be solved because *there is no such riddle*. To put it in a better way, the riddle of history is always identical with the riddle of the present; of our *'Togetherness'*. It must be added that certain prominent critics and adversaries of the philosophy of history are also prone to the same fallacy. They usually denounce as 'Utopian' the image of the future designed by one or another philosophy of history, meaning thereby that it cannot be realized. But how can anyone *in the present know* that there *will never be* a free society of associated producers in the future? How can anyone in the present *know* that humankind will *not* be subjected to total manipulation or will not repeat its history in the future? 'Impossible' and 'necessary' are of similar provenance.

The second fallacy involved in the philosophy of history is the contradiction between its supreme value (freedom) and the ontologization of that same value (together with other, related, ones). If one states that human freedom is progressively decreasing or increasing, or that we are 'thrown' into freedom or that we are subjugated to necessity while the only freedom left to us is withdrawal from the world, or that the same fetters (external or internal forces) limit our thinking and our actions in every society always and in the same way, then in all these formulations, contradictory or different as they may be, freedom is *annihilated*. Even if a statement about the future follows a conditional pattern (if there is a future it will be like this), then the very concept of History which entails the future just as well as past and present, excludes all other future possibilities except the one formulated in the conditional statement. If there is only one possible way to freedom, and all other ways lead to unfreedom, freedom is annihilated to the same extent. This is why the philosophy of history goes 'beyond Good and Evil', and not because it is sceptical about moral motivations and their contributions to historical change (for the better). It has to be repeated that adversaries of the philosophy of history who state with an air of certainty that it is totally impossible that a particular supposition may be borne out in the future, who are haughtily derisive about Utopias (as Popper is) are subject to the same fallacy: they go 'beyond Good and Evil' to the same extent as their opponents.

Chapter Eighteen

The philosophy of history and the idea of socialism

'Socialism is the tendency inherent in industrial civilization', Polanyi rightly remarked. Socialism is a perfectly new idea which should not be conflated with either the longing for a 'just' or 'perfect' society or with the hope of salvation – ideas often expressed in human dreams, in poetry, in religion, throughout human history. Socialism is this-wordly and future-directed, and it regards its final aim, the *transcendence* of present society, as the outcome of the existing society which has to be understood and thereby transcended. Socialism is normally regarded as the product of a historical process which comes about because of the inherent tendency of this very process, both accelerated and realized by human actions (revolutionary or reformist). Even if this idea can be argued for without the theoretical lever of a philosophy of history, it nevertheless has an affinity with the philosophy of history. The actors of one historical period are confronted with similar problems and the theoretical formulations of these problems usually have very much in common, even if their concrete values, social and political motivations, are different or even contradictory. The emergence of a world-historical consciousness as the consciousness of reflected universality was the hotbed of philosophies of history, philosophies that expressed it adequately. Small wonder then that socialist theories have similarly been formulated as philosophies of history, complete or incomplete. As is well known, socialist and non-socialist philosophies of history fertilized each other subsequently, either (often) in the form of direct influence, as in case of the line of descendance: Saint-Simon–Comte–Durkheim, or in the form of transplanting certain basic ideas or theoretical achievements, as in case of the *Kulturkritik* in Fourier, Feuerbach, Marx, Kierkegaard, Nietzsche, Tönnies, Sorel, up until Heidegger, Lukács, Adorno and Marcuse.

The theory of socialism (as well as its practice) has been pluralistic from the beginning. The set of values posited by the theorist was crucial in the construction of the 'image' of the future, which for its part defined *what* was to be transcended and *how*. In the last analysis, this set of values also shaped the whole idea of History, which has allegedly led up to this transformation. It was a matter of philosophical talent and ingenuity as to how closely all these elements could be fitted together by the theorist; how conclusive and coherent the philosophy of history became.

All socialist philosophies of history are *critical*, since their main concern, the future, is contrasted with a present to be transcended. Thus the focal point of theory is criticism of the present. This criticism is basically aimed at those social institutions and motivations the transcendence of which has to be achieved by socialism. The social content of this mission also defines the *meaning* of the notion of 'socialism'. The identification of the concrete achievements of the mission and the meaning of the term 'socialism' has led and still occasionally leads to rebaptizing the projected future society. It may be called communism, a society of associated producers, a self-managed society, substantive democracy, a society of domination-free communication, a radical democracy, and so on. A selection from the many social phenomena that may become main targets of criticism is: commodity production (market relations), the division of labour (social or technical or both), private property (as the source of poverty or of oppression or both), the state, all institutions of domination, individualism, egoism, democracy (denounced as 'merely formal'), production for production's sake (or industrialization in general), manipulation, nationalism, colonialism (war, imperialism), irrationalism, atomization. All models of socialism combine some of these elements but none of them can combine them all. Certain typical combinations exist. These are as follows:

Type A The primary targets of criticism are: individualism, egoism, a way of life based on oppression. The model of the new society encompasses: new forms of life based on communities, immediacy, community, humanization of interpersonal relationships, direct democracy, the abolition of every type of division of labour (including the division of labour between the sexes), the abolition of the state and the institutions of domination, the priority of agriculture, curbing industrial development (or stopping it altogether), the elimination of nations, the replacement of private property with communal property. This conception can be modified in such a way that industrial development should not be impeded and also that the state should not be abolished, but instead should comprise solely of communities, and be controlled by them in the form of a direct democracy. (An example of this is Gurwitch's 'collectivist democracy'.)

Type B The primary target of criticism is inequality of wealth. The model of the new society includes as elements: equalization of property, or abolition of private property, abolition of poverty, abolition of civil society, control over the allocation of needs and need-satisfaction (by a state or a pseudo-state), emphasis on agricultural production (based on collective or individual ownership).

Type C The primary target of criticism is commodity production. The models of the new society include: the abolition of the market through either:

Type Ci the abolition of the state, together with the preservation of the division of labour; technological and scientific development; increasing needs; substantive rationality; an 'equal start' in life; equal access to education; meritocracy, or

Type Cii the abolition of the state and the division of labour (except the technological kind); the end of commodity fetishism, or manipulation, of the subjugation of culture to the market; free development of personality; unfolding of individual abilities.

Type D The primary target of criticism is political domination. The models of the new society include as elements: the abolition of political domination through either:

Type Di the abolition of the state and all political institutions, self-supporting and self-governing communities; no central authority whatsoever; totally free development of personality; the symbiosis of communities, or

Type Dii the decentralization of power; the state being in command of redistribution, and/or as the executioner of the will of all citizens; the market controlled by democratic public opinion; the freedom of individuality limited by self-restriction; real equality of participation.

All models demand the abolition of war and of domination based on the exclusive character of private property. There are, of course, innumerable other combinations of the same patterns, but those described above appear most frequently in philosophies of history of a socialist provenance.

Karl Marx has a bad press these days. His system is usually dismissed by disdainful or sarcastic remarks. The same persons who once clung to every word he ever uttered now turn against him, full of hatred, and tear to pieces the very works that comprised their Scripture for decades. But the image of the Devil is only the obverse of the image of God, and all obsessive hatred of one particular figure is just as much a substitute for religion as having absolute faith in him. Parricide has no rational motivation whatsoever. No wonder then that Marx's system has been mostly replaced by totally irrationalistic myths or other philosophies of history inferior to it in every respect. (An exception is here Cornelius Castoriadis). Anyone who chooses lukewarm Nietzsche, Sorel, Proudhon or Bakhunin in preference to Marx will win nothing: they can only lose, both theoretically and politically. They are, undeniably, strong and sufficient reasons for this *nouvelle vaogue* of irrationalism, cynicism, and the search for new 'prophets', both sociologically and psychologically. This might be a good enough excuse for the man in the street; it definitely is not for scholars, who should know better and who ought to be aware of their responsibilities. Habermas's attitude, that of reflecting upon Marx and his work historically and with the respect that all great theoretical achievements deserve, and at the same time selecting from his system *all the suggestions* and theoretical proposals relevant for us, while leaving behind the others, not in hatred or faith, but with understanding – this attitude is exemplary and, at the same time, more viable.

Marx's *oeuvre* is the greatest system of philosophy of history that socialism has ever produced. It raises all the problems that philosophies of history generally raise, and synthetizes them in an edifice matched by few others (perhaps only by the systems of Hegel, Kierkegaard and Freud). It answers the question about the sense of our historical existence conclusively by making promise (and warning) forceful. Our uneasiness with Marx is due to the fact that his system is a philosophy of history – but it would be most ahistorical to ascribe *this* to *him* as a failure or shortcoming. The philosophically imputed consciousness of the consciousness of reflected universality *is* a philosophy of history and it would be worse than ridiculous to blame a thinker for having responded to the exigencies of his time. Marx was no more 'mistaken' in constructing his philosophical edifice than any great philosopher has been. But since he was the representative philosopher of the history of socialism, he deserves particular recognition by socialists, even if the changing times present us with quite different exigencies. He also deserves recognition by non-socialists as well, for he was as much as anything else a man of genius.

There are various misconceptions in criticisms of Marx. There are adversaries who believe that by 'refuting' Marx, they refute socialism as well. Even if one does not accept Polanyi's statement that socialism is the tendency *sui generis* inherent in industrial civilization, it would be hard to deny that it is at least *one* of its tendencies and that there is a *need* for socialism in these societies. It was not Marx who aroused this need; he merely expressed and formulated it. Even if one formulation of the need is 'refuted', the need itself is not thereby annihilated. The abovementioned critics are like militant atheists who are convinced that if they 'refute' the existence of God, they will put an end to religious needs. Again, other critics contend that Marx has become obsolete because some of his economic doctrines have been falsified. If an economic doctrine is refuted, it is replaced by new ones, and becomes simply forgotten. However, faithful Marxists did not cling to the (economic) tenets of their founding father because they were economically valuable, but because they were indispensable links in a philosophy of history; that is, unless they could be replaced (as occasionally they have been replaced) by functionally equivalent ones. Hence the relevance or irrelevance of the economic theories of Marx hinges basically on the acceptance or refusal of his philosophy of history. Certain critics claim that Marx's system has been proved irrelevant because his prophecies about the future did not come true. This argument tries to attack the master with his own weapons, (with his philosophy of history) but it does so on a far lower level than the target of criticism, for it substitutes instrumental rationality (whose criterion is indeed success) for value rationality (whose criterion is maintaining and following an idea). Notwithstanding the shallowness of the argument, the target is, once again, the philosophy of history; specifically, its claim to formulate true statements about the historical future.

The need for socialism is here, and has to be satisfied. It has to be satisfied theoretically as well, through attempts to give answers to the question about the sense of historical existence. Marx satisfied this need with his philosophy of history because it met the exigencies of his own time. We have to satisfy it by meeting the exigencies of our own times which are different ones. We have to try to do our best with our own particular resources: no one could do it better than Marx.

As mentioned, Hegel's system is a model of the philosophy of history, not only because all its basic elements are completely fitted together but also because the basic contradictions inherent in the undertaking, those of freedom-necessity, contingency-necessity, subject-object, are reflected upon and solved theoretically in the framework of the system. Marx's ingenious remark that in Hegel's system there has been history hitherto but there will be no history hereafter, was a very apt criticism. It must be added, however, that it was exactly this 'double' character that allowed for the circumvention of the basic dilemma pointed out by Mannheim. One cannot ascribe to a system, as a theoretical shortcoming, the fact that it failed to reflect upon itself in historical terms, *if* it considers itself to be the absolute outcome of the teleological development of the historical agent, as realized subject-object identity, as the absolute totality.

Marx's work is a philosophy of history in which all the basic elements are fitted together, but in which the basic intrinsic contradictions could not really be solved. To put it more properly, Marx makes repeated and various attempts to solve them, not only in one, but in different ways. He goes to the end of one solution, then to another one, and so on, and so forth, and in this experimenting spirit lies his greatness. The astonishing fact that he worked on one single theoretical work for his whole life, which he never finished, documents this inner struggle in the clearest way.

Undoubtedly there is a *theory of history* in Marx as well, though it is subordinated to a *philosophy of history*, from the *Paris Manuscripts* onwards. On the one hand, Marx is inclined to identify progress with the consciousness, and so with the existence of bourgeois-capitalist society; on the other hand, he tends to attribute progress to 'History' as a whole. He is inclined to distinguish 'basis' from 'superstructure' only in modern times, but he also posits the dependence of the latter on the former as a universal functional law of History. Though he holds that the paradigm of production is all-embracing, the 'development of the forces of production' is not always regarded as the independent variable throughout the 'whole' of history. A philosophy of history is superimposed on a theory of history in order to make promise more forceful, in his own case as well. Had he stuck to a *theory* of history, communism could have *only* been conceived of as a *movement*, never as the riddle of History solved. However, in this case, the only statement about the future which might be considered as true would be the following: as long as capitalism exists, communist movements (movements with the intention of transcending capitalism) will exist as well. This statement was not considered to be a powerful promise, at least not in Marx's time.

Space does not permit here a detailed analysis of Marx's philosophy of history. Only a brief reference can be made to the interpretation of its elements and to the ways they were fitted together.

History (with a capital H) is the history of the past, the present and the future. Its virtual starting point is the emergence of production, the creation of new human needs. History is in progress. Not all new societies are necessarily 'more' progressive than former ones; there are setbacks and regressive periods which have to be accounted for. But there *is* a succession of progressive 'social formations' which embody the continuity of history, in spite of, or even through, discontinuity. The same social formation can be 'normal' or 'abnormal', 'classical' or loaded with the remnants of preceding social formations, thus 'unclean'. Social formations of different kind (less and more progressive ones) can coexist.

The indicator of progress is the *wealth* produced in different social formations. This indicator is dialectically divided into two: into the wealth accumulated by the society as a whole and the wealth appropriated by individuals of the same society. Hence historical progress is a contradiction: the more wealth is produced, the more need is created on the level of the whole, yet the less it can be appropriated by individuals, at least proportionally. The development of the essence of humankind is alienated from human existence. But, as I have already pointed out, the two indicators of progress fulfil different functions for the very reason that the independent variable is located on the side of the development of wealth. If this were not the case, the theory could not prove any progress in history at all. However, Marx's main value is embodied in the second indicator. This is why the actual character of historical progress could only be defended by positing that the development of human wealth on the level of 'species essence' *will* lead unavoidably to the appropriation of the same wealth by individuals, to the de-alienation of history, to the abolition of the contradiction inherent in 'history hitherto', to a future termed 'true history', to a realm of *freedom*. Hence the future is the stone that closes, as it were, the edifice of the philosophical system: the value of freedom is supreme, it is historicized, located in the future described as 'true' (with all the philosophical implications of the word). Subject-object identity is the conclusion of a history not yet present, only *potentially* so. It is of minor importance in what detail this future is 'described' by Marx. The whole philosophical system serves only one aim: to prove it. As do all philosophers, Marx criticizes existence in order to infer *Ought* from *Is*. Yet his *Ought* is temporalized, and this is why the philosophical deduction had to turn into a philosophy of history.

Even so, Marx does not apply the first indicator of progress in its complexity as the independent variable of progress. According to his paradigm of production, the creation of *material* wealth serves exclusively as the independent variable. The independent variable (the development of the forces of production) becomes the repository of continuity in history *in an unconditional way*. Of course, the independent variable accounts only for development (or progress), not for discontinuity in the same progress, for the distinction of progressive social formations. These are understood as dependent variables, 'relations of production' (economic relations *sensu stricto*, property relations, division of labour, often used synonymously), all *created, sustained* and *annihilated* by the development of the forces of production. It has to be added that the paradigm of production does not involve understanding the production of material wealth as the independent variable with any kind of theoretical necessity. This is the exigency of the philosophy of history. Moreover, Marx was clearly aware of the fact that his 'social formations' or 'modes of production' (a maximum of five in number) were not even the progressive 'embodiments' of the increase in wealth on the level of 'species Being' *(Gattungsmässigkeit)* in every respect. This is why he emphasizes *'uneven'* development (or progress). Should we, however, take 'uneven development' seriously, the whole argument would collapse or end up in a tautology, namely: if production increases, the material wealth (the amount of material needs) of a society increases as well. Production did, in fact, increase, and this is why the production of material wealth increased from one formation to the other. Consecutive formations could be grasped as *different* ones (as different economic relations) but not as progressive stages in a development, since they were not identified exclusively by the increase in production. But Marx was Hegelian enough to adopt the position that – in spite of uneven development – *freedom* increased in the subsequent modes of production. But if freedom only means freedom with respect to nature, the tautology can still not be circumvented. Consequently, the concept should contain the assumption of the growth of the freedom of the oppressed (an increase in personal freedom), an assumption which contradicts the concept of alienation.

Marx did not confront this contradiction; moreover, he solved it 'dialectically'. In terms of his analysis, freedom in fact increased in the subsequent social formations, thus the proletariat is *formally free*, but alienation increased as well, thus the proletariat is *completely subjugated*

Sense and truth in history

to economic necessity, it becomes a class of modern slaves, more unfree than other classes have ever been. As a result, the increase in freedom is not reality, only possibility. But if it is not reality, former 'increases' in freedom cannot be regarded as 'real' either. In this way, former modes of production can only be described as 'progressive' because they *have led* to capitalism, they have led to the possibility of freedom through the deepest deprivation. As a result, no indicator of progress is left but the independent variable, the development of the forces of production which led to capitalism and will lead to its transcendence by the proletariat. The progressive stages of 'History' are conceived of as progressive ones exclusively from the viewpoint of the future, from *Ought*. The future is 'proved' by a past which was constituted by the value attached to this future alone. The argument is circular, the system is closed. But there is a tension in this circularity due to the awareness of human suffering throughout history. A theory which suggests that freedom has increased only in the sense that the development of production enables the actors of history to realize it here and now, is far superior to the positivist argument that the development of production (technology, knowledge, science) has been and is *in itself* and *actually* the 'carrier' of the increase in freedom.

Furthermore, what exactly does this 'development of the forces of production' mean? It means nothing but the progress of *human knowledge* as 'know-how' which follows the internal logic of one sphere of objectivation, that of the means of production. In the final analysis, Marx describes progress in the same terms as Condorcet did: knowledge and freedom make progress, but not in concert. Freedom has to keep pace with knowledge in the future, and it will do so. But the specification of knowledge in its capacity of 'know-how' was meant to combine the idea of progressive knowledge with Hegel's theory formulated in the famous chapter of *The Phenomenology of the Spirit*, 'Master and Slave'. The subjects of 'know-how' progress are the oppressed, the exploited. The development of 'know-how' increases alienation, therefore, it brings about the impoverishment of the productive subjects. The very knowledge which is the source of progress is the source of alienation as well. Human beings pay with blood and sweat for their self-created progress. The tragic aspects of history are stressed more by Marx than anyone else who has pleaded for historical progress. In addition, the ancient messianic idea of justice, by which the most humiliated must be elevated, is taken up again in a rational way. Since the most humiliated are, because of their 'know-how', the repositories of historical progress, their salvation has to be regarded as *self-elevation*, and self-elevation as the necessary outcome of history.

Here, though, Marx recoiled from closing his system as a complete philosophy of history, and tended to replace it, again, by a theory of history. It is only in the case of the proletariat that the self-elevation of the most oppressed, who are at the same time the repositories of 'know-how', is conclusively argued for. No homogeneity is achieved in the concept of 'classes', even though it was a key concept for his system. The meaning of the concept of 'class' in pre-capitalist societies is different from the meaning of class in capitalism. In the first case, the concept is constructed by *conflict* (all types of conflicting interests), whereas the identification of the oppressed with the role of the repository of 'know-how' is completely, or at least partially, neglected. In the second case, it is *labour* which is identical with the oppressed class waging class war for self-elevation. The important distinction between 'class-in-itself' and 'class-for-itself' makes no sense at all in regard to the colliding interest-groups described as classes by Marx in precapitalist societies. Sometimes Marx came very close to the division of History, not into 'progressive modes of production', but into two parts: precapitalist and capitalist, in keeping with the second understanding of the notion of 'class'. This understanding could lead to a theory of history but Marx shrank from renouncing a philosophy of history altogether, since without such a conceptual framework, the *necessary outcome* of capitalist development, its transcendence, could not have been established. He needs the argument of the philosophy of history; the argument that the development of the forces of production has *always* concluded in the destruction of the relations of production in order for a *more progressive* 'social formation' to become established on the ruins of the former one (unless both the forces *and* the relations of production get destroyed). This conceptualization was needed to make the promise powerful that the same thing *will* happen in the future due to the historical tendency of capitalism. Despite this perseverance, the identification of the 'historical subject' within History remains much too vague. The elements that were irreconcilable in cases of the previous historical subjects are reconciled and conceived of together in the case of the present 'world-historical subject' the proletariat.

The internal tension between a theory of history and a philosophy of history is remarkable here, even if the latter is superimposed on the former. The theory of radical needs, scattered throughout all the works of Marx, would imply a theory of history. The argument that capitalism itself gives birth to needs which cannot be satisfied by capitalism, and so motivates human beings to transcend it, makes the concept of History with all its universal laws and tendencies quite redundant and theoretically superfluous. In this understanding the future is a *value* which regulates the actions of those having radical needs, whereas the image of the future depends on the interpretation -of the value of freedom. In this understanding, the theoretical contradiction between freedom and necessity, contingency and necessity, subject and object, disappears. However, Marx could not renounce, at least not as far as the bulk of his work is concerned, the all-embracing concept of a universal law of progress, and therefore he could not escape the contradictions involved in it. Communism is conceived of as a 'free act' of the world-historical class, but at the same time as a mere realization of the historical law, a necessity to which the actors are subjected. In *Das Kapital*, the action of the world-historical class appears only as a *contingent factor* which cannot change the outcome of History, but can only 'ease the labours' or shorten the duration of the delivery. The subject constituted by the theory as the 'carrier' of the transformation is treated as an *object*. Thus the theoretical contradictions of every philosophy of history (those between freedom and necessity, contingency and necessity, subject and object) are restored and reinforced.

As far as the primary target of criticism and the model of a new society was concerned, Marx synthesized all the socialist conceptions of the nineteenth century from the standpoint of his value (the wealth appropriated by every individual). Through this synthesis, he criticized all other attempts made under the auspices of another value commitment. The concept of 'commodity production' was explained in such a way that it could become the focal point of the whole system from which everything else (the world-historical role of capitalism, its necessary transcendence, and the image of 'real history' as a conclusion) could be derived.

All theorists who point out the absence of the notion of 'alienation' in *Das Kapital* miss the basic issue, that the whole construction of the book is nothing but the reconstruction of alienation. In Marx, commodity production is identical with alienated human labour, and the abolition of commodity production is overcoming alienation. It is quite obvious that already the internal contradiction of the commodity contains all the aspects of alienation delineated in the *Economic-Philosophical Manuscripts*, as the alienation of the product from the producer, the alienation of labour as activity (abstract labour versus concrete labour), the alienation of persons from each other (competition, social relations mediated only by the market), the alienation of human essence from its existence (production of use values and exchange values – the first the essence, the latter the existence). Here too, alienation is conceptualized as a contradictory progress (the progressive development of human wealth at the costs 'of the impoverishment of producers). Alienation *is* private property *alias* social division of labour. The labour theory of value, and thus the theory of production of surplus value, implies a reformulation of a concept of property already present in Marx's youthful work. Property was defined in the *Economic-Philosophical Manuscripts* as the source of enjoyment and of disposition. Surplus labour and surplus value are the values embodied in objectivations (the capital) that the labourer cannot dispose of. The labourer produces property which excludes him or her from being the proprietor. The labourer produces domination and himself as a dominated subject. The rate of exploitation is not primarily an economic category but a philosophical one; as a result, the labour theory of value is not primarily an economic theory either. In his *Critique of the Gotha Programme*, Marx protested against the primitive conception that the equivalent of the worker's work could be reimbursed to him or her *in any society*. The main question is not whether the equivalent is reimbursed, it is the question of who disposes of the social wealth which does not flow back into the private consumption of producers. If the disposal is in the hands of the producers themselves, the created wealth is no longer alienated, it is not capital, not private property, but 'social wealth'. This is called the 'positive abolition of private property', as contrasted with its 'negative abolition'. The latter does not transcend alienation, and this is a major issue in Marx, first formulated in the *Economic-Philosophical Manuscripts* and reinforced in *Das Kapital*, in the famous paragraph about the 'negation of negation'.

To sum up: the first volume of *Das Kapital* is, on the one hand, a repetition of the essence of the *Economic-Philosophical Manuscripts*, hence the second Odyssey of alienation; on the other hand, a synthesis of the basic problems of nineteenth-century socialism organized from the viewpoint of the main value: human wealth. The emphasis placed by Marx on the value of wealth led successively to a more positive assessment of capitalist production long before the final version of *Das Kapital* was drafted. He understood capitalism as a revolutionary society, not only because of the unprecedented development of the forces of production triggered by it but also because it revolutionized social relations in several respects by destroying all ancient forms of human intercourse, thus giving birth to modern individuality. This contradiction led to a tension which could theoretically only be solved if de-alienation could be conceived of as the outcome of the internal dynamics of capitalism rather than as resulting from the outcry of the oppressed. The universal law of development reinforced this twist, as did the different 'tendential laws' of capitalism formulated in *Das Kapital* (such as the tendency of the rate of profit to fall).

The paradigm of production does not imply (at least not in a theoretically consistent way) grasping alienation as commodity production, and de-alienation as its abolition, but this theory was highly serviceable as a synthesis of different socialist conceptions. All the main targets of socialist criticism, different from each other, could be homogenized into one. If the target was private property, capitalist commodity production was conceptualized in terms of private property. If the target was the state (and all political institutions), the state and political institutions could be conceived of as mere superstructures of capitalist commodity production which will wane with the disappearance of the latter. If the target was egoism, individualism (not to be confused with individuality!), these trends could equally well be interpreted as the result of commodity production, as competitive behaviour, which will vanish simultaneously with commodity production. If the primary target was poverty, it goes without saying that poverty also disappears with commodity production. If the primary target is inequality, it is also inevitable that the disappearance of commodity production, hence the introduction of the *direct* satisfaction of all human needs, makes the contradiction between equality and inequality an obsolete one. If the primary target of criticism was the lack of culture in capitalism, this lack was ascribed to the commodification of culture. If the primary target of criticism was the impoverishment of human relationships, impoverishment was ascribed to commodity fetishism, to the transformation of human relations into relations of things, and this will completely be overcome with the abolition of commodity production.

All this is a magnificent synthesis, a most powerful philosophy of history. The operation aimed at 'isolating' Marx's criticism of capitalist economy from its philosophical meaning, by transforming *Das Kapital* into a 'scientific' treatise, cuts off the blood-circulation of the work. The corpse can hardly be revived through infusions of the complementary theory of the capitalist state. The work is constituted from the standpoint of the abolition of commodity production, and so *all* contradictions of capitalism *have* to be inferred exclusively from commodity production, from its genesis and its developmental logic, and from nothing else. All students of Marx who have endeavoured to distinguish between 'science' and 'value' in the work of their master, only replaced his values by other ones, or at least by a different interpretation of values, without overcoming philosophy of history. They reproduced the contradiction of freedom and necessity, subject and object, from the viewpoint of necessity and object.

Of course, there can be no objection in principle to an alternative reconstruction of the Marxian philosophy of history; equally there can be no objections to *other*, alternative, socialist philosophies of history. Marx's paradigm can be replaced by another one, as can the independent variable. The basic contradiction can be conceptualized in more than one way. The source of domination can be reconstructed from different angles – there is no theoretical necessity to identify it with commodity production. The different ways of understanding Marx can be reformulated and purposefully fitted into quite different philosophies of history, but this happens against the will of the authors, who, although confronted with new questions, cannot get rid of Marx's weighty (and sometimes burdensome) legacy.

But there is also another course open to us. We can adopt the position that the replacement of the old paradigm by a novel one, the choice of a new independent variable and new indicators of progress (instead of the previous ones), do not make any crucial difference in at least one important aspect. Socialist philosophies of history may vary but they do not cease to express the consciousness of reflected universality which is, on its part, not the only consciousness of our Togetherness. The consciousness of reflected generality is equally the imputed consciousness of our altered being to the same extent, and it has to have a theoretical formulation of its own. The question facing us is whether we have to proceed at all with making true assertions about the historical future as such. If socialism is inherent in our present culture, socialist theory can also be constituted by restricting its assertions to the present and to the future of present. If, furthermore, socialism is inherent *only* in our present culture, socialists could pass true judgments on the present and the past of present without undertaking the reconstruction of History. If the future is not regarded as a necessary outcome of the present, nothing obliges us to infer the future from the present, and, by implication, infer the present from the past as its necessary outcome. Do we really need a theory of universal historical progress in order to make *our* promise and warning powerful? I strongly doubt it. Just the contrary can be argued for: that in our times, the philosophy of history renders both promise and warning *less powerful,* at least for those who are ready to contribute *rationally* to the transcendence of oppression, exploitation, and domination. Both theory and practice suggest the adoption of the position of *theories of history instead of philosophies of history.*

Let me repeat: even though the theory of history is an alternative theoretical solution to the philosophy of history and highly critical towards the latter, the critical attitude does not mean hostility, above all because theorists of history are very much aware of the limitations of their own undertaking. The theory of history is a philosophy too, but an *incomplete one.* It does not infer its *Ought* from *Is* in the same way as philosophies do. In the theory of history, *Ought* is inferred as only an idea, not as the highest *reality:* it renounces the traditional philosophical identification of *ens perfectissimum* and *ens realissimum.* It is a sceptical philosophy and all sceptical philosophies are by definition incomplete. As far as the practical relevance of theories of history is concerned, the theorists are (or at least should be) equally conscious of their limitation. One has to be aware of the fact that not all those who intend to contribute to the transcendence of oppression, exploitation, and domination act in a completely rational way – and the theory of history implies self-reflection as the point of departure. The philosophy of history may serve as a crutch but the theory of history appeals to those who want to discard all crutches. And it is precisely because of this last circumstance that I propose its acceptance.

Part IV

Introduction to a theory of history

Chapter Nineteen

History retrieved?

Vico rightly remarked that every theory must start from the point where the matter it treats first begins to take shape. Thus a theory of history must start where History first began to take shape; roughly, at the end of the eighteenth century. History – with a capital H – is a *project* of modern civilization. It expresses the life-experiences of this civilization: its hopes and despairs, its struggles, its victories and defeats; its hatreds and loves, doubts and beliefs, elevations and humiliations, tensions and contradictions; its catastrophies and its capacity to overcome catastrophies; its crimes and punishments, heroism and pettiness, poetry and prose, and its values.

'History' as such is therefore *not* the history of humankind. 'History' transformed into the history of humankind encompassing past, present, and future is only the *mental construction* of our history, of the modern form of existence and its history.

The distinction between the 'past of present' and the historical past is very fluid. It depends primarily on our theoretical and practical interest whether an event or structure is understood as belonging to the past of our present or to the historical past. Single events and happenings are much sooner transformed into 'past' ones than are institutions, and institutions usually sooner than epochs and eras. I declared History to be the mental construction of modern civilization; of a whole epoch, in its capacity as the expression of this epoch and so also as its constituent. This is why one may repeat the statement that History is not the history of our past, but the history of *the past of our present and so of our present.* Present always encompasses the future of present; as a result, 'History' encompasses to an equal degree *the future of our present.* But the statement that History is also the history of *historical future* (which we know nothing about) cannot be reasonably supported.

'History' as the history of humankind (past, present, and future) has been described as the mental construction of the past of our present and as a project of our present in relation to the future of present. History as the future of our present implied and still implies the project of a *historical future* that we know nothing about.

Hence it is History, this past and future of our present, that constructed and projected History of the past, present and future. This has been and still is the consciousness of its Being. It is a true consciousness in that it expresses its being-History, but at the same time, it is false consciousness in that it substitutes historical past for the past of the present and historical future for the future of the present. Construction and projection of History (of past, present, and future) is the typical (Kantian) *transcensus* undertaken by those who expressed and express the spirit of modern times which *is* History. The life-experience of modern age suggests that the need for metaphysics turned from universe to history. History (with a capital H) is the *metaphysics* of an epoch which *is* History. The need for exactly *this* kind of metaphysics is deeply rooted in our existence and we cannot get rid of it. We can only reflect upon it.

I have set as a point of departure that History, this form of existence of modern times, was born roughly two hundred years ago, and that the concept of 'History' expressed and co-constituted a development unparalleled in any previous history.

But it must be borne in mind that 'History' is the product of Western European civilization and that at the beginning it comprised only a handful of countries. The majority of the peoples of our earth lived in their own histories and wanted to persevere in them. The 'march of History' meant for them the march of armies ready to destroy their culture and way of life. On their part, they were far from being eager to recognize this necessity as their 'freedom' and as the fruit of progress in comparison with the lower historical stage to which they supposedly belonged. However, History is indeed a dialectical process. The same handful of peoples who began to understand their own culture as the goal and outcome of a world-historical process, and who 'civilized' others by the sword, were at the same time the first ones to understand *all* human cultures as equally human ones. 'Barbarians' and 'pagans' became for them the objects of *unbiased* interest. The idea of the superiority of our civilization was born together with the idea of its inferiority. Lukács correctly described *both* Walter Scott and Cooper as the first literary expressions of world-historical consciousness.

History (with a capital H) was understood as the form of existence of modern times. 'Modern age', though, is much too vague an expression. In order to clarify its content, its basic components have to be enumerated, and there are three of these: civil society, capitalism, and manufacturing industry. The *genesis* of History is the development of its three components. It has to be left undecided, at least within the framework of this theory of history, which one of these components furthered the development of the others. This question is left to historiography, and one has to assume that quite different explanations can be proved equally right. The theory of history starts with its reconstruction where History began to take shape; namely, in the periods when these three elements became compounded: around the time of the French revolution, the American War of Independence, and the industrial revolution. Once having come into being, the basic categories of society (in Marx's term, 'forms of existence') have indeed an internal logic of their own. In other words, they possess their own *dynamis* which is tendentially self-unfolding. It is exactly *this* internal logic (this *dynamis*) that has been generalized in the consciousness of the epoch into the internal logic of human history as a whole. The consciousness is the consciousness of existence, that is to say, the understanding of the life-experience as co-constitutive in this same life-experience. It is our consciousness, our existence, our life-experience, and a constituent of our life-experience. When speaking about History, we express this very *dynamis,* and so reinforce its existence.

The internal logic (the *dynamis*) of a social system's *own* categories (which are, as we know, 'forms of existence') was characteristic of every society. (This generalized statement does not mean a relapse into a philosophy of history. I have mentioned that assertions like 'every society undergoes changes' are *platitudinous* and in themselves do not constitute a philosophy of history.) The internal logic of History (our history) differs, however, from the various internal logics of previous histories. In histories, the internal logic (the *dynamis*) of societies is basically *homogeneous:* they unfold according to this logic, or they collapse. Because of external causes, they *may* collapse even if they unfold in keeping with the inherent *dynamis* (even when not yet having exhausted their own possibilities), but this is by no means a 'necessity'. Yet the basic forms of existence of modern society are not homogeneous. Indeed, they are *contradictory.* Not one single logic

– one single *dynamis* – is inherent here, but several ones. Modern society is characterized by *alternatives*. These alternatives are borne by the actors of *this* history. It has often been pointed out that Marx's generalized statement that the history of all societies has hitherto been the history of class struggles misses the point since (precisely in the Marxian sense) capitalism is the only society structured into classes. In my view it is another difference that ought to be stressed: that modern (civil-industrial-capitalist) society is the only one in which the colliding socio-political groups (not only the classes) might – and usually do – embody *alternative logics* of the same social system. In modern society, the future of present depends to a very large extent on the actors of present, since they reinforce one logic of society as against another, and vice versa. The inherent contradiction between the heterogeneous logics is eventually 'solved', only to re-appear again on a different level and in different subsystems. This is exactly why modern history (History) is characterized by the negation of negation.

Space will not permit analysis of all the main contradictions of the modern age here: I can only make hints at the basic ones. The relative independence and autonomy of civil society is in itself a form of existence with *two* internal logics (a double *dynamis*). It ensures the relative independence of the private-economic sphere. Accordingly, one of its logics is the universalization of market, of the exclusive character of private property, of the growth of inequality and domination. At the same time, it establishes the negative but equal freedom of individuals, thus its second logic is the unfolding and enforcement of this freedom (of human rights) in the process of democratization, equalization, decentralization of power. Simultaneously, the development and growth of industry implies a third logic to an ever increasing extent: the limitation of the market through the centralization of the allocation of resources by the state. The repeated 'solutions' of contradictions may tend towards one or the other logic.

Socialism (or, rather, the different types of socialism) represents, on the one hand, a theoretical proposal to solve the contradictions described above; on the other hand, a movement, or, more correctly, different movements promoting the evolution of *one* of the possible logics of modern society. (Better to say: they are promoting *some* of them, and excluding others.) To put it bluntly, socialism belongs to modern society: it belongs to 'History', since it embodies one of the several possible logics of History. For this reason, socialism (as an idea and as a movement) can only disappear together with our History, with History, with the end of the future of our present, with the end of our world, with the end of the *world-for-us*. The *end* of socialism can only be conceived of as the end of History; not, of course, as the end of all histories, in other words, as the end of humankind.

It follows from the foregoing that it is not viable to contrast future socialism with present-day capitalism as a society which ought to be and can be introduced abruptly through a victorious political revolution or through a catastrophe. This outcome sounds convincing only if one assumes, with Marx, that the logic of industrialization and that of capitalism comprise the only, and in themselves the fundamental, contradiction of modern society, and that the former is basic and determining and has the power to eliminate the latter. However, Marx's assumption is theoretically inconclusive. Although he defined the *'carrier'* of socialist transformation as the main element of the forces of production, he never attributed to it the *consciousness of industrialization,* but rather *the consciousness of freedom, equality, and fraternity,* a consciousness which is the manifestation of *the second logic of civil society.* Thus the consciousness of the subject of socialist transformation was to promote the second logic of civil society, while the objective contradictions of society were located in a quite different sphere. If we take the first suggestion seriously, we cannot do so with the second. And if we take the first proposal seriously (as I do), we have to conclude that socialism is a movement which promotes the second logic of civil society as against the first. This can only be conceived of as a process in which the second logic becomes increasingly decisive. But in this case the pathos of the philosophy of history, a philosophy which always advertises that here is the time and 'now the time has come' for an abrupt and total transformation, becomes completely obsolete. The time is 'here' and it 'now has come' because it is *always* here and there is always a 'now' that has come. It is not only 'here' and it has not come only 'now' in the present, but it was in the 'here' and the 'now' of the past of present and it will be in the 'here' and 'now' of the future of present. This is so because our history is History (with a capital H); because its several logics are contradictory; because the actors can act according to one or another of these logics; because they consequently contribute to alternative futures. All this does not mean that 'time is *equally* here' or that the 'now' would have come to the *same extent* in all given moments. In periods in which certain contradictions are temporarily solved (and also re-created on a different level) the pathos of the advertisements of 'here' and 'now' is always stronger than in others, but it is always present because it *is* the present. Every Togetherness has to be aware of *its own* 'here' and 'now', because the moment is its own responsibility, and *not* because it were the *only* moment that is 'here' and that has 'now' arrived. If socialism is conceptualized as the conclusion, as the evolution of the second logic of civil society (which means the enforcement of freedom, of human rights through democratization, equalization, decentralization of power), then socialist transformation does not imply one single 'turning point', but a development from less socialism to more and more socialism; from a society of domination to a self-governed society, to a participatory democracy, a development which does not exclude the possibility of several turning points. As I have mentioned, this logic is only one of several in our society, and no kind of necessity guarantees its subsequently gaining ground against the others. Let me repeat: we can formulate only one true statement about the future (precisely because it is also a statement about the present); that as long as *our* history exists, socialism – as an idea, as a movement, or both – will exist as well.

In addition, one should remember that in the twentieth century a new social formation emerged which is totally different from the one discussed so far. This new social formation is now fairly stabilized (through trial and error) in the Soviet Union and has recently been established in certain Asian and African states. Within it, there is no relative independence of civil society; it does not contain the inherent logics which may lead either to capitalism or to socialism. The only logic (*dynamis*) shared by the two competing social systems is that of industrialization, although one cannot even guess how far this logic will develop in this new society – there is just not sufficient historical experience as yet. It may well be regarded as the 'cunning of reason' that it is just that society claiming to be socialist which excludes a logic leading possibly towards socialism. Regarding this society, the perspective of a total and abrupt *turning point* (as a political revolution or in any other form) can be regarded as a relevant suggestion. Here, the state has to be crushed in order to liberate civil society together with its immanent logic.

To blame socialism and socialism alone (as an idea and as a movement) for the establishment of this new society, and for the annihilation of the values incorporated in *our* history which has accompanied this establishment, is a one-sided view which has to be challenged. One could rather say that *universalization*, a trend imminent in History, has been halted in many of the regions of the world which had, at least partially, a history different from Western regions. The *dynamis* of the second logic of civil society has not been triggered, even if the first has occasionally been 'imported'. But the responsibility of *certain* socialist ideas and movements (not socialism *in general*) cannot be categoricaally denied, since the idea of universalization has been implanted by socialist ideas and movements into this new social body. It was due to this 'fossilized' socialism that the tendency towards universalization was no longer simply halted, but reversed and ideologically underpinned as the universalization of unfreedom disguised as freedom. How far the responsibility of particular socialist movements and ideas is extended is, none the less, an issue which cannot be decided by any theory of history, but only by detailed historiography. However, the suggestion can be legitimately made that the Marxian paradigm of production, transformed into an independent variable within a philosophy of history, served as an ideological lever for the subjugation of the first (though weak) beginnings of civil society. Already I have made brief reference to the fact that Marx theoretically posited the consciousness of the proletariat (the carrier of socialist transformation) in harmony with the second logic of civil society: human emancipation superseded political emancipation. Though serious doubts can be raised about the viability of the model of marketless society, one cannot have doubts regarding Marx's desire to foretell the disappearance of market together with the abolition of the state. The abolition of the market *by* the state, the subjugation of society *to* the state, never even appeared in his theoretical horizon. But when, in keeping with the exigencies of a philosophy of history, Marx remained with the paradigm of production and constructed the basic contradiction of capitalism as the collision between the forces and the relations of production, he, too, opened the way to substitute the consciousness of the forces of production for the consciousness of one specific (the second) logic of civil society. The consciousness of the forces of production is the *technocratic consciousness,* the consciousness of a planning elite already propounded as such by Saint-Simon. Marx would have never accepted a new technocratic elite as the bearer of the socialist transformation. All the same, if the basic contradiction in modern society can be located between the forces and the relations of production, then only a planning elite could become the bearer of this transformation. Thus the establishment of a ruling elite with all the forces of production at its disposal and with the pretension of 'shaping' society 'scientifically' could be underpinned with reference to Marx not without *some* justification, even if with a great amount of mystification.

Due to the contradictions and tensions between its different inherent logics, the equilibrium of modern society is *unstable*. Instability is not a dysfunction of this society, but one of its life elements. The 'social character', in terms of modern American anthropology (that is, the personal character which meets the exigencies of society), is no less unstable. The successive disappearance of communities (except the family), which was by no means a necessary upshot of the development of civil society in itself, resulted from and was fuelled by this growing instability. All traditions have been challenged and all traditional ways of life have fallen apart. The enthusiastic description of the 'revolutionizing effect of capital' in *The Communist Manifesto* gave a true account of this unparalleled structural change. The complexity of this total revolution cannot be accounted for within my framework here. Only some of its aspects need be briefly enumerated.

In the phenomenological description of the development of the forms of consciousness (Part 1, chapter 1), I gave a brief analysis of the consciousness of generality as reflected in particularity. When analysing this, I had in mind the consciousness of the prehistory of History. The different aspects and values of a culture in gestation were, in this epoch, generalized as the 'human ones' *par excellence*; as the basic constituents of 'freedom' and 'reason' as such. No instability was imputed to the new state (and society) which was to be established: just the contrary – this new society was imagined and designed as stability realized; as the embodiment of the eternal-general truth and good, finally accomplished. The society of unstable equilibrium recognized itself as such only after the breakthrough when its three components (civil society, capitalism, industrial revolution) had been compounded, and with disharmonious effects. The 'generally human' became thought of as the *universal*. The first is the *static*, the latter is the *dynamic* conception of the same notion. Being universal means being *universalized*. The 'universal' is the general, but is at the same time that which is not-yet-general, since it has to *become* general in the process of self-development. The universal is the general which claims to constitute humankind. It is Captain Forward. Stable equilibrium has its limits in the framework in which it has to be reproduced. Unstable equilibrium has no such limits. Its identity is preserved in its non-identity; in fact, its identity *can only be* preserved by its non-identity. And precisely this process of universalization, this successive self-transcendence, this self-preservation through self-transcendence, is *universal progress or universal regress* (depending on our viewpoint).

In the world of unstable equilibrium, the sword of fate does not hang above the heads of the creatures; it rests in the hand of actors who believe in their unlimited possibilities. Napoleon is the world-spirit incarnate: the self-made world gives birth to the representative self-made man. Whoever is nothing today can become everything tomorrow – be it individual or class, it does not matter. And who is everything today, individual or class, can tomorrow become nothing. And all this is not due to the capriciousness of fate or to the wrath of the Almighty, but because the individual or class failed to grasp the moment, the great opportunity.

Captain Forward is Janus-faced. The right cheek reflects the glamour of world-theatre, the left cheek the dirt of the prose of world; the right one the plentiness, the left one the emptiness of life; the right one is a challenge to freedom, the left mirrors the burden of necessity; the right bears the mark of self-realization, the left that of the loss of security and personality. But whichever side we look at, the loss of community and the lack of limitations (self-limitations included) have left almost nothing but *success* as the yardstick to measure human achievements. A few basic values have been universalized, but in the process have been stripped of their concrete content. The reinterpretation and redefinition of the same values, and so the reinforcement of their validity, require a high level of reflection. The formalization of values opens the way simultaneously to the revitalization of various kinds of pre-enlightenment fundamentalism. Particularistic irrationalism is substituted for concrete value-rationalism. The tendency of philosophy of history to go beyond good and evil is, indeed, deeply rooted in History, and is also expressed by it.

However, there are certain general substantive values which can be described as the values proper of History. All of them belong to the second logic of civil society; for instance, freedom interpreted as freedom of personality, or equality interpreted as reason shared equally, or civilian courage, or even the so-called 'civility' of human conduct. These values are morally binding and serve as solid, but usually not very effective, counterbalances against the usual identification of Successful with Good.

The society of unstable equilibrium is future-directed. The present is comprehended as the state of affairs which must be superseded, transcended, annihilated: Captain Forward embarks towards the future, and never gets ashore. The future is not only designed and conceptualized as a world which is no-longer-present, but also as a world completely *different* from the present: it is the *unknown*. But being the unknown motivates us to come to know it nevertheless. The unknown or 'that which is to be known' is obviously not the *outcome* of a particular event or undertaking (permanent concerns of human beings), but the outcome of future *itself*, of future as a venture. What is to be known is not whether *this particular* war will be lost or won, but whether there will be wars at all in the future; not whether *this particular* person will manage his fortune well in a certain transaction, but whether he will become a millionaire or a beggar. What was considered as the future in past histories is no future at all for the actors of History. There was once a world in which young men intended to marry, to have children, and continue the vocation of their fathers: this was a *future* for them and a *real* one. Young men of today, if faced with a similar prospect, would say that *they have no future at all*, for 'nothing new will happen to them'. The very *framework* of change has to be changed. The unprecedented has to happen, for only the unforeseeable is accepted as real future. The novel, the unprecedented, the change of the framework of all changes catches the fantasy and raises enthusiasm. But there has never been a history in which people have cared less for their own and their world's future-in-the-present. It is no wonder why. The future of the present is stripped of its content. Those who care for it become empty.

Time is the *fourth dimension* of our history. 'Time is not a container', Hegel remarked, challenging Newton long before the theory of relativity. In philosophy of history, time is always the fourth dimension because History is four-dimensional. And it is exactly because time is no longer a container (as it was), and because history is four-dimensional, that the future-of-the-present – the future inside a stable framework – lost its relevance and became empty. Marcuse's conception of the 'one-dimensional man' expresses human existence in an originally four-dimensional world once the fourth dimension has wasted away. As long as time is a 'container', the future-of-the-present alone constitutes the depth of personality. After the change, it constitutes this depth no longer.

Philosophy of history reflects upon its situation in a twofold way. On the one hand, it recognizes that the 'modern world' is different from all preceding ones. On the other hand, it applies the categories ('forms of existence') of the modern world to all histories of humankind. I reiterate: no philosophy of history applies historical understanding to the present and the future, and it is perhaps understandable why. Philosophies of history historicize humankind in an ahistorical way because their categorical system of historicization is not adequate to the histories *they historicize,* but only to the history of present *against the background of which they historicize.*

Philosophy constructs *Ought* and infers *Ought* from *Is.* Philosophy of History, as the consciousness of History historicized both *Ought* and *Is.* The historicized *Ought* has to be inferred from the historicized *Is.* This inference could only be made if (a) *Ought* is grasped as History; as the history of present and future, or as human relation to both, (b) *Is* is equally grasped as History (history of the past, present and future), and (c) the temporalized *Ought* is comprehended as the outcome of the temporalized *Is* in a positive or negative way. (The development of *Is* gives birth to *Ought,* or the development of *Is* impedes *Ought.* In the second case, the inference is accomplished by a negative temporalization of *Is.*)

Of course, no philosophy can pluralize *Ought.* The greatest concession of the genre is distinguishing between the different levels of *Ought.* Contradictory versions of *Ought* are nonsensical (they are self-contradictory). The dynamic of modern society (of History), however, is contradictory. This is actually why it *is* History (unstable equilibrium). But since no philosophical *Ought* can be pluralistic in character, and since it has to be inferred from *Is,* no philosophy of history can take into account all possibly logics of modern society, at least not as *equally relevant* ones. One logic from among many has to be selected as the *only* or perhaps even the *essential* one. It is this procedure that presses for true statements about historical future. The unknown is pretended to be known as the predictable (because necessary) conclusion of *one logic* of modern society. In this respect it is to no avail whether this logic is supposed to conclude in catastrophe or salvation. So as to prove that there is only one logic of our history, or that only one logic of our society is 'essential' in order to be able to make true statements about 'historical future', this single logic of *our* history had to be mentally transformed into 'the logic' of whole human history. In short, the logic which has been chosen (according to values) as the only one, has been 'proved' to be the only one.

Histories of humankind (different as they were) thus became prehistories of the history of present, lined up and arranged in keeping with the very logic of the present, which the philosopher of history wanted to prove as the decisive one.

It is just this procedure that is rejected by theory of history. The

latter does not revoke historicism, but rather wants to make it conclusive.
It meets the challenge to reflect upon our history historically and
offers an answer to the question about the sense of historical existence.
This is why it must start by reconstructing the contradictory logic of
our history. This starting point alone has many theoretical and
practical implications. One such implication is the complete reformulation of the notion of History.

Our present is no longer the present of a single culture but of quite
different ones. It *became*, in reality and not only in our imagination,
the present of our humankind. 'Togetherness' is now the 'Togetherness' of *all* people living on this earth. It encompasses various cultures
and various social structures that have *various pasts and various past
histories.* We all share our time and our space. We are bound tightly
together not only with ties of economics and politics, but also with
ties of moral responsibility. The future of present depends on all
societies and cultures of the present, whether we are conscious of this
future or not. The very social structure I described above as History is
only one culture from among many. As I argued earlier, this history
has a set of contradictory dynamics, and at least one of them *may* lead
to socialism. There is no overwhelming evidence to convince us that
similar logics are embedded in other cultures which we share our
Togetherness with, though if we are committed to promote this
particular logic (the one leading potentially to socialism), we have to
will that all different cultures which share our Togetherness *should*
develop the same logic. Thus History becomes a *project*, an idea of the
future of humankind. Needless to say, for all those who commit
themselves to *another* logic of modern history, History may represent
a project in the same or similar way. Living up to my own
commitment, however, I am going to argue on behalf of the project of
History from the viewpoint of the *second* logic of civil society.

In this way, theory of history conceives of History as a project from
the reflected standpoint of one of its basic logics. Yet it does not suggest, as philosophy of history does, that this History is a necessary outcome of a past called History, nor does it declare that the whole history 'possesses' one single logic which leads of necessity to the society
of unstable equilibrium. It does not suggest either that the future of
humankind can only be imagined as the continuation of our culture,
although it is its inherent intention that it should be. Hence the project
of History does not imply the reconstruction of the past as the past of
History. Just the contrary: theory of history renounces the *ontological*

constitution of History. If History is only a project, it cannot be constructed as a *factual development*.

Philosophy of history has always dealt with the present: the ontologization of history was the imputed consciousness of the present. It made warning and promise powerful. Theory of history is equally a philosophy, even though an incomplete one. It deals with the present to a no lesser extent, but it is conscious of it. This awareness is nothing but the application of historicity to its own theoretical suggestions. It has to formulate its promise and its warning without the usual overdetermination experienced in philosophies of history.

What can a theory of history tell about the past? If it is conscious of its dealing with the present and of its being the imputed consciousness of the present, is it able to tell anything about the past at all (except about the past of present)?

If the theory of History *projects* History into the future, it has to acknowledge the *unity of the human race*. Here I have to refer back to the analysis of the stages of the development of historical consciousness. The consciousness of reflected generality (identified now as the theory of history) *turns back* in a way to the consciousness of generality reflected in particularity and its basic article of faith by which human beings are born free and are endowed with reason. But since it is formulated as an answer to the question about the sense of our *historical* existence, theory of history is bound to historicize this article of faith as well. The *genesis* of humankind has to be understood as the 'History' of the human race; History with a capital H.

Owing to this, the constitution of 'History' of the past is not *completely* revoked. It is identified with the development of *homo sapiens* and with its *first* life-manifestations. The ancestors of *all* humans were hunters and gatherers in more than 90 per cent of their history. It is reasonable to regard this history as something that was shared *in fact*. All basic human abilities, drives, affections – the abilities of reasoning and of becoming free – have developed in this period. This, and nothing but this, is the foundation of the *promise* that in the future we *might* share a history in common; that we might share 'History' again, not in an unconscious but in a conscious way. Nothing but the *common genesis* can make us think that one logic of the civil society, the logic pointing *towards freedom* and *reason*, is also grounded, even though not in any kind of necessary evolution of historical formations but in the quality of *homo sapiens* shared by all specimens of the race.

If this is accepted, we can drop the whole procedure of constituting the past as 'History' – ontologically. It is a reasonable assumption that the primordial 'History' – history lived unconsciously: history without consciousness of history – has been divided from the neolithic revolutions onwards into *different histories.* 'History' *in itself* is the genesis. 'History' *for itself* might be the future but *there is no guarantee in histories* at all that this will *in fact* be the case. There is equally no guarantee in histories that if this will in fact be the case, 'History-for-itself' will follow the only logic of civil society that the author of these thoughts is committed to. To put it bluntly, neither the genesis nor separate histories are *guarantees* of socialism: they do not even guarantee the perseverance of socialist ideas and socialist movements embedded in *our* history. The most we are entitled to say is that they *do not exclude socialist ideas and movements,* and since I am committed to the latter, *I am also obliged to believe that so it might be.*

If one replaces 'History' by histories (except for the genesis and the past of our present), the whole edifice of the philosophy of history falls apart.

Past histories undoubtedly have to be 'arranged' one way or the other. As has been stated, historiography, the only true knowledge which really deals with the past, cannot cope with its task without applying organizational principles, both synchronic and dyachronic ones. Various philosophies of history might suggest various organizational principles (consistent with their particular sets of values), although they are by no means bound to do so. Nevertheless, one cannot 'link up' historical formations according to their alleged 'inherent developmental logic', inferring a later formation from a former one through the aid of a concept of 'necessity'; nor can one legitimately select one 'world-historical sequence' from the rest. 'History' should not be imagined as a chain of progress or regress, nor should it be grasped as a chain of eternal repetition. Hence the 'indicators of progress' have to be eliminated, as has the common 'independent variable' of the whole historical process. Philosophy should not superimpose itself on history. There is no solid argument that could make us believe that the development of *all* societies followed exactly the same pattern; that change came about in all societies because the *same* component developed in all of them; and that *all* societies collapsed for the same reason. Why a particular society developed and in what way, and what were the basic components in its flourishing and decay; these are questions which can be solved in each case by historiography (and historiography alone) with the aid of meaningful theories.

Instead of regarding ourselves as the goal of 'History' we can regard 'History' as our goal. Instead of being the spectators of all former generations' supposed march in the same dark tunnel whose end is supposedly revealed to us, alone, and for the first time, we may consider them as being detained in different prisons, as fighting on different battlefields, and as occasionally enjoying some well-deserved rest in an oasis.

It has already been pointed out that if a historian accepts a philosophy of history as a 'higher' theory, then he always corrects it in his research, and that this holds true even if someone applies a personal philosophy of history. Historiographical works confined to exemplifying the truth of one particular philosophy of history were always simplistic and could not live up to the expectations of the genre. The real contribution of philosophies of history in the reconstruction of the past was due to their answering the question about the sense of historical existence: the existential question led to the selection and directed the beam of the quest for meaning towards a particular dark spot. This task can be accomplished by the different theories of history as well. The emphasis on one of several logics of modern society, the way it is conceived, the manner whereby the values related to it are interpreted; all this can lead the selection and can direct the beam of the quest for meaning in a fashion wholly equivalent to the *modus operandi* of philosophies of history. It is obvious that the application of generalized sentences and hidden analogies and all other procedures involved in the application of orientative principles are not at all restricted to philosophy of history. They have been factors in historiography long before the emergence of philosophy of history. The assumption that there is no such homogeneous development as the one called 'History', but rather various histories, does not exclude the application of analogies, parallels, typologies, from the scope of inquiry. The claim that the emergence, the flourishing, and the decline of different cultures (social structures) cannot be described by *the same* pattern does not at all mean that no *similar* patterns may emerge or re-emerge in various distinct cultures. All societies have to solve the problems of human coexistence in one way or the other simply because we are human, social, historical beings. If one states that it is, in all societies, a social necessity to produce at least on subsistence level, one is not obliged to say at the same time that the development of the forces of production is *the* independent variable in *all* cultures. If one states that procreation and socialization of children have to be regulated in every

296 Introduction to a theory of history

society, one is not required to say in the same breath that the development of the family is *the* independent variable throughout whole history. If one states that all societies express themselves in meaningful world-views, one is not committed to explain all societies in terms of repeated changes in the spirit of time. If one accepts that statesmen, prominent warlords, or religious leaders contributed to changes in different cultures, one is not bound to regard them as the historical subjects *par excellence*, as motive forces of all changes throughout history. All this applies also to collective authors. If one formulates the generalized statement that 'if power is not subjected to law, the form of political domination will usually degenerate into tyranny', one is not bound to proffer this statement as 'the law of History'.

Here I have to reconsider a previous statement which proposed that all histories (historical pasts) are equally close to humankind. In this formulation, the notion of 'humankind' was interpreted as human-kind-in-itself. All histories share a common genesis and so embody the different possibilities of our human species; all of them *equally embody one* possibility of this species. Despite this, if we construct 'History' as a project, thus as the *idea* of a humankind-for-itself, we should never accept, since we *cannot* accept, the thesis that all histories are equally close to humankind. The decisive criterion for our evaluation of various histories of the past is the circumstance of which one among the logics of our society we choose and how we evaluate it. We *choose* our history (or histories) from among many. The chosen ones will be *closer* to humankind within the framework of our theory related to our commitment.

Various theories of history will choose various histories of the past. In what follows I have to restrict myself to a reference to the possible choices of those theories of history which project 'History' concordant with the second logic of civil society, which I consider to be socialist.

The consciousness of reflected generality historicizes the fundamental statement of the consciousness of generality reflected in particularity: that human beings are born free and are endowed with reason. All philosophies of modernity accept freedom as the supreme value, although they interpret the same idea in quite different ways. Some, though not all of them, render *reason* a part of freedom. However, reason can be interpreted again in different ways, basically either as value rationality or as goal rationality or as both. Goal rationality itself can be interpreted as mere instrumental rationality or as goal rationality proper or as both. A theory of history as the imputed consciousness of reflected generality has to accept reason as inherent in freedom. This is obvious because *every* logic of modern society implies rationality in one or another world-view. This is why the interpretation of reason becomes decisive in the interpretation of freedom. If the project of 'History' is formulated in keeping with the second logic of civil society (radical democracy, self-managed society as equivalent to socialism), value rationality must have the primacy in the interpretation of reason, and consequently the notion of freedom has to involve *moral commitment.*

Because of this, the selection of histories has to prefer those who were *closer* to this project – at least as far as some of their accepted values are concerned – than other ones. Of course, in various socialist theories of history various values can be emphasized, and the fundamental selection can also be made in different ways. One may choose histories with the greatest personal freedom; histories with the least amount of suffering; histories not dominated by a small minority. But every theory of history has to make a selection and none of them can accept the 'inherent developmental logic' of 'History' as leading from a 'remote' to a 'closer' period(s). Despite the innumerable sufferings of its population, why should an Asian despotism be closer to our hearts than societies of peaceful tribes displaying human dignity? Would it be a sufficient reason that the former is 'more complex', or that it developed superior forces of production, or that it is characterized by a sophisticated political structure? A theory of history rejects argument based on the logic of 'in spite of'. Being fully aware of the contradictory logic of modern societies it acknowledges dialectic *only in* modern society. This is why a theory of history has to reject the philosophy of regress and degradation *in toto*, whereas it rejects the philosophy of progress only *conditionally.*

In the next chapter I will analyse this problem in detail. For the moment it is sufficient to stress that a theory of history does not allow for the contemptful treatment of our civilization compared to preceding ones. Since a theory of history adopts the position of one particular logic existing in this society, it has to criticize harshly all other logics embedded in it, yet without choosing any other history devoid of the logic whose position has been here adopted. The project of 'History' and the construction of the common history (genesis) of humankind is the product of *our society*, of our history, no less than philosophy of history. But in one respect it is closer to the vital questions of its birthplace than certain philosophies of history are. Should a Kierkegaard exalt Don Giovanni's grandeur as compared to the 'pettiness' of Don Ottavio because the latter was not ready to take justice in his own hand, but rather subjected the criminal to the law, a theory of history will not share his exaltation and his contempt. No criticism of our society should convince us to choose personal revenge instead of legal justice and law enforcement, mass starvation and mass terror instead of refined manipulation. In my own mind, I share the choice of C. Wright Mills, who referred to Athens and Jerusalem as the symbols of history we are most indebted to. The reason is simple: a 'pre-history' (with all the necessary qualifications of such a concept) of the second logic of civil society (to the evolution of which I am committed), is most recognizable in these two historical *loci.* This is not a new choice. It is recurrent in our history, and it is even accepted, though not openly professed, by several philosophies of history. The selection of these two histories (and perhaps some other ones) has nothing to do with 'lining-up' cultures. Their exemplary character does not imply the assumption that our culture 'regressed' in the last 2,500 or 2,000 years. The choice is not ontologized. It is a value choice and is understood as such.

Apart from the selection of histories from the viewpoint of the project of 'History', a theory of history also entails a general and an all-encompassing criterion for theorizing histories. The value of freedom, interpreted as the freedom of personality and as a value-rational commitment of everyone endowed with reason, functions as a yardstick of assessment of various histories and defines the approach to all of them. Partiality for freedom, if devoid of the image of the 'march of history', of the 'lining-up' of cultures, or the argument of 'in spite of', concludes in partiality for those who are and were deprived of freedom. *It is the partiality for those who suffered the most.* And if it comes to this, to the partiality for those who suffered most, the theory of history no longer selects. It is partial for *all kinds of suffering.* Once this approach is taken, all histories are again equally close to humankind.

Chapter Twenty

Is progress an illusion?

'History', as a construction of the philosophy of history, was comprehended as the reflection on, and the projection of, modern civilization; of the society characterized by unstable equilibrium. The categories of universal progress or regress are thus self-reflections of this civilization ontologized in the process of *transcensus*. Chroniclers and 'cultural lawgivers' of certain high cultures prior to the modern one occasionally related the notions of development, summit, and decline to particular societies, but they never generated the idea of a universal tendency pointing 'upwards' or 'downwards' throughout History as a whole. The categories of universal progress or regress were born in modern times; first, because both progress and regress express the form of existence of modern age; second, because universalization as a tendency and an idea expresses exactly the same thing. There has been only one society hitherto which can be conceptualized in terms of progress and regress adequately, and this is our society. Needless to say, this is far from being a novel idea. However, philosophies of history adopted the position that the specificity of our culture is to induce us to *recognize* the general tendency of progress or regress throughout 'History'. As we have seen, this is the false consciousness of the philosophy of history. A theory of history convinces us of the validity of the theoretical proposal that in societies which did not develop the notions of progress and regress, *there was no* progress or regress at all, and so we are not entitled to 'recognize' it. Progress and regress can only be related to a civilization which elaborates the notions of progress or regress. It follows from this that a theory of history cannot accept the tenet of 'eternal repetition' either. The modern age does not repeat certain previous historical patterns for the very reason that the notions of progress and regress have only emerged from this age. These

300 Introduction to a theory of history

notions reflected on this new form of existence.

Whether the philosopher understands and describes modern age in terms of progress or regress depends on his or her meaningful world-view and value-system applied as regulative ideas in reflection upon the present. In what follows, modern age will be reconstructed in the main from the viewpoint of progress, simply because the theory of history I am going to argue for is led, both theoretically and practically, by the regulative idea of progress.

To select an indicator of progress and to use it as a yardstick to measure the amount of progress in different cultures means to vindicate for ourselves the position of the absolute; of God. In so doing we place ourselves *outside* history, although we have no right to do so because we *are* history. This holds equally true with regard to the indicators of regress and of eternal repetition. When Kierkegaard turned away from the Hegelian concept of world-spirit and conceived of history as a puppet theatre where the strings directing the actor-puppets are pulled by God, he rejected the influence of his great antagonist to a far lesser extent than he himself thought.

Collingwood proposes that if 'there is gain *without any* corresponding loss, then there is progress. And there can be progress on no other terms. *If there is any loss, the problem of setting loss against gain is insoluble.'** No, we are not entitled to select one gain or another and declare that the losses are of secondary importance or inessential. Nor are we entitled to select only the losses and declare that the gains are of secondary importance or inessential. The *nonchalance* of theories of progress and regress for living human beings, for their sufferings and their enjoyments, is astonishing; indeed, it is *shocking.* The application of the two indicators (first of all by Marx) is the only sincere attempt to overcome the arrogance of theories of progress and regress. But despite all the well-deserved respect that a responsible theory of history must pay to this theoretical proposal, it cannot adhere to it, because of the unequal status the two indicators occupy in the Marxian theory. Because all losses suggest human suffering and all gains suggest human enjoyment, every comparison of cultures carried out by the application of the indicators of progress or regress involve the *use of human beings as mere means.* But it is precisely this that is excluded by the supreme value of theory of history. A theory of

---

* R.G. Collingwood, *The Idea of History,* Oxford University Press, 1963, p. 329.

history has to accept the proposal of Collingwood. We are only entitled to speak of progress if 'there is gain without any corresponding loss'. (Just as we would only be entitled to speak of regress if there were losses without corresponding gains.)

It follows that even the development of *our* society, *our* culture – 'History', cannot be described as progressing or regressing either. There have always been, and there are presently, gains *and* corresponding losses. We are not entitled to declare that it was the gains that 'really' mattered while the losses did not, and vice versa. Stating it once again, since the framework of 'History' is the theoretical expression of our history, all philosophies of history decide upon this very question. If they consider the gains in *our* culture to be the decisive ones, they 'signal' progress in 'History'; if they consider losses to be preponderant, they 'signal' regress. Hence the crucial question is that of progress and regress in *our* culture – in the very society in which the categories of *universal* progress and progress were given birth.

If it comes to 'measuring' our culture in terms of progress or regress, then to the description of its *actual* tendency there is no difference whatsoever between the conceptions of progress and regress. And there is a difference still. Let me quote Collingwood again: 'There is one other thing for historical thought to do: namely *to create this progress itself.* For progress is not a mere fact to be discovered by historical thinking: it is only through historical thinking that it comes about at all.'*

I have stated that there is *no* progress or regress in modern society because there are both gains and losses which are incommensurable unless we use human beings as mere means, which we must not do. Yet it still must be emphasized that there *is* progress and regress in modern society in that the *ideas* of (universal) progress and regress were born in this society and these ideas express this society's form of existence. Furthermore, even though *both* of them represent the imputed consciousness of our historical existence, and thus of our historical consciousness, their *function* is different. The idea of progress provides us with a *norm for creating progress,* whereas the idea of regress provides us with a norm for a form of life in an ever darkening world. Consequently, the norm of the idea of progress *can be considered as a universal one* (even though not all theories of

---

*R. G. Collingwood, *The Idea of History*, Oxford University Press, 1963, p. 333.

progress claim universality), whereas the norm of the idea of regress cannot, for reasons of principle, be universalized. The norm rooted in the idea of progress can be viewed as binding for whole humankind; the norm rooted in the idea of regress can only be binding for a chosen elite. I have already mentioned that *universalization* is a basic tendency in our modern world, in 'History'. Hence the idea of progress *expresses* the form of existence of our modern culture in a more adequate way than the idea of regress.

As a result, even if I refuse to acknowledge any *actual* progress in our (modern) society, I feel entitled to say that *there is progress in it* in the sense that it gave birth to the idea of progress as *a value*, as a regulative idea, both in its theoretical and practical uses. *The will to create progress is progress.* The idea of progress and the will to create progress are *realities:* they *exist;* they exist *now;* they exist *here* – they represent *a gain. Were the idea of progress conceived of in the spirit of the norm 'gain without losses', it would become itself a gain without losses.* This is, in fact, what a genuine socialist theory is, or should be, all about. It refuses to compare the incommensurable, to decide whether this or that particular gain or loss was or is more or less important. Its idea of progress is that of gain without corresponding losses because it refuses to use human beings as mere means. This approach is entitled to the claim that, should it be accepted as a theory for social actions, this very acceptance would be a gain without losses.

Viewed from the horizon of the theory of history, progress is not accepted as a fact, but neither is it denounced as an illusion. It is an idea and therefore a reality. But in so far as the idea of progress implies the acknowledgment of progress *in fact*, it is ambiguous, for it involves a *moral contradiction* in that it allows for the use of other human beings as mere means. It is a gain which does not exclude losses, hence it is only a conditional gain. The same idea of progress could become a factual gain unconditionally only if this moral contradiction were solved. Of course, no one knows whether this contradiction will in fact be solved by everyone whose intention it is to create progress. But all those who accept this concept and norm of *progress* are already committed to promote its resolution.

Hitherto it has been taken for granted that the ideas of universal progress and regress express the forms of existence of the culture of unstable equilibrium. But the very emergence of these categories only in modernity seems to be the only proof of the theoretical proposal. This is not a sufficient foundation. It seems to be necessary to return once again to the 'life-world' of modernity.

The society of unstable equilibrium and of contradictory developmental logics is the *dissatisfied society*. Captain Forward elicits this dissatisfaction and is at the same time motivated by it. The phenomenon I am speaking about is not simply dissatisfaction with one's personal lot, or with the corruption of political institutions, or with the loosening of moral ties. These types of dissatisfaction have often motivated human beings in their striving for the 'betterment of life'. The phenomenon in question is a dissatisfaction with the life-world as a *whole*; with the values themselves, and not only with their infruition; with the existing economic and political institutions *in general*; and not only with their insufficient or corrupt ways of application. Because of this it is a holistic dissatisfaction, not a specific one. It emphasises not the wish to restore a previous order or the intention to set right the present one, but the wish to transcend the limitations of social and personal character in their totality. Politically and socially radical trends of different provenance are far from being the only forms of expression of holistic dissatisfaction. The struggle between generations and the resolution of new generations to leave their fathers' way of life behind them became general phenomena, as Ernst Fischer showed, from the French Revolution onwards. No form of life is permanently fixed any more; thus every form of life is experienced as unsatisfactory. But the novel one which replaces it soon turns out to be equally unsatisfactory, and so on, *ad infinitum*. Philosophies of history dutifully followed suit. Most theories of progress promised a change which in itself was a total one: *redemption* from the tension or dissatisfaction. Theories of regress ontologized and justified the same dissatisfaction, and upon either the world, or the eternal struggle between biological and social existence, laid *total* blame for it. Dissatisfaction was transformed into absolute hope or absolute despair.

Theories of history reflect upon the same dissatisfaction, but in a different way. Their principles involve *activating* it, but at the same time *detotalizing* it.

If progress is the idea of gain without any losses, the acceptance of this idea involves dissatisfaction not only by losses *per se*, but also by gains achieved at the price of losses. It obliges us at the same time not to use other human beings as mere means. We too are human beings; as a result, we must not use ourselves as mere means either. No one has the right to be satisfied in a world in which others are suffering. We are obliged to help. We are obliged to do everything in our power to diminish the loss and alleviate the suffering, providing that we never use other human beings as mere means. This proviso is inherent in the norm, for using human beings as mere means causes *new suffering* and *new losses* incommensurable with the possible gains achievable through our actions. But when we have done everything in our power (which is our duty) we have to learn to enjoy our life *as it is.* We have to learn to get the best – the greatest possible amount of *satisfaction* – out of it because we have only got this life, and we should not use ourselves as mere means either. Whoever feels satisfaction will not despair. Whoever does their duty has a right to hope. The question is not whether the state of a 'dissatisfied satisfaction' is easy or difficult to achieve but whether it has to be proposed. Neither the narcissistic cultivation of one's own self nor the activist exaltation of self-sacrifice on the altar of the future are attitudes to be more easily generalized and more viable; perhaps even less so.

One way or the other, dissatisfied society is the society of progress. Total dissatisfaction is at the same time a *universal* dissatisfaction. To put it simply, *everyone* has the right to be dissatisfied, since *everyone's* satisfaction can be taken as a goal. This does not amount to the statement that everyone *is* in fact dissatisfied because of everyone else's situation but that everyone has the right to be dissatisfied with his or her own situation. The notions of freedom and equality are understood as *universals.* Thus everyone who did and does suffer from unfreedom and inequality can justify his or her dissatisfaction by his or her situation, and so claim liberation and equality.

The universalization of dissatisfaction has to be accepted by a theory of history as a gain. Moreover, the idea of universalization has to be deemed *a gain without losses,* even if the actualization of this idea produced not only gains but losses as well. Here, the statement that the idea of progress has to be recognized as factual progress by a theory of history ought to be made more specific. The idea of universalization of dissatisfaction: the idea that every human being, if unfree or unequal, has the right to dissatisfaction, is a progress in fact achieved in the society of unstable equilibrium. It is a conditional one, but this condition is *the* condition for the want of which the new idea of progress (gain without losses) could not have even come about.

To have a right to be dissatisfied presupposes a state of having rights. Only those have a right to be dissatisfied who are inside the political body of a society in which dissatisfaction can be expressed through legally guaranteed channels. Others can *be* dissatisfied without *having the right to be.* They can ask for favours but they cannot appeal to rights. The declaration of 'human rights', the expression of the universalization of freedom and equality, has been the foundation of the right to dissatisfaction, even before several strata of social underdogs could get inside the body politic. To apply any notion of progress to societies that deny the right to be dissatisfied is a *particularistic* procedure which contradicts the universals whose standpoint it intends to express.

It occurred to very few philosophers of history that when they applied the concepts of progress or regress to 'History' as a whole, they completely left out of consideration half of humankind: *women*. It is most astonishing indeed that while 'lining up' cultures according to their 'inherent developmental logic', philosophers have not considered the circumstance that the fate of women has practically never changed. To be exact, their fate did occasionally change, but mostly *inside* the same culture, and not in the course of transformation from one culture to another. (Fourier, the only thinker who was really conscious of this problem, created very arbitrarily a line pointing 'upwards' in this respect as well.) Freedom could (and did) pass from 'one' to 'several' but those 'several' have never been women. The 'development of forces of production' could lead to different 'relations of production', but women never ceased to be the property of men. (Engels, though again one of the few aware of this fact, still used the theory of universal progress together with the argument of 'in spite of'.) Women have never belonged hitherto to any kind of body politic, be it simple or complex, democratic or despotic; for women, all of these polities were equally despotic. Even cultures most exemplary in respect of value-rational freedom excluded women from that same freedom. 'World-historical personalities', be they warlords, statesmen, or scientists, were almost exclusively male. Women's only contribution to history recognized as such was their giving birth to the world-historical men. They were doing the task of nature, not of society; they were given an ahistorical role, not an historical one. Women never *made* history, they only *suffered* it. And they were always in company with those who suffered the most.

When a theory of history states that 'History' is equivalent to modern age, that 'progress' (as an idea and in this capacity, as reality) is the form of existence only of our history, it formulates a statement which is *obvious* for at least half of humankind. It adopts the position of those who, when *all* histories of civilization are taken into account, suffered the most.

Our culture is the first in which women have the right to be dissatisfied. It is the first which gives the possibility for half of humankind to make history, and not only to suffer it. Notwithstanding even substantial losses which may occur during the realization of this possibility, the latter alone is a gain without losses, and as such it is progress. It is related to the novel concept of freedom and equality which encompasses all human beings, all social strata, classes, nations, and *both* sexes, and the right to dissatisfaction for all of them indicates that progress is progress for everyone, and that everyone can contribute to it.

It is obvious that the idea of progress can be (and indeed has been) formulated from the viewpoint of several logics of modern society; thus from the viewpoint of capitalism and industrialization (modernization) no less than from the viewpoint of the second logic of civil society (socialism as the radicalization of democracy). Universal right to dissatisfaction, as related to the universalized concept of freedom and equality, is formulated and claimed by those who promote the second logic of civil society. However, it is the deepest contradiction of the society of unstable equilibrium that while it *expands* its project ('History') and thereby subjugates several other histories together with their own logics, it superimposes several logics of its own development on them, *with the exception of the second logic of civil society.* But at the same time, the idea embedded in the second logic of civil society and which implies everyone's right to be dissatisfied has been disseminated as an idea devoid of the internal logic that it originally expressed. As a result, the internal contradictions of the society of unstable equilibrium have been externalized in a particular way. Different histories revolt against the expansion of the project of 'History', which subjugated them to the logics of industrialization and capitalism, yet without being able to implant the second logic of civil society into these same histories. The ideology of this revolt is borrowed from the theoretical arsenal of the second logic of civil society, but has no roots at all in the life-world and social structure of the societies in revolt. Adopting the standpoint of the second logic of civil society implies acknowledgment that all revolts pursued in the light of its idea are justified, but one should not consider any society coming about as a result of this revolt to be progressive if it does not display the second logic of civil society. The separate realization of the various logics inherent in the culture of unstable equilibrium in separate countries may lead in some of them to an 'unfree emancipation'. But democracy should make no compromise. No despotism or de-enlightenment must be understood as 'progressive', even if it comes about as a result of a movement with an originally emancipatory intent. On the other hand, the process of liberation of different histories from the 'expansion' of our project of 'History' is a totally legitimate one. One may hope (but only hope) that the unity of 'humankind in itself' may lead to a 'humankind for itself' in keeping with the second logic of civil society, and for all those sharing this hope there is an obligation of commitment for it as well. But there is *no knowledge* as to whether this will in fact be our future. Progress is not characteristic of history as a whole. It was born in the modern age and it may well disappear with it. While creating progress and maintaining it by this very act, one can only believe (not know) that it will continue. Future progress is not a necessity, but a value to which we are committed and it is through this act of commitment that it becomes a possibility.

Histories are stories of murder, humiliation, plundering, looting, meaningless toil, suffering. As the culture of unstable equilibrium, History has nothing to boast about; it is an exact copy of its forebears. Our tiny Europe alone has been bled white twice in this century. Progress is made an object of ridicule by monstrous crimes, and by the indifference of peoples of the 'civilized world' who face these crimes unperturbed as long as they can pretend to be ignorant of them. Should this indifference be due to ruthless egoism or should it be a defence mechanism against the feeling of impotence, in both cases it gives free rein to criminals. It is sacrilegious to indulge in the idea of *factual* progress in an era in which the Holocaust, the Gulag and Hiroshima could happen, and, after all the solemn promises to the contrary, Kampuchea (whose name stands here for many genocides in the last two decades) happened again.

No one has the right to blame human nature since no human being is superior to his or her species. In addition, blaming human nature is self-contradictory since it is also an expression of that same human nature that has been blamed. The tasks of our time have become enormous. The world has become *one* even though it is divided. The actors of the present are confronted with items of information coming from everywhere: they are overwhelmed by horror. Formidable events become antiquated daily through other, even more formidable events. Just being conscientious means to behave like Atlas in Heine's poem: to hold the burden of the whole world's suffering on one's shoulder. The whole world weighs on our conscience.

It is a truism of present-day journalese that the first genocide happened in our century. Those who constantly repeat it ignore the fact that the first great work of world literature (another project of 'History') describes a genocide – the destruction of Troy and the extermination of its population. The summit of republican Rome (which everyone learns of in school) was also a genocide. The place where Carthage once stood was ploughed by brave Roman soldiers, and the former inhabitants of the city were killed or sold as slaves. 'Victrix causa diis placuit, sed victa Catoni': even if (as claimed by Lucan) Cato felt sympathy for the vanquished, the deities were with the victor, which demonstrated that one could avoid a bad conscience about what happened. But the assertion that the first genocides have happened in our century is not based upon ignorance. This 'forgetfulness' is the expression of a radically new phenomenon. As there are no less and no more monstrous deeds in present history than in past histories, so there are no less and no more genocides; we simply have a bad conscience about them; 'we in general', since they cannot be accepted as accompanying our project of 'progress' – they lack harmony with our values and in fact contradict them, thereby making us feel outraged. Even so, this in itself would not suffice to elicit the qualms of conscience. One can (and should) feel these qualms only if one is the perpetrator of, or the accomplice in, the evil deed. But we do feel pangs of conscience about infamous crimes without being either perpetrators or accomplices. This can only be explained by presuming that, wittingly or unwittingly, we share another feeling as well: that the crimes in question *could have been prevented by us* if only we had been resolute enough. We feel a *personal responsibility* for all actions which annihilate and revoke the values we regard as valid. This feeling of responsibility could be viewed as imaginary: after all, what can one person do against the powers of the world? Yet this is not an imaginary or affected, but a most authentic feeling. Everyone has the power to do at least *something* against the horrors of the world. If cumulated, this could amount to some weight.

Bad conscience can become a trap as well. We know from Freud that the tension of guilt feelings can be reduced by their transformation into real (factual) guilt. Such tension can also be easily managed through cheap talk about corrupted human nature. It can induce us to abandon the value of progress, to swap it for a fundamentalist ethics of a sort in the process of de-enlightenment. In short, it can promote escapism of all kinds. But it can equally be transformed into the alleviation of suffering: into actions of aid. Public opinion and private sacrifice may prevent crimes, should be they soon enough. The idea of progress can only prove itself valid if everyone committed to it acts in concert. Our century should not be terminated as shamefully as it both began and has continued.

Chapter Twenty-One

The need for Utopia

We have seen that philosophies of history formulate true statements about historical future as a whole. Should they adhere to the theory of progress, they infer Ought from Is so as the former becomes a necessary outcome of the latter. Is and Ought are equally historicized. Ought is split into Ought-to-Be and Ought-to-Do, both being produced by an Is itself considered as a product of 'History' in its entirety. This is exactly why both Ought-to-Be and Ought-to-Do are seen as outcomes of all human history. As a result, both derive from the universal law of evolution. But being necessary conclusions of the development of 'History', they cannot be understood as two forms of Ought but only as two forms of Is. What ought to be, *it is* and *will be*, or it is not but *it will be*. Ought is translated into the present and future tense of existence. Yet this translation is performed with a false consciousness. If Ought is only a figment of imagination and must be grasped as the outcome of Is – as Is temporalized, all previous forms of existence of 'History' have to be identified with Ought no less, and the whole universal law of development falls apart. But the form of Is (in the present and the future) have been put forward as values, and as the realization of the highest value, that of freedom. Hence Ought as Is cannot be located in the past. In philosophies of history they resemble lovers who after thousands of years of engagement meet in the nuptial bed of the present and/or the future. This wedding is the end of history (or prehistory) for which the bell tolls.

I have observed that every philosophy infers Ought from Is, but it is far from being the exigency of philosophy to *identify* Ought-to-Be with 'It-Will-Be' and Ought-to-Do with 'It-Will-Be-Done', only with 'It-Can-Be' and 'It-Can-Be-Done'. But even here the inference must be a valid one. Philosophy has to reconstruct the path from Is to

Ought. This is the case even with Kant, who inferred the categorical imperative from the fact of pure practical reason.

Obviously, the theory of history is an *incomplete* philosophy.

This is so for several reasons.

(a) Since any theory of history applies historicism to itself, it temporalizes both Is and Ought. It reflects on its Ought as on the consciousness of our existence, as on the consciousness of 'History' *alias* the society of unstable equilibrium. In this respect it does not differ from certain philosophies of history. But it does not share their assumption that this Ought is a necessary outcome of 'History' of the past and the present. But if historicized, Ought cannot be completely *formalized;* it must connote certain substantial (material) values as well; those which have emerged or have been universalized in the society of unstable equilibrium. Moreover, the various attempts to formalize Ought are equally reflected by the theory of history as expressions of *our* historicity. All various formulae offered by those attempts are understood as *values* chosen by *our* historicity.

(b) A theory of history infers its two forms of Ought (Ought-to-Be and Ought-to-Do) no less from Is than do all other philosophies. It adopts the position – as most philosophies do – where that 'which ought to be done' *can* be done and that 'which ought to be' *can* be. However, it does not assume that that 'which ought to be' *will* be and that that 'which ought to be done' *will* be done. Marx once suggested that humankind never sets a goal for itself that cannot be realized. This is a statement typical of philosophy of history. Theory of history replaces it with another statement, less ambitious, more realistic, and more *binding:* that humankind never produces values which cannot be observed and constantly upheld.

Thus every theory of history formulates its Ought in the form of Ought (not Is), as ideas and norms, and suggests also that values which ought to be upheld can be upheld simply because they express and embody the consciousness of our very existence and because they were formulated in order to be upheld. The various Oughts of the theory of history exist and are co-constituents of our Being because they regulate both theory and action. They are *not*, however, goals which can or cannot be realized. They are measures of all evaluations, guidelines for *all* goals inherent in all postulates of those actors acknowledging their validity and being ready to uphold them. Whether or not the goals set in the spirit of these two types of Ought will be realized, no one knows. Upholding the values means not more and not less than an obligation to formulate only such goals as do not contradict the two Oughts, that no exceptions can be made, that the argument 'in spite of' is inadmissable; and that concurrent with all this we must strive to realize goals that harmonize with the various types of Ought.

(c) As mentioned, a socialist theory of history works out its two types of Ought through the second logic of civil society. This logic exists. The two types of Ought of the socialist theory of history are the Oughts of this very Is. They are ideas produced by this tendency which react and continuously reproduce it. Let me reiterate: as long as the second logic of civil society exists, these two types of Ought will exist, even if their external existence is unnecessary and even if there is no necessity for them to overpower all other logics inherent in our society. Anyone committed to this second logic of civil society is also committed to its two types of Ought; to setting and realizing goals in the spirit of this commitment, whether or not this logic will break through.

A theory of history is a consciousness of the society of unstable equilibrium, of future-oriented society, of dissatisfied society, of the society in which the concepts of universal progress or regress have been born. In affirming one real logic of this very society, the socialist theory of history accepts the idea of progress. It commits itself to progress, though without assuming that there has been any progress hitherto except the emergence of the idea of progress which it is committed to. Thus the idea of progress (interpreted as gains without corresponding losses) *is the Ought-to-Be of this theory.* It is a value, and as such, the idea of a future society. Plainly, the idea of progress cannot be conceived of without an idea of future. But theories of history, ready to create progress, refuse to formulate true statements about the future. This is why their idea of a future assumes the form of *Utopia.* It is not the future which is inferred from Is but the *Utopia of a future.* This Utopia is an image of the factual universalization and realization of the very values rooted in the second logic of civil society. It is a *holistic image.* Even though it contains the *realization* of all universal values, it does not suggest that they will in fact be realized. What it suggests is that the conflicts of the present and the future *ought to be* and *can be* resolved again and again in a way that would make our society resemble more and more this image. But it does not contain any binding promise that they *will* be resolved in that way. With this in mind, we should set goals adequate to the idea of a Utopia, not expecting the 'realization' of this Utopia but the bringing about of a world which *may* bear a greater *resemblance* to it than the one we live in. If we do everything in our power to create a world resembling somewhat more this Utopia than does ours, we have done our duty, whether we wholly succeed or not. And having done our duty we may enjoy our life, the only life we have.

(d) The Utopia, as an idea of one possible future, as the idea of what Ought-to-Be, implies a commitment and thereby regulates action (that which ought to be done). But it regulates only the actions of those who have *already accepted* the Utopia as a binding idea and so committed themselves to the second logic of civil society. The norm involved in the idea of the Utopia ('gain without losses') implies, however, that no human being should serve as mere means for use. As noted, if we strive to create a world more akin to the Utopia than that presently existing, we have done our duty whether we succeed or not. Even if the validity of our contribution does not depend on success, as is always the case with value-rational actions, *we wish our cause to succeed,* we *will* that the world should more resemble the Utopia in the future than ours does in the present. Otherwise our deeds would become mere outlets for narcissistic self-realizations.

The norm of the Utopia involves the freedom of personality and does not allow for arguments of the 'in spite of' type.* Hence the will to bring about a society which resembles the Utopia more than ours does presuppose that *the others will the same. The maxim of our will* is that every human being *should will the same. The actual universalization of the idea of the Utopia* is therefore the maxim of our will. The second Ought ('that which ought to be done') has to be formulated as follows: we ought to act in keeping with our ideal (utopia) in a way such that our actions can lead to the free acceptance of our utopia by every human being. Again, there is no guarantee (and so no knowledge in advance) whether or not our Utopia will be accepted by everyone, but we should theorize and act in a way such that our theories and actions *could* lead to the free acceptance of the Utopia by everyone.

(e) The Utopia of a completely self-governed society is the idea of progress; the idea of a process of gains without corresponding losses. As such, it has to promote the pluralism of the forms of life. Human beings can be socially equal only if they are unequal in their tastes, inclinations, desires, talents, and interests. The Ought-to-Be can and should be specified in different ways; equally, the Ought-to-Do can

---

* I have worked out this problem in my book *Pour une philosophie radicale,* Le Sycomore, Paris, 1979, pp. 113-41.

and should be pluralistic. All particular goals regulated by the Utopia and all activities mobilized for the realization of such goals, various as they are, equally fulfil the imperative of the 'Ought-to-Do', even if the realization of such goals may contradict each other in the present; this is a proviso for their simultaneous realization that will actually comprise the image of the Utopia. In all these cases the contradiction is not rooted in the supreme values but is due to the priority of need-satisfaction. As a result, it can (and ought to be) solved in practical discourse. Living up to the postulates of the idea of progress involves acceptance of rational argumentation as the means *sui generis* of conflict-solving in the manner proposed in the theories of Apel and Habermas.

Since the Utopia of progress promotes the plurality of forms of life, the socialist theories of history can and should be pluralistic. Various theories may have affinities with different structures of needs, propose various forms of life, and provide various answers to the question about the sense of historical existence. These theories have to recognize each other as equally true (if within them all other criteria of true knowledge are met), and the ways of life they endorse as equally good. If this is so, the arguments of these theories will not be aimed at the refutation (falsification) of the other theories, but at self-verification; in other words, at the justification of their own preferences for a particular form of life.

(f) Even if we accept the idea of progress ('gains without corresponding losses'); even if we promote the second logic of civil society and share the Utopia of universal freedom (in which no one can be used as a mere means by another), we must still face the fact that in our society there are no gains without corresponding losses; that there is no progress (except for the idea of progress); and that human beings *do* use human beings as mere means. People who share the idea of Utopia and set goals consistent with this idea ought to act in a way that their actions *can* lead to the free acceptance of their Utopia by *every human being*. But how can people accept this idea *freely* if their vested interest is in *another* logic of the society of unstable equilibrium, in a logic which contradicts the one rooted in the second logic of civil society? That which is conceived of as gain without losses by those promoting the second logic of civil society is for the advocates of the first logic a *loss*: the loss of their prerogative of using other human beings as mere means. The regulative idea of action signifies the *free* acceptance of all goal-realizations, but a proposal can only be accepted freely if it is rational argument that decides. Rational discourse can only be discussion between the socially equal. If such discussion is in fact intended, all those prepared to *obstruct* discussion with power, prepared to decide matters with force and in consequence to suppress discussion, *have to be forced to listen to arguments.* This force has but one aim: to place the social group of those being dominated into a (perhaps momentary) position of equality with those who dominate; into a position which allows for rational discussion. The other party should have the right to speak freely, but only as an *equally human* being; and his or her needs and interests would not be considered as more or less relevant than the interests and needs of those who are doing the forcing. Should, however, the other party refuse the ideal of the Utopia and defend a different logic of the society of unstable equilibrium, but from the position of (social) equality and *not* from the position of domination, the use of further force for any purpose is, on principle, excluded. Forced freedom is a contradiction that no dialectic can make acceptable. *The wills of all persons* (as *persons* and not as representatives of domination) have to be allowed *equal* status if we desire that our will should be accepted freely and shared by everyone.

(g) Adherents of a socialist theory of history are obliged to act by the norm of the Utopia and create counter-institutions *as well as* argue for their ideas. But *they cannot know* if the Utopia will be accepted, although this is their desire. This is why this theory *forgoes the right* to 'appoint' the bearers of this theory. It is not entitled to prophesy that the transition *will* happen, only that it *can* happen and that it ought to happen. Hence Ought-to-Be and Ought-to-Do are inferred from Is only as *ideas, not* as their *universalization* and universal acceptance. This is why a theory of history is not only *not* a philosophy of history, but, as a philosophy, is an *incomplete* one, and is incomplete on purpose.

A theory of history does not promise the 'realization of this theory's dreams' to humankind; nor does it warn that its nightmares will come true. The promises and warnings of this theory are not embedded in 'History': they are borne by historicity, by human actors who understand themselves in historical terms. There is no other promise but the perseverance by the authors of the promise. There is no other warning but their failure to persevere.

It is very difficult for children to understand what the notion of 'tomorrow' really means. They wake up in the morning and impatiently ask their parents whether today is already tomorrow. The parents smile and explain that tomorrow is not today but that it will come tomorrow. And the whole process is repeated the next day. If you smile, you are at one with the parents in failing to understand that the children, too, are right. Tomorrow is always today, even if tomorrow is never.

The theory of history I proposed can be interpreted as a version of historical materialism. The Utopia of the theory belongs to our (modern) age as one of its forms of consciousness which is in harmony with the second logic of civil society. The theory and its inherent Utopia is in this way rooted in life-experience. It implies a rational choice among the existing sets of values which regulate theory and action and co-constitutes life-experience. It also implies the criticism of all life-experiences which are not in harmony with the second logic of civil society, which hamper its development. Of course, life-experiences are evaluated anyhow; there is no experience exempt from evaluation. Experiences also change and vary according to social classes, environments, and individual situations. The evaluation of life-experiences through the value-set of the second logic of civil society entails the interpretation of this logic which on its part *reassesses* experiences. But there has to be something *in common* in different life-experiences if we assume a propensity in them to reassess themselves with the interpreted (second) logic of civil society; a propensity to produce and reproduce an idea which serves as an *objectivation-for-reassessment*. This 'ingredient in common' has to be a *motivation*, a motivation for the readiness-to-this-idea.

If ours is the *dissatisfied* society, the shared life-experience becomes the experience of dissatisfaction. Dissatisfaction is a life-experience which involves the persistence of the feeling of *want*, the feeling that our needs are not met. In a dissatisfied society the feeling of 'want' is an empirical universal. This 'lack of something' - this 'want' - is felt whether or not we can conceptualize it. Always hoping to eradicate it, we reproduce it again and again. There are only fleeting moments in our lives in which it is not felt; the moments of self-abandon and surrender. But these are (and can only be) moments; 'want' is always present.

The ways through which we try to get rid of 'want' are dependent on the (assessed) life-experiences; these are partly socially inherited, even though they are often modified. The logics of capitalism and industrialization offer an obvious outlet by orienting human beings towards ever more consumption, ever increased 'having', but, of course, *none of these can ever be enough*. Another remedy is forced self-abandon and surrender: life-surrogates; life-substitutes. There is no reason to be disdainful about it; it is not easy to sail on the ship of Captain Forward.

All logics of modern society offer world-views for the interpretation of dissatisfaction; forms of life through which attempts can be made to dispel dissatisfaction.

The need for socialist theories and world-views has been generated by the second logic of civil society. Universal freedom and equality are the ideas of this logic. But precisely because the various logics of the society of unstable equilibrium are contradictory, it is obvious that universal freedom and equality *cannot* be achieved within its framework. The satisfaction of these needs thus implies both the *abolition* of the present society and its total transcendence. As their satisfaction must be viewed as a social issue and not an individual one, these are *radical needs:* their satisfaction means the *radical* transformation of the total social life-world. If life-experience is reassessed by the values and ideas accompanying these radical needs, all other needs and the world-views pertaining to them will be completely devalued or treated with great suspicion. This suspicion has also frequently been extended to need-structures and values that gave preference to the contradictory development itself and to the repeated and relative resolution of the contradiction through its perpetuation.

To be concise, socialist philosophies of history express these needs, and their theoretical proposals are formulated to meet them, though these formulations differ greatly. Far from recounting the various solutions, I can only hint here at some of their basic (and often controversial) tendencies. Despite their differences, there is one common denominator in all these philosophies of history: that 'want' (in all its forms) is thought of as something 'bad'. Their common regulative idea is *satisfied society.* Concomitantly, they identify satisfied society with future society: satisfied society is the future, it is the goal of the present, and it *will* exist. Summed up, their true statement about the future is – satisfied society will be established.

The satisfaction of all needs, which is by implication identical with satisfied society, is a concept very easily challenged. There are needs which can, for reasons of principle, be satisfied only if other needs are *not* met (e.g. the need for unlimited power or wealth). Consequently, in the above theory these needs had to be conceptualized as 'unreal' or 'imaginary'. But even if this theoretical proposal were accepted, we would face other major problems. The satisfaction of all needs presupposes either absolute abundance (unlimited material resources) or relative abundance (stagnation of the structure of needs). The first alternative is not rational (considering that we already encounter limited natural resources) and the second alternative requires another subdivision of our needs into 'real' and 'imaginary' ones whilst still labelling all dynamic needs 'imaginary'. But we cannot judge future generations' needs and we cannot legitimately label our contemporaries' needs as 'imaginary' either. For the philosophers of 'satisfied society', tomorrow will either always remain tomorrow and it will never become today, or they try to convince us that 'it is already today' even if it is not. In the first case, they simply express dissatisfaction; in the second, they tend to deny it, but either way they never undertake to reflect on it in a reasonable manner. Philosophies of history of this kind cannot offer *genuine* satisfaction for radical needs, though they facilitate the transformation of dissatisfaction into despair: if tomorrow never comes today, perhaps there is no tomorrow at all, and if today *has to be called* tomorrow, there is even less of a tomorrow. It is the early Bernstein and his sort of social democracy and *not* Bolshevism that I have here in mind. The latter completely renounced the second logic of civil society and ceased altogether to be a socialist theory. In the case of Bolshevism, the slogan of the 'satisfaction of all needs' was simply transformed into the doctrine of a 'dictatorship over needs', and this has to be left out of the present analysis.*

A socialist theory of history understands itself as an expression of radical needs as well. But it does not promise the future satisfaction of all human needs. Because it disregards the futile task of making true statements about the future, and because of its rational Utopia, its idea and norm do not involve the satisfaction of all needs either. The norm of rational Utopia implies the *recognition* of all human needs except those presupposing the use of human beings as mere means. By the same token, the recognition of all human needs is the recognition of everyone's freedom and equality in his or her capacity as a *social person,* a situation free of contradiction only if one excludes from the recognition of all needs those whose satisfaction makes others unfree and unequal. The recognition of all human needs implies the *norm* of their satisfaction, but not their *actual* satisfaction. Such a theory of history incorporates a twofold promise by which *all human beings decide as equally free persons the priorities of their need-satisfaction and that this decision can result from rational discourse.*

---

* This issue has been discussed in full detail in our collective book: F. Fehèr, A. Heller and G. Márkus, *Dictatorship over Needs* (in manuscript).

The promise to satisfy all human needs is a *false promise*. Even if it expresses radical needs it cannot come to terms with them. To begin with, it lacks an ethical norm for behaviour and action. As no individual can satisfy all human needs, their satisfaction cannot be a binding norm for anyone. Membership of movements which *promise* the satisfaction of *all* needs does not even entail the obligation to *recognize any*. Not even the most particularistic forms of need satisfaction; not even the violation of others' ways of need satisfaction, are excluded from such a member's behaviour. Nevertheless, the claim to *recognize* all needs except those whose satisfaction involves using other people as mere means provides an ethical norm in itself; as such *it is binding here and now*. The capacity to recognise all human needs – both in our personal life and in socio-political action – is universal.

Still, the right to advocate this norm presumes the accepting of it and living up to it. Hence the will to universalizing it (having it accepted by everyone) is not an empty desire or wish, but a real will, a duty, an obligation; *therefore*, tomorrow has also become today in this will even if it remains tomorrow. The demand for the recognition of all human needs can be met here and now if the individual does recognize all human needs, even if the universalization of this norm is projected into tomorrow. 'Tomorrow', with all that it means, may be uncertain, but today is certain, and no uncertainty of tomorrow can rob human beings from the *satisfying* feeling that they have lived up to their duty. Of course, the recognition of all human needs equally involves the recognition of our own needs (in so far as they do not allow the use of other human beings as mere means). The satisfaction of *our needs* is thus justified wherever it does not contradict other people's recognized needs and the needs of those who appeal to us and whose needs we are able to satisfy.

Furthermore, theory of history's Utopia, which promises that priorities in need-satisfaction ensue from rational discourse, is again 'tomorrow', which is also 'today'. This promise brings the following ethical norm: whenever the actor of the present (of 'today') participated in some other person's need satisfaction, he or she should engage in rational discussion about priorities, even if this means recognizing all needs awaiting satisfaction, among them his or her needs as well. If, given two equal claims, priorities cannot be decided rationally, then priority has to be granted to the *other* in line with the norm of *goodness*. In *our* family, in *our* circle of friends, in *our* communities of various kinds, radical democracy can be realized *here* and *now*. If there is no 'tomorrow' already today, there will be no tomorrow at all.

I have proposed that radical needs which somehow 'cling to' the false promise of satisfying every need have either been repeatedly and very easily particularized and de-radicalized or turned into despair. Such radical needs, if bound up with the rational Utopia of the theory of history, do not run these risks. Despair is not totally excluded here either, but it becomes a *moral issue* because only those despair who fail in their duty: those who uphold the norm will not despair, whatever the circumstances may be. Only false promises can be betrayed.

But no one can be 'liberated' from dissatisfaction. Those who observe the norms of a socialist theory of history will not be liberated either. The promise only implies the transforming of dissatisfaction into an *inner tension of meaningful life and outcry*. In the observance of our duty, in doing what we ought to, the world is still full of formidable events which should have been avoided but in fact were not. The norm of recognition of all human needs triggers outcry because needs without recognition prevail. Moral outcry is felt as suffering. No meaningful life can be exempt from suffering as long as there is reason for outcry. And no one can promise that in the future *there will not be* such.

The idea of satisfaction of all human needs in a particular future has been called a 'false promise' not because it cannot be realized. I do not pretend to know anything 'true' about the future, and so I do not know whether this will or will not be the case. There is not even justification enough to state with certainty that this will not be the case. I have emphasized that scarcity is always relative and that the full satisfaction of needs depends on a particular society's structure of needs. I called this idea a 'false promise' chiefly because the idea of satisfying all needs *contradicts* the very idea inherent in the second logic of civil society. From the viewpoint of a theory of history, 'satisfaction of all needs' reduces to a *negative* Utopia; a nightmare.

Every need is satisfied if everyone *feels* his or her needs to be satisfied. This can be imagined as two different models. Model A suggests a completely homogeneous need structure where *no effort* is required by anyone to satisfy these homogeneous needs. This is the image of *Schlaraffenland*, where everyone lives from hand to mouth. Any effort that has to be made for the satisfaction of these needs must itself be a need as well, and a homogeneous one, prescribed completely by tradition. An effort which was not so prescribed could only be regarded as an *individual* act. Should it be considered a collective and non-traditional one, *arguments* for or against the effort could not be excluded and, as such, arguments involve the *priority* of need satisfaction, not everyone's need would be satisfied and the situation would be caught up in contradiction. If we take this model of 'satisfaction of all needs' seriously, we either get a traditional and static society, or no society at all but a loose conglomerate of atomized individuals, none of them partaking in the second logic of civil society. Model B, on the other hand, can be imagined in terms of a completely successful manipulation of needs. Here, the structure of needs can be heterogeneous as well, varying from stratum to stratum, whereas the members of the different strata might be socially conditioned to feel satisfied with their lot. This model does not allow for the individual structuring and satisfaction of needs any more than the first for the simple reason that it is out of question to condition every individual in a different way. This is the model of the 'brave new world', a most abhorrent one. Yet there is no way to imagine the simultaneous satisfaction of all needs other than in terms of these models and their variations.

For Marx, the free human being was the individual rich in needs, and no socialist theory of history can think otherwise. Being rich in needs means the differentiation of the structure of needs in keeping with every personality through the appropriation of social wealth embodied in different objectivations. This ideal implies the recognition of all human needs but it does not imply their actual and simultaneous satisfaction. Although the slogan of the satisfaction of all needs can also be found in Marx – a slogan almost universally accepted by socialist theories of his time – it could not really be fitted into his philosophical system. In fact, in the *Economic-Philosophical Manuscripts* he emphasized just the contrary; that there will be 'want' in a communist society as well, but *a type of 'want' adequate to genuine human nature, to human dignity*. Thus all human needs have to be satisfied which as 'wants' are not worthy of genuine human beings; which *hinder* the development of needs; which on their part are felt as 'want' only by human beings rich in needs.

The rational Utopia of the theory of history also embraces this ideal. Equal recognition of all needs as a 'progressive' project can only be considered if the satisfaction of *at least some needs* is being presupposed. It belongs to the monstrous features of our civilization, and it cannot be formulated in any other way but as an antinomy, that *the equal recognition of all needs creates* ipso facto *a new inequality:* that of millions who will strive for the recognition of their needs on a mere subsistence level, while other hundreds of millions will view the recognition of their incomparably more complex needs as far removed from any problems of mere subsistence. This means *equal recognition* and the (temporary) *fixation of actual inequality* by the same act and at the same time. At the very least, the equal chance to self-articulation should be achieved so that the equal recognition of every need *will not* create a new inequality. As mentioned above, this implies the actual satisfaction of at least some needs for everyone.

I repeat: the Utopia of the theory of history *obliges all those who accept it as an idea to accept it morally, as a norm.* I have argued for the obligation of recognizing all human needs, here and now. All those committing themselves to the Utopia of the theory of history have no right to draw distinctions between 'real' and 'unreal' needs and 'real' and 'imaginary' needs and the like. All needs which are felt as 'want' by human beings are real. This does not mean, however, that we are obliged to place *equal importance* upon each need (which has practical consequences for the hierarchical ordering ensuing from social rational discourse), not even if they preclude the use of other human beings as mere means. If someone mentions the mass starvation of children in South-East Asia and receives the answer, 'this is bad enough, but our children suffer from alienation because of an overdose of television and this is no better', we have cause for outrage and our proper reaction is moral indignation. One mother wants her child to read books instead of constantly watching the TV and the other wishes that her child should survive – both these needs are real *and as such* (but only as such) deserve equal recognition. But should *equal importance* (which concerns priorities of practical urgency of satisfaction) be attached to both? Here, the acceptance of the equal chance for self-articulation as a fundamental precondition of the equal recognition of needs (without creating by the same fact new inequalities) brings the following norm. Although needs deserve equal recognition, those needs have a *practical priority of importance* which *cry with their bare existence without the slightest chance of self-articulation:* the needs of those who are subjected to despotism, who are innocently exposed to violent death; the needs of those bereft of the means of elementary subsistence and survival, of the means of their reproduction as *natural* beings.

Everyone who shares the will to the acceptance of the Utopia (as an idea) by everyone else has to recognize all human needs with the often mentioned restrictions. Since the theory of history upholds the Marxian ideal of human beings rich in needs, it involves an anthropology based on the *unity* of human nature, an anthropology which refuses all divisions of 'human nature' into noumenal and phenomenal halves. Hence the will-to-Utopia cannot be conceived of as a *pure* practical will (in the Kantian sense of the word) but as a will interconnected with, and partially motivated by inclination and desire. In willing that our Utopia be accepted freely, we have to assume that there are human inclinations which do not contradict this will; moreover, which can become motivations for its acceptance. Radical needs – borne by the second logic of civil society – are supposed to be needs of this kind. This does not mean that everyone who feels these needs *will* accept the Utopia, but that its acceptance is in harmony with these needs, and so everyone who feels them *can* accept it. This is so not only because the person in question finds the arguments on their behalf reasonable, but because the Utopia adequately expresses their feelings. Furthermore, if all the goals proposed by the adherents of the Utopia must harmonize with the values of that same Utopia, and the 'Ought-to-Do' inherent in the Utopia demands the recognition of all human needs (with the restrictive formula), it may reasonably be assumed that these goals can freely be accepted also by those whose needs are not radical *per se*. If the Utopia provided goals only for actors with radical needs, it would cease to be the same Utopia which claims the recognition of all human needs.

As a result of this, any socialist theory of history has to combine *anthropological radicalism with political realism.* Anthropological radicalism implies the rational conviction that nothing in human nature prevents humankind from co-operating; that an ever greater resemblance to the Utopia could be achieved. This radicalism also suggests that certain inclinations and motivations exist in us now which could lead to the general acceptance of this norm. Political realism implies the rational conviction that all steps taken in the direction of an ever greater resemblance to the Utopia presuppose the *active* (not only the tacit) *consent of everyone concerned,* and that this consent *does not normally mean the acceptance of the utopia* (in the understanding of a socialist theory of history), but only consent to the particular step taken or to a particular set of goals. The second logic of civil society cannot be 'realized' with a preconceived plan; the very image of such a plan would contradict the logic that this society is supposed to realize. This logic can only be 'intensified' step by step in a slow and often painful process. Whether or not it will actually be intensified no one knows, but it can only be done this way. In this scenario, revolution is interpreted as the transcendence of the society of contradictory logics through the increasing preponderance of the second logic of civil society; as a process which can become our future only if anthropological radicalism and political realism can be combined.

It should be remembered that the needs borne by the second logic of civil society are not the only radical ones. Other needs exist which cannot be completely satisfied in the society of unstable equilibrium, and whose satisfaction necessarily aims at the transcendence of this social structure, but in a totally different (opposite) direction. For instance, the satisfaction of 'the thirst for power' (as this need was called by Kant) is the very need which is limited in the societies of unstable equilibrium by the contrary dynamic of the second logic of civil society. The satisfaction of this need, which would be nothing short of *unlimited power*, triggers off a social trend for the abolition of this very second logic of civil society; it generates a need for the abolition of democracy of all kinds. It would be fatal to underestimate this and other similar needs expressed in certain philosophies of history, and in the exaltation they evince for 'great historical personalities' as for historical subjects *sui generis*. Such needs are all the more dangerous since they can be reinforced by discontentment with instability and with the insecurity so deeply rooted in our culture, and even with the burdens of responsibility thus generated, which are difficult to cope with. An ever-increasing need for stability, for security, for the 'strong men' who should take over all the decisions and so all the responsibility, comes about. The need for unlimited power can also be amplified by the feelings of *ennui*, emptiness, repetition (all adequately described by several theories of *Kulturkritik*), if they are transformed into needs for excitement, for adventure, for 'living dangerously'. One may call these latter needs 'rightist radical' in character, although the notion seems to be somewhat vague, and to locate and identify them is more important than labelling them. They promote the transcendence of the society of unstable equilibrium through the annihilation of the second logic of civil society in a new despotic state.

The radicalism of the second logic of civil society can never recognize the need for unlimited power (as it contradicts its logic and uses human beings as mere means), but *it has to recognize all human needs*, among them those which *might* reinforce rightist radicalism, as *real* ones; that is, in accordance with the Utopia, it is obliged to offer goals, projects, and counter-institutions that might be accepted by people whose needs would otherwise turn towards rightist radicalism. A socialist theory of history has no right to take the position of the 'strong and resolute' who are not bothered by their own insecurity (or perhaps do not even sense it), and who under any circumstances will take the burdens of responsibility. The commitment of a socialist theory of history is a task that can only be accomplished by everyone.

That the motivation for change can be looked for in human needs, in the structure of needs, in a (relative) scarcity felt as 'want'; this idea can be traced back to Marx, and has been elaborated from the viewpoint of one philosophy of history (by Sartre) in our times.

A theory of history I am proposing here also detects the motivation for change in the need structure, but does not look for its application to, or generalization into, the project 'History'. This is not only for the reason that the theory refers to modern age – to the society of unstable equilibrium – and is not aimed at needs in general but at particular needs for particular changes felt in a particular life-world and expressed in particular objectivations and ideas. This in itself would not prevent us from formulating a generalized statement to the effect that 'every change in history is motivated by needs'; it would not prevent us either from transforming *needs* into the independent variable *par excellence* of every change throughout 'History'. But in my view, this generalized statement would be platitudinous. Needs appear in all spheres of social life. The statement that needs constantly motivate change leaves entirely open the question whether the needs for political power, for production, for a meaningful life, for culture, for solidarity, for the division of labour or its abolition, and so forth, are the decisive ones. Need is the 'independent variable' which terminates all independent variables. It allows for the de-universalized statement that in various histories and in various times and in various conflict situations, entirely different types of needs attached to entirely different objectivations and social spheres have been the decisive motivations for change, whilst other needs, even though they existed, could not bring about any change whatsoever.

This is why the application of the theory of need to 'History' (its transformation into a philosophy of history) would be platitudinous unless one picks out a *single type* of need as the 'motivational force' of 'History'. In such a case, not the needs themselves, but rather the spheres of objectivation, the types of social activity that the particular needs are embedded in, have to be singled out as the independent variable of 'History'. Yet this would no longer be the application of a theory of need to history. And so the theory of history, with both its emphasis on the heterogeneity of needs and its conviction that all needs motivate, but that not all of them succeed in instigating change – that in various histories, conflicts and situations, it has been various needs that have instigated change; this theory cannot establish any kind of philosophy. None the less, a theory of history offers an orientation and a norm for historiography. Historians who accept it obtain a theoretical norm both for selection and explanation, and the quest for meaning becomes the quest for needs; those which brought about a particular change in a particular case. At the same time, historians accepting this theory of history must attach greater importance to some needs than to others. The norm which binds in the present binds too in the resurrection of the past. This is why the partiality for those who most suffered becomes the norm of historiography in this theory. In this manner the double indicator of dialectical philosophies of history has been reintroduced, but not as a principle of the philosophy of history, so it ceases to be the indicator of *progress* (or regress). *Change demands explication by the particular needs engendering it, but partiality must be with those who have most suffered.*

In the foregoing I have argued for the thesis that the greatest suffering is always felt by those with needs that cry out with their existence and are incapable even of self-articulation. And precisely because of this incapacity these needs have not brought about change. All philosophies of history which applied a double indicator of progress believed that in the future there will be not two indicators, but only one. This emphasis is taken over by the theory of history in a modified version. If progress is understood as gains without corresponding losses, the two indicators cannot indicate progress at all. The Utopia of the theory of history is the idea of a society in which *every* need brings about change, for every need can express itself *freely* and has an *equal* chance for self-articulation and for argumentation on behalf of its satisfaction. Thus the idea of progress involves the idea of the abolition of the double indicator. Again I reiterate: no theory of history ensures us that this will be the case, it only provides us with the norm that this *should* be the case and that we ought to do everything in our power to that end.

Utopia is the image of what 'Ought-to-Be'. In static societies, where the social structure was reproduced through each society's own (inherent) pattern, value-rational action (that which ought to be done) could prevail without an image of Utopia (that which ought to be). In our dynamic society – in a society of unstable equilibrium and contradictory logics; a society in which the supreme (consensual) value of freedom can be interpreted (evaluated) in entirely different and contradictory ways; a society no longer offering to people traditional sets of values and value hierarchies providing norms for action and for a good life; a society where instrumental rationality has overpowered value-rationality – in this society value-rational action and coherent-value rational behaviour (the 'good life') *become impossible without the guidance of the idea of that which ought-to-be*. Anyone refusing Utopia, refuses thereby the 'good life' and abandons humankind to the mercy of mere instrumental rationality; to the mercy of the thirst for having and the thirst for power, to the mercy of manipulators and dictators. The values offered by the Utopia are few in number, but they are substantial. One can live up to them in entirely different ways, and, because they can be rendered concrete in various actions, in various forms of life, they allow for the combination of a formal and a substantial (material) ethics.* Dissatisfaction from the viewpoint of the second logic of civil society indicates the need for value-rational action. Yet this need cannot be satisfied without the image of rational Utopia. Utopia becomes a need as well.

---

* I have worked out this problem in detail in my book, *Pour une philosophie radicale*, Le Sycomore, Paris, 1979, pp. 113-41.

Chapter Twenty-Two

Some remarks about the sense of historical existence

This book started at the very beginning: with a story about the beginning. I remarked there that historicity is not 'that which happened to us', and it is not something that we just 'slip into', as into a garment. *We are historicity. We are time and space.* Kant's two '*a priori* forms of perception' are the consciousness of our existence. Proceeding from this major point on historicity, I analysed the forms of historical consciousness, the stages of its development. These stages are six in number, although the sixth is yet *in statu nascendi*. Now the time has come to give an account of this highly suspicious concept, the 'beginning'.

In this account, a point of first importance is: how can a *theory* of history start with a generalized sentence and, moreover, build up a *developmental sequence* throughout 'History' - how can it proceed in the fashion of *philosophies* of history which I have here criticized in detail, and proceed in a way resembling the ontological overdetermination of *our* life experiences and ideals? This suspicion should be, to the extent that it *can* be, eliminated without self-delusion. The last remark is important, for the time has also come to confess: it cannot be *completely* eliminated. To replace philosophy of history by a theory of history is in itself an *idea*. We are obliged to live up to it but we cannot live up to it *totally*. The theory of history committed itself to reflect upon itself historically, but this is exactly why it has to reflect on Togetherness as the *absolute present* which cannot be circumvented. I accepted the obligation to understand all histories going by their own norms and not mine, *but it is I who understand them*, and the categorical framework, along with the set of values through which I understand them, are mine. If I make the proposition that 'we are historicity', then by this very act I start to answer the question about the *sense of historical existence*, a question which has only been raised in modern age. We alone identify human existence with historical existence. But this is precisely the question one has to raise and try to answer, here and now. It is the same question raised and answered in different ways by philosophies of history. This is why one cannot completely leave them behind.

If the generalized sentence 'we are historicity' cannot be circumvented, the 'developmental sequence' of historicity cannot be circumvented either. If the question about the sense of human existence *is*, in our Togetherness, a question about the sense of historical existence, then the consciousness of our existence *is* the *self-consciousness of historical existence*. If our consciousness must be understood in terms of the self-consciousness of historical existence, then historical existence *is* the human essence and its self-consciousness *should* be grasped as the upshot of a developmental sequence towards the self-consciousness of this very essence. Either-or. *Either* we resign the attempt to answer the question about the sense of historical existence, and thus forgo philosophy altogether, replacing it with so-called 'empirical studies' that have no bearing whatsoever on our lives, sufferings, hopes, values, personalities, loves, fears and despairs; that is to say, upon everything which is *meaningful* to us, *or* we have to accept a developmental sequence of historical consciousness towards its very self-consciousness.

The theory of history adopts the position of the self-consciousness of historicity even more clearly than does the philosophy of history. When emphasizing that there is no real progress, but only the idea of progress as it appears in modern age, it conceives of the self-consciousness of historicity and the idea of progress *together*. But should this modern age be imagined as something which is *not* the 'necessary consequence' of 'History', how can the 'stages of historical consciousness' be lined up in any kind of developmental sequence at all?

(a) When I described the stages of historical consciousness, I followed in Vico's footsteps in that I recapitulated only the self-understanding of the times in question without adding anything to it. I assumed that the consciousness of past epochs was the consciousness of their existence, and that it expressed this existence adequately.

(b) I have not assumed that any stage in the developmental line of historical consciousness follows its precursor by necessity.

(c) I did not recapitulate the forms of consciousness of all histories, but only those of *our history* ('History') and its genesis. To be more exact, the first stage of historical consciousness was viewed as the consciousness of the *history in-itself,* that of the only *common* history of our species. All following stages (ancient Greece, Judeo-Christian tradition, Enlightenment, modern age) are *co-constitutive of modern* history which was identified with 'History' for the simple reason that it gave birth to the notion of 'History' as a reconstruction and as a *project.*

(d) However, here the ambiguity of the philosophy of history apparently recurs. The project of the philosophy of history called 'History' is nothing but the reflection of our History, even though it pretends to be the recounting of real history in its total development. It seems as if that *modus operandi* had been followed here, even if on purpose. But this is not the case.

In terms of the above expounded theory of history, all historical changes must be explained by the *real needs* producing them, and these needs and their contribution to such changes must in every case be explained in relation to their particular character by historiography. This is why, when the stages of historical consciousness were recapitulated, no attempt was made to recapitulate *any* historical period, *any* history. I did not even try to reconstruct real periods and their real history, but only their self-understanding as historicity. Within the framework of this reconstruction, no single stage of the development of historical consciousness *could be understood* as the outcome of its precursor, for each stage of consciousness was abstracted from *real* development (or 'unfolding') and *real* change; from their own logics and motivations. When, for instance, the consciousness of historicity in the ancient Greek period or in Judaic-Christian tradition was seen as a stage in the developmental line towards *our* historical consciousness, this is not the same as the statement that our society can be understood in any way as the 'necessary result' of ancient Greek, Jewish, or Roman societies, or even that any *real bonds* existed between these societies and ours.

(e) Objectivations survive the real life of societies. The stages of historical consciousness expressed this real life. The real life is gone, but not the objectivations produced by it; they can always be appropriated if the need for their reception exists. The stages of the development of historical consciousness which have been recapitulated in the first part of this book *were the ones 'appropriated' in modern age.* It was through them (and it could only happen through them) that the histories they expressed *became our histories.* This is why the recapitulation of real life has been substituted for the recapitulation of the forms of consciousness: only the latter *is real for us.* They are the particular forms of consciousness which *lead* to *our* historical consciousness simply because we *recognize our* prehistory, ourselves, in them. In communicating with them we communicate with our prehistory, independently of the fact (which has to be decided by historiography) of whether or not the *real* development of the societies that they expressed can be regarded as a precondition or a factor of the 'sufficient ground' for the emergence of our history.

(f) But even if the stages of the historical consciousness are *not* identified with the real development of societies; even if it is emphasized that we *recognize* our prehistory in them through the *objectivations* which survived the real life they expressed, we cannot help conceiving of *our* historical consciousness not only as 'the latest' but also as the 'highest' one. *We are the ones who recognize* and we recognize in them *our* prehistory. The absolute present of a Togetherness is always the highest, even in the theories of regress. Hence the obligation to reconstruct the stages of consciousness as stages of the development of historical consciousness, and our consciousness as the self-consciousness of historicity, the self-consciousness of *exactly this* development. In this respect, but only in this respect, philosophy of history cannot be circumvented, unless one is determined to get rid of philosophy altogether. But such an option would contradict the Utopia and all values of a theory of history. The question about the sense of historical existence has to be answered.

All philosophies of history are anthropologies. So are all theories of history. All philosophies of history suggest a way of life. So do all theories of history. The possible socialist theories of history, one of which I have in this book argued for, conceive of the Ought-to-Be (the Utopia) as a norm for the Ought-to-Do, which for its part provides the will-to-Utopia; and conceive this with the imperative that all empirical subjects (all subjects in need) *should will* the same. Socialist theories of history replace Rousseau's 'general will' by the empirical goodwill of Everyman. Hence *ethics* is an inherent component of such a theory of history. It has been stated that a socialist theory of history allows for the combination of material and formal ethics. Thus, it also allows for different forms of life, equally true and good ones, and all of them may embrace different moralities.

The general outline of a socialist theory of history reaffirmed the relevance of the question concerning the sense of historical existence, and recognized the obligation to answer it, providing this answer is a task already claimed by, and properly lies within, the realm of ethics.

The general framework of such an ethics has already been suggested.

In our century, catastrophes gave birth to absolute hopes, and the same absolute hopes were crushed by or faded away in new catastrophes. The inferno of the First World War ended with the firm promise that it was the last. It is irrelevant whether this hope is attributed to the necessarily coming world revolution or to Wilson's fourteen points and the League of Nations. One way or the other, the idea of 'eternal peace', of freedom, of self-determination, seemed to be on the agenda. These hopes were betrayed. Out of revolutions and democracies new tyrannies arose, economies collapsed, and the world was again pushed into a war, more formidable even than the previous. Concentration camps of various 'new orders', enormous factories of 'processing human raw material', made a bitter farce of the alleged 'superiority' of European culture. But, as an inveterate quality of human nature, out of this new and even deeper chasm fresh hopes were born once again. And where are these hopes now? The fears of the worst, of the self-destruction of humankind, of 'History', of all possible histories, have extinguished them altogether. This is our history, and in its sheer nakedness it is – a history of hopes betrayed. For this, should we blame the world or should we blame our hopes? If we blamed the world, we would blame ourselves: *we are history*. If we blamed our hopes, we would blame *the best in us*, and *we* are history. Blaming is irresponsible. It is responsibility that *should* be taken. It is responsibility that *must* be taken.

A theory of history suggests the *ethics of an active stoicism-epicureanism*. It implies the resolution to undertake value-rational actions irrespective of their success or defeat. Defeat is suffered and success is enjoyed, but both in suffering and in enjoyment *the same* resoluteness has to prevail. We ought to do our duty, we ought to act as if a society resembling somewhat more the Utopia could come about, should our will be universalized as the good will of Everyman. No catastrophe should persuade us that the undertaking is hopeless, for as long as we make efforts, hope exists, and is manifested in and through these efforts. Equally, no hope can permit us to stay at rest in the belief that the deed has been accomplished, for the deed is never *totally* accomplished, the goal is never *irreversibly* attained, and so we can *never* stay at rest. But if we have done our duty, everything which was in *our* power, we may enjoy our lives: *ultra posse nemo obligatur*. If we do not, under the spell of duty and sacrifice, realize that life is beautiful to live, that there is plenty to enjoy, we cannot *sincerely* act in harmony with an idea which entails the recognition of all human needs. Captain Forward should not become a tyrant of our ideas and lives.

Acting by the norm involves learning. Even though all concrete goals must be measured by the yardstick of Utopia, the Utopia itself offers no such goals. Learning from history, from the past of our present, and equally from the past, means to learn which particular goals have to be selected and, from these, which can be shared. Anthropological radicalism is inherent in philosophy, political realism can only be achieved if we are always ready to learn from history, and also from our personal history. Even though our hopes should not be blamed, some of our goals should be, and these should be replaced by other goals, in accord with the lessons drawn from our century.

Everyone who can give a true account of the lessons learned from history; everyone who did everything within their own power to live up to the norm of Ought-to-Be and Ought-to-Do; everyone who can say at the end of their days that, were life offered again, they would accept the offer with delight – these people can also justly claim to know the answer to the question about the sense of historical existence. The norm of truth and of being true in our Togetherness considered as history is in this way accomplished.

Every man is mortal. Only man is mortal because man knows that he will not be. We are confined to one Togetherness along with mortals we share our lives with. The well of our past is indeed deep; our responsibility is indeed enormous. But we only have one life. Therefore, no rush, Captain Forward. At any rate, we can only rush towards our death. 'Time' is not 'here' now because it is always here. We are not in any dark tunnel, with the chance of a glimmering light at the other end which we might see. Godot will not come either; we, however, will certainly leave. We may wish only three times, so we have to wish for something that provides *our* historical existence with sense, and with meaning. There is one wish which cannot be revoked by any other wishes: sharing the responsibility with our Togetherness. We can live an honest life – why should we not try it?